Popular Literacy

Pittsburgh Series in Composition, Literacy, and Culture

David Bartholomae and Jean Ferguson Carr, Editors

Popular Literacy

Studies in Cultural Practices and Poetics

Edited by John Trimbur

University of Pittsburgh Press

ISBN 0-8229-4136-8 (cloth)

ISBN 0-8229-5743-4 (paper)

For the late Lawrence Chisolm, my friend, graduate
advisor, and visionary founder of the American Studies
program at the State University of New York at Buffalo.
He's the person who taught me to think and collaborate
across fields and national borders.

Contents

Preface

The idea for this collection of essays began, I suppose, with some ordinary observations of what students were actually doing in my classes—doodling in the margins of their notebooks, passing notes, reading newspapers and magazines, balancing their checkbooks, doing homework for another class, making lists, writing letters, and more. The longer I've been teaching, the more I've come to notice these uses of reading and writing and to remember my own experience in school and at work. (Department meetings seem especially conducive to my drawing, scribbling, reading the mail, or whatever.) Humans are complex beings and have been multitasking long before the term became a buzzword of postindustrial management gurus. We can actually pay attention to many things at once, use reading and writing for our own purposes while partially participating in the official business or at least pretending to. Sometimes the reading and writing amount to outright defiance, but more often they're carried out as evasive forms of non-compliance. All of this is a matter of what Michel de Certeau calls the "practice of everyday life"—the little ruses and tricks everyone relies on to get by and make do.

At any rate, I became increasingly interested in how people use reading and writing for their own ends—the hidden and unofficial literacies they use to negotiate their way in the world. It seemed to me, moreover, that while my own field of study—rhetoric and composition—was interested in private and community literacies, the goal of such research was largely to explain how unschooled acts of reading and writing enabled or constrained success in the educational system. In a sense, I wanted to begin with a simpler and less pedagogical question—namely, how do people make literacy popular? What's involved when people divert the means of communication from official purposes to serve their own ends—whether in small quotidian ways or linked to popular movements for social change?

There are many people I want to acknowledge for helping me imagine this project and carry it out. I want to thank David Bartholomae and Jean Ferguson Carr, editors of the Pittsburgh Series in Composition, Literacy, and Culture, for believing there was a book here in the first place. It is personally and professionally very gratifying to appear in a series I admire so much. I also want to thank Niels Aaboe, my editor at the University of Pittsburgh Press, for his forbearance and support. Most of all, I want to thank the contributors for their work—and their commitment to a project that seemed to stretch on endlessly. I appreciate their patience and goodwill, and I am delighted that they come from a range of intellectual fields and academic traditions.

—John Trimbur
Cranston, RI
March 8, 2000

Popular Literacy

introduction **Popular Literacy**

Caught Between Art and Crime

When this book was just brewing as an idea, in July 1993, I happened to be in New York City, and my wife and I decided to take our then teenage daughters to see Times Square. At the time, Forty-second Street Now!, the city's redevelopment plan directed by architect Robert A. M. Stern and graphic designer Tibor Kalman, was still in the early stages of a "clean up" campaign to close the sex shops, porn shows, and budget movie houses, drive out the street vendors, pimps, hangers-on, and dealers, and make what was once Manhattan's boulevard of dreams into an urban theme park dedicated to corporate display and real-estate interests. The guiding principle of the redevelopment project, which was more or less followed in ensuing years, is the postmodern architect/oracle Robert Venturi's famous (and typically coy) dictum that "Main Street is almost right."

What we saw on a steamy midsummer day was remarkable—and not only for the hustling, sex work, pickpocketing, and pornography readily apparent. Forty-second Street had already started to move into the "enhanced" space of the postmodern city, if not yet the full pop-culture tourist spectacle its designers were imagining, with rooftop "billboard parks" and fountains gushing ads instead of water, at least in terms of a certain juxtaposition of signs. Above us, on the marquees of Forty-second Street's run-down abandoned theaters were Jenny Holzer "truisms"—samples from her repertoire of ironic commonplaces:

> Boredom makes you do crazy things
> A lot of professionals are crackpots
> Sloppy thinking gets worse over time
> People who don't work with their hands are parasites.

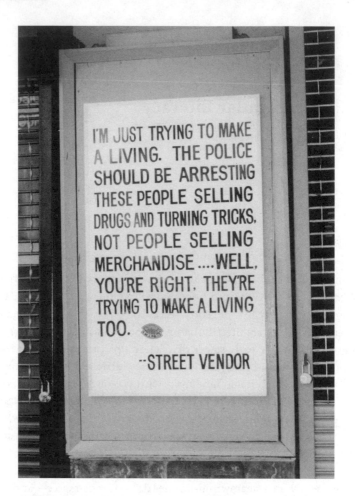

Below, at street level, were statements from street people and passersby gathered by the Forty-second Street Focus Group; posted as notices, they reflected on the meaning of Times Square and the changes about to be implemented by hip urban development.

> I'm just trying to make a living. The police should be arresting these people selling drugs and turning tricks, not people selling merchandise. . . . Well, you're right. They're trying to make a living too.
>
> STREET VENDOR

> The city doesn't want us here. The tourists don't want us here. They treat us like criminals, like we should all be over at Riker's or something. If they had jobs for some of these peoples out here we'd be coming here to go to work, not to hang out.
>
> EDDIE

The signs we saw that day on Forty-second Street have stayed with me, foreshadowing many of the interests and questions the reader will find in this book—what is popular literacy, what is its relation to other literacies, what are its practices and poetics, what are its politics? It could be said that the perspective of the contributors to this collection tends to be at the ground level, with the Street Vendor and Eddie. Working in a variety of fields—ethnography, American studies, history, literary criticism, science studies, rhetoric, and writing studies—the contributors are loosely aligned in a common project to understand how people like the Forty-second Street Focus Group *make literacy popular* by using the available means of communication for their own purposes—by putting up signs to claim an interpretive space.

The Forty-second Street Focus Group's posters, of course, are meant to speak in the voice of experience, to give a popular account from people who have not been consulted by the policy makers—some of whom are about to be driven from their familiar places, pleasures, and livelihoods by the forces of urban re-development. The voice of the people, though, is hardly a unified one, and the posters jostle against each other, expressing outrage, nostalgia, and even qualified approval. Some contest stigmatizing street people as the "dangerous classes"—health risks, public nuisances, unsafe characters put on notice by the planners' and city officials' sanitation campaign—while another notes, "We are in the middle of an experiment to find out how to control an element that we don't like. . . . We have to take Forty-second Street and assume with proper control those people will go away." As the posters indicate and Samuel R. Delaney points out in *Times Square Red, Times Square Blue,* Manhattan's redevelopment plan hinged rhetorically on its ability to portray Forty-second Street and the Times Square area as disease-ridden and crime-infested pockets of vice, perversion, and urban decay. Public health and safety provided the redevelopers with grounds to wage a turf war intent on replacing the "working-class residences and small human services" of a "highly diversified neighborhood" with tourist hotels, office towers, malls, and luxury apartments. From Delaney's perspective, the Forty-second Street Focus Group's posters appeared at a tactical moment in the larger battle for control of the streets, when the Times Square area was under attack as a *popular* space where the classes can mingle—where what Delaney calls "interclass contact and communication conducted in a mode of good will" can take place.[1] You get an idea of how this works from another Forty-second Street Focus Group poster: "When I was in law school—I went to Columbia, and you know that kind of very sedated environment and very closed out from the world. So I would always late at night, just take the 2:00 a.m. train out there and just walk that strip. I saw Times Square as being the best and the worst of war. New York is a battle."

It is tempting to divide the literacies enacted on Forty-second Street by their spatial location and assign Holzer's truisms to a high culture of commissioned artworks and the Forty-second Street Focus Group's testimonies to the urban lowlife of social documentary and social protest. There are indeed consequential differences that need to be analyzed in terms of the productive arts employed in the two cases of sign making and their relationship to the city's redevelopment scheme. Nonetheless, these differences do not map neatly onto a high/low division of the legitimate and the unauthorized. Holzer, after all, is reworking the "aura" of the artwork in the era of mechanical (and now digital) reproduction, and her antiaesthetic has led her outside the museum and gallery to "showings" on theater marquees, public-information posters, T-shirts, plaques, and electronic signs. At the same time, the Forty-second Street Focus Group's posters are working to dismantle the boundaries between art and life from the other end. The posters' account of life on the street has its own poetics, representing the speech of Eddie, the Street Vendor, and the others, one might even say, according to the unities of time, place, and action that Aristotle linked to the mimetic pleasures of intellectual elucidation.

There is no question that the practices and poetics of popular literacy are caught up in systems of valuing reading and writing that are marked routinely by formal oppositions—and the social relationships they call up—such as high/low, expert/lay, professional/client, standard/vernacular, civilized/vulgar. The relationship of popular literacy to these systems of valuing, however, cannot be understood simply as a categorical one of occupying the underesteemed and disparaged term in a familiar cultural hierarchy. Instead, as the contributors show in various ways, the question is better put if we ask how people, like the Forty-second Street Focus Group, use reading and writing to negotiate the boundaries between official and unofficial literacies, the sanctioned and the disreputable. Popular literacy, in this sense, does not demarcate a separate or autonomous sphere of culture, outside and uncontaminated by official literacy. Instead, the cultural practices and poetics by which people make literacy popular are accented at every point by the institutions that regulate the production, circulation, and use of reading and writing—the church, the state, the schools, the market, the culture industry. Popular literacy is caught in shifting relations of forces between the periphery and the center.

The Study of Popular Literacy

One way to describe the work of this collection is to say that the contributors, in one degree or another, bring together two main terms—"popular" and "literacy"—that have their own distinct traditions of use. For one thing, it is difficult to imagine a readership or a place for such a collection without revisionist literacy theorists such as Harvey Graff, Brian Street, and Shirley Brice Heath and of studies in the history of the book and reading by Robert Darnton, Roger Chartier, Elizabeth Eisenstein, Cathy N. Davidson, and others.[2] From various angles, this body of work has been widely influential in redefining literacy as a cultural practice instead of, say, an aesthetic object, a pedagogical subject, a technology of the intellect, or a condition of modernization and economic takeoff. And in turn this redefinition has raised a series of further questions concerning how literacy is used to maintain social networks, exchange social identities, and distribute (and redistribute) power and cultural capital.

The studies in this collection of how people make literacy popular put a particular emphasis on the *making*, and like recent cultural studies of literacy such as Anne Ruggles Gere's *Intimate Practices*, Susan Miller's *Assuming the Positions*, and Margaret Finders's *Just Girls* they pay special attention to what I call the productive arts of popular literacy—the poetics of making signs. In an important respect, this focus on production distinguishes the work in this collection from other currents related to the *popular* in popular literacy that put the emphasis on reception and consumption. Leslie Fiedler and John Cawelti, for example, have used the literary terms "myth" and "formula" to analyze such popular genres as the Western, science fiction, romance, midcult best-sellers, mass circulation magazines, tabloid journalism, and soap operas.[3] This collection certainly shares the antielitist sentiments found in Fiedler's bravura efforts to rescue demotic literature (not to mention the ancient rhetorical understanding of pathos as pity and fear and its modern expressions as spine-tingling terror, tear-jerking sentiment, and erotic arousal) from the censure of official literary culture. The telling difference is that Fiedler wants to read political and cultural meanings off the surface of the text and to make popular genres self-evidently more democratic, subversive, and just plain fun than recognized forms of writing.

By contrast, the studies of popular literacy carried out in the following pages tend to see the question of genre not so much in terms of the myths or formulas that invest a particular genre with a popular essence but as modes of rhetorical action. There are no set political or cultural valences in a genre that can be determined separately from its use—from the genre's articulation in the double sense of how it is put into words (poetics) and how it is linked to social experience (practices). Of course, some genres appear to be associated more readily than others with popular literacy—graffiti, placards, ex-votos, pottery, scrapbooks, cookbooks. But the practices of popular literacy, as contributors show, can also divert established genres from their normal uses to serve popular ends, as in the case of labor dramas at the Bryn Mawr summer school for women workers, biomedical articles in the hands of AIDS and breast cancer activists, or working-class poetry groups.

The studies of popular literacy presented here have much in common with the understanding of the *popular* in such classic cultural studies of readers, viewers, and fans as Angela McRobbie's "*Jackie*: An Ideology of Adolescent Femininity," Janice Radway's *Reading the Romance*, and various "active audience" analyses of John Fiske.[4] The main points of convergence are the relative autonomy ascribed to readers and the location of effective meaning in the uses of reading and writing as much as in the text. To put it another way, instead of positing a direct correspondence between production (the message encoded) and consumption (the message decoded), cultural studies of literacy have created an opening for variable responses and social uses that resist or evade preferred readings. This is the well-known neo-Gramscian "synthesis" in British cultural studies, the Marxism without guarantees that Stuart Hall uses to play the "culturalist" view that people make their own history against the "structuralist" position that they do so under conditions not of their own making. For Hall, people negotiate popular consent in a Gramscian "war of positions" where classes and class fractions vie for moral and cultural leadership. The people are not always right—nor do they speak in a unified voice against oppression and injustice—as they used to in the Popular Fronts of the 1930s. By the same token, the people do not always use the media and popular culture to resist the dominant order in contemporary society, as Fiske and the "new revisionists" sometime make it appear. British cultural studies have been instrumental in developing a view of the popular that doesn't give in to Popular Front sentimentality over the "heroic masses," or the nostalgia for authentic working-class values found in Richard Hoggart's *Uses of Literacy*, while also warding off the mechanical determinism of "false consciousness" in some versions of orthodox Marxism and the cultural pessimism of the Frankfurt School.

I doubt that many of the contributors want to go all the way with Fiske on the subversiveness of popular culture, in part because he puts so much emphasis on consumption in the making of popular literacies. Instead, as I have suggested earlier, one characteristic of the following studies is their attention to production—of texts, knowledges, identities. Although they do not use this language, the contributors are interested in both the *practices* that negotiate the boundaries between official and unofficial literacies and the *poetics* involved in making literacy popular. To my mind, an important feature of these studies is their promise to rescue the term *poetics* from its narrowly belletristic sense as the domain of the "aesthetic," the "literary," and the "imaginative." In this regard, I would go so far as to say that the contributors point back to Aristotle's notion of poetics as mimetic activity with civic instruction as its goal. Or, at least, they stretch that view in a direction that no longer separates poetics from rhetoric.

The Politics of the Popular in the Modern Era

Since the French Revolution, the question of who speaks for the people has been one of great political urgency, put on the agenda when the people burst into the streets, naming themselves the subjects of history. By calling each other *citoyen/citoyenne*, the people emerged in the French Revolution from an act of mutual recognition and pledged it to political agency in its own name, independent of church and state. In the great democratic upsurges—the French Revolution of 1789 and 1793, the democratic uprisings throughout Europe in 1848, and the Paris Commune of 1870—popular forces gathered in the cities against an increasingly isolated ruling bloc, dissolving their internal differences in a collective opposition to the status quo and taking over the streets. The social formation that coalesced as the *people* was a cross-class phenomenon, a momentary alliance—a kairotic moment—of shared grievances, discontent, and frustration and was invested with the universal authority of popular sovereignty.

In this sense, the emergence of the people as a collective subject is a topos that has become one of the stakes of rhetorical and political power in modern class society. In the nineteenth century, European cities periodically clamored with the questions: "Who speaks in the name of the people?" "To whom do the streets belong?" "Who is in charge?" In the French countryside, anticlerical schoolmasters struggled against counterrevolutionary priests for the right to speak for the people. In *What Is To Be Done?*, Lenin says that the vanguard party must be the "tribune of the people," its authority warranted by speaking on behalf of all the oppressed and exploited, and not just the proletariat.

And yet, the *people* are a fragile and unstable formation, for the term refers not so much to a unified political force that can be mobilized on its own behalf when the chips are down but to a molecular social process in which shifting class fractions compose and recompose themselves in cross-class identifications and divisions under the pressure of historical events. By the turn of the previous century, for example, funded by imperialist expansion, the "bourgeoisification" of a sector of the working class—or labor aristocracy—in western Europe and North America revealed that the cross-class alliances that made the people a revolutionary force in 1789, 1848, and 1870 could also lead to class collaboration. With the advent of World War I, the socialist parties of the Second International identified the people's interests with those of their own bourgeoisie and voted for war credits, thereby dividing along national lines an international proletariat that supposedly had no fatherland and only its chains to lose. Consequently, much of the struggle for revolutionary leadership throughout the twentieth century was devoted precisely to this question of the strategic relation of class forces. In China in 1927, Spain in the 1930s, and with the disarming of the partisans in France and Italy following World War II, the composition and recomposition of class alliances played themselves out in the political arena of armed struggle, with the Trotskyist Left Opposition holding to the internationalist line of permanent revolution against the Stalinist doctrine of socialism in one country and the subordination of class struggle to the people's fronts against fascism.

At the same time, the molecular processes of social combination and recombination were taking place in new ways in the realm of popular culture. The boulevards, cabarets, theaters, amusement parks, and dance halls of the nineteenth-century metropolis provided a popular space for classes to encounter each other and exchange identities. As T. J. Clark argues, the "various forms of commercialized leisure which bulked so large in the late-nineteenth-century were instruments of class formation" that operated at the level of the popular spectacle, where nightlife and the new idea of "going out" constructed a petite bourgeois aficionado from fictions of working-class ways of sociability and parodies of middle-class style. By the same token, popular entertainment provided the respectable classes the opportunity to go "slumming" and for elements of the working class, the chance to impersonate their betters. In the reorganization of city life that separated what had been the unity of residence, work, and recreation, the reworking of proletarian beer halls into the popular space of the café, "*generalized* the uncertainty of class, and had everyone's be a question of style." For at least a part of the public, this "masquerade" only confirmed the "sense of class as pure contingency, a matter of endless shifting and exchange . . . a series of petty transfiguration scenes, in which everyone suffered the popular sea-change, the 'real' bourgeois as much as the false."[5]

As Clark suggests, reworking vernacular cultures has been one of the persistent themes of the popular over the past century, and, if anything, it has intensified in the post–World War II period—taking everything from African-American musical styles to strip architecture to gay subcultural expression and articulating their disorderliness and blurred class identities to the market. Repeatedly, cultural practices that had once taken place within communal ways of life have been incorporated into the apparatus of commercial pleasures and corporate structures. It is no wonder, then, as John Clarke puts it, that these rearticulations confronted the popular classes with a culture of mass consumption in which "they were already in place."[6]

In the 1980s and 1990s, with the replacement of the "respectable" middle classes in their traditional role of cultural leadership by an expanding professional-managerial class fraction of baby boomers and yuppies, the popular has itself become a commodity—valued as a marketable sign of danger, transgression, and excess that breaks with the older moral economy of the middle classes and its residual links to an ascetic Protestantism of frugality and accumulation. For the new cultural leadership, the popular is identified along generational lines with the legacies of 1960s and 1970s youth cultures—in particular with media savvyness, style consciousness, appreciation for cultural diversity and the unconventional, commitment to personal choice, and a cosmopolitan outlook in politics and consumption. The cut-and-paste, recycling, and recombinant practices associated with a knowing and ironic postmodernism are in many respects the logical outcome of this new cultural leadership and the underlying expansionary energies of niche marketing, the packaging of exotica, and a permanent revolution of style.

Between Art and Crime

For John Clarke, the problem posed by the popular is whether the "expansiveness" of this new cultural formation "can be matched by an expansion of the cultural and economic conditions of popular participation, extended to those who do not have a niche of their own."[7] Popular participation, of course, involves access to the means of producing and displaying signs of all sorts, and this access is always caught up in the molecular processes by which class identities and divisions are made and remade. Tipper Gore's Parents' Music Resource Center, Bill Clinton's case for V-chips on cable boxes, curfews, and school uniforms, and William Bennett's attacks on gangsta rap and media violence, not to mention the moral panic over black trench coats, Goths, Marilyn Manson, and geek culture in the wake of the Littleton shootings, show that the pull of the "respectable" middle classes to regulate popular style and entertainment is still around, at least residually. Despite the commodification of the popular as a marketable sign of transgression and otherness, the popular retains a certain capacity to shock and frighten "straight" society with its unruly energy.

A telling case about the current status of popular literacy can be found in a 1994 Supreme Court decision. Ladue, Missouri, a wealthy suburb of St. Louis, had in 1991 passed an ordinance to prevent "ugliness, visual blight and clutter," which was then used to ban a small sign reading "Peace in the Gulf" that Margaret P. Gilleo had posted in an upstairs window of her home to protest Operation Desert Storm. The Supreme Court's ruling was a sweeping one, going beyond the lower courts' finding that the ordinance was unconstitutional on

the grounds that it allowed commercial signs, such as those advertising property "for sale," while banning noncommercial ones. The Supreme Court held
that the central issue was not one of equitable treatment (which would have
made a complete ban of all signs—commercial and noncommercial—at least
theoretically permissible) but, as Justice John Paul Steven's opinion for the
Court's unanimous decision put it, of a "special respect for individual liberty
in the home." This principle, Stevens added, "has a special resonance when the
government seeks to constrain a person's ability to *speak* there."[8]

Of special interest in this case is the Court's opinion that signs such as
Gilleo's, displayed in a person's own home, were not only an "unusually cheap
and convenient form of communication" but also a distinctive expression of
the sign maker's identity that could not be transmitted by a sign located elsewhere: "A sign advocating 'Peace in the Gulf' in the front lawn of a retired general or decorated war veteran may provoke a different reaction than the same
sign in a 10-year-old child's bedroom window or the same message on a bumper
sticker of a passing automobile."[9] This seems to me an altogether shrewd rhetorical reading of the speaker's ethos and reader response, and at the same time it
links a person's rhetorical authority and right to speak to forms of private property. For the propertyless, the ability to speak and to make literacy popular remains problematical.

An obvious example of the problematical standing of those unauthorized
by the class standing of property ownership is the emergence in the 1970s of
graffiti and spray-can art by the "crews," "bombers," "taggers," and "burners"
of New York (and very quickly many of the major cities in the United States
and Europe)—and the subsequent attempts to criminalize or aestheticize graffiti
writing. On one side is the nationwide campaign against graffiti, banning not
just graffiti but the sale of spray-paint cans to anyone under eighteen as well.
Inspired by conservative criminologists such as New York Mayor Rudy Giuliani's
advisor George Kelling and political scientist James Q. Wilson and his "broken
windows" theory, the graffiti "abatement" movement has relied on a discourse
linking graffiti to fears of African-American teenagers, gangs, drugs, and hip-
hop culture, to a disrespect for private and public property, and to a pervasive
sense of the fragility of social bonds and the threatened breakdown of civil society. Significantly, as Michael Walsh reports, the war against graffiti became by
1996 a four-billion-dollar-a-year industry, with a host of new clean-up products, prevention campaigns, and rewards for informers.[10]

On the other side, cultural critics and trendy art dealers want to rescue
graffiti from criminalization by the control culture—to validate it instead as
public art that gives voice to the disenfranchised or as the virtuoso performance of a new urban art form. Still others have combined representations of

graffiti as art and as crime by seeking to contain its expression in "approved" places, such as legal murals in the Popular Front tradition of the Mexican muralists and the WPA projects of the 1930s. In some instances, these projects have included grants for individual graffiti artists and sponsorship by local businesses.

The terms of understanding graffiti as an especially powerful indigenous form of urban popular literacy cannot be set simply. Graffiti belongs to the streets, where the right to speak depends on the prevailing relation of forces, not to the home, where ownership, as in the case of the "Peace in the Gulf" sign, warrants the right to public speech. As the writer Eskae notes, graffiti begins as an explicit challenge to property and seeks to unsettle the familiar question "who owns the streets":

> I create illegal graffiti because I see it as a political act against the structure of how things are . . . the whole idea of property ownership, people who think they can own property. . . . What kind of right do they have to say "I own this"? We all own this. . . . Graffiti is a kick in the face to the Gallery/Museum system, where the artist is pimped like a whore for the capitalist system, made into another commodity for people to buy. . . . Graffiti is free for all to come and view—no one can own it, it belongs to all of us.[11]

The writers, however, cannot be represented unequivocally as "tribunes of the people," for graffiti artists, after all, operate in a highly individualistic and competitive culture of ritualized artistic combat, with prime value placed on "putting up" the writer's tag and ironic copyright marks that both draw on and mock the trademarks of corporate ownership. As Krypt says, the values of graffiti artists are in part entrepreneurial: "It's addictive. It gets you high, but high on your own achievement. You created."[12]

To understand what makes graffiti popular, we need to see how its energy and appeal derive from its sources in both art and crime. As Twist suggests, the lure of graffiti depends in large part on the thrill of transgression: "Graffiti's one of the last pure forms of freedom and destruction,"[13] living proof that the writer can evade control by "bombing" the city. For many writers, graffiti is meaningful precisely because it is illegal. In this sense, the relation of art and crime to the formation of graffiti as a practice of popular literacy is a reciprocal one. Without laws to protect property against vandalism, there can be no vandals. This, of course, is a familiar dynamic: rules are meant to be broken, taboos violated. But there is more involved than just the unfolding dialectic of control and transgression. The criminalization of graffiti has also played a key role in making it a marketable art commodity. Despite the hostility of many graffiti writers to the art world establishment, by the early 1980s there had already been important graffiti shows in New York galleries, and the Dutch art dealer Yaki Kornblit featured such New York writers as Dondi, Crash, Ramellzee, Futura 2000, Zephyr, Quik, Pink, Blade, Seen, and Bil Blast in solo shows and organized a major group exhibition at the Museum Boymans-van Beuningen in Rotterdam. With the spread of hip-hop culture as a popular cross-over phenomenon, it didn't take advertisers, artists, graphic designers, and the media long to add graffiti to the image bank. From Keith Haring and Jean-Michel Basquiat in the art world to the 1994 Chrysler billboard that appears to have "tagged" its own display,[14] graffiti has gained "recognition," like jazz and rap, as a uniquely American art form—a visual convention of gritty streetwise authenticity. Like jazz and its symbolic associations with New Orleans brothels and Harlem speakeasies, graffiti is marked by—and valued for—its illegitimate origins outside the control culture of the respectable middle classes.

I don't intend to suggest in this account of graffiti that the popular will always get appropriated by the dominant institutions—co-opted and recoded by the market's insatiable appetite for novelty. That the very notion of authenticity itself is a key word in contested representations of the popular prevents us from drawing easy distinctions between purists and sellouts. From one perspective, graffiti artists who show at galleries are simply changing career paths, though there are, no doubt, real consequences and shifts of loyalty, as is invariably the case in any instance of upward mobility. While there may indeed be reason for concern about the incorporation of graffiti into the market and the media (just as some jazz musicians and critics are worried about the canonization of jazz as a legitimate music, archived in the repertory companies at Lincoln Center and Carnegie Hall), the fact is graffiti's very marketability depends on its illegal aura. To put it another way, graffiti remains suspended in the space between crime and art, between the "abatement" campaigns of the traditional middle class and the aestheticization (and capitalization) of transgression on the part of its postmodern fraction. As an expression of popular sovereignty, graffiti is both an affront to the state and an incitement to the market.

Reading Popular Literacy

The graffiti writer 3-D, one of the first in the United Kingdom, puts it this way:

> In the city you don't get any say in what they build. You get some architect that does crappy glass buildings or gray buildings. No one comes up and says, "We're building this, do you like it? Here's the drawings, we'll take a poll." So why should I have to explain what I do? I live in the city, I'm a citizen. Maybe in the eyes of this

town I'm not so important, because I don't have all that high status, as in class and job, but I live here so I should have as much say as anyone else, and that's why I go out and paint, 'cause I want to say something, and I don't want to be told when I can do it.[15]

How are we to read 3-D's words? That is precisely the problem I think this collection of essays raises. Clearly, 3-D wants to raise the question of who owns the streets and the built environment within which we all live. But exactly on whose behalf? In part, 3-D offers himself as the voice of the propertyless and disenfranchised. At the same time, he doesn't want to be told what he can do. He's a "citizen" but is also, in the "eyes of this town," a marginalized figure. Why shouldn't he have to "explain what I do"? Is this because of his marginalization or because he doesn't want to be accountable? Or are these the same thing? How exactly does graffiti writing answer the problem of voicelessness with which he begins? And what do our own answers to these questions and others we might imagine indicate about our own position and interests?

The problem of popular literacy begins in a tangle. If the term seems to refer to the practices and poetics of the people, it nonetheless keeps pointing back to itself and to those who utter it. For, as Raymond Williams puts it, "popular culture was not identified by the people but by others,"[16] whether they are the clergy and aristocrats in sixteenth-century France gathering popular tales from French peasants and craftsmen, the folklorists of the nineteenth century, whose names are now written into popular story and song as the Grimm's fairy tales and the Child ballads, or collectors like John A. Lomax doing field recordings of cowboy singers and blues musicians, or Jan Harold Brunvand running down urban legends. There are surely questions that need to be asked when one moves peoples' words from their point of origin to the space of a printed page, photograph, sound recording, archive, or museum.

In one way or another, the contributors are trying to address the problem Mariolina Salvatori poses when she confronts Michel de Certeau's argument that "popular culture can only be grasped in the process of vanishing," obliterated by scholarly and critical attention. Is the attempt to bring popular literacies forward for critical examination no more than a quixotic wish, in de Certeau's words, "to suppress the history of a repression"?[17] Now, to be fair, it is hard to deny that this collection of largely white, middle-class, North American academics must account in some sense for institutionalizing what de Certeau calls the "menace" of the popular just by writing about it, analyzing it, topicalizing it as a respectable subject of investigation. But the fear on de Certeau's part about the vulnerability of the popular is not entirely warranted, for the pressure, as always, isn't just from the top down. The real question is the relation of forces, and there is no foregone conclusion that the learned will necessarily overwhelm the unlettered. To my mind, the following chapters contain exemplary lessons about how ordinary, unpropertied, and unsanctioned readers and writers of all sorts divert literacy to serve their own purposes—and the pressure their practices and poetics apply to those of us who study literacy to find more adequate, more generous, and more complex understandings of how people actually use reading and writing.

The first two chapters examine particularly revealing instances of how the subaltern in Mexico and Nigeria draw on the resources of official literacy to produce iconographic literacies that disseminate popular appraisals of church and state. In "Porque no puedo decir mi cuento: Mexican Ex-votos' Iconographic Literacy," Mariolina Salvatori analyzes the Mexican devotional offerings as a productive art of the poor that raises "irreverent and petulant questions," while Charles Keil's "Gypsy Fullstop Punctuates Imperialism" provides a close look at the iconography of punctuation a former colonial soldier and civil servant invented in response to the will-to-power of Western legal and bureaucratic literacy.

The subsequent three chapters explore popular uses of literacy in the Middle Ages and the early modern period and offer reconsiderations of the conventional assumption that literacy amounts to the ability to read and write. Cheryl Glenn's "Popular Literacy in the Middle Ages: The Book of Margery Kempe" examines the "text-based" (rather than "text-dependent") literacy practices of the unlettered medieval spiritualist Margery Kempe, who composed through an amanuensis. In "Giving Voice to the Hands: The Articulation of Material Literacy in the Sixteenth Century," Pamela H. Smith presents the work of the Huguenot potter and writer Bernard Palissy as a telling example of nontextual "artisanal literacy" that generated productive knowledge through experience and labor. Then, Evelyn B. Tribble, in "Social Place and Literacies in John Foxe's Actes and Monuments," reads the depositions of Protestant martyrs under Mary Tudor as challenges by the "lower sort" to learned authority and traditional notions of deference.

The next three chapters examine private and public literacies in nineteenth-century America. Todd S. Gernes's "Recasting the Culture of Ephemera" looks at the way ordinary people assembled commonplace books, scrapbooks, and friendship albums out of the materials of everyday life, creating what he calls a "popular literacy of collecting, arrangement, invention, and memory." In "'We Can Never Remain Silent': The Public Discourse of the Nineteenth-Century African-American Press," P. Joy Rouse considers the "rhetorics of citizenship" employed by the African-American press to weave the polis of the black community into the larger American context and identify racial equality as inseparable from national well-being. Patricia Bizzell, in "'Stolen' Literacies in *Iola Leroy*," argues that Frances E. W. Harper's 1892 novel not only recounts how "stolen" literacies empower its African-American protagonists before, during, and after the Civil War but also reveals how Harper herself "stole" the literacy of literary art in order to represent positively a range of language uses, from oral, dialect-based eloquence to the platform oratory of racial uplift.

The next three chapters investigate various twentieth-century working-class popular literacies and their complex relations to the academy, the market, and the state. In "Plays of Heteroglossia: Labor Drama at the Bryn Mawr Summer School for Women Workers," Karyn Hollis looks at the labor pageants, agitprop skits, and "living newspapers" scripted and produced by women trade unionists at the Bryn Mawr summer school between 1921 and 1938. Stephanie Almagno, Nedra Reynolds, and John Trimbur, in "Italian-American Cookbooks: Authenticity and the Market," examine the contradictory character of this popular genre as celebrations of New World Italians' foodways and commodifications of ethnicity in a cosmopolitan consumer culture. Nicholas Coles's "Joe Shakespeare: The Contemporary British Worker-Writer Movement" reports on the class-based popular literacy of the Federation of Worker-Writers and Community Publishers in the United Kingdom, paying particular attention to the "motivations and structures" for writing and publishing that occur outside the academy and the professions.

The final three chapters consider popular literacies at the end of the twentieth century, in the emergent visual and digital technoculture of contemporary America. In "Changing the Face of Poverty: Nonprofits and the Problem of Representation," Diana George examines how nonprofit organizations such as Oxfam and Habitat for Humanity continue to rely on notions (and visual representations) of the "deserving" and "undeserving" poor in photo documentaries, fund-raising ads, and publicity videos—and the alternative self-representations of the poor and homeless in newsletters and street newspapers. "Popularizing Science: At the Boundary of Expert and Lay Biomedical Knowledge" by Lundy Braun and John Trimbur looks at the relationship between the biomedical establishment and the public and how toxic waste, AIDS, and breast cancer activists are struggling to rearticulate the expert knowledges of official science. Lester Faigley's "Understanding Popular Digital Literacies: Metaphors for the Internet" closes the collection with an exploration of the "easy conflation of information, power, and democracy" and the "hacktivism" of the Zapatistas and Chinese dissidents.

It may be, as de Certeau says, that the "last ruse of knowledge is to reserve for itself the role of political prophesy"[18]—and such an observation, of course, raises troubling questions about the oracular role we might be tempted to take on in writing about popular literacy. By scholarly standards, the chapters in this collection must surely weigh in as accomplished and significant work, and I am proud to present them to you as contributions to knowledge. Still this is not quite the point on which I would like to close. The issue, as I see it, is not simply how skillfully and critically we represent popular literacies but the relationship that this work forms between academics and their subjects, past and present. To my mind, it's not a matter so much of "political prophesy," as de Certeau suggests, but of solidarity and social allegiance—and how academic work might rearticulate its own expertise to popular aspirations.

one **Porque no puedo decir mi cuento**

Mexican Ex-votos' Iconographic Literacy

Mariolina Salvatori

> *Ex-votos*—images on wood or canvas, images embossed on silver or other metal, representative oblations . . . public testimonial of gratitude or of special devotion to sacred images functioning as healthy incitement (encouragement) to ask for graces.
>
> —G. MORONI

> *Santos* —small images of Christ, the Virgin, the saints, or other holy images painted on sheets of tin and intended for private devotional use . . . , ex-votos—small votive paintings, also on tin, left at religious shrines to offer public thanks to a divine image for a miracle or favor received.
>
> —JORGE DURAND AND DOUGLAS S. MASSEY

Mexican *ex-votos* are small votive paintings, usually on tin (although not on "sides of tin cans," as some have suggested.[1] They are religious artifacts that supplicants bring to and leave at a place of veneration (shrine, church, or sanctuary) to offer *public* thanks to a particular divine image for a miracle or favor received. *Santos* are votive paintings as well, but they are household items, meant for *private* devotional practices. It can be argued that while the public devotional function of ex-votos conveys and sustains a supplicant's hope and desire to bring everyday life into the domain of the sacred (in terms of both the pictorial representation they offer and their place of destination, as we will see), the devotional function of santos conveys and sustains a supplicant's hope and desire to bring the realm of the sacred into everyday life.

Morphologically, three elements differentiate ex-votos from santos:[2] (1) a *holy image* of the Virgin Mary, Jesus, usually represented as the Sacred Heart, Saints, and/or the souls of purgatory; (2) *a pictorial rendering* of a threatening oc-

Habiéndose quemado una casa que estaba contigua a la mia, el día 2 de Julio de
1944, viendo que la lumbre empezaba a caer en el patio de mi casa, llena de ang-
tia invoqué a la Sma. Virgen de San Juan pidiéndole que nos librara del incendio,
abiéndonos librado, en gratitud le le dedico este retablo.—Aurelia A. de Castellanos

FIGURE I

currence or miraculous event; and (3) *a written text*, a brief, economic narrative
of what happened and where, who received the miracle, and an expression of
gratitude, more or less formulaic (fig. 1).

Commonly referred to by the generic term *retablos* (a term that is also applied to santos), ex-votos are commissioned by supplicants, who are often illiterate, to semiliterate popular artists (generally called *retablisti*) who can paint
familiar representations of the particular divine figure that is the subject of devotion at a particular site. The majority of retablisti do not sign the ex-votos
they produce.[3]

Gloria Fraser Giffords, a historian and collector of Mexican "folk art," explains the overextension of the word retablo by pointing out that the term, of
Latin derivation (Lat. retaulus, Lat. retrotabulum = a rear table or an area behind the altar), is used in Mexico in a number of senses: "Before 1800 it applied to the great gilded, painted, carved screens created in the apses of
churches behind the altars. . . . After 1900 the word retablo may also apply to
small, votive paintings by popular artists made for clients as thanks or offerings
for miraculous recoveries. Similar materials, sizes, and, in many cases, creators
caused it to be applied to the small paintings of the saints as well" (*Mexican Folk
Retablos*, 2–3).

FIGURE 2

Although I value and respect the equalizing effect (from "great gilded, painted, carved screens..." to "small votive paintings by popular artists") that the adoption and generalization of the term retaulus/retablo in Gifford's excerpt may be taken to suggest, in this piece I shall use the term ex-voto to refer to the particular votive offering (of which the Latin words *ex voto* [for a vow] stand as a reminder) that scripts the story of a miraculous occurrence.[4]

I have known of the existence of ex-votos for a very long time. As a child in Italy I was taken on pilgrimage to various sanctuaries in Puglia, the region where I was born.[5] My mother was praying for a miracle. In my memory, ex-votos are an integral part of early puzzling and haunting religious experiences: the languid smell of lit candles and incense; the sound of incomprehensible prayers and chanted litanies, of heavy sighs and sobs; eery representations of the Virgin Mary, clad in blue velvet and white lace, her heart pierced by a sword; Jesus, his heart cradled in his outstretched hand; God the Father, leaning out of a luminous triangle, his eyes following me wherever I sat or knelt. I remember squeezing my eyes shut to block those visions, until I saw and could follow a nebula of red dust. And I remember the place, the specific sanctuary,[6]

FIGURE 3

where I first saw ex-votos. My mother, a figure of sorrow deep in prayer: attracted by the colorful array of little paintings that covered the walls behind and around the altar, I moved away from her. I was mesmerized and deeply troubled by those little paintings. Some of the images, etched in my memory, still send shivers down my spine: gaping mouths; raging seas; children falling off from trees, walls, cliffs; children being pulled out of wells, or plastered on the ground under the weight of a mountain of bricks, or a fallen horse, a cart, or a truck;[7] people on their death beds, or on rudimentary operating tables, knives midair in the hands of masked doctors who looked more like assassins to me; big spouts of blood poring out of wounds, ears, mouths; a cow giving birth; flames leaping out of buildings, or engulfing bodies. On that, and other occasions, when the images became unbearable to watch, I would shift my attention to the narrative text at the bottom, and I would chuckle—a very literate child, I could pick up at first glance the "scrittura da analfabeta," the semiliterate handwriting, the "poor" spelling, grammar, and syntax the text recorded and put on display. I thought that was amusing.

Since I left Italy and came to live in this country, I never had an opportunity to think or to talk about ex-votos. Not until five years ago, that is, when, in a shop in Philadelphia that specializes in Mexican, Caribbean, and South American artifacts, I came across a little painting on a rectangular sheet of metal, which I recognized as an ex-voto. At first I thought it was Italian. But it was Mexican. I looked for more, began to collect them, to research them only to find out that both collecting (they are being produced less and less while their appreciation by scholars and art dealers is growing)[8] and researching them (scholarship on them is still scanty) were not easy. My interest in them was piqued. As art objects, they appeal to the collector in me;[9] but they especially drew me, emotionally and intellectually (as they did when I was a child), and became *valuable* for the stories they tell, and even more, the stories they cannot openly articulate.[10]

Laconic, humble,[11] simple, and beautiful, Mexican ex-votos document a religious practice of mainly the poor, an art form by the poor for the poor.[12] Simple and humble as they are, they raise challenging theoretical and ethical questions about ways of responding to them, of representing them on their own terms, as much as, or if, that is possible. As objects of popular culture, they bring me face to face with the dividing and alienating power of knowledge— with whether it may be possible to know them according to immanent criteria, whether it may be possible to establish from the outside what "on their own terms" actually means, especially when one starts with a cultural capital of learned knowledge that cannot be forgotten or left behind, and when, to plead my specific case, that learned knowledge is also rooted in another (Italian) culture.[13]

Several months ago, still brooding over this problem but simultaneously pursuing other lines of investigation for other work, I read a particular essay by Michel de Certeau that validated my anxiety about embarking on this writing project. "The Beauty of the Dead: Nisard," a piece de Certeau wrote in collaboration with Dominique Julia and Jacques Revel, is a trenchant critique of what he names as the two founding periods of studies devoted to popular culture: the end of the eighteenth century and the years from 1850 to 1890. The essay opens with an indictment of the very concept of "popular culture." But the indictment might apply to anybody who might want to write about it from a scholarly position.

> "Popular culture" presupposes an unavowed operation. Before being studied, it had to be censored. Only after its danger had been eliminated did it become an object of interest. The birth of studies devoted to street literature (the inaugural book is Nisard's, published in 1854) is tied to the social censorship of their object. They developed out of "a sensitive plan" conceived by the police. At the origin of this scientific curiosity, a political repression: the elimination of booklets judged "subversive" or "immoral." This is only *one* aspect of the problem, but it raises a question of more general concern.[14]

What concerns de Certeau is that the disciplines that since then addressed themselves to the study of the popular—ethnography, anthropology, literary studies, folklore, history, religion—seem to be tainted by an act of repression that is no less violent than the police's original "sensible plan." Studies of popular culture produced from a learned position, he contends, inevitably "pursue across the surface of the texts, before their eyes, what is actually their own condition of possibility—the *elimination of a popular menace*" (128, emphasis added). For de Certeau, not even a scholar's rigorous and responsible reflexivity about the methods he/she uses can circumvent the acts of repression that obtain when learned culture tries to connect with popular culture: "We cannot ignore the fact that it is impossible for a *written* act (ours), an ambition, to suppress the history of a repression, to seriously purport to found a new kind of relation: the last ruse of knowledge is to reserve for itself the role of political prophesy" (135–36).

De Certeau's foregrounding of the "menace" inherent in popular culture is illuminating and unsettling. I understand his argument, and I understand, of course, that my being unsettled by it might be an indication of its force and its power. But I don't want this understanding to immobilize me. I don't want to rule out the possibility of connecting with, of writing about, popular texts in nonrepressive, or nonappropriative ways.[15] As I turn to Mexican ex-votos, then, I shall keep in mind the "menace" that the popular poses to the learned, but rather than focus on the ways in which the latter overpowers and elides the former, I want to foreground moments when the popular confronts (as in "stands up to") the learned and exposes the limits of its various discursive strategies of containment. But before I do this, I want to bring in another theorist of popular culture, one who in a 1976 text seems to call into question the possibly debilitating effects of de Certeau's critique.

In *The Cheese and the Worms: The Cosmos of a Sixteenth-Century Miller*, Carlo Ginzburg, addressing the state of popular culture studies, writes:

> But the fear of falling into a notorious, naive positivism, combined with the exasperated awareness of the ideological distortion that may lurk behind the most normal and seemingly innocent process of perception, prompts many historians today to discard popular culture together with the sources that provide a more or less distorted picture of it. After having criticized (and not without reason) the studies mentioned above on the literature of *colportage*, a number of scholars have begun to ask themselves whether "popular culture exists outside the act that suppresses it." The question is rhetorical, and the reply is obviously negative. This type of skepticism seems paradoxical at first glance since behind it stand the studies of Michel Foucault, the scholar who, with his *Histoire de la folie*, has most authoritatively drawn attention to the exclusions, prohibitions, and limits through which our culture came into being historically. But on second glance, it is a paradox only in appearance. What interests Foucault primarily are the act and the criteria of the exclusion, the excluded a little less so.[16]

What appeals to me about Ginzburg's project is its defense of the excluded. Clearly, that defense is theoretically interested. But the result of that defense is that it lets one of the excluded speak, relinquishing him from the anonymity, or worse namelessness, imposed on him by history, thus making possible a revision if not of history at least of a particular discourse of history. And what I find most instructive about this project is the respectful attention that Ginzburg's remarkable scholarship enables him to give Menocchio, the sixteenth-century miller who thus makes public his own understanding of cosmogony.

📖

Despite their presence in a few museums, galleries, private collections, and churches (Arizona, New Mexico, Mexican border), ex-votos are not yet widely known and appreciated in United States culture. Even as objects of collection, ex-votos remain for many the poor relatives of the much more valued and consequently valuable wood and tin santos, whose stark, half- Byzantine, half-El Grecoesque traits can be readily channeled within a more or less recognizable "Spanish" tradition.[17]

United States scholarship on the subject is still scanty. With the exception of a number of articles in art magazines and museum catalogs, the only three texts that I have found extremely useful in my attempt to write about ex-votos are Gloria Fraser Giffords's *Mexican Folk Retablos*, Jorge Durand and Douglas S. Massey's *Miracles on the Border: Retablos of Mexican Migrants in the United States*, and Sandra Cisneros's short story "Little Miracles, Kept Promises."

The result of extensive and unprecedented study,[18] Giffords's book focuses primarily on santos, but at the end, it gives ex-votos brief consideration, providing an elegant, succinct history of them, and suggesting new, fruitful directions for investigation: "In addition to their artistic merit . . . ex-votos are of great importance as sociological studies. An examination of all ex-votos in any one shrine or church would produce a fascinating record of the people's hopes and fears, their thoughts, lives, and experiences, a record more honest than the fullest statistical study" (147).

Giffords's suggestion that Mexican ex-votos might be more profitably studied as important sociological documents, rather than folkloristic niceties—a suggestion that Durand and Massey were soon to follow—will constitute, I believe, a new and more productive phase of their history. Although indirectly, Giffords herself provides dramatic evidence in her text of the extent to which social and political readings of ex-votos can contribute productive (iconoclastic and irreverent) revisions of what have so far been the two most influential readings of them: the artistic and the religious.

Giffords refers to ex-votos as "dramatic and charming" artifacts, "little story paintings [which] reveal much about the Mexican people and their art." This is the description she provides of them:

> An ex-voto is a votive painting hung on a church wall. . . . [It] is a receipted bill for spiritual or physical boons received. Truly *anecdotal*, the painting illustrates a written text that relates the circumstances of the cure or rescue. The written commentary is often so full of *regional dialect* and *phonetic spelling* that it is *impossible to translate it and still maintain the flavor.* . . . During the colonial epoch and until the end of the eighteenth century the offering of votive pictures was almost wholly confined to the wealthy. After the achievement of independence from Spain, the common man adopted the ex-voto for his own. Now he too made public his testimony of faith, for the ex-voto painting *depicted events in graphic terms for easy transmission to everyone, even the illiterate.* By far the greatest number of *ex-votos were produced for the masses,* for after the custom became popular with the illiterate classes it was abandoned by the wealthy (143, emphasis added).

It is clear that Giffords values ex-votos. And yet, what seems problematical to me about the discourse that frames her reading are the limits that discourse unwittingly imposes on the artist/scribe and on the "common man," the supplicant who needs the artist/scribe to make public his testimony of faith. Each little story is an "anecdote," conveyed in a language that cannot be translated lest it lose its (illiterate) "flavor." Moreover, if, as I assume, "the graphic terms for easy transmission" in the quotation are pictorial, what transpires from this language is that, even in its limited literacy, the written text is not adequate for the masses, who must rely on the visual.[19] I am suggesting that although the thrust of Giffords's reading is to turn ex-votos' iconographic illiteracy into an element of praise, one effect of that reading is that it confines the artists/scribes who produce them to a perpetual state of illiteracy since, were they to outgrow it, their products would no longer be invested with drama, charm, local flavor. What I am pointing out, in other words, are the limits of the traditional discourse of "art as folklore" and its ideology.[20]

In the section titled "The Artists," as she describes the outlook of ex-votos painters, Giffords turns to and cites Roberto Montenegro, one of the few "critical" authorities on the subject she claims she can cite. According to Giffords, Montenegro's *Retablos de Mexico* (1950) provided her with the only written material on ex-votos that is analytic rather than descriptive. She provides this excerpt:

> Stringent needs or rare intuition obliged the Mexican painters of the first half of the 19th century to begin their work painting the so-called "retablos" [ex-votos] and it is to their credit and at the same time to the advantage of these artists that they had no examples to guide them nor school of painting to follow. They pictured nature with the sincerity that is apparent in their work, ingenuously and with no other thought than to set down what appeared before them without hurry and without interest. No foreign review came to disturb their peace not to vary their program. Their creative activity limited itself to work in the endeavor to advance further toward perfection in the immense pleasure of painting. The lack of technique, the discretion of the use of tone and inimitable charm of the fashion of the time, created a school which affords us a sensation of sincerity and makes us see in those old and timeworn portraits the qualities which by their own merit, oblige us to give them a place of preference in our admiration (144).

As I read this passage, I was struck by the logic that leads Montenegro to read the circumstances for ex-votos' painters having "no example to guide them nor school of painting to follow" as complimentary and advantageous, with no mention or interrogation whatsoever of the socioeconomic emargination that deprived them of those examples and schools, or at least of the choice to follow or reject them. And I was struck by, and quite uneasy with, the artistic dicta that enable Montenegro to discern in their work the "sincerity," "the peace[full-ness]," and the "immense pleasure" of its production.[21]

Although Giffords does not overtly register the concerns I am raising, in the paragraph following the quotation from Montenegro, she does turn his words into an opportunity to provide a balanced and noncondescending assessment of the important differences between the painting of retablos and the painting of ex-votos.[22] A bit later, however, her unqualified reliance on another powerful discourse, the discourse of religion, to support her reading of ex-votos' visual composition, produces a disconcerting moment. She writes:

> Hierarchical scaling is used, and the figures are placed above each other, allowing everyone to be seen and counted. Pyramidally arranged groups are common, especially in earlier ex-votos. Such conventionalization of perspective heightens the charm and often intensifies the dramatic quality. The composition of the votive painting is arranged in horizontal bands with the written text appearing at the bottom, the action or miracle portrayed in the middle section, and at the top, less carefully defined, if at all, the area occupied by the image or images invoked. "Man is a kind of deep-air animal crawling on rock bottom, his face lifted to a stratosphere where the holy beings dwell. These in turn bend over the ledge of the dense pool, in search of their faithful" (145).

Up to the last three lines, the excerpt from Giffords's text can be read as a straightforward compositional analysis. But the last three lines suggest that ex-votos disseminate a view of humankind as radically separate from things of the spirit. Indeed, this is the traditional function attributed to them by the discourse of religion.[23] I want to suggest, however, the established hierarchization can also be seen as serving ex-voto artists in a different way: through slight modifications, alterations, transformations of it, they can suggest or convey alternative, perhaps resistant, perhaps wishful conceptions of the supplicant's relation to and submission to the divine (fig. 4). I shall return to this later.

The possibility that ex-votos may express something other than constant and total subjugation to and acceptance of dire fate was perceived by Diego Rivera and apparently by his student and collaborator, Jean Charlot, author of "Mexican Ex-Votos" (1949), who happens to be the source of the unglossed quotation in Giffords's excerpt.

Giffords's text makes Charlot's words function as supporting evidence for the condition of faith that requires and inspires the supplicant serenely to genuflect to God's will. But in their original context, in a context that deploys the discourse of social analysis and critique within which the discourses of religion and art speak with a different accent, the same words grant ex-votos at the

FIGURE 4

least the power to highlight in a potentially critical way "the duality between the human and the divine."

On at least one occasion, Rivera put his admiration of retablos into practice. When during the 1920s the labor leader Vicente Lombardo Toledano wanted to prepare a pamphlet to counter the admonition of conservative priests that land redistribution was against the teachings of Christ, Diego Rivera, the good communist, offered his services to create an illustration for the cover: an engraving drawn in the manner of a retablo.

The picture shows a poor campesino plowing the land behind two oxen while the peasant's wife sits nearby with tortillas in a basket. In the upper right corner of the print, Christ appears suspended in clouds with his sacred heart exposed, and the text states: . . . (The redistribution of lands to the poor is not against the teachings of Jesus Christ or the Holy Mother Church. The Mexican people fought and suffered for ten years seeking to find word of Our Lord Jesus). The religious image, text, composition, and placement of the figures clearly mark the work as a retablo.

Rivera's student and collaborator in the muralist movement, Jean Charlot, saw the power of retablos as emanating from their expression of the duality between the human and the divine. "Like the scaffold-sets of medieval mystery plays, the plastic dramas of the retablos are tiered vertically. Man is a kind of deep-air animal crawling on rock bottom, his face lifted to a stratosphere where the holy beings dwell. These in turn bend over the ledge of the dense pool, in search of their faithful" (Charlot 1949:141)[24] (37–38).

This lengthy passage comes from Jorge Durand and Douglas S. Massey's *Miracles on the Border: Retablos of Mexican Migrants to the United States*. This book makes available especially useful reproductions of beautiful ex-votos and offers an important, well-balanced, and intelligent analysis of them. Durand, a social anthropologist, and Massey, a sociologist, read and convincingly establish the importance of retablos as rare sources of documentation of the migratory experiences of Mexicans to the United States. In other words, their discourse acknowledges a function of ex-votos that exclusively hierarchical types of discourses, as that of highbrow art and religion, cannot acknowledge.

This is not to say that Durand and Massey are uninterested in or unreceptive to the artistic and religious meaning of the ex-votos. Quite the contrary. Like Giffords, whose work they praise and see themselves as continuing and expanding, they also comment on the simple technique, on the semiliterate language, on the "childlike" grammar, on the human and religious traits of these objects. But because, like Carlo Ginzburg, they are intent on reclaiming the agency of the subaltern, the Mexican migrants whose thinking and experiences—they argue—are usually excluded from the copious available literature on migration, whenever they have recourse to the discourses of art and religion, the results are remarkably different. This is how they describe their scholarly goals:

> Studies of Mexican retablos that have been published in the United States so far have focused primarily on *santos*. . . . Less attention has been paid to *ex-votos*. . . . A principal goal of this book is to attract greater attention to votive paintings as meritorious works of popular art.
>
> A second goal of this volume it to shed light on the origins of votive paintings. . . . Understanding the distinct historical and religious roots of [santos and ex-votos] helps to explain the relatively greater influence of ex-votos on the development of Mexican fine arts, a conundrum that has puzzled Giffords.
>
> A third aim of this book is to illuminate the effect of ex-voto on the theory, practice, and aesthetics of Mexican fine arts during the twentieth century . . . in particular on the work of Frida Kahlo, who owes by far the greatest debt to retablo painting.
>
> In presenting retablos commissioned or painted by Mexican migrants to the United States, we seek not only to achieve artistic goals, but also to understand more deeply an important sociological phenomenon—international migration. By carefully examining ex-votos left at key Mexican religious shrines, we hope to explicate the role that holy images play in the lives of Mexicans living abroad. We believe that these icons . . . provide a spiritual and cultural anchor for Mexicans in the northern diaspora, giving them a familiar cultural lens through which they can interpret and assimilate the fragmented and often disorienting experiences of life in an alien land (3–4).

Two points are particularly worthy of attention: Durand and Massey's inversion of the traditional hierarchy, an inversion that establishes the humble ex-voto as the *source of inspiration* for Frida Kahlo's paintings, and the *interpretive and transformative* ("a familiar cultural lens") rather than only the *adaptive* force of their religious function. (The compositional similarity between fig. 5 and fig. 6 is striking. Note Frida Kahlo's use of ex-voto to commemorate Dorothy Hale's suicide, hardly a religious subject. The person who commissioned the painting, Clare Booth Luce, was so horrified by Kahlo's work that she requested she expunge her name, which Kahlo had inscribed in the text at the bottom according to the tradition of ex-votos. An empty space marks its removal.)

A sense of faithful subjugation is all but absent in the ex-votos Sandra Cisneros composes for her short story, "Little Miracles, Kept Promises," a piece that pays homage to while it exposes the incongruity and the potential dysfunctionalism of this votive practice. While the length, the complexity, and especially the humor of the texts that form her narrative mark their fictionality, this fictionality simultaneously pokes fun at the supplicants who ask for mundane things, for material goods, or for divine intervention as a cure for human foibles, as well as the religious practice itself for lending itself to such transformation and interpretation.

In the biographical sketch that introduces the short story, the editor writes: "Cisneros says that she became a writer because she was 'determined to fill a literary void' . . . trying to write the stories that haven't been written."[25] In "Little Miracles, Kept Promises," as she calls attention to the potential for ex-votos to invert the "hierarchical scaling" that constructs the supplicant as distant from and submitting to divinity, she writes a story about ex-votos that available scholarship only fugitively refers to. Through humor she acknowledges a need that many faithful have, more often perhaps than they are allowed publicly to manifest: the need to speak back to, to interrogate, even to inveigh at the celestial powers who sometimes seem unjust or unconcerned. The fact that her examples are not necessarily or always (which might be a deft strategy of deflation) tragic does not lessen the poignancy of that need. Here are three exemplary sections:

> Dear San Antonio de Padua,
>
> Can you please help me find a man who isn't a pain in the nalgas. There aren't any in Texas, I swear. Especially not in San Antonio.
>
> Can you do something about all the educated Chicanos who have to go to California to find a job. I guess what my sister Irma says is true: "If you didn't get a husband when you were in college, you don't get one."
>
> I would appreciate it very much if you sent me a man who speaks pro-

FIGURE 5

Frida Kahlo, Mexican (1907–1954), *Suicide of Dorothy Hale*, 1939. Gift of an anonymous donor. © Phoenix Art Museum.

30 de Octubre de 1868

Recuerdo de gratitud al S.or de Esquipula.

FIGURE 6

nounced. Someone please who never calls himself "Hispanic" unless he's apply-
ing for a grant from Washington, D.C.

Can you send me a man man. . . .

I'll turn your statue upside down until you send him to me. I've put up
with too much too long, and now I'm just too intelligent, too powerful, too
beautiful, too sure of who I am finally to deserve anything less.

Ms. Barbara Ybañez

San Antonio, TX

Dear Niño Fidencio,

I would like for you to help me get a job with good pay, benefits, and re-
tirement plan. I promise you if you help me I will make a pilgrimage to your
tomb in Espinazo and bring you flowers. Many thanks.

César Escandón

Pharr, Tejas

Dear San Lázaro,

My mother's comadre Demetria said if I prayed to you that like maybe you
could help me because you were raised from the dead and did a lot of miracles
and maybe if I lit a candle every night for seven days and prayed, you might
maybe could help me with my face breaking out with so many pimples. Thank
you.

Rubén Ledesma

Hebbronville, Texas

Some of the other texts are more deferential than the ones I cite, and ask
for relief from poor health or grave economic situations rather than from the
ravishing of acne or the specter of a nalgas-less man. I have selected these three
because of the supplicants' confrontational and bargaining stance they convey.

Thomas J. Steele, in *Santos and Saints: The Religious Folk Art of Hispanic New Mexico*,
notices this stance as well, as he writes about people's intimate relationship to
saints in Hispanic New Mexican culture. While this intimacy made the presence
of saints in people's lives a daily occurrence, Steele points out, it also occasionally excessively scaled down and humanized the saints: "If the saint seemed to
refuse the favor or even subject the devotee to an unreasonable delay, the santo
might suffer a punishment of shame by being turned to the wall, put out of
sight, or deprived of some ornament." Having said this much, Steele soon adds,
"Such behavior could not have been typical of a people too intelligent and rever-
ent and realistic to be childishly petulant when disappointed."[26] So, while Steele
acknowledges this human penchant for confronting the divine, he also deftly
controls the potential "menace" it poses by categorizing it as an act of childish

petulance attributable to limited intelligence, insufficient reverence, and lack of realistic expectations.

Cisneros makes no attempt to scale down this petulance, and in so doing she highlights a different kind of "childish spontaneity." Moreover, she suggests the strategic importance of more closely considering that feature of ex-votos that, although constitutive of them (as different, for example, from santos and milagros), usually gets slighter attention: the written text.

Giffords refers to ex-votos as "dramatic and charming . . . little story paintings [that] reveal much about the Mexican people and their art"; (143) Cisneros eliminates the pictorial aspect,[27] the feature that has brought them to the attention of art scholars and art dealers, inserts ex-votos in the realm of literature, reconstitutes them as documents of literacy rather than illiteracy,[28] and indicates their potential for social critique. The ex-votos she produces, examples of *rasquacismo*, turn the table on the traditions that brokered them and on traditional benevolent but limiting readings.

📖

To focus essentially on the naive, the charming, the primitive, and the religious in ex-votos, I believe, risks obfuscating (intentionally or not) their potential to function as records of social indictment, as texts, that can not only document, but also mirror back and critique the dissemination of unquestioning and unquestioned religious practices, of modes of writing history that pass over the deeds of the disenfranchised, and of conceptions of education that deny or are disrespectful of the intellectual agency of the illiterate or semiliterate.

In what follows, I want to propose a reading of ex-votos that examines the kind of literacy they are produced by and represent, and I want to focus on moments when this particular kind of literacy can be made to raise irreverent and petulant questions of the learned cultural and religious traditions that try to contain it. Specifically, I want to look at the iconographic literacy of ex-votos as a *cultural lens* that alters and throws into unexpected relief the following practices: the pictorial composition, the *reconoscimiento* formula, the commissioning of the ex-voto, and the artist's anonymity.

Composition: As scholars of ex-votos point out, the visual composition of these objects is usually simple, two-dimensional, predictable. When this composition is altered, however, when, for example, the space between the human and the divine is contracted, or when, as in fig. 4, the placing of the figures is boldly inverted, the human (in this case, a sister) being placed in the hierarchical space of the divine, the attribute of simplicity usually assigned to them gains a different valence: laconic and effective, direct and incisive, rather than charming and childlike. In other words, simplicity can be imagined as a surplus rather than a deficit category, one that creates rather than occludes a range (albeit limited) of alternatives. Something similar happens with what is considered another "conventional" feature of ex-votos, their iconography. Ex-votos are said to reproduce sanctioned ecclesiastical images. In fact, scholars of ex-votos have argued that they were allowed to flourish because they could function as distributors of such images among the people. Interestingly, however, many ex-votos function as records of local elaborations of available images, reproductions of local saints, regional incarnations of the Virgin Mary.

In Italian scholarship, modifications of the agiographic and iconographic canon are explained as representations of divine entities who appeared to the poor of the area. This explains representations of Mary and Child in or at the foot of a tree (Madonna Incoronata, near Foggia, Puglia), in or on a cloud (a variation of the classic almond?) suspended on a well (Madonna del Pozzo, at Capurso, near Bari, Puglia), or on a fountain (Madonna della Fontana, at Torremaggiore, near Foggia, Puglia)—as apparitions are said to occur. The function that ex-votos fulfill as they represent and disseminate these local religious traditions is worth considering. Although, often, these representations of local apparitions are neither officially recognized nor accepted by the Church, in so far as they remain on the walls of sanctuaries, churches, shrines that attract and draw sustenance—spiritual and monetary—from the pilgrims who choose to visit them to pray and offer thanks, they register a form of cultural resistance from subaltern classes to the dicta of a Church far removed from the supplicants. In other words, by interpreting for and giving back to the subaltern their local iconography (and the unofficial agiography it institutes), ex-votos can be seen as means of *establishing, disseminating, and authenticating* popular cults that enact the belief in or desire for a given Saint's or Madonna's *partiality to* the wretched of the earth.

As far as Mexican ex-votos' adherence to this process is concerned, Durand and Massey argue that occasionally ex-votos replace the divine with common and not necessarily saintly people, people who were perhaps wronged by authorities and began to be invoked as protectors, Robin Hoods. This practice is fascinating but hardly surprising. It may signify an inversion of historical Catholic superimpositions on and appropriations of local, autochthonous pagan cults—an inversion by which the retablista, and the supplicant whose stories he/she mediates, substitutes *his/her own ways* of conceiving of and communicating with the divine for *the ways the Church sanctions*. These are significant ways by which ex-votos may enter or contest official, well established histories of devotion.

Reconoscimiento: Traditionally, supplicants offer ex-votos "after the fact" (although some are promissory notes):[29] the written text that explains the circumstances of the dire situation and its possible or hoped for resolution, is generally rather sparse, schematic. The text says that the ex-voto is being offered *en reconoscimiento*, or *en testimonio* of a grace already received or yet to be granted through divine intercession. The "recording" of gratitude is a fixed and constant formula of ex-votos, just as much as the recording of the supplicant's name, and place and time of the event, and it is traditionally seen as a demonstration of a people's faith. But given the traditional accent of Catholic religion on a faith based on resignation to God's will, on the capacity to offer the other cheek, on the knowledge that real happiness belongs in the beyond, the *reconoscimiento* element suggests that ex-votos may function less as documentations of mystical devotion and ascetic renunciation ("I will continue to pray and accept my lot no matter what"), than as documentations of strong hopes, even requests, to see an earthly realization of faith, in the here and now of life. "Save me and I will. . ."; "Grant me this, and I will." Subtending this votive offering is a certain negotiational *quid pro quo* (one that Cisneros and Rivera have foregrounded). It seems to me that this *quid pro quo*, this act of bargaining, dramatically restructures the relation between the supplicant and the divine entity.[30] Within the small space of the ex-voto, the distance between the earthly/ human/quotidian, and the heavenly/divine/eternal is dramatically contained, made manageable, graspable.

The public acknowledgment of the favor granted, which it is the function of the ex-voto's narrative to perform, and which is the most salient trait of this religious artifact, bears some resemblance to a rather common (popular) Catholic practice: at the entrance of some Churches a book is placed for parishioners and visitors to write down invocations and expressions of thanks for graces received. Yet another popular practice instructs practitioners of Novenas (actually the text of the Novena itself does it) to leave (one or multiple copies of) the text from which they recite the Novena each day for nine consecutive days in a visible spot in Church, so that somebody else might pick up the text, read it, be comforted by it, copy it and extend the devotion. In so far as processes of canonization, beatification and sanctification, as well as the Church's acknowledgment of "holy" grounds and sanctuaries, are based on documentations of devotions, graces, and miracles,[31] it could be argued that the literacy practices inherent in ex-votos, as well as books of miracles and prayers, and novenas, are not acknowledged in and of themselves, but because of their use value for the making of history. Undeniably. But it could also be argued, more constructively and interestingly, that these texts are records of popular culture asserting itself, and finding expression and some comfort, in the language of religion.[32]

Commissioning: Historically, because they were illiterate, whether as painters or readers and writers, supplicants could not personally write and paint their expressions of thanksgiving to the divine image they prayed to. So they commissioned that expression to somebody who could, and would, while remaining anonymous.

Here, too, there is an interesting kind of *quid pro quo* at work: it's the money (quid), albeit a small sum, that the supplicant pays the retablista in exchange for (pro) the commissioned ex-voto (quo). In other words, the tradition of commissioning calls attention to the fact that the documentation and documentability of the miracle rests on a commercial transaction. I am beginning to wonder whether the tradition of the retablista's anonymity might be a way of defusing that economic transaction.

Commissioning works of art has been historically a marker of high culture and economic status, even if such status might have not always been indicative of the supplicant's literacy. In the case of ex-votos, as well, the act of commissioning is a marker of culture and economic status, albeit limited. The supplicant knows of and partakes in certain religious and cultural practices; like a patron, the supplicant pays for the service he/she has commissioned. (The payment might have required considerable sacrifices; nevertheless, it is conceivable there might be some who don't even have that little to give up.) In this case, however, and as many studies of ex-votos point out, the supplicant's need for, rather than the patronlike act of commissioning, becomes the focus of attention. Likewise, the literacy acts of the artist scribe, the "letter writer" for the supplicant, are rendered anonymous, and are focused on for their "color." In this context, both the patron's and the artist's practices are read as markers of illiteracy or inadequate literacy.

Anonymity: *Porque no puedo decir mi cuento. . . . Because I cannot tell my story, I rely on somebody else to tell it for me.* The words that make my title are not a citation. As far as I know, they have not been actually spoken. Had they been spoken, could they have been spoken, the tradition of ex-votos I have discussed might not have "flourished" as it did. "Porque no puedo": what happens if we interrogate "porque" rather than tacitly accept "no puedo"? What does it mean? "Porque no puedo": because I can't? because I don't know how? because I am not allowed to? because I am not allowed to know how? And what about the "porque no puedo" that consigns the work of the artist/scribe to anonymity?[33] These questions still haunt me.

Significantly, recent transformations in the tradition of ex-votos seem to address the questions I have been raising in ways that simultaneously validate them and render them moot.

Production of traditional Mexican (and Italian) ex-votos seems to have decreased around 1950 or 1960. There aren't many retablistas left who practice this art form or can afford to keep this art form alive. The dying out of this tradition has interesting consequences. Let me name two. Once the appeal of this art form has been established and sanctioned in different ways, for different reasons, by scholars in different disciplines, Mexican ex-votos have become highly collectible and marketable. An underground economy has developed. Fakes are produced on rusty sheets of metal and sold as authentic (The artist/scribe's anonymity poses interesting questions about the "author" as the "index" of authenticity.) Although highly perishable, because of their materials and means of production, they have now been given by the law of supply and demand a market value they didn't have in their original economy. In this case, the "arrest" of the tradition renders their religiosity incidental at best, and prevents the literacy practices they document, and the relations between supplicant, divinity, artist/scribe from changing. But it also "fixes" them in ways that make it possible to study their religiosity, their literacy practices, and the divine and human relations they presupposed and reinscribed.

The other consequence makes ex-votos less valuable, and yet it calls for and makes possible interesting changes in their traditional composition, and literacy practices.

The availability of photographic cameras makes it possible for the supplicant to appear in the ex-voto as he/she looks in real life. This "presence" allows for visual recognition and identification on the part of the viewer. For those who can read, the name in the text provides validation. In this version of ex-votos, the Saints or the Virgin appear in "estampidas"/"immaginette" [holy images]. The representations of the divine and the human are pasted to or stapled on a sheet of (often lined) paper. The three partite hierarchical composition is no longer closely observed. The text, whether or not written by the supplicant, may appear at the bottom, in a corner, on the side from top to bottom. The arrangement may be placed in a frame. In this transformation the supplicant reclaims his/her narrative agency from the artist/scribe who has traditionally mediated it, and from a tradition that had established this dependence. (Whether or not this transformation is a marker of supplicants' higher literacy is worth researching.)

Gone is the artist/scribe, his cultural mediation and artistic function no longer needed. Aesthetically, this transformation produces less valuable, less "picturesque" (see, for example, Italian ex-voto in fig. 2), and consequently less collectible ex-votos. It is a loss, one that even I regret, if or when I become oblivious to the price exacted by the continuation of the cultural and economic conditions that led to this art form.

As I said at the outset, I have known of the existence of ex-votos since I was a child. My early exposure to these artifacts of popular religion, and my familiarity with Italian scholarship on this subject, have made it possible for me to recognize the "object" the Philadelphia vendor was selling, to name it, and to re-trace it, through a process of collecting and scholarly research, to a "tradition" that so deeply, so fundamentally connects Mexican and Italian culture. It is in the name of this connection, of which I don't have immediate experience, but which I nevertheless want to contribute to make visible, that I want to reply to de Certeau. He argues that "popular culture can only be grasped in the process of vanishing," and that scholarly works are responsible for much of that vanishing. I argue that it need not be so. In fact I want to suggest that his exasperated awareness of the obliterations that may result from scholarly incursions into popular culture should not make us desist from, but rather assist us in, trying to understand the vernacular eloquence of popular culture.

In lieu of a conclusion

In the summer of 1999, I was shopping for nativity scenes (which I collect) in a store in Tucson, when an embroidered piece, encased in a distressed turquoise wood frame, caught my attention because of its compositional similarity to ex-votos (fig. 7). I asked the storeowner what she knew about its provenance. She handed me an anonymous leaflet, titled "Milagro del Dia. Embroidered Ex-Votos: Stories of Life in Rural Mexico," an account of how this version of ex-votos came to be established. Although the account refers to "we" and gives the first name of one of the two people responsible for this particular adaptation of the ex-voto tradition, their names (Susan White and Tom Baer), in a respectfully self-effacing gesture, do not appear on the leaflet. "Milagro del Dia" provides the following information:

> This collection of work is made up of individual ex- votos drawn and embroidered by women living in a group of pueblitos in the state of Guadanajuato in Central Mexico. These small rural communities are populated by the Chichimecas, who were never conquered by the Spanish, in the sixteenth century. But, as in many rural communities in Mexico, economic conditions have driven large numbers of the men from the land in search of work.
>
> This project provides the women of the rancho a means of supporting their families, as well as a unique avenue of personal expression. It also offers viewers outside the community the chance to appreciate the lives and the artistry of these campesina women.
>
> We began this project in September 1997 in collaboration with the local group

FIGURE 7

Mujeres en Cambio (Women in Change), which is devoted to improving the lot of women in the countryside through projects in ecology and economic self-sufficiency.

Our interest in traditional *retablo* and *ex voto* painting and our desire to work with the women to improve their condition led to our asking them to make work about their lives. It is immediately clear on viewing the collection that these pieces were made by women of deep religious conviction. For the campesinas, every new day is indeed a miracle and every aspect of their lives is imbued with a fundamental sense of connection to a greater whole.

We meet with these women every week, bringing the thread and cloth for the *bordados,* and buying outright the completed pieces. This way, they can work without leaving their families, and they have a dependable source of income. It also allows them the freedom to take creative chances they might not otherwise. Susan, an experienced art professor, works with the women to develop their creative potential, but the stories, the images, and the invention are all their own.

The transformations of traditional Mexican ex-votos brought about by the intervention of a group like *Mujeres en Cambio* and socially committed artists like Susan White and her husband, Tom Baer, are worth noticing. Ex-votos are now produced by women. As the gender of the artist changes, so do the materials of production (from tin to cloth; from paint to thread; from paintbrush to needle), and the immediate monetary value of the artifact: the women embroider and sell their embroideries, and the money they make through their craft benefits them and their communities. In so far as some of the stories these embroideries tell address "the subjects of alcoholism, and domestic violence, the destruction of the natural environment, and even just 'life in the old days'" ("Milagro del Dia"), the artist's role shifts from conveyor of thanks to transmitter of educational messages. Feminized, the genre realigns traditional asymmetries of gender power, becoming a vehicle of social intervention.

As I was writing this postscript, a friend of mine who lives in Tucson and knows of my passion for and work with ex-votos, sent me the winter issue of *Tucson Guide,* featuring an engaging and well-researched article by Nancy Wall, titled "Retablos and Santos." As I do, Wall cites as important sources of information on Mexican ex-votos Giffords's *Mexican Folk Retablos,* and *Miracles on the Border* by Durand and Massey, as well as the work of Susan White and Tom Baer, about whom she writes:

> While living in San Miguel de Allende, in the state of Guanajuato, White encouraged women from nearby communities to tell their stories, their miracles—the brother saved from drowning, the child who escaped uninjured from the burning house—in needlework. The women managed the pictures, but as most of them could neither read nor write, they had to enlist the help of their children in printing the stories on the fabric, making a pattern for their thread to follow. . . . What started out as an experiment with a few women has grown into a project enabling close to 80 women, supporting several hundred children, to make a living from their work.[34]

I am mesmerized by the images this narrative evokes: women, unable to read or write, retrace, with needles as their pens, the words their children have printed on the fabric, their thwarted literacy simultaneously displayed and transmuted through the production of ex-votos. If the reversal of instructional roles induces embarrassment, it neither singles out—the majority of women can neither read nor write—nor incapacitates—women and their children invent their own literacy practices in a cycle of instructional intimacy that lessens their dependence on outsiders. And here I want to call attention to White and Baer's deliberate anonymity, a gesture that richly complicates the anonymity of traditional ex-voto painters/scribes.

It can, of course, be argued that the transformations I have noted are autocratic. Without White and Baer, and their interest in retablo and ex-voto painting, the campesinas might have developed another project. They might have produced bordados of nativity scenes, or weddings, or other colorful scenes typical of Mexican popular art. On the other hand, it can also be argued that the transformations tap into something that is already there, or readily reachable, "the deep religious conviction" of the Chichimecas women. What I find striking about this expression of religiosity is that it does not transfix them in a state of submission; rather, it brings about the articulation of literacy practices instrumental to their subsistence.

I want to end by bringing forth another haunting scene of instruction, another scene where religion seems to necessitate and make possible sophisticated literacy practices. It's a scene that encourages me to focus away from the Bunuellian procession of beggars pushing forward to occupy their accustomed spaces, to observe, respectfully, the literacy and social strategies religion requires of and fosters for those people who feel the need and claim the right to communicate about what matters in their lives:

> It is early morning and the bells in the Church of the Virgin of San Juan de los Lagos are ringing. With the third chime comes the hour to open the main entrance. As the door swings ajar, beggars push forward to occupy their accustomed places on the staircase of the large atrium, and assorted vendors of prints, rosaries, and novena booklets bustle in to set up their booths and stalls. The nuns open up the stand where they will receive the day's alms, and in the sacristy the priest dons his robes to celebrate the day's first mass. . . .
>
> To one side of the sacristy, in the Virgin's Chamber, the daily presentation of votives begins, fulfilling vows made days, weeks, months, or even years earlier. This is the center to which pilgrims come from throughout the region to leave small paintings on sheets of tin to offer thanks to the Virgin of San Juan de los Lagos for a miracle granted or a favor received. People begin to enter; they cross the room and look intently at the pictures, carefully reading the texts on each one. They discuss the miraculous events quietly among themselves, are amazed, and reflect privately on the import. They look with care for a spot to put their own offerings. From crumpled brown bags they take out their own small paintings wrapped in old newspapers, along with a sketch, and perhaps a photo. With pins and tape they arrange the offerings to form a harmonic whole, so that their miraculous story can be seen and known by all, at least for a time (Durand and Massey, 1–2).

The two scenes of instruction with which I bring this piece to closure, not uncommon in literacy scholarship, represent ways of making us hear the silences of history that are neither repressive nor condescending. They suggest the wisdom of tempering, though not forgetting, de Certeau's warning about the dynamics of repression potentially at work in outsiders' interventions in "popular culture."

two **Gypsy Fullstop Punctuates Imperialism**

Charles Keil

> Writing was one of the original mysteries of civilization, and it re-
> duced the complexities of experience to the written word. . . . With
> the advent of writing, symbols became explicit; they lost a certain
> richness. Man's word was no longer an endless exploration of reality,
> but a sign that could be used against him.
>
> —(DIAMOND 4)

I went to Nigeria in 1965 to do my fieldwork for a Ph.D. degree at the University of Chicago. I selected the Tiv people because they were so musical. I transcribed their songs and liked what I had read about them as a tribe without
rulers, radically egalitarian, decentralized, competitive people—"fiercely independent peasants" was the way they were described in the literature.

Sculpture of Gypsy Fullstop by Chiki

And sure enough, the Tiv, settled on both sides of the Benue River in the middle of the Nigerian Savanna country, were independently minded people, very stubborn, honest, blunt, and clear in their responses to any question. Meeting people, talking with them, seeing the great energies they put into music and dance, I became convinced that the Tiv were an exemplary classless society (Keil); not as egalitarian as the Mbuti (Turnbull), Semai (Dentan), Kaluli (Feld),[1] or other hunter-gatherer peoples around the planet, but in comparison with other settled farmers, they had a deep tradition of distrusting authority, a natural skepticism about anybody who was getting more than anybody else. They believed in a zero-sum-game of life in which people who get too far ahead are probably doing it by witchcraft and evil purposes, so if anybody was too successful they were usually ostracized as someone greedy at the expense of their fellow humans.

So it was in this context that British imperialism had a difficult time conquering Tivland. Actually, Tivland was one of the last pieces of Nigeria to go under because the British couldn't figure out how to get control of it. There was no chief to negotiate with, no one who could say "We surrender" and speak for more than fifty or sixty people in a compound. So it was only after World War I that Tivland came under some form of British control. The British tried to develop institutions of indirect rule by appointing chiefs and developing an infrastructure, but had to send a lot of their own people into the territory to rule the Tiv because they didn't have a chief, a king, or an emir to coerce.

Some weeks into my fieldwork I was in the marketplace of Makurdi and ran into a man with a placard around his neck; he was talking fast and arguing with people very insistently, and he immediately asked me to read and sign his text. People said, "This is Gypsy Fullstop." There was a lot of laughter. I read his placard, thought it was interesting, signed it, and suggested that he see my wife in the government residential area, while thinking to myself that since she was the psychologist in the family, maybe she could figure out what he was about.

Gypsy Fullstop's primary document was mounted on cardboard with strings attached so that he could wear it hanging around his neck. The borders of it were made up of British pound signs, with rows and rows of &&&&&&&&& and @@@@@@@@@ as well.

> A. Jurisprudence. Jurisdiction. A. Governorship.
> Justification. or Justifiably. cap 208. to 276.
> Residency or Residencial a Govt. A. Gypsy, Gipsy.
> and heed. Act. Above. cap 216 203 to 224. Both Hnss.
> Secretarial duties and secretary, cap 455. service-
> ableness. service. cap 459. with partnership. as

Police. (1). Warder. and Policy, N:A: Also Clerks.
And Chief clerk. Councillors. cap 99. Govt. cap 385
cap 346. Court Notice. Govt. Above. A. Negro. and Anglo.
Saxon. to A.S. Anglo Saxon. cap 579 to 589. Authority.
Above Staff. London Markurdi Command. 169. Eye-Serve
in the inspection of a employers. and enlistment. cap 169
The above appellational and titled. Act. to be tribune.

        [*tribune crossed out to spell tribal*—C. K.][2]

to Tributarily. Above. Laborious, Slav'ishness. Above.
World. Done. Law. King. the owner. cap 278. to 411.
(f) and resident, Governor, conquered. By Above. Take o-
ver controll.
[*hand written additions*—C. K.] parliament and parliamentary.
The owner. cap 362. Authority. as,
prescribed. owner. Lord R.G.T. Above.
GOVT. cap 208 [*scribbled signature*—C. K.] R.A.S H.L.
    [*typed again*—C. K.]   Sign: . . . .

                               A. Negro and Anglo

               saxon. As A.S. Ang-
               lo Saxon. Pool. Above.

     W EATHER . 558

[*hand written*—C. K.]   Jeopardy. Banks. and Bankly.
    Makurdi. i/c Africa

Over the following months, Gypsy Fullstop would come by with his messages, word salads, coded Fullstop talk on the page. He came punctually; if we
said we would expect him at 1:00, he was there on the dot, even though he
didn't wear a watch. He was always intense, serious, thin, animated, and went
about his business, which included giving us a remarkable wooden statue of
himself, "cruciferous." (The two-foot tall statue of his dead cruciferous self sits
on my desk as I write, and either Fullstop or the sculptor marked it with sergeant's stripes on one arm and a scarification under one eye to make it a portrait.) The word salads fascinated me. And I've been fascinated ever since, always
thinking that someday I would find the time to figure out their fuller and deeper
meanings.

    I've just spent a week poring over them and finding out that I don't know
how to interpret them, that studying them intensely and comparing texts for a

week or two will not make them reveal much more to me than they have in the past. I feel a little foolish that all these years since 1965 I've been building a personal cult around Fullstop, thinking of him as a kind of angel who intervened in my life path, this avatar of literacy, this personification of the period. I've made him part of my life. Part of the reason I've been studying the music of settled Gypsies in Greece over the years is that they are fullstopped Gypsies. I have Fullstop stationery that I use when I'm trying to communicate something about The 12/8 Path, a groovy, anticivilizational religion I've created for myself <128path.org>. I think of him as a kind of spiritual force or soul force, the wampeter in my karass (as Kurt Vonnegut might put it), an orientation point, literally, against which I counterpoint my life of music, poetry, organizing events, and trying to create music-dance pathways for people. Somehow Fullstop is there alongside me as a warning of some kind, an inspiration for getting into my own godhead, a path-clearer, a point that I counterpoint.

So who was this Gypsy Fullstop? That was his main name, what most people called him. He would occasionally refer to Gypsy or Fullstop in his writings, putting (Fullstop) inside the parentheses, but he would also sign all his documents in a little bunched-up scribble "R. G. T. Above"—Royal Government Tyrannical Above. Sometimes he would also sign "J. Jeopardy" with J. probably standing for Jeopardous, and sometimes he would refer to himself as Rolling Stone or Lord Rolling Stone, the form he was in when he created heaven and earth. All of these names combine in the period, the full stop. Full Stop is the core name. He was the period in every sentence that he wrote and, I presume, in every sentence that he saw. Whenever he would read to us his documents he would say the word and then "full stop I conquer," insisting that this point was his act of controlling what preceded the full stop, controlling the word and the world. "Not European. Not African. Gypsy," he would often say. Gypsy Fullstop, a wandering Fullstop, a rolling stone, always in motion and like God, omnipresent. So many sentences in so many different books and every one that ends in a period proves his point. This period . that's Him. His spirit resides in all fullstops.

That's a big claim to make, to be the conclusion of every declarative sentence. Those three dots on the page are not just a break in the narrative. The dots we now call "bullets"? The black spot in Treasure Island? That dot of greeting carried by the messenger from Tralfamadore in another Vonnegut novel? The decimal point? "Laborious" he often put toward the end of a message. "Sweat." "Slavishness." He'd refer to the labor of being this fullstop in all times and places. It's hard work being God.

What of all his other names—Lord Rolling Stone as opposed to Living Stone? I am sure he knew the Stanley and Livingstone story and was positioning himself vis-à-vis Livingstone the white explorer of Africa; he was a Gypsy exploring the world in the other direction. He sometimes carried rounded stones (thunder stones?) from place to place in the "Government Residential Area" on the hill where we lived overlooking Makurdi. I suspect that he thought he was participating in the stones and in each fullstop he pointed to: "I am here, and here, and here, I am everywhere I need to be, keeping things in order, stopping what might otherwise fly out of control." The maddening part of reading the messages is that I know he chose every word with one or more purposes behind each one. There is no binder, fluff, or burble. You know a punctuation mark means something, and no word is wasted, in his mind. Royal Tyrannical Above. Above is the last name, a translation from Tiv "aondo," which means "sky" or "heavens," but the missionaries used it to mean "God" in their Bible translations.

How did he get to be God? The basic information that we pieced together, from his own accounts and from primary school graduates who worked for us as translators, was that he had been in the Burma Rifles, a Nigerian army unit that served the British in the campaigns of World War II. He may have been to Egypt, he probably spent some time in India, so he was sophisticated in terms of seeing the world, fighting in foreign lands. When he came back he served for some years as a sergeant in the Native Authority Police, and his references to cap number this and cap number that, most of the numbers that are sprinkled throughout many of his messages, are references to a law book that I've never been able to find. I'm sure Fullstop knew exactly which statutes and rules he was citing.

As a prosecutor, he was probably responsible for presenting cases to the judge for the government, and so he learned the whole letter of the law and law of the letter by heart. He knew the legalities of the British empire as they impacted on the Tiv people, with all of their distrust and dislike of authority, and their deeply rooted egalitarian ways. At some point the British put him in a bigger bind by appointing him a tax chief or a district chief responsible for as many as one hundred thousand people in one of the major divisions of Tivland.

Caught between the British empire and these egalitarian Tiv traditions, he cracked around 1959. Something snapped; he states that he became "cruciferous," "jeopardous," on trial himself. He often pointed to scars on his knees as proof of being shot or killed. He died and was reborn or "resuscitated" as Gypsy Fullstop, Royal Government Tyrannical Above. These three terms differentiate him from Christ who was crucified, in jeopardy, resurrected, and who seems to be one of Fullstop's many sons in His scheme of things. I was not a son but a "Step-child." The many biblical references, some of which are clustered around the semi-colon—Barnabas, John the Baptist, Adamant Eve—have never become clearly patterned in my mind, and similarly, his "Olympic" references and occasional comparisons with "Al-lah" and "Hinduism" all seem to be contestations and comparisons that occur below his Above status. Put a period after anything and he conquers it. Put a comma after any word and it is designated as lesser, European, secular, and beneath the Fullstop world.

Here is a rough description and ordering of Fullstop's punctuation system. Learn it, and your reading experiences will never be quite the same. This is one discourse in which the punctuation is probably more important and meaningful than the words punctuated.

The period or fullstop is God. Government. Lord Rolling Stone. Above. Conquest. In relational and "comparative" (a favorite word of his) terms, fullstops and capital or big "block" letters show dominance, power-over, final authority. And He, of course, was that Authority in his own mind, an important step or two beyond Buckminster Fuller's "I think I am a verb." "I" know I am a Fullstop.

There is, of course, a lot of power-over in our daily use of fullstops. Stop the flow. Stop breathing here. The fullstop also abbreviates, cuts words down to Inc. and Co. and Ed. and Mr. or Ms.

•

•

Colon stands for "dictum" or sometimes "dark dictum" . . . "branch of creator heaven and earth." "Africa answers dark Africa. Europe answers dark middle ages. I answer dark dictum." (This is from a tape of Fullstop explaining his system.)

In our world the colon does dictate the list that follows it: postcolonial, poststructural, postmodern.

,

The comma is or stands for European, a pause but never conquering. Commas are always subordinate to Fullstop, and he would often give sets of analogies: as MEDICAL is to doctor, as GOD is to Christ, or a Rabbi; indeed all the terms like God, or Gov, with a comma after them indicate a temporal realization of ultimate power, as if Gypsy Fullstop controlled the Platonic forms of God and Government and could designate lesser versions of these forces by putting a comma after them.

Since receiving this Fullstop wisdom, I have been thinking about the pun on coma, Europeans in Newton's sleep, in the cocoon of white skin privilege, oblivious in the false security of empire, a comatose owning class, the clerkish middle classes endlessly articulating regulations in sentences filled with qualifying clauses and their concomitant commas.

‘ ’

Occasionally, he would use the pronoun 'I' or 'my' with single quotation marks around them. Also 'God.' So I think these marks belong with the period and colon.

There is a strong force in general English usage toward the single and double quotation marks used to distance a word or phrase, attribute some word to unspecified people, to indicate irony, to signal "other people say this and I don't," to create imaginary Archimedean leverage points or vantage points outside the text,

("sun addressing sun"   )"moon addressing moon"

The parentheses symbolizing sun and moon may represent the entire natural world or universe in condensed form. In one of the few messages where he spells out (full stop) the words are enclosed within parentheses, and without the capital letters on f and s as I would have suspected. Small (f) enclosed in parentheses seems to stand for the female principle in some contexts.

This might be a big Fullstop contribution to green politics. A reminder of balanced cosmology, natural limits, in every parenthetical expression. (population) (growth) (economics)—if we all shared the Fullstop punctuation code we could bring a new parsimony to bumper stickers.

? and !

Question marks and exclamation marks are "branches of comma." And small block letters are really "in charge of European" too. Commanding Europeans? Or under the control of Europeans? "Fullstop answers Capital. Comma answers small letters."

I'm willing to concede that we Euros do an excessive amount of questioning and exclaiming! Aren't you?

[ ]

My only note on his definition of brackets is about "cross alphabetical contesting before run a cross country race" and something he said about roping off parade grounds. Used rarely in messages.

Quotation marks are also in the hands of Europeans as far as I can figure out. They may mark off the lived world (see His use of "lives" in text below) or problems in that world as opposed to Gypsy Fullstop's mental world. He didn't use them often in his messages.

"Livingstone Adamant Eve, so to, as John the Baptist"

I have puzzled a lot over this definition of a semi-colon, the place where fullstop is above comma. It seems to be the place where Rolling Stone meets Livingstone, God meets mortals, man meets stubborn woman, "+ wife" (see below), father meets son, and it is (V) or fifth in the ordering offered in the text below.

Nor do I have any bright idea about demystifying or remystifying the semi-colon in our normal usage; maybe the Adamant Eves in feminist literary circles will argue for inversion, a comma over the period has a certain logic to it, and we could put this right side up semi-colon within parentheses to naturalize the mystery.

Short dash "borrows shooting draft of god," and sometimes he refers to "dish" rather than dash, or to "cross country race" as if the dash is really about running.

Long dash "of Creator Fullstop. Gypsy government. Fullstop crown of comma."

The main message I get from Gypsy Fullstop's theory of punctuation is that literacy/law/government/monotheism/power-over are all bundled together. I think Fullstop saw the punctuation of exclamation, interrogation, quotation, bracketing, and the short dash of Europeans, the controlling marks of the lesser government, not the symbols of the Royal Government Tyrannical Above, which are the period and colon, block letters, and the long dash. Parentheses and the single quotation mark may be thought of as the natural context for his god head and creativity

What are all these messages about? Grievances mostly. People not answering. Relations coming apart. Things going wrong that R.G.T. Above wanted to correct. He was often consulting with people at the Catering Rest House, people in the Government Residential Area or the Public Works Department, and his documents addressed us as a kind of court of appeal to right wrongs, correct injustices, pass judgment, rebalance things. The assumption seems to be that if you name things right and punctuate them according to his system, the result will be achieved. The vocabulary of naming is everywhere: "titled," "denoted," "appellation," "pronominally," "prescriptable" are all favorite words. A related strategy in many messages is to run all the variations on one word, as if to be sure of covering all the bases, and not letting any meaning escape, e.g., a few lines from the middle of an 13 August 1966 message, a month before the Makurdi pogroms against the Ibo.

then. Asked. Chair the. owner. And of slaughterous.
cap 471. to give destructive murderous. Authority. with
titled. people. refer column 385. Above.
Conquered.
judicable, judicious, judicature, judicial,

judiciary. And
judiciously. cap 274. 275. 276. 575. to of
prejudice Court. All. Asked. titled. judgeship.
justiceship.
Representing by judges and justice also magistrate
under classical names. Employe. to of stykki, stick,
stuck. And presidency. of district, jurisdiction.
the. Above.

That about covers all the ju-words that there are to cover, plus magistrate. If law can be brought to bear Gypsy Fullstop will conquer.

During the time we were getting these word salads delivered to our door there was a great tension building in Nigeria after the first military coup in the country's five-year history of independence. The educated Ibo people who qualified for many of the jobs in northern Nigeria left vacant by the departed British civil servants were disliked and increasingly scapegoated in daily conversations about any and all of Nigeria's problems. A movement to purge them was growing, and Gypsy Fullstop seemed keenly aware of a disintegrating body politic all around him—trying to assert his authority, urging that troops be disbanded, that the sentries at the Mobil gas station be "demobilized," or pointing out people were parading as soldiers, impersonating police, not responding to orders. A lot of his messages seemed to be about replacing people, reordering things, getting an adequate response to God. With a state apparatus rushing toward disintegration, Gypsy Fullstop had more work to do than ever before.

How he fed and housed himself I don't know, but he seemed to know everyone in the area and must have had a variety of people feeding him or letting him sleep under a porch here or in a backyard quarters there. He made extensive rounds all over Makurdi, copying down the information on sign boards and traffic signs to work into his messages, picking up every variety of paper— old receipts, vouchers, blank forms from offices, pieces of newspaper, anything that he could write on. We would often get five messages on five different kinds of paper clipped together. He would try to tailor his message to fit the piece at hand, an avid recycler before recycling. Come to think of it, we can look at the words in the messages, the content in between the punctuation marks, as a recycling of English.

Here is a one page of a Gypsy Fullstop word salad (a typed transcript of what he wrote in script) that may be slightly more interpretable with the punctuation definitions in mind. Say to yourself "fullstop. I conquer." Whenever you see a period. Think of commas signaling subordination. Use the definitions above.

Head of "lives". Denoted On.

(1). R. Goth. As. God. titled. Govt. Capital. 5.

(1): dictum God: Govt: branch of.

2. thunderbolts, titled, God, Govt, x,

III = Noah branch Moses titled diana Goddess

IV   = Jesus christ n the sons titled God

(V);   = living Stone Adamant; + wife;

the above titled and appellational.

to appellation, also of: have

various titled for Compatibles.

And Comparative. As. Seen (1).

has another titled. Gods. And

al-lah 'God.' In Arabic word.

to Else. Then have of his,

as 2. God, God! God?

Goddless, "God" to else, titled

Contesting where above the

throne of "lives." Olympic. By.

(1.) R. Capital. And qualifying figure.

1. creation. 1. Mghetar,³ Vocabularly

illustration the cne.

{scribbled R.G.T. Above signature}

J. Jeopardy   Acc.

I wish I could tell you that reading lots of other messages has enabled me to work out some sure interpretations for this one. But I don't know why "lives" is within quotation marks in the first line, or further down, "throne of 'lives.'" In other texts, he correlates elements of the five lists with the fingers of the hand: Fullstop and Colon as thumb; God, Gov, as forefinger, and so forth to the little finger standing for Adamant Eve, Livingstone, and in other contexts John the Baptist. There are ordering principles at work—God. as Fullstop, God: as giver of dark dicta, God, as Govt, here below. There may be gender and generational principles in there somewhere—no punctuated conquering of the Hebraic-Greco connections leading to "diana Goddess" in the middle or in the flow of Christian sons under (IV); perhaps the equal sign says that these are areas of equality below God's dark dicta, and "2. thunderbolts, titled, God, Govt, x," mediates between the Fullstop world above and the living world below.

The problem with the preceding paragraph is that it begins to reorder, resequence, make logical the Fullstop unbundling of the civilization/literacy/

imperialism bundle. But if he had wanted prosody, a sequence of sequential sentences, he would have used sentences. He doesn't. Verbs, active verb processes, are rare. "Titled" over and over again. "Denoted on." "Appellational./ to appellation." Naming and punctuating. Name it. Conquer it. Control it. Again and again and again.

But then there is the J. (Jeopardous?) Jeopardy side of him. God as Royal Government Tyrannical Above comes to your door as a beggar asking for help. I think it was only as the crisis deepened and after we left Makurdi for Ibadan that the messages began or ended with requests for assistance on matters of nutrition, shelter, controlling the "gangs of jealousy," getting out of Africa, and going to Europe. Before the crisis and pogroms, he was coming to our door to explain things, give us the latest titlings and appellationals, show His Step-child what he had figured out within his world. The whole second half of the message above could be read as a divine or Olympian anthropologist at work on compatibles and comparatives. Summing up the problem of comparative religion as "God, God! God? Goddles, 'God'" could save you a lot of time reading tomes by theologians.

If I were more of what Kenneth Burke called a "logologist," if I had done some extensive struggling with the classic texts of deconstruction and post-structuralism, I am sure I could extract more meanings from Fullstop's messages and show some great affinities between his deconstructions and those of our contemporary literary critics. As they say in jazz, I don't have the chops for it. I'll let Gypsy Fullstop have the last appellations and punctuations in hopes that they will echo in the minds of people concerned with literacy as both a warning and an inspiration.

In the days leading up to the September 1966 pogroms against the Ibo in the market of Makurdi, led by a regiment of the Nigerian army that came to town for the purpose of leading the mob and "giving permission" to plunder and kill, my wife and I would read messages from Fullstop and think that in his own way he was responding to the disintegrating society around him more effectively than anyone around us; at least he wasn't denying that the tensions and hatreds existed. The day after the pogrom we received a message that began "'I' beg of you, can assist 'me' with Gangs of jealousy." And this short note on a small piece of paper the day after that:

> 'I' demanded. British
> troops. who, may claimed,
> british West African frontier
> force who deformed to be
> the federal of (ct.) while

above abbrev of chief Barnabas
has no titled of Army why
Army should be of his titled
head national as bad
Europe, command. Report.
Immediately.
By. pronominally.
ellimitable. Gypsy. T. Govt.
titled. Above. Traced. Appositle.
of 'who' King. ? parley. Chiefs.

{R.G.T. Above signature} R.

three **Popular Literacy in the Middle Ages**

The Book of Margery Kempe

Cheryl Glenn

However wide-ranging twenty-first-century views of literacy might be, whether scholars refer to Shirley Brice Heath's studies in the American Piedmonts, Sylvia Scribner and Michael Cole's Vai project, E. D. Hirsch's cultural literacy, Geneva Smitherman's work on black American language use, or Walter Ong's and Eric Havelock's theories of orality and literacy, our literate culture privileges the written word. Even scholarly explorations and discussions of Vai and Piedmont literacies—no matter how respectful—are implicitly situated in comparison with schooled literacy.[1] Contemporary concepts of literacy are inevitably colored by our culture's dependence on the physical, material artifact and on a deep-seated insistence that reading and writing are inseparable language arts. Thus, the text dependency—our reading books, writing books, and reading and writing *about* those books—in our own documentary culture and noetic world makes very difficult an accurate conception of medieval literacy.[2]

Background, or the Range of Medieval Literacies— Text Based to Text Dependent

Through our contemporary lens of literacy, it is easy to envision the medieval, preprinting equivalent of mass production: the secluded scriptorium, hushed in the vocalized reading of transcribing monks. We can also readily focus on a class of courtiers and clerics, the *litterati*, who read, wrote, and spoke in Latin, using the language of the learned among themselves as they discussed classical and continental texts. We can imagine those accomplished men (the *litterati*) using a vernacular to impress their governmental, scholarly, and religious opinions onto the *illitterati*, that monolingual populace limited by their vernacular, by their own popular literacy.

Our seeming facility at determining the powers and limits of medieval literacy, however, belies the complexity of the task, especially given that the term *litterati* indicated those schooled in Latin, regardless of individual expertise or accomplishment. The only lexical provision for those who read or wrote or spoke only in their vernacular—with any measure of manual proficiency or expertise, or in any number of languages or dialects other than Latin—was the apologetic and imprecise *illitterati*.[3]

No person, not even those *illitterati*, remained unaffected by literate practices and totemic texts. Medieval society at large conducted its affairs orally within what Brian Stock calls a "textual community" of texts, publicized by a few readers and more interpreters to an even wider audience of listeners. In fact, in *Listening for the Text*, Stock assures us that "the text did not have to be written: oral record, memory, and reperformance sufficed. Nor did the public have to be fully lettered. Often, in fact, only the *interpres* had a direct contact with literate culture."[4]

The strong oral component of medieval popular literacy meant that "the masses of people read by means of the ear rather than the eye, by hearing others read or recite rather than by reading to themselves"[5]—those who could decipher print mediated writing to the *illitterati*. The use of memory, the persistent habit of reading aloud, and the preference, even among the educated, for listening to a statement rather than scrutinizing it in script comprised popular literacy practices. And interpreters of texts were readily available: the Catholic Mass might be held in Latin, but other parts of the church service were in the vernacular, and public testifying was common; proclamations might be written in Latin, but they were read aloud by town criers in the vernacular,[6] and public discussion was always necessary for common understanding. Literacy mattered. Its repercussions stratified the social scale "from the king issuing directives, and the nobleman endowing a monastery with books, to the freed slave clinging to his new social status by means of a written charter"[7] and the commoner participating in the church liturgy and in religious life.

Despite the preponderance of evidence relating to schooling of the regular and secular clergy, it would be a mistake to assume that education and learning were confined to clerics (or that all clerics were learned, for that matter). Laymen could attend the vernacular petty school (not the aristocratic grammar school) or be tutored at home; their sisters might also meet with a tutor or be educated in a convent. Diversifications and diffusions of elitist literacy practices existed among the laity to the extent that people at all levels of textual expertise functioned according to an awareness of key cultural texts, be they religious or legal. Thus it was that both lay men and women alike heard about texts they probably had not read, listened to texts they perhaps could not read, composed texts they probably could not themselves write, and talked about texts that they had in some measure committed to memory. Theirs was a literacy based on texts (*text based*) rather than dependent on texts (*text dependent*) as is the case with our modern documentary literacies.

As literacy scholars (re)consider medieval literacy practices, then, we must look beyond those hushed, secluded, privileged, and sometimes solitary documentary and orthographic practices. We must render visible those oral-aural social events that created textual communities of shared understanding, communal performances contingent on the art of memory. After all, in her *Book of Memory: A Study of Memory in Medieval Culture*, Mary Carruthers reminds us that "the ability to 'write' is not always the same thing as the ability to compose and comprehend in a fully textual way, for indeed one who writes (a scribe) may simply be a skilled practitioner, employed in a capacity akin to that of a professional typist today. The distinction of composing (or 'making' in Middle English) from writing-down continued to be honored throughout the Middle Ages. Similarly, learning by hearing material and reciting aloud should not be confused with ignorance of reading."[8]

Our understanding of medieval popular literacy becomes skewed if we think of literacy in terms of generalized abstractions (e.g., to be civilized, the ability to function within literate society), or if we think of literacy as a set of developmental techniques or "basics" (the ability to produce and process print), the two sets of concepts most pervasive today. Brian Stock's sophisticated concept of textuality describes that popular literacy (as opposed to "schooled" literacy) most aptly; he argues that a text does not have to be written but can instead be spoken, its structure and coherence safe within an oral textual community: "One can be literate without the overt use of texts, and one can use texts extensively without evidencing genuine literacy. In fact, the assumptions shared by those who can read and write often render the actual presence of a text superfluous."[9] We must allow for a range of competencies in reading, writing, and other literate behaviors, especially when considering the Middle Ages, during which time reading and writing were never acquired concurrently, writing being the superior and certainly more expensive and difficult skill. The range of writing skills—calligraphy, cursive, printing, illumination, taking dictation, composing, transcribing—makes writing a technical skill far more involved than reading, even without considering the medieval difficulties of keeping quill, ink, and parchment in order (which I will explain in more detail below). Moreover, the scene of one knowledgeable person reading aloud while all the others listened carefully ("read" aurally) and memorized automatically was the centerpiece of medieval literacy practices at all levels of expertise, regardless of the language. People often memorized their educations, having received them aurally from the recitations of those who had learned the "texts" first. And the only distinction made between writing on the mind—memorization—and writing on parchment was made in order to endorse memorization, a skill widely used by litterati and illitterati alike.

Tantalizing though they be, it is beyond the scope of this essay to survey or taxonomize the full range of medieval literacy practices in Europe, many of which have already been expertly investigated (see Chaytor, Clanchy, Graff, Patterson).[10] But I call to mind that broader vision in order to provide background for my focus, and I will circle around (and around) issues of orality, memory, and religion as I investigate the literacy practices of the comparatively unschooled populace in medieval England, in particular those so richly demonstrated by Margery Kempe.

Circling in, or the Text-Based Literacy of Margery Kempe

The case of bourgeois, unlettered Margery Brunham Kempe (1373–ca. 1439) best demonstrates medieval popular literacy. Daughter of a prominent family, wife of a less prestigious burgess, and mother of fourteen children, Margery left her relatively comfortable life to answer God's call to weep (her "gift of tears") and to pray for the souls of her fellow Christians—and to do so not in a cell or convent, but throughout England, Europe, and the Holy Land. But before she embarked on her missionary travels, she lived in cosmopolitan Lynn, where she would have been exposed to popular Continental trends in fashion, religion, language, and thought.[11] And in Lynn, Margery composed her spiritual autobiography, The Book of Margery Kempe, a nexus for the English church, the vernacular, and text-based literacy practices.

Although never before recognized as significant by literacy scholars, Kempe's fifteenth-century Book has rightfully become an investigative site for scholars of other stripes (medievalists interested in mysticism, travel literature, women's writings, and autobiography) attracted to her ability to elaborate with considerable sophistication her religious convictions and practices, her Franciscan affective piety,[12] her fluency with biblical texts, her place in the mystical tradition, her marriage and unmarriage, and the rhetorical technique of her autobiography.[13] Therefore, she has come to be recognized as one of the most important English women who participated in the elitist, masculine medieval literary tradition that has long excluded her. After all, this illitterata did not practice her literacy in what has come to be seen as its traditional sense; instead, she inscribed it in an alternative literacy practice that complicates and enriches any picture we might have of medieval literacy practices.

Composed in the early 1400s, Margery's Book lay neglected, but preserved, until 1934, when Hope Emily Allen identified and helped Sanford Brown Meech edit the unique manuscript, which was long the possession of the Butler-Bowdon estate. The Early English Text Society's 1940 publication of Meech and Allen's literal copy of the *Book* established Margery as the first woman to compose her life story in English.[14] Hers is the earliest extant autobiography in English, and, in fact, the earliest extant, large-scale narrative written in English prose.[15]

In her *Book*, she gives voice to a largely silent and unsung force: the *illitteratae*, medieval women having little opportunity or need for formal education unless they joined a religious order.[16] In the process of recounting the limitations and possibilities for deeply devout, ambitious women of "extreme" holiness[17] (women like herself), Margery demonstrates in her *Book* how medieval popular literacy provided her with her formidable store of scripture and religious doctrine. God, she claims, provided her with the determination to breathe life into her spirituality. Styling herself as "this creature," a common medieval usage akin to "servant of God" as well as a reminder to her readers that she herself did not do the actual writing of the text, Margery recounts her call to "write":

> This creature was inspired with the Holy Ghost . . . that she should . . . make a book of her feelings and her revelations. Some [clerks] offered to write her feelings with their own hands, but she would not consent, for she was commanded in her soul that she should not write so soon. And so it was twenty years . . . before she did any writing. Afterward, when it pleased Our Lord, he commanded her and charged her that she should write down her feelings and revelations and the form of her living that his goodness might be known to all the world.[18]

The case of Margery Kempe, then, evidences that medieval literacy practices extended far beyond those within a prestigious, male-only institution contingent on both a separate, learned language (Latin) as well as the text-as-physical-artifact.

Circling Again, or Orality, Collaboration, and Popular Literacy

Margery knew well what the written word and its strong oral component implied: she was literate despite her inability to read and write.[19] That seeming paradox of "illiterate literacy" is a prominent feature of medieval popular literacy, a feature meriting reiteration. Describing the culturally determined literacy conventions to which a woman such as Margery Kempe would have subscribed, Franz H. Bäuml writes that "a literate culture is defined . . . by the characteristics of literacy and their effects on those dependent on it. This dependence does not require the ability to read on the part of the individual: it *does* require access to written information by means of the individual's own or someone else's ability to read. . . . The point is that they relied—if not on their own—then on someone else's literacy for the knowledge necessary as a basis for their actions."[20] Accordingly, medieval literacy becomes a mode of communication rather than a set of personalized technical skills. Literacy becomes a medium of textuality (both in the creation and reception of texts) limited only by the range of the human voice and the capacity of the human memory. I want to emphasize that the ability to "write" was not necessarily the same as the ability to compose and comprehend in a fully textual way, and the ability to "read" a "book" could mean learning both by hearing material and by reciting from memory. The common medieval practices of reading aloud (and the concomitant listening) and reciting from memory meant that a knowledge of letters and book-learning were compatible with little direct contact with print itself. These popular literacy practices were text based without being text dependent; people used the information in texts without using the actual texts themselves: contact could be vicarious. In short, whereas our contemporary literacy practices are often concentrated on seeing and inscribing, medieval practices emphasized hearing and remembering.

People, especially those of high rank, employed a secretary to write letters, contracts, and wills for them.[21] Given her social and financial standing, Margery Kempe no doubt knew of such practices when she employed an amanuensis for didactic rather than legal reasons (and when she contracted to study or "read" with a priest, which I explain below). By her own account, she was convinced that her life, both as she lived it and as she recorded it in a story, would help her audience (whether they be contemporary witnesses to her or future readers and listeners) achieve greater knowledge and appreciation of God's ways. Her autobiography provided her yet another, more lasting locus for displaying her vast memory and understanding of the Scriptures and Church doctrine, which she could neither read nor write about herself. Her text-based (not text-dependent) *Book*, then, the story of her life, needed only to be transcribed by an amanuensis.[22]

Ironically, the primary obstacle to her goal seemed to be her first amanuensis:

> Then had the creature no writer that would fulfill her desire nor give credence to her feelings until the time that a[n] Englishman dwelling in Deutschland . . . having good knowledge of this creature and of her desire, moved I trust through the Holy Ghost, came into England . . . and dwelled with the foresaid creature until he had written as much as she would tell him for the time that they were together.

> And since he died. Then were there a priest which this creature had great affection for, and so she communed with him of this matter and brought him the book to read. The book was so evil written that he could little skill [apply] thereon, for it was neither good English nor Deutsch, nor were the letters shaped or formed as other letters were. Therefore the priest knew fully there should never man read it, except by special grace. Nevertheless, he promised her that if he could read it he would copy it out and write it better with good will (Proem. 2b. 2–20).

This passage bears scrutiny, for it reveals the practices of popular literacy. Readers can follow the unlettered Margery as she locates and then interacts with her inexpert and expert scribes. Readers are then privy to the second (expert) scribe's frame of mind when he's faced with the odious task of recopying the first scribe's "evil written" script, and perhaps it is more important that readers are made aware of a proficient scribe's power. An expert scribe can intrude into the author's narrative, whether to record his own tribulations in transcription, his empowering "special grace," or his opinions of why the previous, inept scribe had agreed to do such work (the second scribe writes that the first scribe was "moved, I trust, through the Holy Ghost"). As might be expected in a primarily oral culture, Margery's text was intelligible when read aloud to her, although that same text was problematic to both her reader-scribes.[23] This particular passage illuminates the distinction between the faculties of aural readers and scribal readers: for Margery, the ear and mouth were connected; for her scribes, the eye and hand.

Given the various capabilities with the range of literate behaviors, both oral and written texts edified and informed the populace. Clearly, medieval popular literacy was a literacy of secondary orality within an oral culture strongly linked to written texts. Throughout the classical and medieval periods, no written texts made the slightest distinction between writing on the mind (memorization) and writing on some surface (books and manuscripts) except in terms of true learning. Those who rely on writing for their information are not truly learned; those who truly know have imprinted their memory with the information—in the manner of Margery Kempe, who displays a tremendous store of biblical and doctrinal information as she dictates her *Book*.

The Sphere of Authorship, or Memory and Literacy

According to extant primary and secondary evidence, Margery Kempe was the earliest English writer to commit to writing an intimate, revealing, and personalized account of life and thoughts. Her religious experiences, her conversations with religious men and women, and the oral Church teachings, all become inscribed in her memory. With no independent recourse to books or manuscripts, Margery relies on her memory, calling up her text-based literacy.

The reasons for such memory and recitation practices are manifold, not the least being the scarcity of books and manuscripts, the supply never equalling the demand. The scarcity and high value placed on books related directly to the cost of their production.[24] Books were valuable because of the raw materials (parchment, ink, pens) needed to produce writing and because of the skill (the craft literacy) necessary for actually executing it (tanning skins, mixing inks and grinding pigments, sharpening pens). But the written text itself accrued value according to the extent and complexity of its colored illuminations and the richness and ornateness of its binding and cover.[25] Written texts (books and manuscripts) reflected the material wealth and status of their owners, and, not surprisingly, books were a favored loot and a source of rich ransom to thieves. Until the development of rag paper and the invention of mechanical means of reproduction, then, books remained moveable property, treasures, irreplaceable in their religious and intellectual import. Furthermore, book ownership outwardly symbolized skills acquired and public functions performed, an intellectual status perhaps even more impressive than that of mere wealth (although the possession of books never did certify that book owners themselves could actually read, let alone write).

In a world of few books, then, and the majority of those in library holdings, accessibility to texts—written or oral—was always uncertain, for "one could never depend on having continuing access to specific material."[26] Few individuals—whether priests, lawyers, or university teachers—owned more than the few books of their office. And few individuals other than the rich and powerful had access to library collections, which were mostly attached to cathedrals, collegiate churches, and monastic orders.

Having no ready or usable access to books or manuscripts of her own, Margery seems not to have cluttered her mind with half-remembered scriptural or doctrinal passages (the likes of which we text dependents carry around in our heads). Neither was her book variegated with half-understood passages. Instead, her locutions are clear, emphatic, and effective—so as to make a lasting impression on the soul—and her phrasings lend credence to her claim of serious religious study with clergymen.

In her *Book*, Margery records an example of such a locution. When a clerk asks her how the biblical phrase "Crescite and multiplicamini" should be translated, she answers his Latin with her own language: "'Sir, these words are not understood as only the begetting of children bodily, but also as the purchasing of virtue[s] . . . such as the hearing of the words of God, giving good example, meekness and patience, charity and chastity, and such others, for patience is more worthy than miracle working.' And she through the grace of God answered so that clerk was well pleased" (51.58a.3–10). The clarity of her memory is awesome, especially given the exhaustive detail of her recollections (the manuscript comprises 124 leaves in eleven gatherings). The uncanny accuracy of her retellings is confirmed in her Book, whether she recounts her (what has been documented as a typical) pilgrimage itinerary or her doctrinal discussions with bishops. David Knowles writes that Margery provides "an early, if not the first, example in English prose literature of the skil[l]ful use of dramatically appropriate dialogue based on the substantial memory of what had taken place."[27] When, for instance, the Archbishop at Caywood "put to her the Articles of our Faith," "God gave her grace to answer well and truly and readily without any great study so that [the Archbishop] might not blame her, then he said to the clerks, 'She knows her Faith well enough'" (52.60a.5–11). Indeed, her memory served her well.

The following retrospective account of Margery's stay with a priest and his mother also demonstrates the caliber of her memory. Not only can she tell a compelling story, she can also explain a measure of her unlettered Bible learning:

> There came a priest newly to Lynn who had never known her before, and, when he saw her in the streets, he was greatly moved to speak with her. . . . [He invited Margery to visit him and his mother in their chambers.] Then the priest took a book and read therein how Our Lord, seeing the city of Jerusalem, wept thereupon, foreseeing the mischiefs and sorrows that should come . . . . When the said creature heard read how Our Lord wept, then wept she sore. . . . And afterwards, the same priest loved her and trusted her full much and blessed the time that ever he knew her, for he found great ghostly comfort in her and began to look at much good scripture and many a good doctor [of the Church] which he would not have looked at were it not for her. He read her many good books of high contemplation and other books, such as the Bible, with doctors' views thereon, Saint Bride's book, Hilton's book, Bonaventure, Stimulus Amoris, Incendium Amoris, and such others.[28] . . . The aforesaid priest read her books for the most part of seven or eight years, to the great increase of his knowledge and his merit (58.69a.29–31; 69b.6–10, 20–36).

Perhaps only a woman untrained in and unconscious of institutionalized literary practices would feel comfortable explaining her "book" learning this way, learning constructed and interpreted by her secondary orality. Her judicious and dramatic use of the Gospels and other devotional literature throughout her Book reflect her remarkable memorizing power and oral learning, commonplace accomplishments in a predocumentary (pre-text-dependent) culture.

H. J. Chaytor articulates the significance of memory within a culture wherein the population-at-large lacked text-dependent literacy skills and a minority guarded those few and treasured books: "The feats of memory involved were probably less surprising to a medieval audience than they would be to ourselves. Our memories have been impaired by print; we know that we need not 'burden our memories' with matter which we can find merely by taking a book from a shelf. When a large proportion of a population is illiterate and books are scarce, memories are often tenacious to a degree outside modern European [and American] experience."[29] The capacious medieval memory, untrammelled by associations with printed text, seems alien to our contemporary culture. But the belief in the power of memory dates at least as far back as Plato's *Phaedrus,* in which Socrates warns his interlocutor that "this invention [letters of the alphabet] will produce forgetfulness in the minds of those who learn to use it, because they will not practice their memory. . . . They will read many things without instruction and will therefore seem to know many things, when they are for the most part ignorant . . . since they are not wise, but only appear wise."[30] (275a–b). For Plato, as for medieval culture, writing on the memory is the only writing truly valuable for one's education, rational abilities, judgments, and (later) salvation, for the memory is portable and ever-accessible, unlike written texts. Since the time of the ancients, then, the trained memory was coextensive with wisdom and knowledge.

Encircling Christianity and Literacy, or the Power of the Word

The Christian religion was a major force in textualizing medieval popular literacy practices of reading, listening, reciting, and memorizing, with religion and literacy overlapping to the point of pleonasm. Christianity simply cannot be separated from the written word, be it the written laws of God or the written teachings of Christ. The Word—literally and figuratively—is the Christian God: "In the beginning was the Word, and the Word was with God, and the Word was God. He [the personified Word] was in the beginning with God; all things were made through him, and without him was not anything made that was made" (John 1:1–3). God's word, as speech and action, is irrevocable and brings to reality whatever it expresses: creation, redemption, salvation. Because Christianity binds itself inextricably to the word, then Christians must have access to the words of God: moral exhortations, prayers, and psalms serve as guides for both faith and daily life; knowledge of biblical texts validates piety and faith. Christianity elevated the status of the written word and thereby promoted a literacy with crucial, afterlife consequences for all Christians.

Margery realized the power of the word in a real sense: the spoken word, her witnessing, was indeed effective, but the written word, her *Book,* could carry further and preserve longer the trials and triumphs of her worldly and spiritual pilgrimages. She was, after all, witnessing and writing in response to God's call to weep, pray, preach—and travel—widely. She needed religious literacy to carry out her mission. Her medieval Christianity stressed the essential link between a variety of literacy practices and the word of God, the scriptures, and the wisdom of the holy Fathers. Her Christian literacy educated her in the organizing principles of the faith as well as in basic social altruism.

Thus for Margery, as well as for all other Christians, availability of biblical teachings was a paramount concern in her life. And her *Book* is replete with accounts of her educational opportunities coming to fruition: "Thus, through hearing of holy books and through hearing of holy sermons, she ever increased in contemplation and holy meditation. It is impossible to write all the holy thoughts, holy speeches, and high revelations which Our Lord showed to her" (59.70a.5–9). When she is examined on her faith by the Abbot of Leicester, she is found orthodox, her aurally derived knowledge of Church doctrine being sound:

> The Abbot and his assessors . . . made her swear on a book that she would answer truly to the Articles of the Faith, as she felt about them. And first they rehearsed the blissful Sacrament of the Alter, charging her to say just as she believed therein. Then she said, "Sirs, I believe in the Sacrament of the Alter in this way: that man who has taken the order of priesthood, be he ever so vicious a man in his living, if he say duly the words over the bread that our Lord Jesus Christ said when he made His Maundy among His disciples where He sat at the supper, I believe that it is His very flesh and His blood and no material bread; nor never be unsaid once it be said." And so she answered forth to all the articles as many as they asked her; they were well pleased (48.55b.5–20).

And when the Archbishop of York forbids Margery to teach or challenge the people in his diocese, she responds according to biblical teachings, and she witnesses for her Lord:

> I shall speak of God . . . until the time that the Pope and the Holy Church have ordained that no man shall be so bold as to speak of God, for God almighty forbids not, sir, that we shall speak of him. And also the Gospel makes mention that, when the woman heard our Lord preach, she came before him with a loud voice and said, "Blessed be the womb that bore thee and the teats that gave you suck." Then our Lord said again to her, "Truly so are they blessed that hear the word of God and keep it." And therefore, sir, I think that the Gospel gives me leave to speak of God (52.60b.2–13).

Margery's "illiteracy" seems to have fueled her abilities to listen to and learn from her readers—and to memorize; she was especially canny regarding Church doctrine as the spousal scene (to come) demonstrates (see also *Book*, chaps. 12, 13, 16, 50–55). Although the lower clergy might harass and taunt her, the high churchmen listened to her and protected her, even when her actions were considered irregular.[31] For instance, the Bishop of Lincoln, authorized by the Archbishop of Canterbury, examines her and her husband and gives Margery permission to live apart from her husband, wear white clothes and a ring (inscribed *Iesu est meus amor*), go on pilgrimage, and receive Communion weekly; he even encourages her to compose her life story:

> [The Bishop] was right glad to hear [her meditations and high contemplations] . . . and counseled her . . . that her feelings should be written. And she said that it was not God's will that they should be written so soon, nor were they written until twenty years later. . . . And then she said, "My Lord, if it pleases you, I am commanded in my soul that you shall give me the mantle and the ring and clothe me all in white clothes. And, if you clothe me on earth, our Lord Jesus Christ will cloth you in Heaven, as I understand the revelation." . . . And the [Bishop's] clerks asked this creature many hard questions, which she, by the grace of Jesus, resolved, so that her answers pleased the Bishop right well and the clerks had full great marvel of her that she answered so readily and pregnantly. . . . Then he asked her to go to the Archbishop of Canterbury . . . "and ask him to grant leave to me, Bishop of Lincoln," to give her the mantle and the ring, because she was not of his diocese. This cause he feigned through the counsel of his clerks, for they loved not this creature. . . . Then she took her leave of the Bishop of Lincoln, and he gave her twenty-six shillings and eight pence to buy her clothing with, and to pray for him (17a.10–14; 17b.2–6,28–33; 18a.37–40).

Her steadfast conviction that Christ had singled her out to suffer, learn, testify—and be saved—kept her in good stead both with all the high (and better educated) clergy who scrutinized her orthodoxy and obedience as well as with the many lower clergymen who took the time to read to her and discuss the readings with her. Her conferential relationship with the clergy adds to the believability of her *Book*, supporting her presentation of popular literacy practices and indicating that medieval English clergy felt more pastoral responsibility than has generally been believed.

A Circle of Commerce, or Religious Activism and Active Literacy

Nonconformist religious activism was the most vital spiritual commerce of the day, and Margery's religious knowledge (scriptural, biblical, doctrinal) was her currency. Given her learning, Margery succeeded by doing what the great Franciscan writers had directed the devout—illiterate and literate alike—to do: love

Jesus in his humanity, attend the Virgin, and participate emotionally in the joy and grief of the Christian story, duties predicated on biblical knowledge. In *Mystic and Pilgrim*, Clarissa Atkinson explains the permeation of the fifteenth-century Franciscan teachings: "[Margery] followed closely the example set forth by [the Franciscan] authors of Meditations on the Life of Christ. The distinct and specific influence of such works in the prayers of an illiterate woman shows us how religious instruction was transmitted (and transformed) in the Middle Ages. Margery's book is valuable because it is a *response*. Generally, our sources are limited to the writings of the experts—teachers and professionals; here we find some of the results of their work."[32] Hence, Kempe's *Book* provides us a look at an oral-aural learner's active response to her religious teaching.

Margery preserved the raw material of her experience—spiritual, emotional, intellectual, and interpersonal—as a memorable narrative that would persuade the future of its worth and demonstrate Franciscan affective piety. The narrative of her "subjectively determined performance"[33] could be easily memorized and recited in episodes like the stories of religious and professional storytellers so prevalent in the Middle Ages. Her oft-unorthodox religious activism provided colorful material for those brief episodes, each of which follow a predictable course: she is suspected of heresy, threatened and harassed, examined in her faith, perhaps jailed. These vivid sequences resolve in her vanquishing of her prosecutors, her exoneration, and the eventual conversion of her prosecutors (see *Book*, chaps. 13, 46, 52, 53, 55).

> She was brought into the Archbishop's chapel, and there came many of the Archbishop's men, despising her, calling her "Lollard"[34] and "heretic," and swearing horrible oaths that she should be burned. And she, through the strength of Jesus, said to them, "Sirs, I fear you shall be burned in hell without end unless you amend yourself of your oaths and swearing, for you keep not the commandments of God. I would not swear as you do for all the good of this world." Then they went away as though they were ashamed (52.59b.36–37, 1–8).

What twenty-first-century readers might see as a loosely organized narrative, medieval listeners might instantly recognize as a story akin to the homily in structure and the sermon in theme, two genres Margery and her unlettered audience would know well.[35]

Yet her story is memorable—though neither predictably coherent nor conventionally chronological—major features of our written tradition. Perhaps its ostensible lack of chronology has always made Margery's story seem to lack logical coherence as well, for not even her second scribe could realign her story: "This book is not written in order, every thing after the other as it is done, but *as the matter came to the creature* in mind when it should be written, for it was so long before it was written that she had forgotten the time and the order when things happened. And therefore she wrote nothing except what she knew right well for the very truth" (Proem. 3a. 12–18 [emphasis mine]). Conscious of her memory lapses, Margery composes the Book as cyclical and associational, structures perhaps familiar in an oral culture. Using her memory as a conceptual filter for image formation and recollection, however, she orders her impressive, self-contained vignettes so that they render the whole message, much as Bible stories and poems work together to depict the holism of Christianity. Any defects in her chronology, then, would not have been noticed by those who heard her story episodically and were deriving momentary excitement from following her adventures.

Her composing technique, therefore, seems intended for oral performance, the composition genre most familiar to the laity. Margery effectively marshals the information within each short scene like the best of storytellers, commingling homely, even commonplace, events with rather self-satisfied descriptions of her great devotion, her intimacy with Jesus, and the gradual routing of those who oppose or mock her.[36] Thus, her tellings represent the intertextual compositions of medieval popular literacy, the easy commingling of autobiography, hagiography, social history, scripture, and Franciscan practices for the edification and pleasure of her intended audience. Her tellings also emphasize the dependency of her literacy practices, which were contingent on others in bringing her story to light. "This creature," as Margery consistently styles herself, projects a sense of radical dependency on God (and Jesus) and constant collaboration with scribes for her ongoing creation.

"This creature" and her audience were particularly impressed by hagiography, stories and lessons of the virgin saints. Every medieval child would have been familiar with those women admitted to Heaven's center stage by virtue of their virginity, their heroic defense of that state, or their tarnished virtue redeemed by special graces (or martyrdom). Wanting easy admittance to Heaven as well as permanent release from the bonds of marriage, Margery negotiates her chastity with her husband.[37] And the scene of that negotiation typifies Margery's strikingly effective use of gossipy anecdotes, fresh dialogue, and figurative language as she develops her narrative for an unlettered audience:

> It befell on a Friday on Midsummer Eve in right hot weather, as this creature was coming from York bearing a bottle with beer in her hand and her husband a cake in his bosom, that he asked his wife this question, "Margery, if there came a man with a sword and would smite off my head unless I should commune naturally with you as I have done before, tell me the truth of your conscience—for you say you will not lie—whether you would suffer my head to be smitten off or else suffer me to meddle with you again, as I did at one time?" "Alas, sir," said she,

"why raise this matter when we have been chaste these eight weeks?" "For I will know the truth of your heart." And then she said with great sorrow, "Truly, I would rather see you slain than we should turn again to our uncleanness." And he said again, "You are no good wife" (11.12a.9–24).

Bringing her long experience as audience to her role as author, Margery knew well that her contemporary audience could not be treated tenderly. Thus, Margery brings her characters to life by presenting them in conversation with each other, changing voices, intonation, and gestures.

The preceding scene is typical of her rigor in emphasizing religious or moral points or subtle Church doctrine (in this case, the recovery of God's most valuable gift, virginal purity). As she composed each scene of her evangelical Book, she relied on the narrative techniques of oral, text-based tellings: the acknowledgment of familiar books and stories (the Bible and other devotional stories, lais, fabliaux); repetition; digressions for the purpose of moralizing, explaining, or describing; speaking in character. Her Book resonates with the popular literacy practices of telling, listening, explaining, and retelling.

Just as Margery Kempe embodied Christianity, she embodied the conflation of literacy and religion, especially in her Bible stories. Not only does she accurately remember the stories included in her Book, but she constructs those stories with an audience awareness that makes them unforgettably appealing (and bordering on the hyperbolic). The Franciscan tradition of personal involvement in well-learned Scripture[38] as well as the narrative techniques of oral culture served well Margery's fictional envisioning of such scenes—as both narrator of and actor in those scenes, she is ever mindful of her audience. Thus, her recollections spring from a mind both retentive and inventive, from one skilled both orally and aurally.

For instance, when her visions transport her to the scene of Jesus' interment, Margery enters the story as the central figure. Mary's description is largely in terms of Margery's ministrations: Margery treats the mournful Blessed Mother as a needy Christian, giving Mary unsolicited care and advice: "Then the creature thought, when Our Lady was come home and was laid down on a bed, that she made for Our Lady a good caudle [a warm, medicinal beverage] and brought it to her to comfort her, and then Our Lady said unto her, 'Take it away, daughter. Give me no food, but mine own Child.' The creature answered, 'Ah! Blessed Lady, you must needs comfort yourself and cease of your sorrowing'" (81.95a.5–12). The scene of the resurrection provides Margery an opportunity to demonstrate her scriptural literacy.

Her Book is replete with her detailed, participatory scriptural envisionings (the birth of Mary; the birth of Jesus; the adoration of the Magi, after which Margery accompanies Mary to Egypt; the Passion, crucifixion, resurrection, etc.). The scene of the resurrection demonstrates Margery's Christian education in the basic social precepts of generosity and kindness, which she applies to Mary. Her *Book* is also laced with "good works": nursing and serving the poor and the sick, counseling the bereaved and insane. Margery prays for a widow whose husband is in Purgatory; she gives away her money; she nurses lepers; and she consoles the tempted.

Christian literacy was, indeed, more than an education in generosity and kindness, for those principles overlay cardinal tenets of the Christian faith: prayer, penance, baptism, and witnessing, all accomplishments that Margery records. Her constant interchange with "Our Lord" depends on her prayer and petition; he always answers her prayers, almost always with a pleasing answer (cf. the issue of white clothes or of pilgrimage). She writes about her great penance: she fasts on bread and water, tears her skin with her nails, and wears a hair shirt— that is, until Jesus appears to her and asks her to stop. Moreover, her witnessing becomes the mainstay of her narration, connecting her, in one way or another, with people of all ranks. Hence, Margery's literacy stressed the link between the uses of Christianity for daily living and communion with others as well as its use as a vehicle for the word of God. For her, literacy and Christianity were irrevocably linked as one.

The Orb of Significance, or Margery Kempe's Literacy

The Book of Margery Kempe is an invaluable archeological find: it provides twenty-first-century readers an actual contemporary account of popular medieval literacy practices, both their reception and production; it gives us running commentary of the author's composing process and of her second scribe's transcribing process. When the second scribe finishes copying the original text, he writes that the first scribe had "made true sense . . . of herself that had all this treatise in feeling and working," which he himself had "truly drawn out of that copy into this little book" (89.106b.22–24).

In a world where readers provided the unlettered access to religious texts and where belief was communally negotiated, the appearance of an unlettered woman's autobiography is extraordinary. Her extraordinary accomplishment paradoxically confirms ordinary literacy practices, for as a spiritual autobiography and a window into literacy practices, her *Book* may be part of a trend of which we have no other account or examples. Other than her reference to saints' lives, we have no documented explanation for why or how Margery thought of recording her life story other than to celebrate and tell about her relationship with Jesus, who said to her soul: "You could not please me more than you do with your writing, for daughter, by this book many a man shall be turned to me and believe herein" (88.104b.4–20).

While accomplished readers, writers, and interpreters were rendering material texts superfluous for the rest of the believers, unlettered Margery was launching her own story into the world of textuality, the effort spent in order to justify her ambition to be heard and validated. Autobiography specialist Philippe Lejeune finds that women such as Margery who take the initiative to produce their life stories are determined that their audience will "understand their lives and validate them." And in *Writing a Woman's Life*, Carolyn Heilbrun tells us that "power is the ability to take one's place in whatever discourse is essential to action and [power is] the right to have one's part matter."[39] Margery followed the course of medieval literacy practices opened to the unlettered (being read to, memorization, and conferencing) and located herself within the particular discourse that overlay Franciscan affective piety.

Margery's story also indicates the ubiquitous employment of English. Because Latin had become remote from the secular side of society, greater use was made of the vernacular in all areas of administration and social regulation. As early as the Roman invasion of England, missionaries realized that they had little chance of success unless they quickly came to terms with the English vernacular, which was essential for preaching, for the instruction of English youths and communication with their royal patrons, and for the establishment of the priesthood. But perhaps, most important, the *Book* provides us an opportunity to trace the author's movement during her composing process, beginning with her gathering of material (experientially or textually), contemplating the arrangement of that material, locating an amanuensis, racking her memory, and ultimately producing and delivering her text despite a lifetime of obstacles.

The Book of Margery Kempe expands and redefines our traditions of literacy, making a place within that tradition for her "illiterate"—text based, not text dependent—popular literacy. In composing her innovative example of purposeful and persuasive prose, she depended on both sources of words—the pen and the lips—to inscribe her life story, a story without an audience for some five hundred years.

As academic inquiries continue moving forward and backward in history, up and down class and race lines, through language and so-called literacy barriers, and across gender and genre lines, various scholars will recover other such examples of (il)literate activity, uncover a range of different stories of literacy, and then revise our conception of literate practices. Like the case of Margery

Kempe, each story will disrupt and then enrich what is now a neatly packaged, text-dependent, test-measured literacy. Our steady focus on elitist, separatist literacy practices broadens into a panoramic vision of all the effective, prevalent, and useful popular literacies. Only then will we begin to appreciate the richness, otherness, and multiplicity of those literacies both inside and outside the academy.

four **Giving Voice to the Hands**

The Articulation of Material Literacy in the Sixteenth Century

Pamela H. Smith

> Practice: I have had no other book than the sky and the earth, which
> is known to all, and it is given to all to know and to read in this beau-
> tiful book.
>
> —BERNARD PALISSY (1580)

Circa 1400 an anonymous master mason compiled a historical introduction to
masonry, setting out the customs and regulations of the masons' craft in England. This artisan believed Euclid to be the inventor of masonry. The master
mason does not, however, mention Euclid's authorship, or his book, or proofs,
but contends instead that Euclid had been a clerk of Abraham in Egypt and had
learned geometry from him. Euclid had subsequently taught geometry to the
Egyptians, but not a theoretical science of geometry. Rather, it was an emi-
nently practical one. Indeed, for this master mason, geometry and masonry
were the same activity:

> Then this worthy clerk Euclid taught them to make great walls and ditches to hold
> out the water [of the Nile]. And he by geometry measured the land and departed
> it in divers parts, and made every man to close his own part with walls and
> ditches, and then it became a plenteous country. . . . And they took their sons to
> Euclid to govern them at his own will, and he taught to them the craft [of] ma-
> sonry and gave it the name of geometry because of the parting of the ground that
> he had taught to the people.[1]

The master mason established a genealogy for masonry that traced its lineage
back to Abraham through Euclid, thus grounding it in biblical history. Euclid
was a cipher in his story. The historical personage of Euclid (as third century
B.C.E. author of *The Elements of Geometry*) was unimportant; in fact, the master

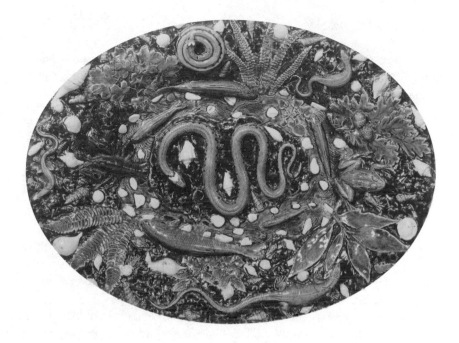

PALISSY WARE DISH

mason and medieval masonry in general made no use of Euclidean geometry, and the mason probably was not able to read the Latin version of Euclid's *Elements* that had existed in the West since the twelfth century. Euclid here functioned as an "authority" from a dimly sensed canon of Greek and Roman authorities in the Latin West, but he was understood by the mason as embedded in the much more central biblical context. We may draw two lessons out of this incident. First, although the mason seemed to reach into "high" culture for an "authority" to legitimate his craft, the authority that "high culture" gave to that figure had no meaning for the master mason. Instead, the mason understood Euclid within the terms of his own craft and "culture." Second, the mason did not perceive geometry and masonry to be different activities. From his perspective, the "high" culture of geometry and the "low" culture of masonry were not separate. The mason's conflation will be useful to keep in mind throughout this essay, for one of the tasks will be to attempt to understand how an artisan in the early modern period viewed his own activity, and if we assume that he began by understanding his craft as "low" culture, we may go astray. In other words, the view from "the bottom up" should not always assume that those at "the bottom" see themselves as occupying this "lowly" position.

Reading Earth and Sky

In the year 1580, a book written by another artisan, the Huguenot potter Bernard Palissy, appeared in Paris and was framed as an always antagonistic dialogue between theory and practice:

> THEORY: And how do you know that, and what is your basis for undertaking to contradict so many learned philosophers who have written such fine books on alchemy? You who know neither Greek nor Latin, nor scarcely good French. . . .
>
> THEORY: And where have you found this written down? Or tell me, what school have you been to, where you could have heard what you say?
>
> PRACTICE: I have had no other book than the sky and the earth, which is known to all, and it is given to all to know and to read in this beautiful book.[2]

What does it mean to read earth and sky? I shall argue that this is not just a radical social and intellectual claim, but that it expresses a specific artisanal epistemological radicalism, one that can be termed "material literacy."

A particularly persistent feature of Western culture has been a division between those who work with their minds—scholars—and those who work with their hands—artisans. Throughout much of Western history, these two groups have been separated by a social and intellectual chasm. The Greek disdain for manual work as deforming to mind and body was carried on in Western culture up to the seventeenth century and beyond. Artisanal knowledge was separated from the realm of school knowledge by the fact that the mechanical arts were neither taught in the schools nor written down, and a certain unclean odor clung to them as the "illiberal" arts, for in antiquity they had been the work of slaves. The knowledge of artisans was transmitted by doing and imitation, rather than by the study of books, and artisanal guilds, their rituals, apprenticeship training, and unwritten techniques constituted the means by which artisanal knowledge and techniques were reproduced.

Such training led to what I shall call an "artisanal literacy," which had to do with gaining knowledge neither through reading nor writing, but through a process of experience and labor. Rather than producing a "lettered man," such literacy had the goal of making knowledge productive. We might regard this as a nontextual, even a nonverbal[3] literacy. If scholars conceived of problems, or indeed of reality, primarily in terms of words and the manipulation of words, artisans might see reality as intimately related to material objects and the manipulation of material, which could be thought about and understood as a "material language." If this material literacy is nonverbal and nontextual, how might we come to understand it? We must look for expressions of the artisan's view of the relationship between himself and the matter he works.[4] We can turn to the material objects that the artisan produces for these expressions, and we can look to texts written by artisans to help us understand what such a material language and literacy might be. I shall explore this problem by examining the work of Bernard Palissy (ca. 1510–ca. 1590), a Huguenot potter, who was literate (in a conventional sense) in French but not in the language of learning, Latin, and who produced both extraordinary texts and pottery. The evidence of Palissy's writings and objects will be employed to infer this artisan's understanding of his own process of creation.

I shall first consider his claim that literacy in the book of nature is superior to literacy of texts and that sky and earth are given to all to know and to read. We should make no mistake about it; these are radical claims. This is evident in a trial argued before the Paris Parlement in 1579, just a year before Palissy's book appeared. In this contest, the plaintiff was the Medical Faculty of the University of Paris, which charged the defendant, a Paracelsian chemist, with practicing medicine without a license. On the first afternoon of the trial, the defendant stated that he could not speak Latin, and for the rest of the day the court debated this assertion. While the chemist refused to express himself in Latin, the plaintiffs maintained they could not examine him in French, for medical knowledge was expressed only in Latin. Against this, the chemist asserted that disease was not healed in Latin or in Greek, and, as Hippocrates had spoken Greek and Avicenna had healed in his native tongue of Arabic, he, a native of France, could pursue his art in French.

The Faculty of Medicine did not recognize this argument and turned instead to the education of the defendant. How could he be a true doctor, if he couldn't speak Latin, for medicine was taught in Latin? He could not possibly have passed the disputations and examinations in medicine. The court granted him a chance to translate a sentence from Latin. At first he refused. Under pressure, he admitted he could read Latin better than speak it. After much discussion, the judge allowed him to present a written translation to the court, but with the stricture that he perform it on the spot with no time to take it away or study it. As the judge read out the chemist's translation, the Latin was so bad that the court burst into laughter. The court recorder noted all the mistakes in translation and then by analogy listed the illnesses treated "incorrectly" by the chemist. The court finally concluded that a man who did not know even the basic rules of Latin conjugation and declension could hardly understand anything about medicine and, consequently, must be irresponsible and lacking in good character.[5]

The lesson we may take from this episode is one of a recognition of the social and intellectual threat represented by a claim to literacy in the language of nature in the sixteenth century. The language of learning was Latin, and a person must be literate in this language in order to make claims to legitimate knowledge and to the authority that conferred. An institutional structure embedded within a political and social hierarchy mediated and guarded this literacy.

Palissy's statement that he read earth and sky, a book open to all, thus challenged established educational structures and a social elite that worked with texts in ancient languages. It opened an epistemological controversy about the aims and method of knowledge, and it raised the specter of religious confrontation between personal illumination and institutionalized intercession. It is worthwhile considering what these statements mean and how they came to be made, for they tell us first about the self-consciousness of the artisan, which may help us to understand how he viewed his own capacity of production, and second about the way he viewed knowledge itself. What is the goal of knowledge, and how should it be pursued? Can we reconstruct what the Huguenot potter understood himself to be saying when he made this radical knowledge claim?

It is important to note that the rhetoric used by the potter would become important in the scientific revolution of the early modern period and that Palissy is part of the story of the process by which practice and sensory experience gained legitimation in Western European culture. Some historians have viewed Palissy as the source for Francis Bacon's inductive method.[6] Instead of taking part in that debate, this essay will attempt to understand what kind of a claim to knowledge and legitimacy the potter was making when he said he could read earth and sky, and to delineate the parameters of his "material language" and literacy. We will see that in the sixteenth century a conjunction of events, both religious and intellectual, made possible Palissy's and others' articulation of this claim to knowledge.

Bernard Palissy

Bernard Palissy (ca. 1510–ca. 1590), the Huguenot potter, is remembered at a span of time of almost 500 years because he produced signed objects and three published texts. Palissy apprenticed as a glass painter, traveled as a journeyman gaining experience in his craft, learned to draw and survey, and settled in Saintes, southeast of La Rochelle. In the 1540s, apparently after seeing a white enameled cup probably produced in Italy or Germany in imitation of Chinese porcelain first brought to Europe only decades before, he taught himself pottery making. Pieces from his own hand are rare, but Palissyware, as it is called, is based on extraordinary models of Palissy's design: large-scale tableware—sauceboats, ewers, large platters, covered with three-dimensional objects and glazed in deep greens, blues, browns, and pure white—produced for the tables and curiosity cabinets of the highest nobility of France. The majority of these pieces imitate a shoreline, or a marshland, a deep blue center with fishes thrusting out of the plate, swimming down the length of the platter, or a snake coiled on a small island protruding out of the surface, every scale of the wet reptile perfectly imitated from nature.[7] Around the rims of the platters are snails, salamanders, crabs— all amphibious creatures creeping along the edges of the water, surrounded by deep green vegetation.

Palissy's larger works, the grottos and pleasure gardens he designed and built for his noble patrons, exist no more, but he described one such garden of delight in his 1563 text. This garden was to be situated at the foot of hills so that a stream might run through the grottos built and glazed by Palissy. Four grottos, or "cabinets" as he calls them, were located at each corner of the garden, their interior ornamentation ranging from classical decor to (artificial) untamed nature. Palissy's description of a single one will suffice to give some idea of their ambitious scale:

> Note then, that at the base and foot of the rock [a pottery imitation rock glazed in many strange colors] there will be a natural trench or receptacle for water, which will be equal in length to the said rock. For this cause I will make projections on my rock, along the said trench, upon which projection I will place several frogs, tortoises, crabs, lobsters, and a great number of all kinds of shells, the better to imitate the rock. Also, there will be several branches of coral, whereof the roots will be at the foot of the rock, in order that the said corals may have the appearance of having grown within the said trench.
>
> Item, a little higher on the said rock, there will be several clefts and concavities, on which there will be some serpents, aspics, and vipers, which will be couched and twisted on the said projections, and within the clefts: and all the rest of the height of the rock will be sloping, tortuous, and lumpy, having modelled over it a number of kinds of herbs and mosses that commonly grow about rocks and moist places. And above the said mosses and herbs there will be a great number of serpents, aspics, vipers, and lizards, which will appear to run over the said rock, some upwards, some to one side, some downwards, disposed in many pleasant gestures and agreeable contortions; and all the said animals shall be modelled and enamelled so like to nature, that the natural lizards and serpents shall come often to them with wonder, as you see that there is a dog in my workshop, that many other dogs have growled at seeing, thinking that it was natural. And from the said rock will distil a great number of jets of water, which shall fall into the trench which will be in the said cabinet, in which trench there will be a great number of natural fishes, and of frogs, and tortoises. And because upon the bank adjoining the said trench there will be fishes and frogs, modelled according to my art of the

earth, they who shall go to see the said cabinet will think that the said fishes, tortoises, and frogs are natural, and that they have come out of the said trench, inasmuch as in the said trench there will be some that are living. Also, in the said rock will be formed some kind of recess, to hold the glasses and cups of those who may feast within the cabinet: and in the same way there will be formed in the said rock certain bins and little receptacles for the cooling of the wine during a repast, which receptacles will always contain cold water; because when they shall be full according to the prescribed measure of their size, the superfluity of the water will flow over into the trench, and so the water will always be fresh within the said receptacle. Also, in the said cabinet there will be a table, like in material to the rock, which also will be supported on a rock; and the said table will be of an oval fashion, being enamelled, enriched, and coloured with divers colours of enamel, which will shine like a mirror. And they who shall be seated to banquet at the said table will be able to put fresh water to their wine without quitting the said cabinet; for they will take it from the jets of the fountains of the said rock.[8]

After seeing his work in provincial Saintes, Catherine de Medicis, the Queen Mother, called Palissy to Paris in 1567 to decorate the halls and gardens of the Tuileries Palace. Palissy proceeded to build a grotto, and he continued to work in Paris with short interruptions for the rest of his life.

Palissy's texts—two published in 1563 and one in 1580—are of equal interest to his objects. In 1563 he published a short description of a grotto built for the Duke of Montmorency and a book, *True Recipe by which all the men of France would be able to multiply and augment their treasures.* The *Recepte véritable*, organized as a dialogue between unnamed interlocutors, contains a diversity of subject matter ranging from farming and fertilizing methods to an account of the Reformed church in the town of Saintes. It contains a plan for the garden of delight (which was also a refuge from the persecutions of war and religious conformity) and a design for a fortress, shaped after nature in the form of a shell. The book also contains observations of nature and theories about the genesis of rocks, crystals, metals, springs, and other natural formations. This work of natural history is also, perhaps primarily, a religious testament, and in it Palissy is concerned to make clear his commitment to the Reformed faith and to the promulgation of its tenets. He appears to have helped found the Reformed church in Saintes, and he views even his garden as a work of worship. He claims to found the garden on Psalm 104, and, indeed, we can almost see the words translated into Palissy's design:

He sendeth the springs into the valleys, which run among the hills.
They give drink to every beast of the field: the wild asses quench their thirst.
By them shall the fowls of the heaven have their habitation, which sing among
the branches.

He watereth the hills from his chambers: the earth is satisfied with the fruit of
  thy works.
He causeth the grass to grow for the cattle, and herb for the service of man: that
  he may bring forth food out of the earth;
And wine that maketh glad the heart of man, and oil to make his face to shine,
  and bread which strengtheneth man's heart.
The trees of the Lord are full of sap; the cedars of Lebanon, which he hath
  planted;
Where the birds make their nests: as for the stork, the fir trees are her house.
The high hills are a refuge for the wild goats; and the rocks for the conies.
He appointed the moon for seasons: the sun knoweth his going down.
Thou makest darkness, and it is night: wherein all the beasts of the forest do
  creep forth.
The young lions roar after their prey, and seek their meat from God.
The sun ariseth, they gather themselves together, and lay them down in their dens.
Man goeth forth unto his work and to his labour until the evening
O Lord, how manifold are thy works! in wisdom hast thou made them all: the
  earth is full of thy riches.
So is this great and wide sea, wherein are things creeping innumerable, both
  small and great beasts. . .⁹

Palissy's work, with its interest in springs and fountains and the innumerable
creeping creatures of his watery blue-green platters, derives from his religious
vocabulary but coincides with his patron's interests in garden decor. Palissy
never ceased declaring his faith (even through his work) and was only saved
from religious persecution (and probably from death in the St. Bartholomew's
Day Massacre) by the protection of his powerful Catholic patrons, whose gardens and grottos he was building.¹⁰ His patrons died before him, however, and
he spent at least the last two years of his life in prison where he died in 1589
or 1590.

Palissy published his second book, *Admirable Discourses on the nature of waters and
fountains, either natural or artificial, on metals, salts and salines, on rocks, earths, fire and enamels.
With many other wonderful secrets about nature. Plus a treatise on marl, very useful and necessary,
for those who practice agriculture. The whole arranged as dialogues, in which are included theory and
practice*, in 1580. The *Discours admirables* is similar to the *Recepte veritable*, containing
treatises on springs and fountains, metals, alchemy, potable gold, theriac, ice,
salts, rocks, clay, potting, and marl. It assembles the material Palissy presented
in public lectures in Paris between 1575 and 1584. While public lectures by
practitioners were not wholly unknown in the 1570s, Palissy's lectures, according
to his own evidence, drew not just practitioners, but also physicians and sur-
geons of the court, as well as nobles and gentlemen. Palissy kept a collection of

rocks, fossils, and earths with which he illustrated his lectures and demonstrated his theories.

Even from this brief overview of Palissy's life, we can already begin to see how he came to make his radical claim to knowledge. The analogy between individual reading of Scripture and the unmediated reading of nature leaps out at us first. Palissy's claim to "read" nature without an intermediary set of authorities is of course analogous to the Protestant's reading of Scripture without the mediation of a priest. While unmediated Protestants had proven dangerous for those trying to overturn social hierarchies—such as the peasants around Salzburg in 1525 and the Anabaptists in Münster in 1534—it nevertheless was an activity advocated in the works of Luther and Calvin. These writings no doubt strengthened the resolve of an individual such as Palissy to rely on the authority of his own conviction in resisting religious and civil authorities, but we must remember that his specific claim was about the reading of nature, not of Scripture. This claim too had a religious context. Paul had charged that the pagan Romans had no excuse not to worship the God of the Christians; even if they had not read of him, his works stood open to their sight: "All that may be known of God by men lies plain before their eyes; indeed God himself has disclosed it to them. His invisible attributes, that is to say his everlasting power and deity, have been visible, ever since the world began, to the eye of reason, in the things he has made. There is therefore no possible defence for their conduct; knowing God, they have refused to honor him as God, or to render him thanks."[11] Augustine had echoed this sentiment, calling for the Christian to praise God through the Creation.[12] In Palissy's own time, Luther and Calvin had reiterated and brought back into prominence the idea that a Christian can come to knowledge of the Creator through the Creation.[13] Palissy could thus view his reading of nature as a simple extension of his reading of Scripture.

We might be tempted to go no further than this religious context for an explanation of Palissy's claim of knowledge, but his religious convictions cannot explain his use of natural objects to demonstrate his theories in his lectures and in the *Discours admirables*. In claiming to be able to read earth and sky, Palissy was also making a statement about his access to the experience of nature and his ability to produce valuable objects out of this experience. In the most immediate sense, his knowledge and productive abilities constituted power: they saved his life. He possessed knowledge in demand by the nobility, and patronage by the powerful made possible his publishing and practicing, despite his unorthodox beliefs. Palissy benefited from the political developments in France during his lifetime. In the sixteenth century, the court of the king began its struggle for the hearts, minds, and tax revenues of the aristocracy of France. Palissy himself was given the commission of mapping the saltworks of the

Saintonge in order to institute the king's *gabelle* salt tax.[14] This political struggle manifested itself not only in religious and constitutional disturbances but also in the building projects of the king and Queen Mother, which would help to draw the provincial nobility to Paris and hold them there by a lavish and lucrative court life. That he was aware of his own power is clear from the opening exchange in the *Discours admirables* in which Theory asks Practice to instruct him in finding water and constructing fountains because he has "a property on which there are no fountains and there is only a well which is subject to drying up, like others."[15] Practice (Palissy) possesses *productive* knowledge useful to Theory, a landowner and patron engaged only in consumption. What more productive knowledge could there be for a landowner than where to find water? In the circumstances of his life and in his consciousness of his own power, Palissy takes part in an epochal encounter between an old order of consuming aristocracy, written texts, and contemplative knowledge on the one side and on the other a world in which labor and practice give power, and knowledge is active and productive.

Productive Knowledge

I shall consider more closely this notion of "productive knowledge." Palissy made the assertion that his literacy of earth and sky was superior to the literacy of texts in a society in which productive knowledge was becoming increasingly important and practice and practitioners were rising in status. Texts and school learning were effective in producing a learned man—the possessor of a body of knowledge—but not at all effective in making knowledge productive. For productive knowledge, an artisan—a creator of things—must be sought out.

In a view of the organization of knowledge that went back formally to Aristotle, productive knowledge in the sixteenth century was understood to be the province of art. It is in the *Nicomachean Ethics* that Aristotle discussed the organization of knowledge. He distinguished between the contemplative life and the active life, each of which had its own end, type of knowledge, and degree of certainty. The life of contemplation concerned itself with the pursuit of the unchanging and eternal good. The result of contemplation was epistemic or theoretical knowledge about the immutable objects of nature, things that existed by necessity and contained within themselves the source of their change. Theoretical knowledge was proven by demonstration in the form of syllogisms and based on certain, demonstrable principles.[16]

Practical knowledge, or praxis, on the other hand, concerned mutable affairs that could be directed and intervened in by humans. This knowledge was based in action and derived from either "things done" or "things made." The sphere of practical knowledge pertaining to things done resulted in "prudence," and it was the knowledge required by rulers and men of public life. Aristotle dealt with this knowledge particularly in his practical writings on ethics, economics, and politics. Prudence could not be called a science, and was not of absolute certainty, for it could not be proven by demonstration based on certain principles. Prudence might never be certain, but it could be used as the basis for action if it were based on experiences, or particular facts.[17] Prudence apprehended only the particular, not the general (which was the basis of theoretical knowledge), and achieved this apprehension by (often fallible) sensory perception.[18]

The practical knowledge concerning "things made" was *techné*, or art. Art did not deal with things that already existed or had come into existence of necessity. Instead, art itself brought its objects into existence. Art was the only one of the three types of knowledge that was productive, for the efficient cause of its objects lay in the maker and not in the objects themselves.[19]

Science, prudence, and art were different types of knowledge for Aristotle, and his distinctions continued to be observed in the course of European thought. The Roman concern with political life in the forum focused the sphere of practical knowledge on "things done," and praxis came to refer to the type of knowledge necessary for a life in the service of the *res publica*. Beginning as early as the twelfth century in the medieval universities, the development of a course of education that focused on the systematization of the liberal arts and excluded the mechanical arts as incapable of similar ordering widened the gap between theoretical and practical knowledge. At the same time, however, the practitioners of the mechanical arts, organized in guilds, took on increasing economic importance and political power in public life. The humanist reform of knowledge of the Renaissance, reacting against the life of contemplation as exemplified for the humanists in the medieval universities, renewed the Roman perception of the value of the active life and developed a rhetorical strategy that set the life of contemplation and theory against the life of political activity and practice. Concurrently, the practical knowledge of "things made" became a source of power and a subject of great interest to scholars, literati, and princes by the sixteenth century. The mechanical arts came to be seen as the foundation of the wealth of cities and republics. Scholars and their republican and princely patrons began to look to artisans and artisanal knowledge as productive and valuable, an integral part of the common good.[20]

In 1531, for example, Juan Luis Vives encouraged scholars not to "be ashamed to enter into shops and factories, and to ask questions from craftsmen, and to get to know about the details of their work."[21] The Parisian pedagogical reformer Petrus Ramus (1515–1572) visited the workshops of artisans in Paris and Nuremberg and formulated a notion that "natural" or "practical" reason should guide humankind in the acquisition of knowledge. He wrote that this method of reasoning had been known to the ancient natural philosophers, but in the course of history it had become distorted. This natural reasoning could be learned from the daily experience and observation of the trades, such as navigation, medicine, agriculture, and bookkeeping. As a humanist, Ramus believed he was returning to ancient sources in positing this method, for the practice of these arts was more ancient than the theories of scholars.[22] This interest in practice and the mechanical arts would culminate in the seventeenth century in a complete reorganization of knowledge by which practice and its effectiveness in bringing about a "product" would in fact prove theory.

Knowing Nature

When scholars such as Vives and Ramus went into the workshops of artisans, they sought there not just the techniques, but the very knowledge that made the artisan capable of producing. What was that knowledge? To this the universal and ancient answer was that artisans had a knowledge of matter and nature, for "ars imitatur naturam" (art imitates nature). Artisans also considered themselves to be imitating nature; Palissy repeated over and over his claim that his art imitated nature so well that they could not be differentiated. Witness his ceramic dog that brought growls from passing canines and his crafted fish that the beholder would perceive as swimming in the grotto alongside real fish. But the artisan did not simply possess the ability to imitate the objects of nature, such as dogs or fishes, but also possessed experience (and thus a kind of knowledge) of matter and an ability to imitate the very processes of natural generation and growth—of creation—in his production of crafted objects. How can we, while keeping in mind the injunction to pay attention to the artisan's own self-representation and perception of hierarchies, apprehend the artisanal experience of "knowing nature"?

In order to explicate this concept of the knowledge of nature, I shall turn to the medical and religious reformer Philippus Aureolus Theophrastus Bombast von Hohenheim, called Paracelsus (ca. 1493–1541). Paracelsus elevated the knowledge of the artisan above the learning of books because the artisan worked with the objects and the matter of nature. He challenged medical doctors and university instructors to learn from those who work with their hands: "Learn of old Women, Egyptians, and such-like persons; for they have greater experiences in such things than all the Academians."[23] He collected remedies from the miners and common people to whom he ministered, and he maintained that the knowledge of those closer to nature and a state of pure labor was more valuable than knowledge from books. He proclaimed observation and experience in the "Book of Nature" as superior to the books of authorities for gaining medical knowledge: "For this I would prove through nature: He who would explore her, must tread her books with his feet. Scripture is explored through its letters; but nature from land to land. Every land is a leaf. Such is the *Codex Naturae;* thus must her leaves be turned."[24]

I turn to Paracelsus not because he was an artisan, but because Paracelsus, in setting out the method of "reading the Book of Nature," articulated an "artisanal literacy" by which artisans thought about their relationship to matter and nature, and their own processes of creation. Paracelsus was not an artisan, but he was a medical doctor (a theoretician), a surgeon (an artisan), and an alchemist (an activity that combined work in the laboratory with extensive textual study). These were all activities acknowledged to have a substantial component of manual work, but more importantly it appears that Paracelsus gathered experiences and remedies from peasants and artisans. He questioned miners on their remedies for diseases contracted in the bowels of the earth, and he drank with peasants in village taverns, gaining a thorough knowledge of vintages and *aqua vitae.* In 1527 he issued a broadside against traditional medical education at university and advocated instead a curriculum based on firsthand experience of nature and the treatment of patients. He lectured in the vernacular and admitted barber-surgeons to his courses.[25] Throughout his life he worked in the laboratory and practiced alchemy, which he understood not simply as the transmutation of base metals into silver and gold, but as a search for the principles that would make such a transmutation possible. For him, alchemical works were directed toward gaining knowledge about the creative principles of nature and imitating them by human art. Being both art and science, alchemy illuminated the relationship of the artisan to his material and the productive process and provided him with a language in which to talk about this relationship and process.[26]

Paracelsus believed that the person who worked with his hands was more closely attuned to nature, because by his art he imitated nature. Thus he was interested in the knowledge of nature not just because he viewed it as necessary to the practice of medicine but because it formed for him the path to an understanding of God's Creation. Moreover, the art of the craftsman "reformed" nature by creating valuable objects out of the raw materials of nature. The manual labor of refining nature for human needs, common to all work with the hands and thought by Paracelsus to be exemplified in the refining processes of alchemy, brought about the reformation and ultimately the redemption of the world and humankind. All manual arts (but for Paracelsus, especially medicine and alchemy) carried out in microcosm the macrocosmic process of human redemption after the Fall.[27] By this work of redemption artisans produced useful goods; and for Paracelsus, material works were more powerful than words as a form of worship. God expected works, for He provided humans with the fruits of nature, but humans had to labor by the arts of the artisan to enjoy them. Paracelsus believed the method of the artisan, who taught his apprentice with his hands rather than his tongue and words, was superior to that used to transmit knowledge in the universities because it rested in experience and manipulation of nature.

Paracelsus emphasized experience with the things of nature themselves. As quoted above, the Book of Nature must be read with one's feet, in travel and observation. For Paracelsus, "Erfahrung" (experience) in fact meant "the result of travelling with open eyes."[28] Experience, which was becoming a catchword for the humanists involved in the active practice of public life, meant for Paracelsus something different. Paracelsus's notion of experience had little to do with public life or common sense. Rather, his was a deeply gnostic understanding. Paracelsus believed human beings possessed both a divine and corporeal nature and were capable (at least in the case of the chemist/physician) of quasi-divine powers. From the gnostic beliefs that God is present in all matter and that this divine power inheres in human beings came Paracelsus's idea of experience.[29] Knowledge of nature was gained not through a process of reasoning, but by a union of the divine powers of mind and of the entire body with the divine spirit in matter.

In explaining this method of experience, Paracelsus drew on the terminology of theory and practice, but inverted the traditional understanding of these terms in a remarkable way. The universities taught a *scientia*, meaning a body of knowledge formed into a discipline by its logical structure and based on the learning of a certain group of books. In contrast, Paracelsus defined *scientia* as the divine power in natural things, which the physician must "overhear" and with which he must achieve union in order to gain knowledge of medicaments. The physician then put *scientia* to the test by creating medicines from this knowledge and curing the sick. This testing yielded *experientia*, which was the goal of knowledge. Thus Paracelsus turned the traditional relationship between *scientia* and *experientia* on its head. Where *scientia* had previously connoted a corpus of knowledge defined by the books of authorities, Paracelsus used it to mean the innate virtue inhering in natural objects, while *experientia* was the fruit of testing:

> Now note the difference between *experientia* and *scientia*. . . . *Scientia* is inherent in a thing, it is given by God; *experientia* is a knowledge of that in which *scientia* is proven. For instance, the pear tree has *scientia* in itself, and we who see its works have *expe-*

rientia of its *scientia*. . . . Thus follows the book of *scientia*, that we experience *scientia*. . . . It is *scientia* to make a patient healthy. But this *scientia* is the medicine, not the physician. . . . These are the books of medicine.[30]

Experientia constitutes the only true knowledge of objects, and it is gained by testing the *scientia* of the object.[31] Similarly, in his constant reference to the Book of Nature, Paracelsus used familiar concepts, but reversed the traditional primacy of words over things.

In this important passage Paracelsus articulated the experience of the artisan, that is, he expressed the meaning of the phrase "knowledge of nature" for an artisan in his creation of objects from natural materials. Paracelsus used the terminology—*scientia* and *experientia*—of "high culture," but the experience that he articulated was alien to that culture. In this he reminds us of the master mason with whom we began. Although this artisanal experience of knowledge, this "artisanal literacy," had been present in artisanal life perhaps for centuries, its first articulation occurred in the sixteenth century.

Experiencing Matter

This articulation of artisanal experience can be found in the texts of Bernard Palissy also.[32] It emerges with particular clarity in a chapter of Palissy's second book, the *Admirable Discourses* (1580), entitled "On the Art of the Earth." The book as a whole discusses processes of generation, growth, and change. Palissy writes on springs and waters, alchemy, ice, salts, and their central place in the generation of terrestrial bodies, on stones, clays, and on marl earths and their potential for agriculture. Between the chapters on clays and on marl earths is the "Art of the Earth," a dialogue in which Theory attempts to pry out of Practice the secret of his enamel making.[33] Theory begins by accusing Practice of attempting to divert him from his aim to learn the art of the earth. Practice scoffs, "Do you believe that a man of sound judgment would thus wish to give away the secrets of an art that has cost dearly to the man who has invented it?" Theory responds that Practice is "misusing the gifts of God," but Practice contends that while "the word of God" and the "sciences that serve the whole state must not be kept secret," yet his "charming invention" will only become common and cheap if he yields to Theory. When Theory promises to keep it secret, Practice tells him instead that he is not "wide awake, quick, sympathetic and hard working" enough to carry it out, nor does he have the requisite capital needed to bear the losses incurred in practicing the art of the earth. Theory retorts that if Practice teaches him in writing the fruit of his experience, he will not need these prerequisites. To this Practice replies: "Even if I used a thousand reams of paper to write down all the accidents that have happened to me in learning this art, you must be assured that, however good a brain you may have, you will still make a thousand mistakes, which cannot be learned from writings, and even if you had them in writing, you wouldn't believe them until practice has given you a thousand afflictions."

Palissy here asserts that practice cannot be learned in writing, but must be learned by doing and labor. In this assertion he again opposes the consuming, barren, and written culture of theory to the productive, active world of practice. He finally agrees to tell Theory his secrets, but not before he has told him "the calamities I have endured before attaining my goal . . . because you will see that nothing can be attempted or completed, to render it in beauty and perfection without great and extreme labor, which never comes singly but is always accompanied by a thousand anxieties." In telling the story of his calamities, Practice makes clear to Theory what he means when he says that practice must be learned by labor—in fact, Practice means nothing less than a Paracelsian union with his material.

Palissy begins his story by relating his encounter with the porcelain vessel, an "earthen cup, turned and enameled with such beauty that I was immediately perplexed." At once he "started to look for enamels, like a man who gropes in the dark." He began by crushing all sorts of things that might be used; he bought earthen pots, painted them with his glazes, and wrote down which mixture he had applied to each piece. But nothing worked. "For several years, with sadness and sighing," it went on this way, now sending off "three or four hundred pieces" to a nearby pottery, then putting them into the kilns of glassworks, until finally "God willed that just as I began to lose hope, and for the last time had gone to a glass works with a man carrying more than three hundred kinds of experiments, it happened that one of them melted within four hours of being put into the kiln which was so white and polished as to cause me such joy that I thought I had become a new man." Palissy experienced rebirth of himself and his hopes with the melting of the enamel. He spent "seven or eight months" making earthen vessels, then building his kilns by his own "incredible labor," mixing his mortar, drawing the water, fetching the brick on his own back. He worked "like a desperate man," spending six days and nights (the span of Creation) at the kiln tending the fire. Still the enamel would not melt. He crushed new materials for the enamel, fired up his kiln again, whereon running out of wood, he began to burn the wood of his garden, then his own house: "I was forced to burn the tables and the floor of my house, in order to melt the second mixture." He describes his situation vividly: "I was in such anguish as I could not describe: for I was quite dried out because of the work and the heat of the kiln; for more than a month my shirt had not dried on me, and moreover, to console me I was jeered at, and even those who should have helped me, went about the town shouting that I was burning up the floor: and thus I was made to lose my credit, and I was thought to be crazy." At the end of his nine-month labor, he still did not bring forth progeny.

He fell into a "sad and puzzled mood" and finally hired a potter to turn the vessels. In tearing apart his last kiln to build a new one, the flesh of his hands was so torn that he was "forced to eat with my fingers wrapped in bandages." But this kiln ruined an entire load of pots when the pebbles in the brick exploded and stuck to the glaze. The next kiln load was ruined by ash blowing into the glaze, then the enamels would not melt at the same time, until "all these mistakes have caused me such labor and mental anguish that before I had made my enamels fusible at the same degree of fire, I thought I would be at death's door." And indeed his body suffered the ravages of his unsuccessful labor: "Also as I worked at such things for more than ten years my body was so wasted away that my arms and legs had no form or trace of muscles, but on the contrary my legs were like sticks." His home was no refuge: "I could obtain no patience, nor do anything that was considered good. I was despised and jeered at by everyone." He ends his lament dwelling on this sad situation:

> For several years, having nothing to roof over my kilns, I was every night at the mercy of rains and winds, with no succor, aid or consolation, except for the owls hooting on one side and the dogs howling on the other; sometimes winds and storms sprang up which blew so hard over and under my kilns that I was forced to leave everything, losing my labor; and it happened often that having left everything, without a dry rag on me, because of the rains that had fallen, I went to bed at midnight or at dawn, dressed like a man who has been dragged through all the mud holes of the city; and in retiring thus, I stumbled about without light, and falling on one side or another, like a drunkard, filled with great sadness: because after having worked a long time I saw my labor lost. Now, in retiring thus dirty and wet, I would find in my bedroom a second persecution worse than the first, which makes me wonder now that I did not die of sadness.

But Theory knows Practice eventually attained success, and so, impatient with Practice's stories, Theory demands that Practice tell him his secrets in a straightforward way. Practice responds with the ingredients of his enamels but not the precise doses, saying "the mistakes I made while I found out the dose for my enamels taught me more than the things that were easy to learn: therefore I judge that you should work to find this dose, just as I have done; otherwise you would esteem the knowledge too lightly." Theory gives up in disgust, calling the art too mechanical to be prized in any case. Practice expostulates that it is an art far from mechanical and, in addition to that, useful to all facets of human civilization. And there, not for the last time, the dialogue between Practice and Theory breaks off.

In this vivid account of his trials, Palissy makes clear the bases for his authority in speaking. He possesses knowledge inaccessible to Theory, for despite Theory's superior status, Theory has not the requisite habits of observation, the material skills, or the stamina. Practice possesses productive knowledge, by which he can get his bread, and this economic reality gives him power over Theory. Practice gains his knowledge through experience, literally through trial by fire. His body and the shell of his body—his home—are consumed in the process, forming a unity, like Paracelsus's experience, with the materials he works. In the end, his labor redeems him and his household, an experience denied to Theory because theory does not labor.

It is clear that for Palissy knowledge of nature was sacred knowledge and manual labor was worship. In contrast to the Greek insistence on the deforming aspects of manual work, Christian thought had elevated the laborer and focused on the reforming potential of work. The Fall of humankind had made all humans laborers, condemned to get their bread in the sweat of their face, but the monasticism of the Middle Ages established the life of *ora et labora* (prayer and work) as work that redeemed not just the individual, but the whole of society.[34] Much has been written about the place of vocation and work in the thought of Martin Luther and Jean Calvin, and while reformed ideas doubtless affected Palissy's conception of his call to form a church and preach God's word, the understanding of his own labor was closer to that of Paracelsus's artisan as redeemer of self and the world through work and knowledge of nature.

In a brilliant reading of Palissy's text and work, Neil Kamil further explicates Palissy's artisanal understanding of the process of creation in his own labor. He shows in some detail how Palissy's account is imbued not only with analogies to sexual generation, but also a religious understanding of his work, and he notes the Paracelsian union between the artisan's body and the matter itself, which results in the process of death and rebirth. Kamil finds evidence of this artisanal worldview in both Palissy's account of the art of the earth and in shoemaker and mystic Jacob Boehme's experience of work, and particularly in Benvenuto Cellini's account of casting a bronze statue of Perseus in his *Autobiography* (dictated 1558–1566, first published 1730).

In this account, Cellini contracts a sudden, intense fever just before the metal being heated to cast his statue is liquified. He must leave the work, but a phantom enters his bedroom saying the statue is spoiled. He drags himself back to the workshop and stirs up the fire so vigorously that the roof begins to burn and the workmen are left under the elements. Finally the cake of metal comes "back to life," at which point "such strength surged through my veins that all the pains of my fever vanished." But still the metal does not flow quickly enough to be let through the channels and ducts into the mold. So Cellini begins to melt his pewter plates and dishes, as Palissy had burned his floorboards and furniture, until the mold is filled, and he "fell on [his] knees and with all [his] heart gave thanks to God." Like Palissy, Cellini experiences the death and re birth of the matter he works; his body, his home, and his earthly possessions were drawn into the cosmic process. Kamil comments that "the Paracelsian artisan, exploiting his special transformational relationship with materials, could . . . experience a spiritual rebirth every time he performed artisanry to externalize his internal millennial event."[35]

Giving Voice to the Hands

While Cellini's knowledge of Paracelsus is not known and Palissy mentions Paracelsus only in passing, I believe that we can still view Paracelsus and Palissy as "giving voice to the hands," that is, articulating the language in which artisans understood their own relationship to the matter they worked. The vocabulary of this language was formed primarily from religious expression, the dominant and most familiar language for both the Catholic and Huguenot artisan. The understanding of work as redemption and of the process of creation as one in which the artisan's body unites with the material to experience death and rebirth need not be millennial, but can be drawn from a combination of religious and sexual imagery and observation of natural processes of generation and growth. If we follow Paracelsus's articulation, begin from the artisan's notion of *scientia*, and apprehend that for him *scientia*, or certain knowledge, resided not in theory but in matter, we can begin to understand the material literacy of the artisan and the claim to read sky and earth.

When Paracelsus and Palissy claimed to *read* the book of Nature, they took a model of literacy from the world of texts, from "high culture." Perhaps the articulation in words of artisanal experience could not have had any other model than that of an already articulated epistemology. But the "reading of nature" in which Palissy engaged consisted in what we might call an experience of matter and the process of creation, rather than an artisanal approximation of the "high culture" activity of reading of texts. In the same vein, Palissy maintained that peasants laboring on the land engaged in philosophy. Not surprisingly, Theory scoffed at this, "one would suppose, to hear you speak, that some philosophy is needed by labourers—a thing which I find strange."[36] What Palissy attempted to convey here, however, was that labor on the land—humankind's first vocation in the struggle of redemption—demanded, as much if not more than any other art, an understanding and a harnessing of nature's generative powers. The peasant knew and read nature; Palissy said this peasant engaged in philosophy. Like the medieval master mason, Palissy translated the model of literacy borrowed from high culture into his own understanding of what knowledge was and how it was obtained. Such a translation admits of no simple binary opposition between high and low culture.

In the *Recepte véritable* Palissy states that in the face of the evil nature of the world he "found nothing better than to fly the neighborhood and the acquaintance of such people, and to withdraw [him]self to labour on the earth, which is a just thing before God."[37] It is this power of labor both to redeem and to produce a refined and valuable product that gives Practice the right to speak, to claim that his literacy—his ability to read earth and sky—is superior to the books of Theory. A powerful mix of religiosity and economic self-consciousness informs Palissy's statement, and although we may be tempted to try to separate these components, it is not possible, for his works and books are as much an account of his religious faith as they are a rendering of accounts to his patrons and an advertisement of his skills. More than this, however, we have seen that his works also give access to an experience and to an epistemology that until the sixteenth century was expressed only in the work of the hands. If we view artisanal literacy as beginning in a grammar of matter (in which things really do have primacy over words) and a sacramental understanding of labor and human creation, we can come to understand what it meant to be literate in the reading of earth and sky.

five **Social Place and Literacies in John Foxe's *Actes and Monuments***

Evelyn B. Tribble

In April 1571, a Convocation of the English Church meeting at St. Paul's ordered that the "holy Bible in the largest volume as it was lately printed in London and also that full and perfect history which is entitled 'Monuments of Martyrs' be made available in hall or chamber for the use of strangers and servants."[1] The Bible "in the largest volume" is the Bishops' Bible, the revised translation authorized by Queen Elizabeth in 1568; the "Monuments of Martyrs" is John Foxe's *Actes and Monuments of These Latter and Perilous Days*, better known as the *Book of Martyrs*. Foxe's work, a massive two-million-word record of the martyrs of the Protestant church primarily focusing on the reign of Mary Tudor, is now one of the great unread books of Anglo-American culture. No twentieth-century edition yet exists, probably due to the formidable difficulties of editing and production the two-million-word book presents.[2] Nor is it an easy read; modern readers are apt to be put off by its huge bulk and its encyclopedic tendencies—deposition after deposition. Letter after letter is reproduced, each exhaustively recording the interrogation and burning of martyr after martyr. Yet it is arguably one of the most important and influential books ever published, both in the Elizabethan period and in its afterlives, as the book is reprinted, rewritten, and redisseminated at moments of perceived crisis in the Protestant church.

Because of its enormous influence with a diverse audience, and because of its concern throughout with pitting the learned against the unlearned, the *Book of Martyrs* provides a unique opportunity to study the interplay between "high" and "low" literacies in the early modern period. In what follows, I read the *Books of Martyrs* to examine the strategies by which nonelite readers appropriate and deploy literacies. Two related points emerge from this study: (1) what counts as "literacy" is vigorously contested in this period. Many of the "lower sort" that Foxe chronicles are highly literate in that they have a firm grasp on the spatial and rhetorical configuration of the Bible, but are in fact unable to read at all; (2) the social consequences of this access to learned culture are profound and potentially unsettling to a hierarchical society such as Tudor England. Elite readers wish to allow access to such "full and perfect" books as the Bible and the *Book of Martyrs*, but they also wish to control how they are read. On their part, the lower orders show alarming tendencies to read and to dispute in ways that threaten traditional patterns of deference. As Foxe presents it, the struggle between high and low is fought over the broadly conceived issue of "place," as lower-class ability to use Scriptural citations or "places" challenges traditional models of social place.

📖

In the last decade, students of early modern literacy have increasingly begun to question the assumptions behind the binaries of "orality" and "literacy," or "literacy" and "illiteracy." The essentialist nature of these categories, along with the implicit hierarchizations characteristic of binary pairings, have been challenged by theorists and historians alike. Historical studies of early modern England have shown the two categories instead to be permeable and shifting. Literacy is a socially embedded concept and cannot be discussed outside of a context.[3] As David Cressy has remarked, "It is important to talk of the margins of literacy, and of the uneven incidence of literacy in a partially literate society, rather than the simple dichotomy of literacy and illiteracy."[4] Keith Thomas has argued persuasively that we must think of *literacies* rather than a monolithic and static "literacy" in this period. In early modern England, the meaning of literacy was various: it was much more common to be able to read than to write, since the latter was taught separately and primarily in schooled settings; black letter or gothic type was easier to read than roman type; roman easier than deciphering the complex and various manuscript hands then current; and vernacular literacy of course much more widespread than Latin literacy. Literacy and illiteracy, orality and literacy thus should be seen as forming a continuum rather than a divide.

It is also important to consider these issues at least in part within the categories the culture itself provided. In the case of the early modern period, the opposed terms are "learned" and "unlearned"; implicitly, those in the former category are to instruct those in the latter. In his dedication, Foxe represents his book to Elizabeth in exactly this way: "Though the story being written in the popular tongue, serveth not so greatly for your own peculiar reading, nor for such as be learned," he begins, "yet shall I desire both you and them to consider in it the necessity of the ignorant flock of Christ committed to your government in this Realm of England."[5] These "ignorant" he characterizes as "wrapt in blindness" for lack of both Scripture and "the light of history." Accordingly he proposes to relieve their ignorance and instruct their simplicity: "Though they be but simple and unlearned yet not unapt to be taught if they were applied." Yet much of the content of the *Book of Martyrs* precisely inverts the hierarchy of these terms, as again and again in Foxe the powerless and unlearned prisoner wins a symbolic victory over the powerful and learned inquisitor. The victory is invariably won by the martyr's ability to deploy his or her own reading of the Bible to the embarrassment of the tormentor; as the textual "place" —the apt Scriptural quotation that exposes the lies and tyranny of the Papist— temporarily unsettles social place—the educational, gender, and status hierarchies of early modern society. In the *Book of Martyrs*, then, Scripture becomes a site for the renegotiation of social relations.

Indeed, the history of the circulation and reception of Foxe in many ways mirrors that of the Bible. On the one hand, in linking Foxe and the Bible, the English Church assumes that the reading of these texts will assure good order. This assumption is perhaps best epitomized by Archbishop Cranmer's preface to the Great Bible of 1540. Cranmer claims that the text will teach ordered behavior: "Herein may princes learn how to govern their subjects, subjects obedience, love, and dread to their princes, husbands how they should behave them unto their wives, how to educate their children and servants, and contrary, the wives, children, and servants may know their duty to husbands, parents, and masters."[6] According to this account, the text will ensure the perpetuation of existing social and political hierarchies and thus provide a handbook in which men and women can find and rehearse their social place. The famous title page by Holbein visually confirms this desire; it depicts Henry VIII handing the Bible to his prelates. The prelates in turn pass the book to the clergy and then the laity, appropriately positioned at the foot of the page, most of whom spout little cartoon bubbles reading "vivat Rex" or "God save the king."[7] This representation of the orderly transmission of the text exemplifies Tudor optimism about the socially conservative function of the Bible. In this vision, the learned will pass on the word of God to the unlearned, who will in turn receive it obediently and quietly.

But this is rather less than half the story. The insistence on order and hierarchy also reveals the fear of proliferation and diversity, of an entropic shift from locating authority within traditional institutions to its location within potentially recalcitrant, willful, and heady subjects. The latter years of Henry VIII's reign clearly reveal such fears, as a series of proclamations sought to ensure that reading the Bible did not disrupt good order. A proclamation shortly after the first authorized Bibles were placed on display in churches admonished parishioners not to read the Bible aloud during church services:

By the which injunctions the Kings royal majesty intended, that his loving subjects should have and use the commodities of the reading of the said Bibles, for the
purpose humbly, meekly, reverently and obediently; and not that any of them should
read the said Bibles, with loud and high voices, in time of the celebration of the
holy Mass and other divine services used in the church, nor that his lay subjects
reading the same, should presume to take upon them, any common disputation,
argument or exposition of the mysteries therein contained, but that every such
lay man should humbly, meekly and reverently read the same, for his own instruction, edification, and amendment of his life, according to God's holy word therein
mentioned.[8]

Rather than ensuring good order, the book becomes a focus of disorder,
setting up a competition between unruly lay readers and church hierarchy.
Foxe reprints a number of presentments or accusations made in Henry's time
for the offenses the proclamation seeks to eradicate. Among the presentments
are these: "Brisley's wife, for busy reasoning on the new learning, and not
keeping the church"; "Mrs. Castle, for being a meddler, and a reader of the
Scripture in the church", "William Plaine . . . with loud reading the English
Bible he disturbed the divine service"; "Christopher Erles . . . for looking upon
his book at the time of elevation" (5:444). These accusations demonstrate the
steps taken to eradicate a perceived rivalry between orderly reception and disorderly reading. "Setting up" the Bible in churches results not in meek reverence, but in a cacophony of voices loudly and busily competing with the priest.

If the Tudor state desires men and women to find in the Bible their social
place, Reformers were more interested in the issue of textual place, or the
"order, process, and meaning" of the Scriptures. And as the many narratives of
lower-class martyrs reveal, these two models of "place" were at least potentially
in conflict. As Foxe describes it, just such a motive underlay William Tyndale's
decision to translate the New Testament into English. According to Foxe,
Tyndale

perceived by experience, how that it was not possible to establish the lay people in
any truth, except the Scriptures were set before their eyes in their mother tongue,
that they might see the process, order, and meaning of the text; for else, whatsoever truth should be taught them, these enemies of truth would quench it again,
either with apparent reasons of sophistry, and traditions of their own making,
founded without all ground of Scripture; or else juggling with the text, expound-
ing it in such a sense as it were impossible to gather of the text, if the right
process, order, and meaning thereof were seen (5:118).

The desire that lay men and women should know their way "through" the
Scriptures is at the heart of reforming theory. This has profound implications

for the instruction of the "unlearned," whether conceived of as those entirely unable to read or those marginally literate. That is, simple instruction, divorced from its grounding in the Scriptures, is not sufficient. Without a knowledge of the territory of the book—its organization and process—one is at the mercy of Papist jugglers who will exploit the inequality of access to the Scriptures to their advantage.

Yet it is important to realize that this knowledge of the Bible is not dependent on possessing "literacy" in the way it is ordinarily understood. The narratives about lower-class martyrs that Foxe recounts demonstrate a striking variety of forms of access to the Scripture. A number of the martyrs were nearly illiterate by any measure, yet they have "heard" and internalized books through more educated relatives, friends, or neighbors. We are told of John Maundrel, for instance, that "after that the Scripture was translated into English by the faithful apostle of England, William Tyndale, [he] became a diligent hearer, and a fervent embracer of God's true religion, so that he delighted in nothing so much as to hear and speak God's word, never being without the New Testament about him, although he could not read himself. But when he came into any company that could read, his book was always ready, having a very good memory, so that he could recite by heart most places of the New Testament" (8:102–03). The book takes on almost a talismanic quality here (we must always keep in mind the extraordinary power that the newly available Bible in English must have had for those accustomed only to hear Latin services).[9] It is portable, concealable, and can be carried "about" one. Yet Maundrel's case also shows the fluidity of orality/literacy in this period, for he does not simply carry it about as one would a saint's image; rather, he seeks out opportunities to have it read aloud and from there to memorize and thus internalize it. Thus even without being able to read, he nonetheless knows his textual places.

Foxe's narrative of the life of the fisherman Rawlins White provides another instance of the capacity of the "unlearned" to hear and internalize Scriptural place:

> Under Edward VI, White began to be a diligent hearer, and a great searcher-out of the truth. But because the good man was altogether unlearned, and withal very simple, he knew no ready way he might satisfy his great desire. At length it came into his mind to take a special remedy to supply his necessity, which was this: he had a little boy who was his own son; which child he set to school to learn to read English. Now after the little boy could read indifferently well, his father, every night after supper, summer and winter, would have the boy to read a piece of the holy Scripture. . . . And to this his great industry and endeavour in the holy Scripture, God did also add in him a singular gift of memory; so that by the benefit thereof he would and could do that, in vouching and rehearsing of the text, which men

of riper and more profound knowledge, by their notes and other helps of memory could very hardly accomplish; insomuch that he, upon the alleging of Scripture, very often would cite the book, the leaf, yea and the very sentence: such was the wonderful working of God in this simple and unlearned father (7:29).

Memory provides an oral means of constructing aids superior to those employed by the learned, allowing White to negotiate the terrain of the book expertly.[10] What is interesting in this instance is the text-based nature of White's facility; without being able to decipher in the way we ordinarily understand the textual marks on the page, he nevertheless is presented as having a firm spatial grasp on the Bible, a knowledge of the "leaf, yea and the very sentence."

Foxe is also concerned to make the point that women as well as men are capable of such feats of memory and understanding. Of Alice Waste he writes: "And though she was of herself unlearned and by reason of her blindness unable to read, yet for the great desire she had to understand and have printed in her memory the sayings of the holy Scripture contained in the New Testament, she acquainted herself chiefly with one John Hart [who read to her]; By the which exercise she so profited, that she was able not only to recite many chapters of the New Testament without book, but also she could aptly impugn, by divers places of Scriptures as well sin, as such abuses in religion, as then were too much in use in divers and sundry persons" (8:747). The book and the self are imprinted analogously, as the printed book, mediated through the sighted reader, impresses itself in the memory of the blind unlearned woman.

📖

But the case of Joan Waste raises other important issues for this study: the question of how readers read, how they deploy this access to learned culture. For in learning their textual places, these men and women "forget" (or attempt to redefine) their social places. Waste is able to use her knowledge of the Scripture to "impugn" sin and "abuses," the latter presumably referring to the reinstitution of the Catholic Mass under Mary. Once the reader or hearer of Scripture has internalized the book, he or she is able to stand in for the Bible and produce readings resistant to institutionally sanctioned interpretations. And these readings may not be in the interest of an ordered society. One of the inquisitors Foxe records provides a strikingly frank rationale for forbidding the circulation of the Bible in English: "Lest the ignorant vulgar sort, through the occasion therof, might haply be brought in danger to leave their vocation, or else to run into some inconveniences: as for example, the ploughman, who heareth this in the gospel: 'No man who layeth his hand on the plough, and looketh back is meet for the kingdom of god,' might peradventure, hearing this, cease from his

plough" (7:449–50). We see here a recognition that the Bible contains within it many passages at odds with the sort of hierarchical society that was the model for the Tudor state.

Despite such fears of an overly naive literalism, the real problem for the Marian church was an overly figurative reading of the Eucharistic symbol, particularly the role of the bread. When, in Matthew 26:26, Jesus says "this is my body," is he speaking literally or figuratively? The Catholic doctrine of the Real Presence depends on a literal reading of the verse: Jesus plainly says that the bread "is" his body; therefore, when consecrated by a priest, the bread mystically is transformed into Christ's flesh. Reformers, by contrast, argued vehemently that the words "this is my body" were to be taken as a trope or figure. We are no more to believe that the bread is Christ's body than we are to believe that Jesus is a vine when he says, "I am the vine." These may seem like unimportant distinctions to us—a matter of "semantics"—but they were of profound importance in the sixteenth century. Under Edward VI, a reformed prayer book went forth, one which emphasized the participatory nature of the Eucharists, or the Lord's Supper as it is called in Reforming circles. The eating of Christ's body and the drinking of his blood changes from a mystical transubstantiation into a participatory rite of remembrance. When, under Mary, the sacrament is refigured as something one watches rather than something one does, there is resistance on all levels.

In fact, the primary focus of nearly every interrogation Foxe records is the reading of this sacrament. Crucially, the reforming argument depends on metaphor—which is in itself a "displacement," a use of language in a place other than its "proper" one. And such a displacement, like the social displacement feared as a result of lay reading, is potentially threatening. In one of the disputations between Cranmer and his inquisitors recorded in Foxe, Cranmer's interlocutor (himself using a trope) posits the following analogy to prove his point that "no tropes" can be found in the account of the Eucharist: "The good man of the house hath respect that his heirs, after his departure, may live in quiet without brabbling. / but they cannot be in quiet if he do use tropes; / therefore I say he useth no tropes" (6:450). Tropes result in "brabbling" because they introduce polysemy into Scripture; figurative language opens potentially uncontainable proliferative possibilities.

Foxe's book is designed to equip readers to use textual places to confute their social betters on this central issue. By reading even casually in Foxe's book, readers cannot help but learn the primary issues in this debate. Foxe actually provides a sort of kit for trying out disputation at home: "And for the reader's sake, to make the matter more largely and evidently to appear, concerning the distinction made of the bishops in this disputation, here have we, as in a brief

sum or table, expressed, as well their arguments, as the distinctions and answers . . . thus hast thou, gentle reader, in this aforesaid table set forth unto thee
the diverse respects how the real body of the Savior is eaten . . . by which table,
if thou mark it well, thou mayst answer easily to the most part of the arguments which the papists bring" (6:521). Readings based on such tables proliferate in Foxe, who is careful to ascribe them to the workings of God on weak
vessels of unlearned men and women. But in chronicling the spiritual victories
of the subordinate classes, Foxe also produces models of reading and speaking
profoundly challenging not only to Roman Catholic versions of hierarchy, but
to Elizabethan versions as well. What Foxe praises as a God-given ability to impugn on the part of Waste is perceived by the inquisitors, who use the same set
of gender and social hierarchies predominant throughout the Tudor period, as
profound challenges to normal order.

In fact, so profound are some of these challenges that Foxe himself is put
into difficulties by the narratives he recounts. The crucial line between religious and political challenges to Mary's reign is at times very difficult for Foxe
to maintain, as the difference between heresy (a religious crime) and sedition
(a secular crime) becomes increasingly blurred. For instance, the case of George
Eagles, otherwise known as Trudgeover-the-World, presents some problems of
framing. Foxe invests him with heroic qualities: "That he, having little learning, or none, most manfully served and fought under the banner of Christ's
church . . . is not to be neglected for his base occupation . . . he expressed and
uttered his manly stomach." Yet Eagles is accused of the secular crime of rebellion rather than the religious crime of heresy. Foxe is compelled to explain "albeit it was well known that poor Eagles did never any thing seditiously against
the queen, yet to cloak an honest matter . . . and to cause him to be the more
hated of the people, they turned religion into a civil offense and crime" (8:395).
Eagles is hung, drawn, and quartered (the civil penalty for treason) rather than
burned (the religious penalty for heresy).

Alice Driver, first presented for likening Queen Mary to Jezebel, presents a
similar difficulty. Foxe is careful to claim that she makes the comparison on the
sole basis of Mary's persecution of the faithful, rather than on grounds that might
be considered seditious by his readers. Nevertheless she receives the secular
penalty for speaking slander against the Queen: "her ears are cut off." In the
examination that follows, Foxe presents her as continually transgressing gender and social boundaries; she enters with a "smiling countenance" and tells
the examiners she laughs at "what fools ye be." As is typical, she is asked about
the sacrament—"dost thou not believe it is very flesh and blood, after the words
be spoken of consecration?" (8:493–94). She begins by expressing an ignorance
that quickly proves to be disingenuous:

Sir, said she, "pardon me though I make no answer, for I cannot tell what you mean thereby: for in all my life I never heard nor read of any such sacrament in all the Scripture."

SPENSER: "Why, what Scriptures have you read, I pray you?"

ALICE: "I have (I thank God) read God's book."

SPENSER: "Why, what manner of book is that you call God's book?"

ALICE: "It is the Old and New Testament. What call you it?"

SPENSER: "That is God's book indeed, I cannot deny."

ALICE: "That same book have I read throughout, but yet never could find any such sacrament there; and for that cause I cannot make you answer to that thing I know not. Notwithstanding, for all that, I will grant you a sacrament, called the Lord's supper; and therefore, seeing I have granted you a sacrament, I pray you show me what a sacrament is."

SPENSER: "It is a sign."

And one Dr. Gascoine, being by, confirmed the same, that it was the sign of a holy thing.

ALICE: "You have said the truth, sir," said she: "It is a sign indeed, I must needs grant it; and therefore seeing it is a sign, it cannot be the thing signified also. Thus far do we agree; for I have granted your own saying" (8:494).

As Foxe presents it, this passage marks an extraordinary reversal of the terms of the inquisition, as Driver's skillful manipulation of her underdog position elicits the response she desires. She actually performs this feat twice, as immediately thereafter she engages Gascoigne in another dialogue designed to confute him on the basis on the impossibility of Christ's body occupying two positions at once, another favorite trump card of the Reformers:

Such a doctor, such doctrine. Be you not ashamed to teach the people that Christ had two bodies? In Luke xxi: "He took bread and brake it to his disciples, saying, 'Take, etc. and do this in remembrance of me.'" St. Paul saith 1 Cor xi: "Do this in remembrance of me; for as often as ye shall eat this bread and drink this cup, ye shall show the Lord's death till he come; and therefore I marvel you blush not before all this people, to lie so manifestly as you do." With that Gascoine held his peace and made her no answer for, as it seemed, he was ashamed of his doings. Then the chancellor lifted up his head off from his cushion and commanded the gaoler to take her away.

"Now," said she, "ye be not able to resist the truth, ye command me to prison again. Well, the Lord in the end shall judge our cause and to him I leave it. I wis, I wis, this gear will go for no payment then" (8:495).

Foxe's marginal comment reads: "Gascoine's mouth stopped." This scene plays
out in miniature several of Foxe's favorite points: the ability of Scripture, even
or especially as read and interpreted by the common folk, to confute the so-
phistical and arid theology of the Papists; the reliance of the Catholics on force
rather than Biblical authority; and the ultimate victory of the faithful at the
Last Judgement. These themes are underscored at the next examination, when
Driver asks her interrogator to prove something by Scriptural quotation. He
stalls: "'I cannot tell the place, but there it is.' With that she desired him to look
in his Testament. Then he fumbled and sought about him for one, but at that
time he had none; and that he knew well enough, though he seemed to search
for it" (8:495).

Foxe's margin reminds us of her victory: "The papists put to silence by a
simple woman," but Driver also makes the point herself: "Have ye no more to
say! God be honored! You be not able to resist the spirit of God in me, a poor
woman. I was an honest poor man's daughter, never brought up in the university, as you have been, but I have driven the plough before my father many a
time (I thank God) yet notwithstanding, in the defence of Gods truth, and in
the cause of my master Christ, by his grace I will set my foot against the foot
of you all" (8:495). It is indicative of the extraordinary power of the book that
the spiritual high point for Foxe occurs when a priest is unable to find his place
in the Bible. Here textual place provides a site to unsettle social place, as the interrogator's inability to negotiate the terrain of the Bible allows Driver to claim
spiritual superiority over her social betters.

The case of "Prest's wife," whose Christian name Foxe is unable to obtain,
provides an example of an even more socially marginal figure than Driver. Foxe
presents her as "certain poor woman, and a silly creature" (8:497). More, she is
a masterless woman, who seems to provide living confirmation of the fear that
the lower classes will read the Bible literally and abandon their proper social
place. For religious reasons growing "in contempt of her husband and children," she leaves "and so taking nothing from them, but even as she went, de-
parted from them, seeking her living by labor and spinning as well she could,
here and there for a time. In which time notwithstanding, she never ceased to
utter her mind as well as she durst" (8:497). The Bishop to whom she is presented for this "uttering" scolds her: "Fie, for shame. Thou art an unlearned
person, and a woman. Wilt thou meddle with such high matters, which all the
doctors of the world cannot define? Wilt thou talk of such high mysteries? Keep
thou work and meddle with that thou hast to do. It is no woman's matter, at
cards and tow to be spoken of" (8:498). When Prest goes on to condemn the
mass as "idol worship," the Bishop says: "See this prattling woman. Dost thou
not hear, that Christ did say over the bread, 'this is my body,' and over the cup 'this

is my blood'?" Prest replies: "Yea, forsooth he said so; but he meant that is his body and blood, not carnally, but sacramentally." The Bishop responds: "Lo, she hath heard prattling among these new preachers or heard some peevish book. Alas, Poor woman! Thou art deceived. . . . I promise you, you are a jolly Protestant! I pray you, in what schools have you been brought up?" Prest responds: "I have upon the Sundays visited the sermons, and there I have learned such things as are so fixed in my breast, that death shall not separate them" (8:498). Foxe comments later: "Albeit she was of such simplicity and without learning, yet you could declare no place of scripture but she would tell you the chapter; yea, she would recite you the names of all the books of the Bible" (8:501).

The angry question of the Bishop—"in what schools have you been brought up?"—demonstrates his attempt to locate authority in traditional institutions, away from the dangerous and unpredictable "breasts" of the unlearned. Like White, Prest's inability to read this does not prevent her access to the book; indeed, she has internalized it and has become a walking concordance. Foxe seems concerned to stress that she knows the "order, process, and meaning" of the book, to quote Tyndale. That is, her "simplicity" does not prevent her from acquiring a strong sense of the spatial and rhetorical configuration of the Bible.

It is important to realize, however, that Foxe does not valorize breakdown in social hierarchy for its own sake. Rather, he is careful to frame the narrative to emphasize the workings of God in the simple and unlearned. Indeed, much of the rhetorical force of his narratives of the spiritual victories of the unlearned comes from playing off of assumptions about hierarchy. Thus one reading of Driver's case is that the Papists are so benighted, befuddled, and duplicitous that even the most marginal of social figures can confute them. Further, of course, their "victories" are "symbolic"; they are all burned and thus are subsumed into the continuing narrative of the monuments to Papist cruelty.[11] Yet despite Foxe's continuing efforts to collapse book and body, to see lower-class and female martyrs as "vessels" of God rather than agents, the social implications of allowing the possibility for the internalization of the book are potentially explosive.

This fact did not escape the attention of Foxe's detractors, including Thomas Harding, who vigorously condemned "huge dunghill of your stinking martyrs . . . heretics, thieves, church-robbers, murderers, rebels, and traitors."[12] The social sneers are made even more explicit in Robert Parson's seventeenth-century confutation of Foxe. Parson claims that Foxe,

> being broken, by heresy, from the forsaid communion of Saints in the Catholic Church, and from their association and participation, both brought himself, and his Protestants that follow him, into the communion & society of a most impious

and infamous company of condemned heretics, and wicked malefactors, some condemned for lewd life, co[n]spiracies, rebellion, and murder, some for atrocious behavior, in hurting and wounding quiet and innocent men, some for witchcraft and sorcery and conjuring even to the destroying of their Prince's person, some for theft and manifest robberies, or rather sacrilege, some for heresies confessed, and detested by the Protestants themselves.[13]

He concludes by directly addressing the reader, asking what "he thinketh of this new association, communion, and fellowship, with such sort of people." That this contempt is class based is made clear by his summary reckoning of the estates of those burned: "Husbandmen, weavers, sawyers, shoemakers, and curriers, smiths and other such like occupations 282. poor women and spinsters 64. Apostate monks and friars 25. Apostate Priests 28. ministers 10 Public malefactors, and condemned by the laws for such 19&c" (3:[29]). Parsons pauses here, because, after all, this is a lot of dead people. While professing to sympathize with the readers' "horror of mind" at reading of so many deaths, he goes on in a letter to the reader to explain that "it was necessary justice and no cruelty" (3:[A1r]).

To underscore this point, Parsons produces a calendar of Roman Catholic martyrs designed to confute Foxe's calendar of Protestant martyrs. The competing calendars are organized on facing pages—on the right are Parson's martyrs, presented with a build-up of authority, social and textual, as in "this was a Lady" or "this was a Noble man" accompanied by buttressing learned citations of the Church fathers. On the left are the rabble of Foxe's martyrs, identified scornfully with their occupation or social place: "This was a proud arrogant fellow, by occupation a cook, who joining with a painter as insolent as himself used intolerable and contemptuous words" (3:[4]). For Parsons, the social differences between the Catholic martyrs and those of Foxe speak for themselves, as he reworks Foxe's praise of the working of God in weak vessels back into the traditional social categories of the period—insolence, arrogance, pride.

📖

Parson's commentary raises the question of the readership of the *Book of Martyrs*. I tend to agree with Mark Breitenberg that "the book's impact and valorization was as diverse as the literacy levels of its audience."[14] The reception history of *The Book of Martyrs* shows that, like many encyclopedic books (of which the Bible is only one example), it contained material capable of supporting a number of different ideological positions. In its originative moments of publication, when the primary enemies were perceived to be Catholics rather than heterodox Protestants, Foxe's book worked as a kind of prose epic commemoration of the Elizabethan settlement. But in the Stuart period, Archbishop Laud apparently saw precisely the dangers in it that Parsons describes, for he is said to have refused to license an edition during the reign of Charles I (the Parliamentarians licensed an edition in 1641).[15] And there is evidence that later readers saw in it precisely the models of inversion I have described. In his discussion of Foxe and Richard Hooker, Richard Helgerson discusses the ways in which John Bunyan, imprisoned after the Restoration, uses the *Book of Martyrs* to model his own responses to his inquisitors.[16] A much longer study could be written about the later uses of *The Book of Martyrs*, a book periodically reappropriated and contested until the early twentieth century.[17] Because of its quasi-canonical status and widespread dissemination, it provides a striking test case for the varieties of literacies in the early modern period, as textual place is used to renegotiate social place.

six Recasting the Culture of Ephemera

Todd S. Gernes

Fiske's General Store, located in the center of Holliston, Massachusetts, was established in 1863 as a haberdashery and whatnot shop and later evolved into a general store, selling newspapers, postcards, books, arts and crafts supplies, and a variety of blank books and albums. The goods have changed over the years, but the general categories and their arrangement on the shelves have remained in comforting stasis against a tide of trophy homes, cell phones, and sport utility vehicles. When Fiske's teenage daughter, Annie, started her first friendship album in the early 1880s, commonplace books, autograph albums, scrapbooks, and chromolithographed dye cut gleanings were all the rage. Her family's store, attuned to domestic trends, would have stocked an enticing variety of blank books with tinted, gilt-edged pages, ornate frontispieces, and bindings of stamped leather or velvet. How did Annie begin her collection? A visiting cousin wrote the first lines in Annie's album: "When you are old and cannot see / Put on your glasses and look for me." In time, her album gathered signatures, sentimental tokens of affection, and fanciful hieroglyphics, like the grinning monkey faces stealthily drawn on the frontispiece in blue crayon by Annie's little brother. At first glance the pages of nineteenth-century American commonplace books, scrapbooks, and albums appear lifeless and remote, turning to dust even with gentle handling. On closer inspection, however, they are general storehouses of information about childhood, growing older, love, spirituality, language, and learning.

This essay examines how ordinary people created meaning, art, and history by assembling and patterning the short-lived, transitory objects and materials of everyday life in eighteenth- and nineteenth-century America. Crafting and shaping meaning from the material culture of ephemera constituted a popular literacy of collecting, arrangement, invention, and memory. Ordinary

A typical friendship album page (c. 1840) anatomizing, in coordination with an image of the biblical Hagar, the sentimental language of flowers. The caption reads, "1. A Garden Anemone: Forsaken. 2. Great Flowered Heath: Solitude. 3. Honeywort Flowered Heath: Solitude." From the collection of Barton L. St. Armand.

Americans used household materials—blank books, pen and ink, wax, hair cuttings, paper, or fabric scraps—to process information about the world and their own historical being. Poetry, fiction, recipes, emblems, and obituaries were clipped, preserved and arranged into a richly textured historical and cultural fabric. Commonplace books, friendship albums, scrapbooks, and amateur artists' portfolios contained similar information and materials, but the various genres gave shape to diverse patterns of reading, writing, and social interaction—all fueled by the unruly passion of collecting.[1] Barton Levi St. Armand, discussing "the essentially private nature of the portfolio genre, its function as a loose repository of musings, views, portraits, copies, caricatures, and 'studies from nature,'" points out that nineteenth-century portfolios and related genres were "a means of preserving the secret self in the face of . . . growing technological exposure."[2]

Compilers of assembled books transformed the everyday prose of the object world into poetry, infusing domestic artifacts with historicity, familiarity, and selfhood. They created collections that, by virtue of their cultural complexity and incompleteness, transcended mere accumulation.[3] Indeed, objects had the power to shape collectors' personalities and concretely expressed psychologically important aspects of their interior lives,[4] whether that expression was a projection of childhood,[5] adult autobiography in fragments, or multifaceted, historical perspectives on America's recent past.[6] Because the culture of ephemera represents a somewhat nebulous tradition of language use and learning, I shall recast it in the following pages as a popular medium of expression shaped by the human impulse to collect material objects and invest them with meaning, producing, in many cases, what Krzysztof Pomian has called "semiophores."[7]

In the mid-nineteenth century, a technological shift in the means of textual production, especially the introduction of the penny press, dramatically altered the environment of alphabet and image.[8] Handicraft constructionism, the process of selecting, arranging, and reusing material and linguistic scraps to evoke meaning, was a tradition of language use that was verbal and visual but also tactile. It preceded and nourished the Arts and Crafts tradition of collective labor and later gave birth to the modernist "art of assemblage," the aesthetic of cubist collage,[9] but its roots lay in the shaping and reshaping of the material culture of ephemera by common people in response to technological developments in mechanical reproduction, particularly the ephemeralization of communications technology and the proliferation of cheap print media. Handcrafted assembled books of ephemera were frequently given as gifts, passed down intergenerationally, and acquired new inscriptions, signatures, and layers of meaning with use and reuse. With varying degrees of craftsmanship and skill, men and women, professional writers and amateur compilers, shaped paper worlds of miscellaneous fact and imaginative fancy. Catalyzed by sharp increases in general literacy,[10] readers became actively engaged in the production of meaning through the manipulation of textual scraps and images. Commonplacing, the tradition of copying extracts of poetry and prose into blank books, and scrapping, the art of cutting and pasting, became widespread practices of active reading in eighteenth- and nineteenth-century America. I shall examine these historical reading practices in the following pages with regard to hand-assembled books and their ephemeral contents.

Turning the pages of Annie Fiske's friendship album, one comes across a nonsense rhyme scrawled in the margins by the compiler's great-great-grandchild (it was common for albums to be passed down and reused): "Roses are red / Violets are blue / You've got a figure / Like a B-52!" A nutrient and generative medium of alphabet and image, the culture of ephemera embraces orality and literacy, the sacred and the profane, and commonsense aphorisms as well as nonsensical humor. Here is a whimsical gem from a late-nineteenth-century album in my own collection: "I hope you're sweet / I hope you're nice / I hope you eat / A lot of mice." "Nonsense," says Susan Stewart, "stands in contrast to the reasonable, positive, contextualized, and 'natural' world of sense as the arbitrary, the random, the inconsequential, the merely cultural. While sense is sensory, tangible, real, nonsense is 'a game of vapors,' unrealizable, a temporary illusion."[11] The culture of ephemera is a medium of many contradictions and dialectical tensions: sense and nonsense, sacred and secular, adulthood and childhood, joy and sorrow, order and disorder, history and nostalgic reverie—or even slavery and freedom.[12] These are contained but rarely resolved within the collector's "magic circle," to borrow a phrase from Walter Benjamin,[13] or within the ornate covers of an album. Although radically tactile in its historical incarnation, the word "ephemera" has come to symbolize the inconsequential, arbitrary, or "merely cultural" uses of language and other sign systems.[14] Reading the culture of ephemera demands archival specificity and attention to the rule-governed, intentional use of meaningful scraps and fragments in various sociohistorical contexts.[15]

Commonplace Books

Assembled books, unique volumes compiled by human hands from textual and material fragments, reflect an aesthetic of salvage and assemblage as old as quilt making or other economies of scarcity. Stitched, glued, torn, scented, underlined, overwritten, or gnawed, assembled books clearly display their histories of use, collaboration, and intergenerational reuse. Although these traces and historical imprints seem evident, even familiar, like teeth marks on a beloved baby book, interpreting them is another matter. The literary remains of ordinary Americans lack a beginning-middle-end structure and a finished or finishing form, and most often they constitute an array, a collection, "which establishes its referential connections beyond the text, in the world of social space and referential event."[16] As arrayed texts constituting idiosyncratic collections, assembled books resist conventional historical emplotment and narrative closure,[17] are in turn garrulous and taciturn, and are products of a creative, social, tactile, and embodied cultural practice that I have called "active reading"[18]

Roger Chartier has called for an archaeology of historical reading practices and a deeper understanding of communities of readers. "Reading," he says, "is not uniquely an abstract operation of the intellect: it brings the body into play; it is inscribed in a space and a relationship with oneself or with others. This is why special attention should be paid to ways of reading that have disappeared in our contemporary world."[19] In contrast to the classical image of the reading public produced by the modern age, Chartier argues that "'the people' is not always to be sought in the plural, but rather in the secret solitude of the humble practices of individuals who cut out the images of the *occasionnels*, who coloured printed engravings, and who read the chapbooks for simple enjoyment."[20] If, as Chartier suggests, reading brings the body into play, then assembled books exemplify a universal but neglected dimension of reading—tactility. Active reading, with the tactility that the term implies, should be considered in conjunction with other physical and corporal modes of reading, including oralized reading and silent, visual reading, and other styles, such as intensive and extensive reading.[21] Commonplace books typically provide a context for acts of reading because they often contain concrete details about the compiler's choice of books, reading environment, and everyday life.[22]

An archetypal assembled book form, the commonplace book has a long history. Although it has come to be associated with Locke's Enlightenment version, Aristotle recommended the habit of keeping written handbooks of arguments arranged under topical headings, such as "On Life" or "On Good," accompanied by pertinent references to individual authors. Commonplace books supplemented the mnemonic technique of the topics, a system of visually spatialized locations in which knowledge could be readily stored and retrieved.[23] The rhetorical commonplace, or *locus communis*, was particularly important to medieval memorial culture that, as Mary Carruthers has illustrated, was emotionally charged, ethically motivated, and conceived in material and therefore spatial terms. "Memoria was also an integral part of the virtue of prudence, that which makes moral judgment possible. Training the memory was more than providing oneself with the means to compose and converse intelligently when books were not readily at hand, for it was in trained memory that one built character, judgment, citizenship, and piety."[24] Carruthers emphasizes the highly active nature of medieval reading, describing it as a "*hermeneutical dialogue* between the mind of the reader and the absent voices which the written letters call forth, at times literally in the murmur of ruminative meditation."[25] While the medieval scholastic took up the memory arts in a practical way, using the low faculty of imagination to form corporeal similitudes to help his memory, the art of memory was transformed in the Renaissance into a Hermetic or occult art and infused with new life, magic, and celestial resonance (Yates).[26] On a more prosaic level, commonplace books were typically kept by Renaissance schoolboys for use as oratorical primers[27] and were among the most important textual sources influencing the development of the Renaissance emblem.[28]

Students of the Renaissance commonplace book have argued that commonplacing was a complex practice of critical thinking and reading, encompassing all the aspects of rhetorical invention defined by medieval scholasticism. *Inventio* was the process of finding material for an argument and involved *collatio* (the bringing together of texts), *cogitatio* (reflection), *intentio* (concentrated attention), *ruminatio* (digesting reading), and *meditatio* (contemplation), all of which generated copiousness in speech and writing.[29] Ann Blair, writing about Renaissance natural philosophy, argues that the seemingly endless cycles of text gathering, selection, and assessment used in compiling a commonplace book reflected the humanist method of seeking truth: vigorous reading, comparison, and critical judgment. This "method of commonplaces," she says, serves as a metaphor for the ways in which natural philosophers created physical knowledge. In the process of sorting and placement, "the commonplace book offer[ed] opportunities for new critical confrontation of material," and yet the indefinite multiplication of separate topics and headings left ample room for contradictions that seemed to undermine the critical faculties demonstrated elsewhere in the book. "As a tool for composition which opened many possibilities but required none in particular," Blair concludes, "the commonplace book [was] supremely tolerant of cognitive dissonance."[30] In her discussion of the influence of "the commonplace mentality" on Renaissance poetry, Ann Moss claims that the essence of commonplace critical thinking lies in thematic variation, allegorical interpretation, and subtle allusion. "The critical reader," she says, "was a knowledgeable reader, but more pertinently still, a reader who could make informed comparisons between texts. Indeed, the commonplace-book may be said to have invented the critical reader, in a modern sense."[31]

A survey of American encyclopedia articles, tracts, and popular educational guides bears out this statement. Beginning in the eighteenth century, the domestic practice of keeping commonplace books became a widespread tool of general education and active reading. Enos Hitchcock, a New England minister and educator born in Springfield, Massachusetts, in 1744, was particularly concerned with the problem of free and universal education in young America. "What will be the state of American governments," he asked in 1785, "if they are not nurtured by general education and strengthened by public virtue, let the fate of many fallen republics tell! . . . If the means of education should be neglected," Hitchcock continued, "the rising generation would grow up uninformed and without principle; their ideas of freedom would degenerate into licentious independence; and they would fall a prey to their own animosities and Contentions."[32]

In Hitchcock's *Memoirs of the Bloomsgrove Family* (1790), a fictionalized guide for child rearing in the New Republic, the parents of Osander and Rozella direct them "to keep a commonplace book, to note the material occurrences, the books they read, the subjects on which they treated, with their comments about them, and to transcribe some of the most remarkable passages they contained." This practice, according to Hitchcock, proved to be advantageous, for it preserved the knowledge they acquired and matured their judgment. "While many other young people, who had read no less than they, could recollect little more of a book than the author's name, they could give a good account of their contents." Hitchcock admonished instructors of youth to develop systematic, active reading habits. "Much time is lost by a confusion of studies," he warned, "and by a promiscuous manner of reading books."[33] A 1798 American encyclopedia, significantly, defines commonplace-book keeping as a practice of active reading for the common man, a man of "no extraordinary genius," making him "read with accuracy and attention" and "inducing him insensibly to think for himself."[34]

From the American Revolution through the nineteenth century, commonplace books became a tool of self-cultivation in the garden of American culture. In 1832 *The American Annals of Education and Instruction* included an article promoting the use of "Common Place Books" as a practical method for "collecting and retaining the greatest amount of knowledge . . . , as the farmer, who adopts the best plan in the management of his agricultural affairs."[35] In contrast to medieval memorial culture, with its emphasis on meditation, rumination, familiarization, and emotional intensity—reading, in Carruthers's words, as a "hermeneutical dialogue between two memories"[36]—American popular culture defined memory in moral yet pragmatic terms[37] and stressed the importance of self-discipline, industry, work, vigor, and vigilance against "promiscuous reading," particularly novels. The culmination of the commonplace-book genre was a ready-made, fill-in-the-blanks version for the nineteenth-century professional man. Dr. John Todd designed his *Index Rerum; or, Index of Subjects* (ca. 1835) as "a manual to aid the student and the professional man in preparing himself for usefulness," in contrast to the Lockean commonplace book, which required "too much time and too much labor."[38]

John Locke's popular "New Method of a Commonplace Book" gave text precedence over image and emphasized rational classification and "natural Order,"[39] but in everyday domestic practice commonplace books retained elements of myth, mystery, and magic, revitalized by the folkloric confluence of rhyme, nonsense, and laughter. Commonplace books contain fragments (both verbal and visual) that stand in a metonymic relationship to common sense, such as proverbs or realistic prose, and fragments that stand, ironically, in a paradoxical and metaphorical relation to common sense, such as riddles, anagrams, and nonsense verse.[40] Commonplace books and other assembled-book forms reveal, in Susan Miller's words, "the intersections of social vectors, forces that produce discursive actions that have simultaneous material, aesthetic, and ideological consequences."[41] They are, in a word, scrappy. Although postmodern interpreters may take delight in the seemingly scattered fragments, fluid subjects, and simultaneity of these cultural artifacts, the act of assembling books was—historically and essentially—an integrative practice of internalizing word and image, an expression of the need and desire to make the self whole.

In many cases that historical "self" was female. Educational guides, self-help manuals, tracts, and encyclopedias encouraged the "fair sex" to keep commonplace books, and the majority of nineteenth-century examples that survive today were assembled by women. Keeping in mind that women were historically excluded from institutions of higher learning, one should not be surprised that their commonplace books are peppered with comments about female education and extracts that both praised women's intellectual capacities and scorned the denigration of their intellects by patriarchal culture.[42] Betsy Lawrence of Ashby, Massachusetts, affirmatively echoed the sentiments of an oration about female education in her commonplace book (ca. 1800): "Is it not a melancholy truth that man too often prostitutes his boasted faculties to the destruction of female happiness?" (BULH, MS 12.4). Later in the century (ca. 1830), Caroline Russell of Wilmington, North Carolina, transcribed a critique of female education into her commonplace book (BULH, MS 12.24), bemoaning the emphasis on mere behavior. "We do not encourage intrepidity and independence of thought," she wrote.

Prevailing ideologies of gender—Republican Motherhood or True Womanhood, for example—are reflected in the pages of late- eighteenth- and nineteenth-century commonplace books. These ideologies, however, were recontextualized by the compiler's act of selection, juxtaposition, and commentary, clear evidence of "intrepidity and independence of thought." From Thomas

Jefferson's genteel commonplace book, steeped in an intellectual tea of Erasmean and Lockean flavors,[43] to the scrapbook of a nineteenth-century schoolgirl soaked in sentimental tears, assembled books bear traces of a process of active reading that involved collecting, extracting, selecting, and reassembling texts and images. Poems, prayers, hymns, popular songs, ballads, histories, recipes, aphorisms, diary entries, captivity narratives, epistolary novels, biblical extracts, political tracts, parables, penmanship exercises, and riddles, to name only a few "speech genres,"[44] were extracted, collected, assembled, remembered, integrated into speech, used in daily life, and passed on to future generations.

Scrapbooks

As the manuscript commonplace book decreased in popularity in the mid-nineteenth century, scrapbooks rapidly filled the void. In many cases, early commonplace books were literally transformed into scrapbooks, as news clippings and steel engravings overlaid and all but obliterated handwritten, extracted gems. Visually expressive, colorful, garrulous, and interactive, the scrapbook fit well with the material culture of childhood, which flourished with the decline of Calvinism in America after about 1820.[45] By midcentury, stationery stores advertised a wide array of blank books and sold engravings, gleanings, and colorful cut-outs of all kinds. Newspapers and magazines featured children's sections designed especially for young scrapbook assemblers—"Scraps of Fun," "Leaves from Our Scrapbook," and "The Scrap Basket," to name only a few examples. Although both boys and girls compiled them, scrapbook keeping became associated with domesticity and femininity by the end of the nineteenth century, part of the material culture of girlhood.

Printed scraps evolved in the nineteenth century from simple black and white engravings to heavily embossed chromolithographed reliefs printed in sheets. The color and texture of scraps evolved over the decades. In the 1830s and 1840s, paper embossing and ready-made albums were popular, whereas the period from 1850 to 1880 was characterized by cut-out paper material and juxtaposed scraps in glossy relief. After the golden age of the printed relief scrap in the 1880s and 1890s, the demand for mass-produced scraps declined in the twentieth century. "Scrapiana" was the term used to describe this pervasive culture of scrapping, one that influenced graphic design, printed book production, and the decorative arts. Popular during the last quarter of the nineteenth century were fancy boxes, panorama and diorama boxes, and scrapped and lacquered furniture of all kinds, including chairs, clocks, tables, cabinets, and especially Victorian Scrap Screens. "Decalcomania," the application of water transfers to furniture and other household objects, was also used to decorate the inside of glass jars and bottles.[46] Books on domestic economy, such as *Our Homes; How to Beautify Them* (1888), illustrated a fanciful "[Fire] Screen of Crazy Work," while Clara Andrews Williams's colorful children's book, *The House that Glue Built* (1905), featured dye-cut home furnishings ready for pasting in empty, two-dimensional rooms. In *The Girl's Own Book* (1833), Lydia Maria Child explained how to make scrap-boxes, ordinary cardboard or wooden boxes that were painted, decorated with cut-out engravings, and varnished. "It is common," she said, "to cover center tables and fire-boards with engraved scraps, in the same manner as boxes. When done with great neatness and taste, they form very beautiful articles of furniture. Colored engravings, if not too gaudy, are more beautiful than plain ones."[47]

Compilers of scrapbooks and albums combined commercially produced scraps with found objects from a variety of sources, creating a fine textual melange. Scraps from fancy stationery stores supplemented newspaper clippings, manuscript fragments, advertising cards, and other ephemera in assembling scrapbooks. E. Walker, a New York book bindery, advertised "books of engravings, scrap-books, albums, and portfolios." Blank books and albums could be ordered through the Spellman Brothers' Bazaar and Bargain Catalogue or through *The Youth's Companion*. Scraps and gleanings were also sold door-to-door by young-people-turned-itinerant-peddlers through firms such as The Haverfield Publishing Company or J. Jay Gould, who especially encouraged young ladies to participate.[48]

Although it is tempting to discuss the process of assembling scrapbooks in terms of *bricolage* and authentic folk culture, to think of scrapbooks as being, in Henry Glassie's terms, "composed of objects produced out of a nonpopular tradition in proximity to popular culture,"[49] mass-produced "how-to" books and books of children's handicrafts containing recipes for scrapbooks were available throughout the nineteenth century. In her book, *Scrap Books and How to Make Them* (1880), E. W. Gurley effusively extended the metaphor of the scrapbook life: "Our life is a living Scrap-book. Clipped from the scroll of Time and pasted in by the hand of Fate, every day brings its contributions, and leaves accumulate until the book is filled." Gurley concluded that the scraps that made up the books were the record of everyone: "We are all Scrap-books; and happy is he who has his Pages systematized, whose clippings have been culled from sources of truth and purity, and who has them firmly Pasted in his Book."[50] In *The American Girl's Home Book of Work and Play*, an activity book published in 1884, Helen Campbell suggested scrapbook making as a rainy-day amusement for younger children, along with coloring pictures, picture-puzzles, paper dolls and furniture, home newspapers and home post offices. She advised her young readers to "have the leaves made of strong, thick cotton cloth; and after they are filled a bright cover can be made, and the whole thing sewed together." Campbell also encouraged her readers to "begin with a common paper book, an old copy-book being quite as good as a new one."[51] Significantly, compiling a scrapbook, a tactile process of clipping, sorting, ironing, arranging, placing, pressing, dabbing, and pasting, was wedded to an oral tradition of telling improvised stories based on the scrapbook's fanciful sequence of images.

Unlike the Lockean commonplace book, with its neoclassical aesthetic and orientation toward public oratory, mid-nineteenth-century scrapbooks revealed a private and expressive literary sensibility appropriate to the age of popular Romanticism. Early commonplace books were filled with hand-copied extracts from various sources and reflected a relative scarcity of reading material. After the Civil War, scrapbooks became a pragmatic response to an over-abundance of mechanically reproduced words and images. Olive E. Dana, writing in 1891 about her particular "way with scrapbooks," emphasized the importance of leisurely literary judgment in the process of clipping, sifting, and compiling. She noted that "many people say, 'Paste at once.' But one's selections will not be nearly so valuable if pasted too soon. With a goodly accumulation made before sorting, there is less danger of duplicates or repetition; and by waiting a little, one has a choice of critiques, and can present a thing in its most valuable form. How rich will be the stores of information concerning Mr. Lowell! It is well to be liberal in clipping, but very critical when it comes to pasting."[52] Scrapbook keeping involved a process of literary judgment but was also a multilayered articulation of individual sentiment, a visually expressive form of storytelling and autobiography that seemed to capture the spirit of the times.[53]

Much like the crazy quilt (considered a "Japanese" fashion in the nineteenth century),[54] which gives the appearance of free-style folk improvisation while conforming to established and often printed patterns, such as the popular Ladies' Art Company's *Miniature Diagrams of Quilt Patterns* (1879), the cutting and pasting of scraps was a structured means of expression that intersected with educational practice and the American ethos of self-improvement through active, disciplined reading. As Ellen Gruber Garvey has pointed out, the popular practice of keeping trade-card scrapbooks reflected the discipline of the marketplace and of consumer culture as well, reinforcing traditional gender roles yet opening up paper worlds of imaginative fancy.[55] The process of cutting and pasting scraps became a popular educational technique in the nineteenth century. German educator Friedrich Froebel used collage in his kindergartens to encourage visual creativity, and Maria Montessori subsequently developed it in her schools.[56] Many cut-and-paste books of the late nineteenth century were designed to improve children's creativity, dexterity, and visual memory. Grace

Goodridge's *Scissors and Paste: Designs for Cutting and Pasting with Suggestions for the Work* (1899), for example, included chapters on "The Value of Cutting as Seat Work" and "Cutting as a Means of Expression." Like the commonplace book, the scrapbook, with its grammar of cut-and-paste collage, was promoted by journalists and educators as a method of cultivating taste through disciplined reading. James L. Elderdice, writing in 1884, was enthusiastic about the practice of "acting as one's own editor, accumulating material from every field of literature, passing judgment upon, rejecting, selecting and classifying articles for the 'make-up' of the volume which is under your supervision, and which is to bear the stamp of your individuality almost as much as if you had written the entire book yourself. It is one of the best methods of developing taste and judgment, as we know of nothing that can compare with it as an intellectual pastime, unless it be playing the role of an amateur journalist."[57]

Amateur journalism clubs and literary societies were often formed on the premise of keeping scrapbooks and collectively sharing their contents. Beginning in the early nineteenth century and reaching a peak of popularity in the 1880s, amateur journalism brought newspaper production into the home. Weekly newspapers, handwritten, or typeset, and printed on miniature presses, transformed kitchens across the United States into domestic newsrooms, and children and adolescents became overnight cub reporters, literary correspondents, and hometown editors. Although Nathaniel Hawthorne published a handwritten parody newspaper before he entered Bowdoin College in the 1820s,[58] this rainy-day amusement for young people was popularized with the publication of Louisa May Alcott's *Little Women* in 1868–1869. The Pickwick Club, based on Alcott's own family history, was the name of the fictional March girls' literary society, reflecting their admiration for Charles Dickens. Jo, Beth, Meg, and Amy met every Saturday evening in the big garret and, becoming Samuel Pickwick, Augustus Snodgrass, Tracy Tupman, and Nathaniel Winkle, produced the *Pickwick Portfolio*, a publication that would inspire a minor nation of youthful imitators —proud ephemerals, who found their rhetorical and literary voices in this nineteenth-century equivalent of amateur radio and on-line chatrooms.[59]

Helen Campbell, citing the example of *The Pickwick Portfolio*, promoted either handwritten or printed amateur newspapers as a fun and pleasurable pastime and stressed inclusivity in the editorial process: "Nobody's feelings get hurt by rejected articles; for whatever is written has its place, and it may be made as large or small as seems best."[60] E. W. Gurley suggested that a "delightful and profitable mode of literary culture may be adopted in a neighborhood by forming a scrapbook club or association." Gurley recommended that members meet on certain evenings, compare their books as to the number and quality of the selections, trade duplicate articles in a kind of literary exchange, and read selections aloud.

"This one is to read a Poem, another a page of Fun, another a short Story, while others will furnish selections from Science, History, General News, etc. All of which have been gleaned from papers and magazines since the last meeting." The object of this game was to discuss the topics "in a plain, sensible way," laying a good foundation for mental culture and the advancement of morals and manners. A scrapbook, Gurley concluded, "is not a grave in which you have buried all these good and beautiful thoughts, but a living treasure always open to your mind."[61]

The practice of keeping scrapbooks typically continued into adulthood as a method of life-long learning. Importantly, scrapbooks were often shared, displacing dominant conceptions of intellectual property and individual authorship with an ethos of community building and mutuality. Nineteenth-century women's literary clubs, as Anne Ruggles Gere has argued, fostered this kind of intellectual culture, encouraging collaboration and communal ownership of texts. "Terms such as fusion, fluidity, mutuality and continuity defined their relationships and shaped their use of texts as they borrowed language across generations."[62] Club women were great scrapbook keepers but certainly had their counterparts in the male sphere. Men and women from all walks of life pasted miniature speeches into their books and stressed the importance of "systematic reading"[63] or admonished readers to "start a little library." According to an item in a late-nineteenth-century Maine scrapbook, the reading of challenging books would promote "mental health." The author went on to warn readers, in language reminiscent of Victorian admonitions against masturbation and its debilitating effects, that passive reading, worse than desultory reading, would leave the reader inactive, "in a sort of indolent reverie," rendering the mind incapable of analysis and synthesis. "Passive reading takes the spring and snap out of the mind, until the brain becomes languid, lazy and disinclined to grapple with great principles and hard problems" (WLDC, fol. 123).

In 1903 an anonymous writer for the New York Sun observed, "This is an age of albums. A score or more of different kinds of albums, portfolios, memory books and diaries are in current use." The writer went on to discuss the technological advantages that modern album-keepers enjoyed. While the "old-fashioned girl" had to charge her memory with events and experiences, many of the new-timer's private experiences had already been recorded in photographs and printed accounts. "People now keep albums of the public events they have witnessed and the celebrations they have participated in, of inaugurations, funerals and anniversaries of importance, triumphs celebrated, monuments unveiled, society reunions. They might not do it so commonly but for the newspaper clippings on all subjects so handy to paste in."[64] As the journalist made clear, basic changes in the processes and technologies of mechanical reproduction affected the ways in which people processed information about their lives. In earlier days, keepers of albums and commonplace books transcribed much of the verse and prose by hand. After about 1850, with the proliferation of cheap print and photographic media, scrapbooks and photograph albums soon outnumbered handwritten commonplace books and albums. The age of mechanical reproduction brought about basic changes in the historicity of the individually constructed book, from the point of view of the compiler, who could more easily record and preserve private experiences and public events,[65] and from the point of view of the historian, whose job was facilitated by the compiler's act of preservation. If the culmination of eighteenth-century commonplace book was Dr. John Todd's preprinted *Index Rerum; or, Index of Subjects*, then the high-water mark for the nineteenth-century scrapbook was "Mark Twain's Patent Self-Pasting Scrapbook," invented by Samuel Clemens in the 1870s. Clemens wrote enthusiastically to his brother Orion on 11 August 1872: "My idea is this: Make a scrap-book with leaves veneered or coated with gumstickum of some kind; wet the page with a sponge, brush, or rag or tongue, and dab on your scraps like postage stamps. . . . [A] great humanizing and civilizing invention." As of 1877, twenty-five thousand self-pasting scrapbooks were sold, Clemens's only commercially successful invention.[66]

Friendship Albums

As we have seen, commonplace books and scrapbooks provided the verbal-material basis for intellectual reflection, literary selection, and aesthetic production. It is possible to interpret these artifacts—most often the creation of individual compilers—as assemblages of autobiographical fragments and, collectively, as a type of intimate, expressive rhetoric of words, images, and objects. Whereas commonplace books and scrapbooks metonymically represent the individual consciousness of the compiler, friendship albums, which often were the products of many hands, reflect the kinship, community, and affiliation central to the lives of nineteenth-century men and women.

The *album amicorum*, or friendship album, enfolds the culture of ephemera in its ornate leather bindings and variously tinted leaves. An unstable book genre containing everything from riddles to recipes, from Hebrew poetry to miniature hair wreaths, the friendship album grew out of sixteenth-century European scholasticism and flowered in the hothouse of nineteenth-century American sentimentality. In American culture, friendship albums (often called lady's albums) became a stage prop in the parlor theatrical of middle-class adolescence. In the 1830s, Maria C. Jones began her album with the following declaration: "This shall be the Record of my Youth—*Maria*," and she marked her place with a colorful, hand-stitched bookmark (BULH, MS Harris Codex 1229). Album writing was a communal ritual of linguistic play in which young women and young men exchanged verses and emblematic images to memorialize the present moment as a stay against the future. The ritualistic exchange of samples of handwriting authenticated both near and distant relationships, friendship and kinship, because handwriting was held to reveal an individual's true character and culture. Because Mary Abba's mid-nineteenth-century album (BULH, MS Harris Codex 1242) was considered to be an emblem of her life, she was admonished by friends to "let no foul spot upon its page appear" (BULH, MS Harris Codex 1242). The album was a wonder-book that reinforced the individual's identity and social status through webs of friendship and affiliation.

The American friendship album has a variety of names and forms: *album amicorum*, forget-me-not album, lady's album, *poesie* album, floral album, memory book, autograph album, or *album of the* heart. It was generally a blank book containing bits of prose, poetry, and drawings by family members, friends, acquaintances, schoolmates, or teachers, and dedicated to the compiler.[67] The poetry and prose were most often signed and dated, and the residence of the inscriber given. Owners assembled much more than prose and poetry on the surface of the album's paper, silk or faux vellum pages. Albums absorbed the various odds and ends of everyday life, anything that would fit conveniently between the covers of a book: drawings, watercolors, calligraphic flourishes, miniature hair wreaths, silhouettes and paper cut-outs, pressed flowers and dried leaves of grass, tintypes, fabric scraps, recipes, or miscellaneous lists. Tinted pages in various hues were often decorated with some sort of art or craft, such as watercolor, crayon, sketching, stenciling, or "mezzo-tinto," skills that were often perfected at dame schools, female seminaries, or mixed-gender academies. The culture of ephemera is located at the intersection of literature, bibliography, folklore, and material culture, and the American friendship album marks this crossroads with its colorful perennial blooms and coded language of flowers.

The practice of keeping an autograph album probably originated in mid-sixteenth-century Germany. The *album amicorum* or *Stammbuch* was the proud possession of itinerant European students, who would gather and bind together in an interleaved book of recommendations, sentiments, signatures, and emblematic proofs of descent from intimate friends, patrons, protectors, companions, and comrades.[68] With the rise of Romanticism, the German *Stammbuch* became more fanciful and decorative than official, and it came to be called the "*poesie* album."[69] The custom of album keeping quickly spread from Germany to England and first began to proliferate in America in the 1820s and 1830s, increasing in popularity through the 1880s and beyond. The aristocratic friendship album, however, underwent a sea change as it crossed the Atlantic. Innovations in paper making, printing, and book production during the mid-nineteenth century led to the assembly-line-style mass production of albums, which soon became popular among Americans of moderate means with an occasional hour of leisure.[70] Although both men and women kept friendship albums, they were primarily marketed to young women, as the published titles suggest: *The Floral Album, Flowers of Loveliness, The Rose Bud Album, The Young Lady's Album, The Young Lady's Remembrancer,* or *The Mother's Joy.* Inscriptions, often written in the language of flowers, praised beauty, chastity, moral purity, and true womanhood. Verses, epigrams, and witticisms deemed beautiful, elegant, or witty were embalmed between stamped leather covers, committed to memory, and used to adorn the owner's conversation and correspondence.

The evolving physical structure of friendship albums in the nineteenth century reflects technological innovations in book manufacturing in the United States, which remained largely a localized, artisan-based industry until after the Civil War. In the pages of friendship albums, traditional orality, manuscript culture, and industrial production conjoined in a dynamic interplay of cultural figures and forms. During the first two decades of the nineteenth century, albums were primarily manufactured and distributed by small binders and stationers. Craftsmen like Amos H. Haskell bound small blank books in simple marbled paper covers with plain leather spines, sometimes with the names of the owners lettered in gold on the front. Haskell, a Boston bookbinder by trade, according to the *Boston City Directory,* bound the Album of Hannah S. Haskell, of Salem, Massachusetts, in 1826. She filled the "variegated pages" of her "fair volume" with maxims and poems from family, friends, and acquaintances about friendship, happiness, human nature, and good fortune (AAS, ca. 1830).

A remarkable number of mid-nineteenth-century albums were produced in the fourth-floor, tin-roofed bindery and press rooms of John C. Riker, a New York City binder, publisher, and bookseller. Riker specialized in popular albums and gift books, and an extraordinary number of existing albums dating from 1830 to 1850 have his imprint on their engraved or lithographed title pages. On 1 August 1856, Riker sold the contents of his shop to Hezekiah S. Archer. The inventory on the bill of sale gives some idea of how Riker's albums were made. Riker's shop must have been a steamy, clamorous place, filled with smells of leather, glue and machine grease, and ringing with the cacophony of industrial production. The rooms were crowded with standing presses and press boards; stamping and backing presses; cutting machines for books and boards; stabbing and sewing machines; steam and gas pipes; hammers and stamps for backs and sides; iron screw presses for gilding edges; iron plates and glue kettles; gold knives, gold cushions, and a box for loose gold; benches, tables, and

shelving fixtures; and a graining machine and punches. Added to this industrial hodgepodge was an array of friendship albums and gift books in various
stages of completion, a jumble of album backs, corners, and sides, soon to be
assembled into the Jenny Lind Album, The Gift Album, The Album of Beauty, Gems from Flora,
Forget-Me-Not, Moss Rose, Excelsior, Bouquet, Fountain, Scrap Book, Remembrance, and more.[71]
Riker's albums were ornate, textured and slim, a pleasure to look at and to han-
dle. They literally called out for inscriptions.[72] After Riker went out of business in
1856, the publishing firm of Leavitt and Allen, among other publishing houses,
produced albums in a variety of colors, shapes, and sizes.

Because nineteenth-century friendship albums were often embellished with
pencil and ink sketches, crayons, watercolors, theorem painting, calligraphic
ornaments, or hair embroidery, they have been placed within the collector's category of "schoolgirl art." This designation encompasses a wide range of artifacts, such as hand-colored geography maps, mourning pictures, sand-paper
drawings, samplers, embroidery, and herbarium folios, which were produced
by young women at schools, academies, and seminaries during the early and
middle nineteenth century. Historians of education generally refer to this aspect
of female education as "ornamental," placing it in a class below "intellectual
improvement,"[73] emphasizing the historical inequality between the education
of men and women in the United States. While friendship albums exemplify the
fruitful conjunction of ornament and intellect, they also contain within their
stamped leather covers the unwritten history of young women's experience in
schools, academies, and seminaries in nineteenth-century America. The friendship album was a reflection and reminder of the seminary student's youthful
days of self-cultivation and creativity. Although the student could not bring
home the seminary's library, mineral cabinets, or herbarium, she could certainly
fill her album with poetry, art, and souvenirs of youthful friendships. Like the
ornately engraved, allegorical diplomas issued by many of these institutions,
the album became an outward sign of the compiler's intellectual cultivation,
aesthetic literacy, and verbal grace—"trophies" of culture.[74]

Friendship albums were part of the fashionable paraphernalia of lady's
academies and seminaries, and reading their inscriptions within this context
highlights the aesthetic orientation of women's education during the first half
of the nineteenth century. Cynthia Bragton Angel, for example, attended the
Smithville Seminary in North Scituate, Rhode Island, in 1840. During that year,
Cynthia kept an album containing poetry, colored lithographs, and a fine example of hair embroidery (BULH, MS Harris Codex 1250), a testament to her
appreciation of art, poetry, and handicraft. Cynthia had the opportunity to study
"the Greek, Latin, French, Spanish and Italian languages, the various branches
embraced in English literature, the different Natural Sciences, Mathematics,

Metaphysics, &c. &c." Cynthia could also avail herself of instruction in "Draw-ing, Painting, and instrumental and vocal Music." According to the Seminary's *Catalogue* (1841), students displayed their talents and knowledge at public exhi-bitions, which typically consisted of performances by a brass band, poetry read-ing, orations, prayer, and dramatic dialogues.[75]

Nineteenth-century friendship albums illustrate the convergence of folk art and academic design and reflect multiple aesthetic orientations. Dominant among them is what I have previously referred to as the process of *bricolage*, in which "an artist partially accepts a new idea, fusing the new with the old."[76] When Sarah Barnes attended Worcester School of Design and Academy of Fine Arts (ca. 1859), she kept an *Album of Friendship* (AAS), which she filled with prose, poetry, and designs from talented schoolmates. Toward the beginning of the volume, Hannah J. Reynolds drew a geometric "Magic Square" with Sarah's name radiating outward from the center in a pattern reminiscent of a quilt or a piece of embroidery. Under the square Hannah wrote, "As from the center in the square above you must read up or down and right or left towards either corner, so may your influence from you as a center extend to the 'four corners of the globe,' and be as harmonious as the sounds in your name, is the wish of your friend." The "Magic Square" combined traditional visual patterns and word-play with the geometric precision of academic design.

Perhaps the most often repeated metaphor in nineteenth-century album inscriptions equates the album with the intellect. As numerous introductory album inscriptions suggest, album pages were literally *tabulae rasae* in the Lock-ean sense, as Ann Eugenia Tyler's album (AAS, ca. 1840) makes clear: "The mind is an Album, unsullied and bright, / Just opened for angels and spirits to write." As a "book of youthful acquaintance," the album was emblematic of character formation and intellectual growth. Central to this growth was a young woman's spiritual development, expressed here as a veil of sentimental mysticism adorned with angels, spirits, demons, and incantations. "The mind is an album" in Tyler's book, suggesting that albums give shape and substance to memory. In Sarah E. Webb's book, the album was "designed to be a faithful mirror of the minds" of her friends and relations. As time passed, the thoughts and affections inscribed on the album's pages became both a mirror of history and a memorial of de-parted youth: "History and tradition shall alone tell that we have lived. The past throws a mantle woven of mysterious charms over departed excellence" (AAS, ca. 1845).

In looking closely at album inscriptions, we can see that they reveal inter-active networks of productive people and forces, rather than indolence, shal-low emotions, or social clichés.[77] When William Lloyd Garrison inscribed the album of Lillie Buffum Chace (BULH, MS Harris Codex 3019), daughter of

Elizabeth Buffum Chace, Rhode Island abolitionist, suffragist, and prison reformer, his words welcomed her into a social and political community. Garrison's 1861 inscription conformed to the conventions of mid-century Christian
sentimentality, but his message was transformational and politicizing:

> Virtue, dear Lillie, is not asceticism, or prudishness, or sentimental feeling, it is a
> living principle, deriving its strength from activity in the performance of benevo-
> lent actions and the daily duties of life. Its best investment is made, and its largest
> returns are found, in striving to raise the fallen, comfort the distressed, succor the
> outcast, and deliver the oppressed. It finds its root in disinterested love, whereby
> self-sacrifice to reclaim the lost, and save the world, opens a fountain of blessed-
> ness, and the cross is made the instrument of salvation.

Garrison turned the capitalist metaphor of investment and return into
an aphorism about community, self-sacrifice, and "disinterested love," what
Jonathan Edwards in 1765 called "benevolence to being in general."[78] Review-
ing the colorful and ornate pages of nineteenth-century friendship albums reveals communities of readers and writers actively engaged in practices and
processes of literacy, inflected with political or theological accents. The historical record confirms that the social practice of assembling books was often an
experience-driven process of personal reflection and renewal, an active con-
stituent of the theological imagination,[79] integrating body, mind, and spirit. In
fact, the most common topoi in eighteenth- and nineteenth-century assembled books were spiritual in nature.[80]

When we pick up the black leather, gold-stamped covers of Ellen M. Bowen's
friendship album (AAS, ca. 1845), turn over the white and green tinted leaves,
and examine the engravings of "Washington's Mount Vernon" and the "Baltimore and Washington Railroad Viaduct," it is difficult to imagine that Ellen had
any role in the print communications circuit other than that of a consumer.
As her album inscriptions reveal, however, Ellen belonged to a community of
young women attending the Charlestown Female Seminary in Massachusetts,
as its 1846 catalog reveals. Significantly, the young women at Charlestown had
an active "Social Circle," formerly a tract society, which sustained an itinerant
"Colporteur," or book peddler, who distributed the Bible and religious tracts
in the distant American West. Their "Colporteur" sent the Social Circle letters at
regular intervals throughout the year, letters that were likely read aloud at meetings. "His labors . . . consisted principally in efforts to promote the circulation
of the Bible and such books of moral and religious character as are regarded
standard works of an inestimable influence by all who know their claims." The
young women of the Social Circle hoped that only good would come "from a
free distribution of the 'Word of Life.'"[81] With the knowledge that young women

in seminaries, academies, and female societies functioned as producers, financial backers, distributors, and consumers of printed texts, the conventional portrayal of young women as passive consumers of literary culture begins to fade, replaced by an image of active learning.

Codex

In the heterogeneous pages of assembled books, "words and speech genres gradually accumulate meaning over centuries of diverse experience that layer evaluation upon evaluation, place intonation over intonation."[82] The longevity of these book genres, the intergenerational transmission (and subsequent reuse) of individual artifacts, and their historical ubiquity attest to the value of assembled books as a resource for illuminating the history of popular literacy. Assembling commonplace books, scrapbooks, and albums was a way of creating the past, a form of complex thinking, in Vygotski's sense of thinking concretely in associative complexes,[83] and a life-long process of forming an integral self. Assembled books were products of collecting, reading, and memory, everyday practices in which users adapted and transformed the ordinary details of life within a dominant cultural economy for their own purposes and their own ends. Family stories and textual property (books, manuscripts, and ephemera) were commonly preserved and passed down along generational lines, and these narratives and objects were understood in relation to the life cycles of birth, coming of age, adulthood, and death. The practice of assembling books, of extracting choice bits from reading materials and intertwining texts, images, and family history into an intergenerational, cultural fabric, is significant in its sociocultural breadth. It was a pattern that varied according to context, but was nevertheless replicated across boundaries of race, class, gender, and region.[84]

Language is marked by uses and contains the imprints of its enunciative acts and processes of articulation.[85] Like hand tools burnished with time and use, mending and reuse, assembled books exhibit traces of collective and often intergenerational processes of fabrication, the stitches and seams of handicraft constructionism. William Gilmore has discussed the concept of "mending" with regard to reading practices in rural New England: "Capturing a distinctly rural approach to change, the ideal of mending encouraged people to reuse land, material objects, and ideas as long as possible. The objective in mending was to perpetuate something while altering it as little as possible, whether the thing in question was a dam, a fence, clothes, shoes, farm implements, or conceptions of heaven and hell, natural history, or government. In the powerful opinion of the *New England Primer*, regular reading of the Bible could even mend a life."[86]

The art of assembling books, rich in intellectual, aesthetic, and spiritual possibilities, involved processes of cognition as well as communion. It was a practice of popular literacy involving cycles of textual selection and assessment, allegorical interpretation, and the critical confrontation of material, a practice tolerant of cognitive dissonance yet rooted in classical conceptions of order. Commonplacing, scrapping, and inscribing were also methods of cultural production, of textual assemblage by one or many hands. The culture of ephemera, that nutrient and generative literary medium of alphabet and image, nurtured less powerful literary voices, like those of young women, whose means of literary production were often limited to handicraft constructionism and ephemeral textuality.

seven "We Can Never Remain Silent"

The Public Discourse of the Nineteenth-Century African-American Press

P. Joy Rouse

> Cease agitation? Yes, when you repeal the Fugitive Slave Law, reverse
> the Dred Scott decision, and give use the right of citizenship in the
> free states, abolish slavery in the District of Columbia, break up the
> internal slave trade between the slave states, and guarantee unto us
> the privileges which the Federal Constitution guarantees to all men.
> Then, and not until then, may you expect us to be silent. . . . When
> the people of our common country shall be willing to accord to us
> the political rights which are enjoyed by other natives of the soil, we
> shall then be prepared to cease warring against the government and
> rebuking the church of its hypocrisy. But just so long as the enemies
> of the colored men's rights is to be found skulking behind the pillars
> of the church, and seeking security in the strong arm of the law, we
> can never remain silent.
>
> —*Weekly Anglo-African*, 20 August 1859

The above epigraph represents many characteristics and goals of the nineteenth-
century African-American press;[1] from its beginning in 1827 with the publication of *Freedom's Journal*, the press served to bring African Americans into public
discourse and to represent the interests, needs, and opinions of the African-
American community. The nineteenth-century African-American press functioned to shape community thought and action, and to argue and advocate for
the common good of the African-American community. That function situates
these texts as rhetorics of citizenship because the editors and writers identified
the common needs of the African-American community and wrote to make
the issues they identified a matter of public discourse. They contributed to a
public literacy grounded in action and critical consciousness of the political
and social dynamics within and involving the black community. Although the
press was certainly a venue for news reporting, the construct of "rhetorics of

citizenship" provides a way to see the press, and articles within it, as tools for persuasion. Locating themselves first within the *polis* of the black community and then within the larger American context, these writers made racial discrimination a public issue and argued for the African American's right to government protection. In many texts within the history of rhetoric, the *polis* (city or city/state) is a reference used to form public opinion about the common good of a political collective, as in the current or future stability and strength of a country. Texts from the African-American press model a sophisticated navigation of constructions of the black community and of the United States that weave together these constructions so that national well-being is inseparable from real racial equality. In fact, in article after article, advocates for race pride and racial equality are ultimately the protectors of the central, American values of justice, virtue, and liberty.

The papers also offered a representation of African Americans that countered racist stereotypes and worked to establish a citizen-specific African-American identity. Whether in New York in the early nineteenth century or in New Orleans just after the Civil War, or in Washington, D.C. well after Reconstruction, the press had at least a dual role. It delivered a service to the black community by providing news and perspectives that were otherwise unavailable in a public format; the very nature of news items that were selected, however, carried strong persuasive power for advocating social, cultural, and political change in the interest of equality. This essay draws heavily from the African-American press because these writers best represent the emerging construction of African-American citizenship.

This essay necessarily assumes a rather broad-reading audience for the newspapers discussed here. Readers were very differently situated depending on both year and geographic location. Publications before the Civil War had a primarily free black audience who were struggling to make sense of their "free" position within an American polity that saw them as deficient and unworthy of citizenship. Reconstruction publications, from the Civil War through 1877, had a free black audience that sometimes included northern African Americans as well as freedmen (former slaves) who were posed to seize and embrace a citizen identity within a context that required nothing less than a complete overhaul of American citizenship. Post-Reconstruction publications had an audience that struggled to thrive in an era of intense Ku Klux Klan activity. This audience also faced a federal government that allowed a complete unraveling of the rights they had fought for and gained. Throughout this essay I refer to "the black community"; it is this reading audience that I encapsulate within that concept, as well as the larger African-American population the papers advocate for. "Community" does more to capture the underlying spirit of *polis* and the arts of citizenship than the word "population" can encompass.

The following three sections provide a broad discussion of three topics pertinent to the nineteenth-century African-American press. Section one discusses the role the press played in forming a strong community cohesiveness, naming racist violence and initiating the defense of the African-American citizen. Section two continues the discussion of racist violence and discrimination and shows how emerging African-American citizens were positioned in opposition to the government that failed to protect their civil rights. Finally, section three offers a brief discussion of how one publication, Ida B. Wells Barnett's *Free Speech*, was attacked for exposing the racist and economic-driven lynchings of African-American males.

Martin Dann has observed, "The history of black people in America is one of self-determination and self-definition, to be included as 'Americans' with full citizenship rights or to be granted the privilege of establishing a separate and independent political entity." This view of history is embedded within the black press as it provided a forum for arguments for inclusion and the opportunity to work "through the system" and arguments for exclusion that counseled to avoid an already corrupt system.[2] Although there were just over forty publications before the Civil War, Armistead Pride writes that 1,187 black newspapers were founded between 1865 and 1900; by 1890, 575 papers had been established in the South.[3] Antebellum northern black publications focused on gaining social mobility and political/social rights for northern blacks.[4] Papers established in the South after the war "functioned as [instruments] to help the newly freed slaves bridge the gap between slavery and freedom."[5] There are numerous explanations for the increased growth rate of African-American publications after the Civil War. After the war there was better education in the African-American population in the North and the South than before the war: literacy increased. The freedmen began earning money and collectively were able to support papers financially (if only for brief periods in many cases). Financial support was also offered from various social groups, and religious organizations began sponsoring their own publications. Politically sponsored publications increased because of the black vote; and finally, the community recognized the influential position that editors claimed, and many people sought this profession. Wolseley also suggests that enforced segregation led to a community consciousness that the papers both reflected and participated in.[6]

In her history of the African-American periodical press, Penelope Bullock writes that the growth of the press was in flux with the status of African Americans. From the 1830s to the 1860s the press was active because of political and social dangers the community faced. The periodical press began, she continues, "as a part of the organized activities of black people who were working for the emancipation of the slave and for the liberation of the free Negro from inequities and restrictions. As the status of free Negroes deteriorated during the 1850s and the early 1860s, they became increasingly alarmed about their situation." From 1865 to 1879, when the community was hopeful of gaining full citizenship as a result of the Civil War and reconstruction, the periodical press was basically "dormant"; in the post-Reconstruction years from 1880 to 1909, the press experienced a resurgence as black civil rights were stripped away and violence against the community increased.[7]

From the beginning of the press in 1827, with the publication of Freedom's Journal, it has assumed a key position in the African-American community by offering news related to the community, teaching African-American history and race pride, and confronting racism. Writing about the cohesive function of the press, Dann observed that the editors, "who were often self-educated, brought to their community a spirit of racial pride and encouragement that were essential factors in keeping the community together."[8] An awareness of oppression was presented along with success stories from within the community. Offering an interpretation of the press as a reaction to white racism, Lawrence Fortenberry argues that although many publications of the black press were started for different reasons and supported various causes within the community, "overall they were largely fostered by the white media's unwillingness to promote a positive and thorough image of blacks to the public. . . . From its outset the black media have existed in this country because the larger white media have failed to uphold the standards of equality and freedom of speech."[9] The dual purpose of race uplift and confronting institutional and interpersonal racism has been one of the mainstays of the black press. Freedom's Journal began this tradition, but the publications that followed—newspapers, journals, periodicals, and magazines—continued to use this public medium to counter racist attacks and to foster community.

"We wish to plead our own case": The Function of the Black Press

> Because the wise and good awake and consecrate themselves to our cause, we ourselves must have proclaimed our oppression and wrongs from the HOUSE-TOP.
>
> —SAMUEL CORNISH, The Colored American

Freedom's Journal began publication in New York City in March of 1827. Dann notes the significance of its publication in New York instead of Boston or Philadelphia, which had large African-American and abolitionist populations. Due in part to several proslavery New York City newspapers, racial tension and discrimination were higher there; the need for a paper to represent the black community was immediate.[10] Community leaders in the city met in 1827 to discuss the "anti-black propaganda" produced by the New York Enquirer and other papers and to decide on an appropriate means of action. They decided an "independent black newspaper" was called for and invited Samuel Cornish and John Russwurm to be the editors.[11] Although this team was short-lived, Cornish and Russwurm agreed to edit the paper and thus began the first publication of the African-American press. In a short article titled "To Our Patrons," they explained the need for the paper to their audience: "We wish to plead our own case. Too long have others spoken for us. Too long has the public been deceived by misrepresentations in things which concern us dearly, though in the estimation of some trifles; for although there are many in society who exercise toward us benevolent feelings, still (with sorrow we confess it) there are others who enlarge upon that which tends to the discredit of any person of color."[12]

With this short statement Cornish and Russwurm made a case for the need of African Americans to influence public opinion and to speak for themselves. They also placed immediate value on concerns of the community that others, notably supporters of the proslavery Enquirer and Evening Star, either completely ignored or trivialized.

In "Proposals for Publishing the Freedom's Journal," the editors spoke more directly about race uplift.

> We deem it expedient to establish a paper . . . for the moral, religious, civil, and literary improvement of our injured race. Experience teaches us that the press is the most economical and convenient method by which this object is to be obtained. Daily slandered, we think there ought to be some channel of communication between us and the public through which a single voice may be heard in defense of five hundred thousand free people of color. . . . We believe that the time has now arrived, when the calumnies of our enemies should be refuted by forcible argument. . . . As the diffusion of knowledge, and raising our community into respectability, are the Principal motives which influence us in our present undertaking, we hope our hands will be upheld by all our brethren and friends.[13]

The editors' goal is a strong community voice. Given the variety of voices and topics represented in the journal, their use of "a single voice" is more symbolic of community than proscribed views and political stances. Contributors' open debate of issues, especially citizenship, indicates that the editors sought a variety of opinions; they wanted to raise the level of African-American participation in public discourse. The reasons that Cornish and Russwurm gave for publishing Freedom's Journal are representative of the goals of subsequent publications. In a growing number of journals and special-interest periodicals established in the years that followed, African Americans demanded equal treatment under the law and were increasingly committed to confronting racial and economic oppression. Printing announcements for political meetings and follow-up reports of the gatherings, these publications documented and called for direct social involvement. The press practiced a rhetoric of citizenship that Dann characterizes as a "quest for national identity" that challenged the continuous attempts of white society to deprive African Americans of their rights; editors and contributors were defining for themselves what being a citizen meant. This process involved "an awareness of a collective responsibility, a resistance to racism, and a commitment to self-definition and self-determination."[14] Instead of an emphasis on individual rights, the focus was on community, racial pride, and social action. Although shared oppression was certainly a major topic in the newspapers and demonstrated an identificatory rhetoric, the African-American community was rarely left in the position of victim without a means of action. The racism they faced in everyday life was used to call for resistance, and to support a historical consciousness that named their oppressors.

Russwurm and Cornish had intense disagreements about colonization that resulted in Cornish leaving *Freedom's Journal*; Russwurm eventually gave up his position as well and moved to Liberia.[15] Cornish returned to the paper and renamed it the *Rights of All* in May of 1829.[16] He later became the editor of the *Colored American*, which was in publication from 1837 to 1942. In the proposal for the *Colored American*, Cornish maintained that the paper was to function as a platform for the community; he intended it to "open a channel of communication for the interchange of thought, . . . through which light and knowledge may flow to instruct, enliven and fertilize all." In "Why We Should Have a Paper," Cornish maintained that the *Colored American* was necessary in order to contend with the "multiplied ills of slavery" that pervade the land and the church, to unify the black population of the free states scattered over five thousand towns —"to rouse them up. To call all their energies into action—and where they have been down-trodden, paralyzed and worn out to create new energies for them." Finally, he wrote, "No class of men, however pious and benevolent, can take our place in the great work of redeeming our character and removing our disabilities. They may identify themselves with us, and enter into our sympathies. Still it is ours to will and to do—both of which, we trust, are about to be done, and in the doing of which, this journal as *an appropriate engine*, may exert a powerful agency."[17] Firmly positioning himself and the paper within the community, Cornish aimed to make the *Colored American* an agent for social change; likewise, he recognized the ability of his community to fight back and intended the paper to be used for creating more energy in the face of oppression.

After the Dred Scott case began in 1847 and the Fugitive Slave Law was passed in 1850, the papers paid even closer attention to the precarious position of free blacks in the recognition that their freedom of movement and social involvement were at risk. The *Aliened American* (1853), a product of the Ohio Conventions of Colored Citizens, edited by Charles Howard Day, Samuel Ward, and J. W. C. Pennington, responded to these changing conditions. Describing the rationale behind their title, the editors wrote in their announcement: "Born under the United States' Constitution, and entitled by it, to all the rights and immunities of other citizens, the State and national Governments have not only disfranchised, they have ostracized—have made [African Americans] aliens— through their Law, the Public Opinion and their Community Regulations."[18] They took as their goal to "make our way where our personal presence would be excluded" and to aid in the educational development of the community.

In the years just before the Civil War there was a heightened sense of urgency in the free black community as a result of several political set-backs. In 1854 the Kansas-Nebraska Act was passed and repealed the Missouri Compromise of 1820, allowing slavery in the western territories. In the 1857 conclusion of the Dred Scott Case, Chief Justice Roger Brooke Taney declared that Scott could not, under the Constitution, be considered a citizen and would have to return to slavery.[19] Free blacks as well as escaped slaves were subject to capture and trial, and free blacks without free papers were in a precarious position if seized and claimed as fugitives. Free blacks often assisted fugitives and provided shelter and a way into Canada; they were central to the fugitives' defense and rescue in the case of capture. While certainly defending individuals, this assistance was also a defense of African-American freedom and citizenship. "Shall we resist Oppression? Shall we defend our Liberties? Shall we be FREEMEN or SLAVE?" asked a writer in the New York *National Anti-Slavery Standard*. Frederick Douglass also determined that the Fugitive Slave Law "virtually made every colored man in the land an outlaw . . . hunted by any villain" and made him vulnerable to treason charges if he defended himself.[20]

Within this political climate Thomas Hamilton began editing the *Weekly Anglo-African* in New York and stated there was a need for advocacy for the black community "from our own stand-point." Hamilton listed eight aims for this publication: to "set forth our cause in a true and clear light, by a . . . review of our condition, past and present"; to promote industry, perseverance, economy, and self-reliance; to promote "that kind of education really essential to our present condition and future development"; to support "elevating employments" such as agriculture and mechanics; to connect with other African-American communities; to give an account of activities within the community; to report on "all that transpires" in the country or world related to African Americans; and, finally to promote justice and virtue."[21]

Although Hamilton's goals are similar to those of previous publications, the sense of urgency is carried out through his goal to foster an educated, self-reliant, virtuous, working community and to keep the community informed about political changes. Dann characterizes the *Weekly Anglo-African* as supportive of militant resistance;[22] this tendency is evident in the opening epigraph for this chapter. Calling for black participation in public discourse and characterizing resistance as "warring" against the government, this article constructs the African-American citizen in opposition to the government. This was a recurring rhetorical maneuver as writers equated African Americans with the "American" principles of liberty and justice while pointing out the pervasiveness of "caste prejudice." Writers used instances of racism in everyday life to call for suspicion and careful evaluation of political institutions. The *Weekly Anglo-African* advocated critical evaluation as a way for African Americans to avoid becoming pawns of political parties: "We feel . . . that in striking us down, liberty and justice are also stricken down in the land. . . . With us it is not parties, but principles. . . . Parties as such, be they of whatever name, are to us as the mere scaffolding to the building. If in examining the platform of the party, or in looking through the antecedents of men, we find either void of sound principles, we shall utterly reject the one and cast the other forth as a branch that is withered."[23]

In "The Irrepressible Conflict," resistance is characterized more specifically as a conflict between "right and wrong" that pervades all aspects of society: "No matter what way we turn our eyes, we find an irrepressible conflict going on, and one which has been going on since the foundation of the government. It is everywhere rife in the land and to evil doers is fearful. In church and in state, in the moral circle, in the social circle, there it is, ceaseless and irrepressible, and will so continue till the last vestige of human oppression is extinct, or society itself in the land is destroyed. This conflict between right and wrong—between human bondage and human oppression on the one hand, and human freedom and equality on the other—between the robber of rights and the robbed."[24]

Conflict seems "fearful" to "evil doers" because oppression is being resisted. Clearly positioning the black community on the side of "right," the writer predicts that society will destroy itself if oppression isn't stopped. The author argues that "we have no fears for the ultimate result. As much as we love country, government, law and order—yea, even life itself—we love liberty, right, equity, and justice more." Given the political betrayal of the black race through the acts discussed above, country, Government, law and order are pitted against liberty, right, equity, and justice in a rhetorical maneuver that positions African Americans as defenders of democracy and virtue—as a force to be reckoned with: "Repress this conflict? Conquer it?" the writer asks, "What arm is sufficiently powerful—what force, either in the press, or in the government, or in the combination of demagogues is equal to the task. . . . They cannot check an atom of the conflict. Like a terrible volcano, it will break out with tenfold violence and tenfold fearfulness."[25] As a rhetoric of citizenship, this passage identifies equal rights for African Americans as the common good of the American *polis* and predicts entire societal dissolution if these rights are denied.

Confronting Power: Publicizing Violence and Prejudice through the Press

> There is nothing of which men are generally so unwilling to give up a part in order to secure the whole, as they are of power. . . . I cannot recollect a single instance . . . in which men have voluntarily surrendered any part of their power over others, from a discreet regard to the preservation of the remainder. There is not . . . a single example of power given up, without constraint. It has always been taken.
> —*Freedom's Journal*, 20 April 1827

> They have fanned a flame which they now fear is to consume them. . . . Acts of injustice like the holding of our fellowmen in slavery, very naturally suggests to guilty parties fear of retaliation.
> —*The Leader*, 24 December 1865

> Why do not our city dailies mention some of the outrages committed daily and nightly by white men against the freedmen? If a freedman commits an offense against a white man, it is immediately heralded, but when the freedmen suffer, the world seldom hears of it.
> —*Loyal Georgian*, 27 January 1866

While Hamilton, as editor of the *Weekly Anglo-African*, played up conflict and used it for momentum, other voices in the African-American press indicate that the community response to conflict, specifically to racial violence against blacks, should be to highlight citizens' rights to protection and freedom from harassment. This argument was even more prevalent during the Civil War, Reconstruction and post-Reconstruction days in the southern African-American press. Writers positioned the community in opposition to a government that was failing them. Making violence and racial discrimination a matter of public interest, they named their oppressors as the mainstream white press remained silent or justified cases of violence. The epigraphs for this section demonstrate how power, as a commodity, and violence, from the struggle over power, came together in articles from the press. In the South, fears of possible retaliation from the freed slaves were used to justify white violence; with time the justifications changed, but the violence continued and the mainstream media, as the last epigraph shows, continued to focus on any wrongdoings of African Americans. "When the freedmen suffer, the world seldom hears"; the press provided one way to affect public opinion by making sure acts of violence and discrimination were reported.

In the antebellum north, David Ruggles, of the Mirror of Liberty wrote about the usefulness of the press in forming public opinion in 1835. He didn't support the black press exclusively, but encouraged community support for the antislavery press in general and wrote occasionally for the Emancipator and the Liberator.[26] The press may not make laws, he wrote, but it does influence public opinion, which feeds into lawmaking. "It may be urged that the press cannot alter the laws of our country which make us slaves; this I admit. It cannot directly, but it can indirectly, changing the public opinion which creates the laws. What is the public opinion? It is the opinion of the majority of the intelligent people who inhabit our country, who are of the opinion that we ought to be banished to that Sepulchre, LIBERIA, for the crime of wearing a sable skin. It is the opinion of those who repudiate us as being by nature inferior to themselves."[27]

Within the Mirror of Liberty Ruggles adopted a policy of describing specific acts of violence and racial discrimination as well as the names of the "actors." He was well aware that some people would find this practice objectionable, but insisted, "[the Mirror of Liberty] will never attempt to treat questions of public interest in a manner to avoid giving offence to men, when principle is involved; even if we possessed that art, we question the propriety of describing errors without showing the actors with them."[28] When papers were established in the South, continuing this practice put publishers and editors in immediate danger; printing the details of white violence could result in lives being threatened or businesses burned.

Frederick Douglass also used his newspaper to construct the African-American citizen. In the November 1862 issue of his paper, Douglass' Monthly, he addressed the position of slaves freed during the Civil War in "What Shall Be Done with the Freed Slaves?" He dedicated his paper to the abolition of slavery and to gaining full citizen's rights for all black Americans.[29] On behalf of the freedmen Douglas wrote: "Putting aside all the hay, wood, and stubble of expediency, I shall advocate for the Negro, his most full and complete adoption into the great national family of America. I shall demand for him the most perfect civil and political equality, and that he shall enjoy all the rights, privileges and immunities enjoyed by all members of the body politic. . . . This is the only solid, and final solution of the problem before us."[30] Douglass argued that the freedmen must become equal members of the American polity; by arguing for bringing the freedmen into the "great national family of America," he sought to position them as contributing members of the polity during the time of Reconstruction.

Subsequent publications expressed anger and horror over the daily occurrences of violence with which the freedmen lived. Some writers supported self-defense, while others appealed for government protection; they shared the impulse to make racial violence and discrimination a matter of public discourse and to establish African Americans' identity and rights as citizens. A writer for the New Orleans Tribune lamented the lack of aid for the freedmen. Although some attempts were being made to protect the freedmen's "interest," they had been "very imperfectly protected." "In many parts of the State, a system of terror has been inaugurated, to keep down the Freedmen; several have already been murdered and many more will be if we do not resist. The right of self-defense is a sacred right. We read in the American Constitution that it is an immunity of its citizens of the Republic that they can bear arms." This writer suggested arming black troops to protect the communities or punishing the "would be murderers" as a way to stop the violence. One way or another, the writer concluded, "these people must be taught to respect the lives of their fellow citizens."[31]

In the New Era, a Washington, D.C.-based paper, discrimination was approached through government protection. Here a writer charged that the government had failed to lay a sound foundation for the rights of African Americans. Slavery had been "struck down," but "the element of slavery predominantly in our local government still crippling enterprise, withholding education, and sneering at loyalty" was left intact. In other words, an official mandate did little to address pervasive institutional and social racism. The writer continued: "It was felt that a solid foundation for liberty and justice had not yet been reached. It was seen that in a Republic all must be citizens on the basis of equality, enjoying like protection and like privileges." Although African Americans in Washington, D.C. had been given the ballot and had used the vote for effective social change, because "each fe[lt] that he [was] a part of and ha[d] an interest in the welfare of the city, the District, and the nation," "old fogies" tried to undermine their opportunities to exercise the right to vote. Although they had been granted the "privilege" to vote, that right wasn't protected, which made equality impossible. Inequality reverberated through businesses, schools, and political practices.[32]

Government Reconstruction ended in 1877, but left in its wake numerous political and social problems that the African-American community still had to face. Although the Enforcement Acts of 1870 and 1871 had been passed to curtail

Ku Klux Klan activities, in the early 1880s these laws were declared unconstitutional. The Amnesty Act of 1872 allowed ex-confederates to return to political activity in an official capacity and set the stage for antiblack white Americans to regain control of local and state governments. Although a second Civil Rights Act was passed in 1875 to give African Americans access to public accommodations, in 1883 it was declared unconstitutional. In post-Reconstruction America, clearly, the rights of the community were unprotected, and the press continued to respond with biting criticisms that reflect disillusionment with political parties and the government in general. In response to the 1875 Civil Rights Act being repealed, a writer for the *Globe* asserted, "the colored people of the U. S. feel today as if they had been baptized in ice-water. From Maine to Florida they are earnestly discussing the decision of the Supreme Court declaring the Civil Rights Law to be unconstitutional. Public meetings are being projected far and wide to give expression to the common feeling of disappointment and apprehension for the future."[33]

With government restriction of Klan activity declared unconstitutional, the Supreme Court said that the "U.S. was powerless to protect its citizens in the enjoyment of life, liberty and the pursuit of happiness." Positioning the African-American community and the government in opposition once again, the writer asks: "What sort of Government is that which openly declares that it has no power to protect its citizens from ruffianism, intimidation, and murder? Is such a Government worthy [of] the respect and loyalty of honest men?" Having neither protection for their political rights nor civil rights to safeguard equality, the community was faced with a Supreme Court that declared: "Railroad corporations are free to force us into smoking cars or cattle cars; that hotel keepers are free to make us walk the streets at night; that theatre managers can refuse us admittance to their exhibitions for the amusement of the public." Showing frustration and anger with the "system," this writer adopts a civic-minded rhetorical stance that positions the black *polis* and the white American *polis* at odds with one another. He asserts, "We are aliens in our native land; we are denied an equal measure of that protection which flows from citizenship and which is denied to no other class of American citizens . . . the Democratic party is a fraud—a narrowminded, corrupt bloody fraud; the Republican party has grown to be little better."[34]

In their rhetorics of citizenship, African Americans insisted that black citizenship could not be partial, that social and political equality are inseparable. Articles and editorials in the black press repeatedly challenged the notion of political equality without social equality. Full citizenship was impossible without both because, as a writer in the *Colored American* argued, "to talk about elevation, social or moral, without civil and political rights; is to talk about an elevation which never did, and . . . never can exist. No man is either socially, or morally elevated, . . . who is proscribed and oppressed; who has not civil rights —who is half way between slavery and liberty."[35]

The Suppression of Public Discourse:
The Press as a Target for Violence

> A government which has power to tax a man in peace, draft him in war, should have power to defend his life in the hour of peril. A government which can protect and defend its citizens from wrong and outrage and does not is vicious. A *government* which would do it and cannot is weak; and where human life is insecure through either weakness or viciousness in the administration of law, there must be a lack of justice and where this is wanting, nothing can make up the deficiency.
>
> —FRANCES ELLEN WATKINS HARPER, 1891

Like teachers of the freedmen, editors, publishers, and other community members who agitated publicly for the rights of African Americans and called for their resistance often faced threats, violence, and scorn. Some whites especially took exception to the publicizing of white violence and the "exposure" of their racist violence through public discourse. The end of Reconstruction brought an escalation of violence targeting African Americans as well as any white Americans who advocated for the black race or who displayed sympathy or generosity toward them. As this violence escalated through Klan raids, home burnings, and intimidation, the press often also escalated its response. This was the case of Ida B. Wells Barnett's *Free Speech* in Memphis, Tennessee. After Barnett became half owner of the paper, she used it to foster race pride and resistance and was outspoken about white violence against the African-American community. Her well-known antilynching campaign was an attempt to stop the violence, expose the criminals, and provide the "real" reasons behind white hatred.

Barnett wrote to disassemble the justifications for violence aimed at the black community. When three black men from her community were hanged, Barnett responded in the paper by arguing that the motives of the murderers were economic. While she was out of town, her office was burned and she was warned not to return. This experience made her even more outspoken and determined to expose "lynching [as] an integral part of the system of racial oppression" and to show that such violence was more related to political and economic motives than to crimes committed by African-American men.[36]

After her office was burned, Barnett published an antilynching pamphlet,

A Red Record, in 1895 to report on the incident and to historicize white violence against the African-American community. She asserted, "Not all or nearly all of the murders done by white men, during the past thirty years in the South, have come to light, but the statistics as gathered and preserved by white men, and which have not been questioned, show that during these years more than ten thousand Negroes have been killed in cold blood, without the formality of judicial trial and legal execution."[37]

In the same amount of time, she recorded, only three white men had been "tried, convicted, and executed" for all the murders of black men. When "public sentiment" called "the Southern white man" accountable for his "barbarism," he gave excuses that have, over years, "adapted themselves to the emergency." Barnett then gave and refuted the three main reasons used to justify the murder of black men. First there was the fear of "race riots" and the necessity of keeping blacks in control for the safety of the white community; "this story," Barnett reported, "wore itself out." Despite the violence and predictions of insurrections, "no insurrection ever materialized; no Negro rioter was ever apprehended and proven guilty, and no dynamite ever recorded the black man's protest against oppression and wrong." The second common excuse came after African American males were enfranchised. In the face of antiblack arguments like "This is a white man's government" and "No Negro domination," African-American voters faced angry mobs and the Klan as they tried to exercise their right. Reflecting the widespread disillusionment with what the vote was thought to promise, Barnett asserted, "He believed that in the small white ballot there was a subtle something which stood for manhood as well as citizenship, and thousands of brave black men went to their graves, exemplifying the one by dying for the other." Given pervasive intimidation, violence, fraud, and murder, the ballot became a "barren reality" and the community found itself "voiceless in the councils of those whose duty it was to rule." Since "Negro domination" was not a valid threat, the third justification given was the rape of white women by African-American males. Barnett asked, "Does he mean the crime which the statutes of the states describe as such? Not by any means." Since there was seldom any recognition of voluntary associations between white women and black men in the southern white community, rape was redefined in this context to mean any contact at all between black men and white women. Barnett pointed to slavery days and the practice of white families being left alone for days at a time while the male was away on business; during the Civil War, "while the master was away fighting to forge the fetters upon the slave, he left his wife and children with no protection save the negroes themselves."[38]

After historicizing white violence against African Americans, Barnett made her paper, the *Free Speech,* the point of her argument by relating how her office had been burned. Barnett's self-appointed function as advocate for "all victims of the terrible injustice which puts men and women to death without form of law" was a threat to the agents of that injustice. Their response was to squelch her primary means of influencing public opinion; they wanted to prevent her from exposing them for the murderers they were and from characterizing their excuses for violence as groundless justifications for barbarism. Ultimately holding the public responsible for tolerating punishment without "judicial trial and legal execution," Barnett asserted in 1894: "There were 132 persons executed in the United States by due form of law, with in the same year, 197 persons were put to death by mobs who gave the victims no opportunity to make a lawful defense. No comment need be made upon a condition of public sentiment responsible for such alarming results."[39]

The African-American press had a number of functions in the nineteenth century. Roland Wolseley asserts that the papers were "of far more consequence as persuaders than as news organs."[40] Their functions as "persuaders" and as "news organs," however, weren't mutually exclusive. That is, gathering and dispersing material taken to represent "news" is a persuasive act. Writers located themselves within the *polis* of the African-American community and offered news that was particularly relevant to that community. Through the antebellum, Reconstruction, and post-Reconstruction, editors, writers, and supporters of the African-American press sought to form public opinions that would recognize the citizenship, the humanity, of African Americans. They provided news that was often left out of the mainstream media and argued that African Americans' participation in public discourse was a community responsibility. The civil rights of African Americans depended on their merging the arts of discourse and the arts of citizenship as a way to demand protection of their rights, to expose white violence and discrimination against them, and to create an image of the African-American citizen that embodied the "American" values of justice, virtue, and liberty. Ultimately, writers for the nineteenth-century African-American press worked to construct and foster an image of the African-American citizen that countered a government that failed them.

eight "Stolen" Literacies in *Iola Leroy*

Patricia Bizzell

Iola Leroy, published in 1892, is the best-known novel by Frances Ellen Watkins Harper, a member of a prominent free-born black activist family and a feminist, prolific writer, and eloquent speaker for civil rights.[1] The story is set during and immediately after the Civil War. The first scene presents two male slaves hailing each other on the way home from market. They are laughing and joking in the manner of a "Sambo" or "Step-n-Fetchit" black male stereotype, and in the process one informs the other that the butter for sale that morning was very fresh. They walk along together and encounter other slaves who also inquire about the state of the butter, fish, or eggs.

We soon learn that one of these seemingly ignorant slaves, Robert, has been reared from infancy by a mistress who defied the law and taught him to read, although not from purely benevolent motives: as Harper puts it, "She had fondled him as a pet animal, and even taught him to read."[2] Robert turns her deception to his own purposes, reading the newspapers to get information on the progress of the Civil War and passing that information along to his fellow slaves through the code references to the state of the market goods.

This information is crucial to the slaves' planning to escape and aid the Northern war effort. White Southerners attempted to discourage such efforts by lying to their slaves about both the progress of the war and the reception that escaping slaves were likely to meet in the North. During one planning session, Robert rebukes his friend Tom Anderson for believing such lies: "Tom, you must not think because a white man says a thing, it must be so. . . . Somebody else can read the papers as well as Marse Tom and Frank. My ole Miss knows I can read the papers, an' she never tries to scare me with big whoppers 'bout the Yankees."[3] Robert, Tom, and other men at this meeting do subsequently escape and become soldiers in the Union Army.

Thus the theme of what I am calling "stolen" literacy emerges at the very beginning of Harper's novel. Robert's literate abilities are "stolen" in several senses. His mistress in effect stole literacy for him, by teaching him to read in defiance of the law that prohibited such knowledge to slaves. She has given him these stolen goods, however, only to serve her own amusement and convenience. Teaching him to read is for her like teaching a pet dog to retrieve the newspaper from the driveway. She finds the process entertaining, and the literate slave is more useful to her in running errands.

Robert, however, has stolen this literacy away from the mistress who, in giving it to him, anticipated controlling it. He uses his literacy for his own purposes, namely, to aid in the subversion of the social system that keeps him a slave for whom education, and other basic human rights, are denied. And even more striking, his literacy aids this subversive process by allowing him to rewrite the version of history the slave-owners attempt to impose on the slaves. Robert's literacy enables him to counter the slave-owners' version of the war with another version more hospitable to the hopes of rebelling slaves. Significantly, Harper ratifies this theft by having Robert, Tom, and the others successfully escape and go on to fight as Union soldiers against the slave system. Furthermore, the fact that Robert's literacy assists not only himself but also his comrades to act effectively against oppression suggests that Harper sees literacy for African Americans as serving not only individualistic but also collective social ends.

"Stolen" literacy also ends up empowering the novel's title character, Iola Leroy, and points the way for her from silence imposed by the brutal oppression of slavery to eloquence used on behalf of African-American self-determination. What I find striking about Iola's situation, as Harper depicts it, is that Iola "steals" literacy, as it were, from the dominant social group. Iola is the child of a white plantation owner and his light-skinned African-American concubine, and she is educated as a wealthy white girl even though she is legally her father's slave. Thus Iola "steals" literacy or acquires it under false pretenses, given the law against slave literacy. Indeed, Iola herself does not even know she is black.

Harper underlines the irony of this theft by depicting Iola as sold into oppressive bondage directly from her elite Northern boarding school after her father's unexpected demise. Harper orchestrates the scene by showing Iola talking innocently with her school chums about the institution of slavery. Iola defends it, insisting that none of her papa's slaves are discontented! While she eloquently defends her papa, cheeks flushed and eyes flashing, the two white lawyers who have come to claim her as an asset in her father's estate are eavesdropping and commenting salaciously on her beauty, heightened by her ardent oratory.

Iola then spends a brief period of time "offstage" in the novel while she is in the hands of a brutal white playboy. Harper does not tell us much about what happens to Iola while she is his slave, but we can infer much from what we see of the change in Iola after she escapes. The once lively and loquacious girl has become mournful, physically subdued, and above all, silent. At this point in her story Iola works as a Union army nurse and we most often see her sitting quietly by the bedside of a dying soldier.

Two events seem to shock Iola out of her passive state. One is the death in a concluding Civil War battle of Robert's friend Tom Anderson, the former slave who helped Iola to escape. Tom is very black and depicted as speaking a black dialect; he is barely literate, although we are told of attempts he had made while a slave to receive instruction secretly at night. Some readers have been critical of the distance Harper creates between Tom and Iola; in the novel's terms it is unthinkable that they should become lovers. But at Tom's deathbed, Iola tells him that his friendship has meant as much to her as her mother's love. And it's not that Iola wants a "whiter" partner. The other galvanizing event in her life at this time is an offer of marriage from the white Dr. Gresham, who wishes to take her north to a life of domestic comfort and racial deception (he proposes that as his wife, she pass for white). Iola rejects him.

Iola's grief when she loses Tom and her resolve when she rejects Gresham — both feelings surprise her with their intensity—awaken what we would call a race consciousness in Iola. She tells Gresham that she is rejecting him not only because she now sees herself as black, but because she wants to work for her black race. At this point in the story, Iola sets herself on two parallel quests: she makes a series of attempts to find work for herself that will be of service to the black race, and she gives a more personal expression to her racial solidarity by attempting to find her black mother and brother, from whom she has been separated in the turmoil following her father's death and the war's end. Once again, individual and collective goals are intertwined.

Moreover, the goals of these quests are defined in terms of racial solidarity, and the experiences Iola has as she pursues them serve to deepen her identification with the black race. When seeking housing and work, she is discriminated against if she reveals her race; and she finds that black people, not white people, are willing to help her. When seeking her mother and brother, she comes in contact with a wide variety of black people, light- and dark-skinned, well educated and illiterate, and as they sympathize with her quest and try to help her, she finds that what all of them have in common is far more important than what may separate them.

The novel's end finds Iola associated with a black literary group, of the sort Anne Gere describes as flourishing among both white and black middle-class women in nineteenth-century America. The members, in this case both male and female, read their work to the group, for example, a scholarly paper on the pros and cons of black emigration to Africa and a poem entitled "The Rallying Cry." Iola delivers a paper on "The Education of Mothers," underscoring, both in its scholarly format and in its content addressing the power of mothers who retain the right to educate their children, the improved conditions black women such as Iola had after slavery. The group members also discuss the ideas presented in these writings, and Iola is depicted as not only contributing to these discussions but momentarily striking dumb the professionally educated men present, ministers and doctors, with admiration at her eloquence.

Thus Iola has changed dramatically from the silent mourner who came out of slavery. These concluding scenes seem contrived to demonstrate empirically that Iola's literacy is of a high order, and that it is now used not to defend the cruel patriarchal order of slavery, as in the scene at boarding school, but to attack white supremacy and, presumably, to help other black people find voices to do the same. When we last see Iola, she is married to a black doctor and working as a teacher.

Readers who do not focus on the trajectory of Iola's literate abilities, as I have suggested here, may see her as an example of a stock figure that can be found in white and black writers' works in nineteenth-century America, namely, the beautiful slave who is especially, abusively desired for her nearly Caucasian appearance. Recent black feminist literary criticism, however, has argued that Harper does not merely reproduce this stock figure, but rather uses it to advance an anti-white-supremacist agenda. I would argue that Harper advances this agenda particularly through her treatment of the ways Iola Leroy and other black characters in the novel acquire and use literacy.

Barbara Christian has termed the stock character that Iola seems to represent as the "tragic mulatta."[4] This is one of four stereotypes of the black woman that Christian identifies in nineteenth-century American literature, and all four stereotypes are defined in terms of the black woman's sexuality under slavery. The "mammy" is defined in terms of stereotypical maternal qualities: her body is swollen from repeated childbearing, and with her own children sold in the manner of livestock, she is depicted as performing nurturing activities, such as cooking for the household. The "loose woman" stereotype is defined in terms of the licentiousness supposedly aroused by the fact that slaves' sex lives under the chattel slavery system could not be regulated by marriage: she is depicted as handsome, voluptuous, and sexually aggressive. The "conjure woman" seems to be the only image that allows the black woman to escape a sexual definition, but only because she is depicted as old and witchlike, with a withered, unattractive body and dangerous supernatural powers of self-protection. Finally, the "tragic mulatta" is a very light-skinned and well-educated, ladylike slave whose intelligence works against her by supposedly intensifying the pain she feels at her servitude as a white man's sex object.

Harper's character Iola does indeed resemble the tragic mulatta. She is light-skinned, with long, wavy dark brown hair and blue eyes. She is so Caucasian in appearance, in fact, that neither she nor any of her acquaintances realize that she is, as it were, "legally" black until the truth comes out after her father's death. She then suffers the typical tragic mulatta fate of being sold to a white master who abuses her in an attempt to gain her sexual submission. But as Barbara Christian points out, all these tragic mulatta trappings are assigned to Iola very early on in the story, and almost immediately, the Civil War draws to a close and Iola is freed from bondage both to her cruel master and to the tragic mulatta role. It is as if Harper casts her in this role temporarily only so that Harper can reveal its inadequacies by Iola's subsequent career. Hazel Carby adds that Harper uses Iola's near-white beauty to emphasize the evil of slavery: her appearance, we know from the experience of both her and her mother, is the result of generations of sexual assault by white men on black women.[5] P. Gabrielle Forman goes even further and suggests that Harper makes Iola nearly white so as to capitalize on white readers' concerns about the so-called white slave trade, in which European-American girls were kidnapped and forced into prostitution, in hopes of persuading these readers to transfer some of their outrage to the prejudicial treatment of African American women, both within and outside slavery.[6]

Moreover, Barbara Christian argues that Harper is at pains to show that the liberated Iola fits none of the four black woman stereotypes. Her subsequent life, far from being "tragic," leads to her establishment as a happily married black intellectual. Her marriage to a black man, and the platonic relationship depicted with her husband, help preserve Iola from any taint of the "loose woman" stereotype; her childlessness distances her from the "mammy" stereotype; and her strong Christian faith is at odds with the witchcraft of the "conjure woman" stereotype.

Iola's identification as a religious woman is also important because Harper depicts African-American Christianity as morally superior to that of the whites. Indeed, Frances Smith Foster has pointed out that this theme is important in Harper's earlier novels as well.[7] The white masters allow a minimum of Christian learning to the slaves in hopes of giving them a religion that will make them passive in suffering. Harper depicts black Christianity as being indeed a powerful comfort in suffering for enslaved black people. But black Christianity also fosters a moral perspective that allows black people, whether slave or free, to criticize the hypocrisy of the whites. For example, Robert explains to a white captain in the Union Army that black Christianity is superior to white, by describing the kind of religion exhibited by the long-suffering slave mother:

"Now, Captain, that's the kind of religion I want. Not that kind which could ride to church on Sundays, and talk so solemn with the minister about heaven and good things, then come home and light down on the servants like a thousand of bricks."[8] As usual, Robert is expert at providing counter-versions to white history; here he depicts white Christians in a way different from how they would like to see themselves.

Robert later tells another story about black Christianity, focusing on Uncle Jack, a slave who frequently stole chickens and other foodstuffs from his owner's farm. Robert's captain questions whether such a man could be a true Christian, since he is a thief. Robert explains that Uncle Jack's owner once detailed a white minister to tax Uncle Jack about the stealing. But Uncle Jack argued that his thefts really comprised modest reimbursements for all the unpaid labor he contributed to make the farm productive. Uncle Jack's eloquence persuaded the minister that the white owner was in fact the real thief, and the minister turned his remonstrances on the owner, thus demonstrating both the moral and the rhetorical superiority of black Christianity. Iola Leroy, too, makes use of the power of black Christianity both in a concluding speech in which she compares the suffering of the enslaved black race to the suffering of Christ, and in her practice of her teaching vocation in connection with a black church.

I have been arguing here that Frances Harper's novel Iola Leroy presents a diverse and positive picture of black literacy. We see a variety of black characters acquiring literacy in a variety of ways, even when they are not legally permitted to do so, and using literacy to subvert the white-supremacist order and foster the interests of the black race. In making this case, I have admittedly glossed over some features of the book that might grate on modern readers: for example, Harper's critical deployment of black stereotypes is not always handled so skillfully that we can be sure she intends to debunk them, especially in the case of some of the more uneducated and dark-skinned characters; conversely, the speeches placed in the mouths of Iola and other educated black characters may seem so flowery as to protest too much about these characters' intellectual powers.

Alice Walker sees Iola's whiteness as an example of the light-skin prejudice that exists among black people, itself a product of assimilating the white-supremacist consciousness of the oppressors.[9] But Hazel Carby disagrees, pointing out that the group of black intellectuals whom Iola joins at the end of the novel includes several men and women who are described as being very black or "African" in appearance. Iola's light-skinned brother Harry marries a very black woman. Carby argues that what is significant here is Harper's creation of a male and female black intelligentsia, similar to the "Talented Tenth" invoked by W. E. B. Du Bois, who can speak for black civil rights to both black and white audiences.

One could still argue, of course, that this elitist approach is disrespectful of the less literate characters, whose dialect may grate on modern readers. But I would contend that Harper represents positively a range of language abilities. Robert, for example, although literate, is clearly not as well educated as Iola, yet he is depicted as bright, critically acute, and effective, functioning as an intellectual among his group of escaping slaves. Also, consider the positive depiction of Uncle Jack, whose oral, dialect-based eloquence overcomes the much more highly educated and socially privileged white minister and works effectively to protect Jack from retribution by his white owner. Indeed, P. Gabrielle Forman has argued that for Harper mere literacy is never enough; rather, characters must use their literacy for politically acceptable ends, which in Harper's view mean racial liberation and uplift. Forman suggests that Harper's imperative to evaluate literate practices in political terms induces her to endorse the wide range of literate practices that I have tried to point out, as well as "communal ways of knowing" that may be based in forms of what Forman calls "oral literacy," such as the ability to read faces.[10]

Nevertheless, I think it's legitimate that Harper would want to idealize and praise the "high literate" abilities of Iola and her circle. Iola's speeches often do seem so flowery that they might almost be cribbed from Harper's own platform speeches, but what if they are? Harper herself was a dark-skinned black intellectual whose platform eloquence was so powerful that some hearers attempted to denigrate it by claiming that she was actually a man, or perhaps a white man, in disguise.[11] Someone whose public voice suffered such appropriations might well want to retaliate by creating powerful images of black people, especially black women such as Iola, who transform stolen literacies into strategies for social justice.

Furthermore, in integrating a style supposedly more appropriate to platform eloquence into a work of fiction, Harper herself, in effect, steals literacy. She appropriates and adapts cultural elements from the dominant group—such as accepted conventions for a work of fiction—while transforming them for her own purposes and adding other elements from her own culture. We see Harper mingling genres here, interpolating black dialects and black cultural content. The very structure of *Iola Leroy*, then, could be considered an instance of stolen literacy. Written late in Harper's career (she was sixty-seven when it was published), the novel exemplifies her lifelong practice of using literacy acquired as a free-born black woman on behalf of African-American rights, as well as women's rights, temperance, and other social causes. Harper does not want her white readers to forget, in spite of the focus on slavery in her work and that of other African-American writers, that a literate and activist free black community had existed in America since at least the eighteenth century.

Harper steals literacy also in that she forthrightly offers a book with a message, something that is supposedly taboo to "high" literary art. The message, of course, makes a political statement about what black people can be and can do, but the offering of the message also makes a political statement, insisting on the black artist's right to use art in her own way, and for her people. Furthermore, as Forman points out, this message is coded within the references in the novel that black readers would be more likely than white readers to recognize, a strategy that parallels the coded references we saw Harper foregrounding in her opening scene in which slaves are using print literacy covertly. An example of such coding is Harper's choice of the name "Iola" for her title character: black readers would instantly recognize this name as the pen name of Ida B. Wells, the late nineteenth century's most radical young black woman activist and a worthy heir to the mantle that Harper herself had borne for so long.

Harper's idealization of black uplift and her uses of dialect and oratory may pose problems of taste for academically trained readers. But I would argue that such readers ought to consider how their own reading practices school their emotions. It is not the case, I would contend, that canonical reading practices do not allow for the transmission of messages, but rather that the messages are heavily culturally coded. This might be seen in a comparison of *Iola Leroy* with a more canonical text published in the same year, *The Awakening* by European-American author Kate Chopin.[12]

Both of these novels deal with a sort of awakening experienced by a central female character. In Chopin's novel, Edna Pontellier awakens to a sense of her own needs, not to any race or other group consciousness. Also, both awakenings require rebellion against prevailing social norms. But in Chopin's novel, the rebellion is a failure, and the story ends with the main character's suicide. This ending would seem to school us in gentle regret at the ironies of life's complexities, that is, if we follow canonical close reading practices. A more vigorous feminist criticism might repudiate this quietist emotional schooling or redirect it into rage that such an ending seemed necessary to Chopin. Harper is similarly vigorous in her willingness to school her readers to a sense of hope and enthusiasm for bettering the African-American condition. Academically trained readers ought to be at least as willing to consider this as they are to consider (white) feminist interpretive strategies.

Now is not the only time in history that people have had to self-help themselves to literacy in spite of oppressive obstacles, as Harper's novel suggests, and to use literacy to attack these obstacles. On a number of levels, as I have tried to show, *Iola Leroy* can serve as example and inspiration for those trying to "steal" literacy for their own purposes today.

nine **Plays of Heteroglossia**

Labor Drama at the Bryn Mawr Summer School for Women Workers

Karyn Hollis

It is surprising how little difficulty the students have writing their own plays. They use the newspapers and magazine accounts of current events as a source of material. These provide plenty of material on labor problems, such as the wage and hour bill, strikes, unemployment, and numerous other important matters.

One excellent example was the play *The Wage and Hour Bill*, written and produced by the students this summer. It was presented in the form of a "Living Newspaper." These subjects are so vital to the working people that the students not only act their parts, but actually live them. Some of the lines were improvised as they went on the stage, which was very effective, because it was so realistic. Another good example was the skit *You've Got Something There*, which brought out clearly the advantage of collective bargaining.

The technique that students develop remains in their minds, and that helps them to carry on dramatics education in their own communities and unions.

—ANNE D. BADEN, Student, Bryn Mawr Summer School

As revealed in the words of this student, labor drama played an important role in the educational agenda of the Bryn Mawr Summer School for Women Workers. Several extensive productions and numerous skits were performed every summer of the school's existence, from 1921 to 1938. The dramatic activity was part of a liberal arts curriculum that also included English composition and literature, the natural sciences, social sciences, and labor economics. The summer school's academic and aesthetic agendas evolved out of a focus on the experiences of the working women and a desire to help them improve their lives in terms they themselves articulated. The creation of a workers' theater offered a number of benefits along these lines. Labor drama, in its essence a public and collective endeavor, provided the discourse for the transformative social project envisioned by the summer school. Because creating plays and skits calls for synthesizing experience into a performative mode, workers conceptualized, evaluated, and critiqued their lives, often forcefully (re)writing themselves personally and collectively into current events and public discourse. Furthermore, in researching and writing plays, the students encountered academic discourse and the discourses of public policy and journalism. Since these discourses had to be "translated" into appropriate registers for summer school, union, community, church, or YWCA plays, the women gained a great deal of rhetorical sophistication.

Another benefit of dramatic activity was that it linked the working women to the important working-class cultural aesthetic of the time, with its roots in the more distant tradition of folk performance. The richly varied discursive context of the summer school exemplifies Bakhtin's concept of "heteroglossia," which Diane Price Herndl defines as "multiple voices expressing multiple ideologies from different strata of language-in-use."[1] As will be seen in the excerpts and commentary to follow, the working women brought their own marginalized voices to the summer school where they encountered other discursive forms, forging more powerful voices in the process. Their strengthened discursive subjectivities countered the bourgeois hegemonic discourse that textually oppressed and even erased them. Indeed, of all the summer school's literacy practices, labor drama was likely the most transformative, by enabling the women to grow intellectually, politically, and aesthetically.

The school was established in 1921 by M. Carey Thomas, the President of Bryn Mawr College, after she heard the National Women's Trade Union League call for women's colleges to attend to the educational needs of working women. She chose Hilda Worthington Smith, committed social activist and former Bryn Mawr Dean, to direct the summer school. During its seventeen-year existence, approximately 1,500 women attended the school on scholarships financed largely by alumnae clubs of "regular term" Bryn Mawr graduates. Democratically run by administrators, faculty, and students, the summer school aimed for diversity in its student body, recruiting women from a variety of racial, religious, ethnic, and geographic backgrounds. The largest number of students worked in the needle trades and came from the Northeast, but they also included Italian Catholic telephone operators from Philadelphia, Jewish immigrant bead stringers from Russia, and Baptist textile workers from the deep South. In response to student demand, African-American women were invited to attend in 1926 and thereafter. The school required an eighth-grade education and recruited women eighteen to thirty-five years old, with the average age being twenty-five. Many were unmarried. Several follow-up studies have shown that almost all graduates did indeed assume leadership positions in labor, education, community, government, and religious organizations.[2] The end of this remarkable educational project came in 1938 when the Bryn Mawr Board of Trustees, wary of the summer school for years, objected to two summer school faculty attending a rally in support of striking workers at Seabrook Farms in New Jersey. The Trustees voted to cancel the relationship between the College and the summer school. It was reestablished as the coeducational Hudson Shore Labor School and continued as such until 1950.

The curriculum at the summer school was amended in response to student suggestions and criticisms as well as the faculty's perceptions of what worked and didn't work. One basic principle, however, remained constant: that workers' own experiences should be central to their education. Since personal experience was to play such a key role in the course of instruction at the summer school, it is not surprising that student-centered genres such as autobiography, poetry, fiction, and the collaborative essay were typical assignments in English composition classes. Dramatic productions, from complicated pageants to improvised skits, also became an increasingly important activity. Several extensive productions and numerous skits were performed every summer. For example, over thirty-five theatrical pieces were produced during the summer of 1936 alone.[3] Two goals predominated in accounts of the school's dramatic activity: to help the working women reconstruct more powerful subjectivities and, ultimately, build an egalitarian working-class culture that reflected their interests, needs, and desires.

Workers' Culture: Building on the Past

In examining the summer school's theatrical arts program, one should understand that dramatics there occurred in the context of a larger workers' theater movement, which had its own history harking back to European folk performances. A more recent precursor, however, was the participatory pageant performed in the United States in the 1910s and 1920s by civic associations, churches, unions, immigrant groups, and even corporations, the purpose of which was to involve cast and audience in a morale-building spectacle. These pageants combined song, dance, mass chants, and often spectacular costumes, scenery, and orchestration to make their dramatic point. The *Paterson Strike Pageant* of 1913 offers an influential example. Organized by the Industrial Workers of the World (Wobblies) and directed by John Reed, it was performed in Madison Square Garden with a cast of about 1,500 striking immigrant silk workers before a crowd of 15,000 to protest the oppressive conditions leading to a three-month strike at a local mill.[4]

A continent away, participatory pageants were being used to build support for the Russian Revolution, but the need for a more mobile and adaptable stage led to the development of an extensive *agitprop* theater by the Moscow Blue Blouses, a revolutionary acting troop inspired by the early Soviet workers. The *agitprop* (agitation and propaganda) theater spread with the Communist movement to other working-class organizations of Europe. Drama historian Daniel Friedman credits a German immigrant workers' theater called the *Prolet-Buehne* with introducing this type of labor drama to American workers in the New York area.[5] A majority of the Bryn Mawr plays can be characterized as such.

Workers' theater groups formed in unions, left-wing political groups, the Y's, and churches, wherever workers' concerns predominated and energy was available for combining educational, organizing, and aesthetic endeavors into plays or skits. At the height of the workers' theater movement "hundreds of troupes and tens of thousands of workers . . . wrote, directed, performed and attended their own theatrical pieces." In 1935 a national organization called the League of Workers' Theatres reported a membership of 400 theater groups in 28 cities across the United States. The League published a monthly journal, *New Theater*, which at its height had a circulation of 18,000.[6]

Workers' Theater: New Genres from the Working Class

Productions developed at the Bryn Mawr Summer School fit easily into the dramatic styles common to the workers' theater movement of the 1930s. The most popular theatrical form was the "mass recitation" adapted from the early participatory pageants.[7] Often combined with group movement and musical or rhythmic accompaniment, the mass recitations were typically performed by a worker's chorus reciting verse in a dramatic context that pitted workers against a capitalist boss. The point, usually political, was simple and direct. The acting style stressed clarity of voice and gesture.[8] The *agitprop* skit, which usually included mass chants, was the other popular form of the day. Friedman writes that it involved radical political content, an extremely physical acting style, and a montage plot structure based on political concepts, rather than linear development of character and plot.[9] Many *agitprop* skits combined short, scenic episodes into longer plays, a la *Waiting for Lefty*, the workers' theater hit of the 1930s written by Clifford Odets. This form is seen frequently in the summer school repertoire.

Another popular workers' theater style used at the summer school was the "election script." In these skits, the various political parties, Democrat, Republican, Communist, Socialist, or Fascist were poked fun at or praised, depending on the political tendency of the theatrical group.[10] Another genre of Russian origin, also frequently produced at the summer school, was the "living newspaper," or dramatized news story. Made famous in the United States by the Federal Theater project under the direction of Hallie Flanagan, these productions portrayed important current events, emphasizing their effects on the working class.[11]

Other well-liked forms included "cabaret-style revues, vaudeville-like comedy routines, political circuses, . . . and pantomimes."[12] Music and percussion instruments were often used in all genres to energize the audience; spectators and actors often sang together a spirited rendition of *L'Internationale* at the end of a production. Humor and satire were staples in this theater, and as with other forms of working-class art, "contents and forms [were drawn] from folk and popular tradition."[13] Thus, the summer school students used melodies from popular songs and nursery rhymes in their productions and rewrote the words to suit their purposes.

In characterizing theater for working-class audiences, Bruce A. McConachie and Daniel Friedman argue that what most separated the workers' stage from the mainstream theater of the day was the blurred distinction between actors and spectators.[14] Summer School student Victoria Grala wrote an account of this phenomenon in the 1937 issue of *Shop and School*, the student publication. "A unique and somewhat startling technique which was used over and over again in our drama this summer, was that of actors speaking from different parts of the audience. . . . We discovered that an emotional feeling of unity resulted from such drama, because we were sympathetic with these audience actors and felt in our own hearts what they themselves were speaking in the play. Then again, it broke the sharp line which is usually found between actors and audience as we were as one with the players."[15]

McConachie and Friedman point out that unlike the more mainstream drama of the 1930s, workers' theater did not delve into the psychological make up of its characters, but chose instead to stress themes of social morality.[16] They also emphasize the strong emotional effect of many working-class dramatic productions, designed for the most part to build class consciousness and underscore the need for social change from the workers' perspective.

Goal: Advancing Workers' Culture

According to Friedman, the ultimate goal of the workers' theater was to "create a distinct working class culture which . . . would reflect and inspire . . . workers in their economic and political struggles."[17] The words of an anonymous summer school student echo this intention. Her unusual use of the feminine possessive pronoun indicates her belief that this culture will include working-class women's perspectives also: "Real labor drama is only now beginning to be written and produced. Its unestablished place in the field of the arts means that anyone and everyone can contribute her [sic] own experiences and feelings to the experimental performance which will in the end build a firm Workers' Art."[18] Director Smith also mentions this goal in the extensive book she wrote on the summer school in 1929. In her characteristically visionary style, she commends this "new and living drama of the people, drawn from the deep sources of daily living, with potential power to re-create new life for the workers themselves and for others."[19]

Goal: Reconstructing Subjectivities through Drama

Feminist post-structuralists and compositionists indicate that having access to a variety of powerful discursive subjectivities is crucial to producing empowered subject positions in women.[20] In assigning drama a central pedagogical role and in recognizing its catalytic function in the reconstruction of subjectivities (although not in post-structuralist terms, of course), Bryn Mawr Summer School was at the forefront of the worker education and organizing movements of the age. Many summer school faculty and administrators were leaders in the field of worker education, and their views on labor drama and other issues were frequently published in leading scholarly journals. In 1935, for example, the *Journal of Adult Education* published a symposium of articles on "Creative Expression" in which Jean Carter, instructor and later a director of the summer school, published a piece entitled, "Labor Drama." Arguing from a philosophical as well as pedagogical perspective, she discusses the benefits of using drama in the classroom. In making drama out of their fragmented life and work experiences, she explains, workers "find a medium for reconstruction and expression . . . which thereby creates a unity between life and art—a higher mode of living than is normally open to the worker."[21] In another article, Carter praises schools, such as Bryn Mawr, whose dramatic productions have as their "primary aim, the education and the re-creation of the workers taking part in the play rather than the converting of a prospective audience."[22]

In the same issue of the *Journal of Adult Education*, Esther Peterson, the talented and energetic Director of Dramatics and Recreation who was later to serve in several presidential administrations, describes how she used the enthusiasm and experience of working women to help them develop skits and dances from their own lives. She also explains how material studied in the "academic" subjects found its way into the students' productions, again achieving a unity of mind and body typically denied to workers. In a more recent interview, Peterson recalls another innovative dramatic technique: the summer school's use of role-playing to boost the women workers' morale and self-confidence. "We started that back in the 20's and 30's long before there was anything else like it," she recalls. In the role-playing exercise she describes below, the women practiced standing up to and appropriating a hostile and powerful patriarchal discourse: "They [the workers] said that they would never dare to stand up in union meetings . . . in front of all the men. But we developed them. We'd put on plays. They'd take parts; they played that they were men. They experienced the kind of heckling they would get. They took the parts of the boss, the citizens."[23] Student Victoria Grala, writing in the summer school publication *Shop and School* in 1937, praises dramatic activity for other reasons that underscore its transformative potential. She points out that group planning produces a feeling of solidarity and unity among those putting together a play, and the process usually requires research that "forces [the workers] to face problems and to think clearly in an attempt to solve them."[24] Thus, in learning how to best portray their own difficult working conditions, students began to use the discourses of economics and the social sciences to call for a better life for themselves.

The process used to develop the skits, plays, recitations, songs, and dances performed at the summer school also contributed to the experience of self (re)presentation and (re)construction. The actual writing down of a play was the last step in a long procedure, or may never have occurred at all. Indeed, references to the benefits of improvisation are frequent—one such mention was made in Baden's remarks that opened this essay. If dialogue was not written down, of course, it could be personalized and tailored to fit different individuals and situations.

The importance accorded the dramatic activity is best revealed by the fact that Summer School Director Smith was herself primarily in charge of it during the first ten years of the school's existence. In her autobiography, she describes a way of organizing a series of spontaneous skits, encouraging workers to find the dramatic in their own daily experience. The girls divide into groups —perhaps according to industry—as they prepare for the "Trade Party," an annual event in which the various trades represented by the students at the summer school are presented in skits. For ten minutes they are to develop a scene.

Then "without stage, scenery or curtain," the brief scenes are acted.[25] Afterward, the audience discusses their merits and criticizes their faults.

In their writings, faculty repeatedly emphasized the importance of the reconstructive experience for students. Calling the work "experimental," Carter describes how a group of students critique and improve their skits. After viewing one together, she asks them what they liked. Responses such as "I could hardly wait to see how it was coming out" or "people don't act like that in a real shop" lead to discussions about "climax, suspense, economy of words, and the effectiveness of expressing ideas through a movement, a gesture, or a look." After this discussion, the actors might continue to polish a piece. Eventually, writes Carter, "in the course of several weeks something may be produced that seems worthy of being written down and presented to a larger audience." She concludes that "the instructor discovers, however, that presenting a play has become less and less important to the students as the interest in making the play has developed, and that the real satisfaction is in the *reconstruction* of one's own experiences."[26]

In her 1936 report on "Dramatics and Recreation," Peterson discusses how the play *America You Called Us* was developed by the dramatics group from a poem written in the creative writing group. She remarks that the students seemed to have "a real feeling" for the material. "This was probably because the content was discussed so widely before it was written by a smaller group. Miss Lockwood and Mr. Cummins [English and economics instructors] gave excellent assistance in building in the student body a vivid understanding of the dramatic quality of those periods of American history. This, plus the general [antipathy] toward war, made the performance mark a stage in the thinking of the students rather than a dramatic production."[27]

This consolidation of the dramatics and academic program was one way dramatics evolved over the years. A related trend was the increasing importance dramatics assumed in the overall curriculum: at first an extracurricular, evening project, it eventually became a central activity in itself with a director, assistant director, and a place in the morning academic schedule. Another trend was that subject matter for the skits and plays was to come increasingly from the students' life experiences mediated by material they were studying in classes.

The Development of a Dramatics Curriculum

The evolution of the dramatics curriculum can be observed through internal memos, project reports, and curriculum committee minutes, which record the important insights and struggles of the students and faculty who pushed for more theatrical activities. Writing in 1929 about the importance of dramatics at the school, Smith comments that on numerous occasions the faculty argued about how much time to allot to drama and other "recreational" activities. Smith asserts that in spite of the concern with the time taken away from "more serious" academic subjects, both faculty and students alike seemed to want to stick to the large festivals and performances. She comments that an effort is made to include all students in the programs, so as not to divide the audience into actors and spectators.[28]

By 1932 the minutes of an instructional committee meeting recommend that three elective projects be set up for the following summer session: a science project, a history project, and a project in dramatics. The minutes stressed that "the values gained for the students of former years through putting their ideas into dramatic form were recognized. It seemed important, again, that a small group have a fairly intensive interest in this project throughout the summer and that this group do some writing. A larger group would take part in the dramatic productions." It was also pointed out that the students would find the knowledge of methods of producing labor drama invaluable in their local communities. In this regard, a faculty member suggested that help in staging the summer school productions might be obtained from the Group Theater. Smith, however, objected, reporting that she would prefer to work with a senior from Vassar College "who had a great interest in labor drama and wanted to be of assistance."[29] Thus Smith underscored her desire to forge links between students from the women's colleges and the working women.

In the 1936 summer session, recreation, music, and dramatics were put under the direction of Esther Peterson. She remarks in her end of the session report that combining these three activities was very effective, although the staff still needed to be increased. She reports that the year's dramatics work grew out of the "experiences of the students as these were given significance through the class work." Peterson laments the fact that the dramatics staff did not spend as much time with the "unit instructors" (of English and economics) as they would have liked. She was pleased that many of the women were able to pick out dramatic situations from their own experience and to use the dramatic method to express ideas. She reports that faculty tried to give the students enough experience developing original material so that they would be able to put together their own dramatic presentations when they returned to their homes. Peterson goes on to report over thirty-five short plays, skits, and mass recitations, many including song, interpretive dancing, and folk dancing, that the students had participated in over the summer.[30]

By 1937 Smith was intensely involved in the Teacher Education Project of the WPA, and Jean Carter, former summer school teacher, had become the school's director. This seems to have been the crowning year in terms of summer school dramatics. In her "Report to Faculty . . . May 1937," Carter notes that, in addition to the regular division of the student body into units concentrating on English and economics, instructors for science, dramatics, recreation, and workshop will cut across the units to work with the entire school. She announces that morning periods will be scheduled for dramatics so that the dramatics instructor can count on some regular time for meeting all students in small groups.[31] In her report for this year, Peterson praised this new system saying it was now possible for her to develop a greater degree of continuity in the program by seeing students regularly and getting to know their class work. She could also visit economics classes "to help students and faculty see opportunities for relating the dramatics and economics class programs." She also mentions the great benefit of learning about "newer stage techniques for expressing important ideas" that was acquired when the students went to a production of *An American Tragedy* by the Hedgerow Theater.[32]

Dramatic Production at the Summer School: A Closer Look

Although it is largely ignored in histories of the workers' theater movement, as has been seen, "some of the earliest regular work in labor drama in America was done in connection with the resident labor colleges and summer schools for workers."[33] Even though the height of the movement was around 1934, the Bryn Mawr Summer School, for example, had put on labor dramas since the early twenties. Unlike their autobiographies that were occasionally about the students' personal concerns of family or education,[34] the student plays almost always centered around their work lives or current political and economic events that directly affected them. The plays often projected the women into the public arena in powerful roles. In my research among student publications and reports on the dramatic activity, I encountered over fifty-two labor dramas written at the summer school. Certainly there were numerous others that were not preserved in writing. A brief chronological account of the dramatic activities recorded in *Shop and School*, curricular reports, and memos will show how the plays and skits evolved over the years in terms of style and content.

In 1922 Haroldine Humphreys, Director of Dramatics, reports on the workers' dramatic activities in the *Bryn Mawr Alumnae Bulletin*. In praising two of the performances that were to become annual events at the summer school, the International Peace Festival and the closing Lantern Ceremony, Humphreys keys in on characteristics that were to continue to be important over the years. "Here was drama 'of the people' freed from stage tradition and as pure as Greek ritual," she writes. "The same principle of disregarding the spectator and emphasizing the ceremonial significance" was observed.[35] The "Calendar" of the 1924 *Bryn Mawr Daisy* records that the students from the advanced economics class staged a mock arbitration case based on an actual happening between an employer who had broken his contract and the Union with whom the contract had been made. "The discussion was quite spirited besides being educational, and the debate was enjoyed by both audience and actors."

In her chronicle of the daily events published in the 1928 *Echo*, student Ruthella Stambaugh mentions that her favorite skit was by the laundry workers who humorously acted out the tortuous path of a sheet in its journey through a laundry. She also reports on plays attended by students that year at the Hedgerow Theater: Susan Glaspell's *The Inheritors*, Shaw's *Arms and the Man*, and Ibsen's *Pillar's of Society*.[36] The 1929 *Echo* reports that a class studying American civilization put on a skit at night during which workers, dressed in colonial costumes, read the *Declaration of Independence* amid much applause. A "page" distributed copies to every table so that all could follow along. The reading was followed by everyone singing *The Internationale* and *The Star Spangled Banner*.[37]

Instructor Florence M. Pharo used a good bit of dramatics in the speaking component of her English course in 1930. She and her students worked up a series of short sketches about Bryn Mawr. "Four girls, wearing hats and carrying suitcases, pretended that they were traveling back to New York from Bryn Mawr. In the train they discussed Bryn Mawr naturally and informally."[38] Another skit from her class showed southern girls organizing a "club" (probably a YWCA). The southern girls sang a duet that one of them had composed. In their calendar report for 1930, students Ruth Epstein and Margaret Sofia mention dramatizing different kinds of union activities. The students in these skits showed how meetings were conducted and important matters were settled.[39]

In a report entitled "Experiments in Labor Dramatics at the Bryn Mawr Summer School for Women Workers in Industry," written in 1932 by workers and an unnamed undergraduate "Dramatics Assistant," the following "Animated Press" (living newspaper) appeared in outline form:

Characters:
    Editor-in-Chief
    Foreign Editor
    Domestic News Editor
    Fashion Editor
    Society Editor
    News of the Day:
        Domestic:

    1. Dies Bill[40]

    2. Political Campaign Speeches

    3. Stamp Tax

Foreign:

    1. Lausanne Conference

    2. Great Britain vs. Ireland

    3. Recognition of Russia needed

    4. Tragedies of recent Kings—a song

Society:

    1. An extravagant society wedding

Fashions:

    1. Show of dresses and hats from the Co-Operative Store (run by the workers at the school)

Amusements:

    1. Modern version of *Alice in Wonderland*

    2. Music by Edith Berkowitz

Newsboys on the street selling "Extras."

In *Labor Dramatics*, the scrapbook of the Dramatics Project Group 1933, it is reported that students in the Palmer-Finck Unit (class) attended a hearing on sweatshop conditions in Norristown, Pennsylvania, on 7 July 1933. When they returned, the students acted out what they had seen for the rest of the summer school. They portrayed a judge, a representative from the Central Labor Council, and several witnesses. The hearing concerned a complaint waged against the Pioneer Coat Company where the employer kept the employees' drinking water in dirty barrels. Previously prosecuted, the employer refused to improve work site conditions. The wages were also very low. Girls doing piecework for a full week received from one to three dollars, and one hand sewer, aged nineteen, received one dollar for a full week's work. The students acted out another complaint against the Reading Clothing Company where a sixteen-year-old girl worked in unsanitary conditions for two and one-half cents an hour. There was no rest room on the premises.

    Labor Dramatics also contained the following "Mother Goose Depression Pantomime" by student Jennie Previti, first published in the 1933 issue of *Shop and School*.

    Stage Directions: *The characters assemble backstage. Mother Goose comes forward and reads the opening verses:*

        Mother Goose Land is unhappy these days

        Her children have brought her despair

> They have nothing to eat
> No clothes and no heat
> There's misery everywhere.

The sheriff swaggers in, examines everything in sight, and walks off with a large market basket. Mother Hubbard appears with her dog under her arm, looks in her cupboard, and sits down and weeps.

> Old Mother Hubbard went to the cupboard
> To fetch her doggie a bone
> When she got here
> She found the house bare
> The sheriff had come and was gone.

Jack Horner runs in with an empty pie plate and curls up dejectedly on the floor. He sticks his thumb into the empty pie plate with great disgust.

> Little Jack Horner sat in a corner
> Without his Christmas pie
> The next time I hope
> For Labor we'll vote
> His unemployed father did sigh.

Peterson's 1936 report to the director describes in detail how the year's Trade Party was produced. As the students were looking for the year's unifying theme, someone complained that the Supreme Court had worsened the plight of the workers in almost every trade by declaring various parts of the National Industrial Recovery Act unconstitutional. "So 'Unconstitutional' became the cry and theme of the Trade Party."[41] The theme song was written to the tune of *Are You Sleeping, Brother John?*:

> Null and void, null and void
> Unconstitutional, unconstitutional
> We cannot enforce it,
> We cannot enforce it,
> Null and void, null and void.

This refrain was sung at various times during the production of *It's Unconstitutional*. A chorus of workers read offstage from the Declaration of Independence and the Constitution, while a group of judges in stylized robes and masks quoted from the balcony parts of famous decisions that declared certain legislative acts "null and void." Against this setting, more than thirteen groups presented their trades. "In 'Push Press,' the paper maker, through work motions and work sounds, typified the rhythm and monotony of the press." In "Buttons" a worker sat at her machine sorting buttons: large, small, plain, fancy. Her thoughts were revealed through a poem she had written. The most humorous part of the year's Trade Party, according to Peterson, was the skit given by the service workers, "Tarts and Flours." "It had a freshness that was delightful for the students acted so naturally. New lines and incidents appeared in the production which were never heard in the rehearsals." The Trade Party continued with "Lies from Above," as the jewelry workers revealed the need for regulated working conditions in their shops. The skit showed "the plight of the sympathetic forelady who has to enforce unfair rules to keep her job." When she exclaims: "It was so much better under the N.R.A.," the Supreme Court becomes lighted, rises and says "Unconstitutional!" In "Shop Talk," radio makers portrayed work on the conveyor belt. "The noise, smoke, and rackety rhythm of the equipment, the tension and speed of the workers to 'keep up production' leads to exhaustion when the bell rings."[42] While the tired workers are trying to keep up the pace, a radio broadcast comes on announcing that the Supreme Court had declared the minimum wage law "unconstitutional." An analysis of The Prelude, the introductory skit to It's Unconstitutional, follows below.

In addition to the skits and sketches developed and improvised by the students, Peterson also mentions that they put on "Free Tom Mooney," a mass recitation obtained from the Brookwood (labor college) Players as well as a skit originally produced by the professional Theater Guild. Peterson concludes that throughout the summer, "the students learned that the most effective dramatic productions are possible without even memorizing parts, and without all the paraphernalia of production."[43]

In her director's report for 1937, Carter praised Peterson's work with the students in dramatics. "It offered opportunity for expression of both experiences of individuals and activities of the classroom." She remarks that "in addition to a large number of original skits worked out by individuals and groups, two long plays "of real significance were developed." The first play, Who Are the Workers, grew out of an attempt in an economics class to define the term "workers." It was a kind of pageant that involved the whole school. Each trade group worked out the dramatization of its industry, and the foreign students introduced the idea of the "interrelation of workers of the world." The other play, Packing! Packing! Packing!, was the result in one class of an intensive study of the Supreme Court issue. In the form of a "Living Newspaper," the forty-seven-page play presented the entire history of the court from 1790 to the present day, exposing the continuing political nature of its composition, and concluding with some indication of how it might be pressured to evolve in a more worker-friendly fashion in the future. Carter again writes that "the dramatics instructor and all others concerned considered the process and not the product of primary importance. The analysis and research that went into the preparation of the material and the planning of the presentation had immediate educational value, for knowledge and understanding were subjected to the test of expression."[44]

The year 1937 had the most activity at the summer school, if we judge from the commentary on dramatics in *Shop and School*. The "Calendar of Events," lists an impromptu skit, *The Workers' Spirit*, along with six other productions: *The Whistle Blows*, *May Day*, *Who Are the Workers?*, *Packing, Packing, Packing*, *The Pied Piper*, and *War Drums*. In addition, the workers attended *An American Tragedy* and *Aria Da Capo* by the Hedgerow Theater.[45] In the 1938 issue of *Shop and School*, the last to be published on the Bryn Mawr campus, student Anne Baden made the remarks that began this article. Sally Russian records the summer's events and lists the following student productions: *You've Got Something There*, *Wages and Hours*, *Stop Those War Drums*, and *We Tomorrow*. She also mentions attending *A Moral Entertainment* by the Federal Theater Project and the Hedgerow Theater production of *The Frodi*.[46]

As we have seen, students were often taken to see socially relevant plays staged by professional and workers' theatrical groups, or they watched plays staged on campus by such groups. Below is a partial record of plays seen from 1924 to 1938.

1924 - Susan Glaspell, *The Inheritors*, Hedgerow Theater, Rose Valley

1925 - Henrik Ibsen, *The Pillars of Society*, Hedgerow Theater, Rose Valley

1926 - Lady Gregory, *Spreading the News*, read by tutors

1928 - Susan Glaspell, *The Inheritors*, Hedgerow Theater, Rose Valley
- George Bernard Shaw, *Arms and the Man*, Hedgerow Players
- Henrik Ibsen, *Pillars of Society*, Hedgerow Players

1929 - George Bernard Shaw, *Misalliance*, by the Hedgerow Theater, Rose Valley
- George Bernard Shaw, *The Devil's Disciple* by the Hedgerow Theater, Rose Valley

1930 - Tom Tippett, *Mill Shadows*, reads play he wrote

1936 - Brookwood Labor College, *Free Tom Mooney*, reading of labor play

1937 - Theodore Drieser, *An American Tragedy*, Hedgerow Players
- Edna St. Vincent Millay, *Aria Da Capo*, Hedgerow Players

1938 - *The Frodi*, Hedgerow Theater, Rose Valley, PA
- *A Moral Entertainment*, The Federal Theater Project
- Marc Blitzstein, *The Cradle Will Rock*, reading of labor play

The plays listed below were frequently recommended on syllabi and reading lists to students in English classes:

1921 - John Galsworthy, *Justice, Strife, The Silver Box, The Mob*
- George Bernard Shaw, *Man and Superman, Pygmalion, Major Barbara*

- Israel Zangwill, *The Melting Pot*
- Edward Sheldon, *The Boss, The Nigger*
- Gerhart Hauptman, *The Weavers*
1926 - Karl Kapek, R.U.R., *The World We Live In*
1927 - Henrik Ibsen, *The Doll's House, Enemy of the People, The Pillars of Society*
1934 - Eugene Brieux - *Maternity, Damaged Goods*
- John Golden - *Precedent*
- Eugene O'Neill - *Beyond the Horizon, The Hairy Ape*
- Elmer Rice - *The Adding Machine*
- Paul and Claire Sifton - *1931*
- Israel Zangwill, *The Melting Pot*
1935 - Albert Maltz, *The Black Pit*
- Clifford Odets, *Till the Day I Die, Waiting for Lefty*
- Paul Peters and George Sklar, *Stevedore*
- Elmer Rice, *Street Scene, We the People*
- Ernst Toller, *The Machine Wreckers, Man and the Masses*
- George Sklar and Albert Maltz, *Peace on Earth*
1937 - Paul Green, *In Abraham's Bosom*
- John Wesley, *They Shall Not Die*
1938 - Susan Glaspell, *Trifles*

The plays watched and read added to the rich discursive context that the workers drew on to create their own productions. What follows is the analysis of a workers' skit that illustrates well the rich intertextuality typical of summer school dramatic productions.

A Play of Heteroglossia: The Prelude to It's Unconstitutional

VOICES OFFSTAGE: We the people of the United States in order to form a more perfect union, establish justice, insure domestic tranquility, provide for the common defense, promote the general welfare, and secure the blessings of liberty to ourselves and our posterity, do ordain and establish the Constitution of the United States of America.

MALE VOICE:

The judicial power of the United States shall be vested in one Supreme Court. The judicial power shall extend to all cases, in law and equity, arising under the Constitution.

JUDGES:

The Constitution is the Supreme Law of the Land.

The Supreme Court has taken an oath to uphold the Constitution.

When an Act of Congress conflicts with the superior law, the Supreme Court cannot enforce it, but must declare it null and void.

VOICES OFFSTAGE: . . . all men are created equal . . . life . . . liberty . . . happiness.
 Whenever any form of government becomes destructive of these ends, it is the right of the people to alter or abolish it and institute new government, laying its foundations on such principles and organizing its powers in such form as to them shall seem most likely to effect their safety and happiness. . . . justice, tranquility, . . . blessings of liberty.

JUDGES: (Woven in with above speech of voices offstage.) When an Act of Congress conflicts with the superior law, the Supreme Court cannot enforce it, but must declare it null and void.

Clatter of girl's heels walking to work.

GIRL'S VOICE: Come on, Mamie, I can't wait all day.

MAMIE: I'm not going in.

VOICE: What's the matter, laid off?

MAMIE: Tough luck. See you later.

THE UNEMPLOYED

The scene is an employment office—one or two benches. Waitress enters and sits on bench. Office worker enters and sits opposite waitress.

WAITRESS: What's your racket?

OFFICE WORKER: Aw, just another of the unemployed. Office work,—in a bank I used to be. Yes, used to be.
 And then we merged with another bank. They had no place for me, so— (with a shrug)—

WAITRESS: Tough luck kid.
 I wrecked myself
 Waiting on tables
 For a dozen years
 Luggin' a tray
 Just couldn't take it
 Ten hours a day.

OFFICE WORKER: But the N.R.A.?

DEMOCRATS: We, the democrats, made the N.R.A.

G.O.P.: We, the republicans, are here to say: Boondoggling, waste.

SUPREME COURT: It's Unconstitutional!

WAITRESS: Yeah, the N.R.A.

Negro girl enters and sits down. Old woman enters shortly after and sits down beside her.

OLD WOMAN: How hot it is!

NEGRO: Do your feet ache?

WAITRESS: I'll bet they ache!

OLD WOMAN: Can't get back! Too old to work!

NEGRO: And I'm too black!

WAITRESS: Aw, don't take it—You've got the same right as ANYONE else. Why don't you raise hell about it?

NEGRO: Have you heard of the chain gang, or lynching, or Herndon?[47] We united
    in protest but they used an old, old, law on him,—insurrection they called it,
    My Lord! My Lord!

SUPREME COURT: The conviction stands.

OLD WOMAN: I've worked for years, seven dollars a week. Can't save a cent.

DEMOCRATS: But we've taken care of social security.

REPUBLICANS: Boondoggling, Waste!

OLD WOMAN: That's not for me
       There is a law that could help, you see
       But that would be

SUPREME COURT: Most unconstitutional.

Farmer's wife enters and sits.

High school student also enters.

FARMER'S WIFE: Will we have to wait long?
       I have children at home
       If you can call it home.

WAITRESS: Kids, oh?
       I like kids.

FARMER'S WIFE: But they'd better be dead
       Than grow in a sty.
       We did have a farm
       They could see the sky
       And speak to the sun
       And the earth was warm
       And the hay smelled nice
       Now their playmates are
       Cockroaches and lice.

WAITRESS: Kids
       Cockroaches
       Lice!
       My God! I feel sick!

HIGH SCHOOL STUDENT: But what about the A.A.A. [Agricultural Adjustment Ad-
    ministration]?

DEMOCRATS: T'was an awful wrench
       But after a while
       Came the A.A.A.
       And the sunshine of our smile

REPUBLICANS: Boondoggling, Waste

SUPREME COURT: It's unconstitutional.

College student enters with diploma in hand.

COLLEGE STUDENT (TO WAITRESS): Move over, sister.

W.P.A. worker enters.

DEMOCRATS: We love our youth
    We see their rights.
YOUTH: Six dollars a month
    To sit home nights.
W.P.A. WORKER: Six dollars a month
    That should have been ours;
    But there's plenty that went
    To the great War Powers!

Laundress enters as the youth says; "six."

LAUNDRESS: O, I'm one up
    Six bucks a week;
    I did get twelve
    I could get by.
WAITRESS: That's what you'd call
    A fifty-fifty cut.
YOUTH: But what about the minimum?
LAUNDRESS: A minimum, Huh!
    We'd scrub and sing
    For the minimum.
    A minimum, Huh!
    There's no such thing!
    Or haven't you heard
    Like everything else
SUPREME COURT: It's unconstitutional!

Coal miner's wife enters on the "unconstitutional."

WIFE: Unconstitutional?
    Guffey Act,[48] eh?
    My husband works, did work
    In a mine, but its unconstitutional
    Work, employment, coal to burn
    That is if you steal it
    It's unconstitutional
    What does it mean?
SUPREME COURT: When an Act of Congress conflicts with the superior law, the
    Supreme Count cannot enforce it but must declare it null and void.
UNEMPLOYED: We want so little, the N.R.A.
POLITICIANS: Interference with American rights.
SUPREME COURT: Unconstitutional.
UNEMPLOYED: Insurance, Child Labor Amendment
POLITICIANS: SHSSHH! That's dangerous (*aside*)
    Interference with American rights.
SUPREME COURT: Unconstitutional.

UNEMPLOYED: Minimum Wage Protection, Anti-Lynching, Youth Act, Housing
SUPREME COURT: Unconstitutional.
POLITICIANS: The natural forces of recovery will re-absorb them into industry. . .
    will absorb . . . will absorb
(VOICES OFFSTAGE): In order to form a more perfect union. . . .
    justice, tranquility, blessings of liberty. . . .
SUPREME COURT: Null and void . . . unconstitutional.
VOICES: . . . government becomes destructive of these ends . . . right of people. . . .
    nay, . . . duty of people, to alter, abolish it.
UNEMPLOYED: Let the corpses lie!
        New millions risen
        From school and shop
        From mine and soil
        Together reach
        Together toil.

        Let the corpses lie!
        Here, take my hand
        And in our grip
        There shall be power
        There shall be power
        To sense rebirth
        To know the hour.

Feminist dialogics, a gendered interpretation of Bakhtinian concepts such as "heteroglossia" and the "carnivalesque," is helpful in understanding how this skit resisted hegemonic discourse and generated empowered discursive subjectivities for the women workers. As will be illustrated below, there is a gendered dimension to many of the dialogic interactions in The Prelude. These interactions include those between "official" and "unofficial discourses," languages of black and white workers and the working class and the bourgeoisie. Elements of the carnivalesque can also be found in The Prelude. Indeed, the discursive appropriations and parody, textual embodiments, costuming (masquerade), music, and humor of the workers' stage mirror the potentially subversive activities of the carnival.[49]

The characters in The Prelude present a colorful gallery of the silenced. They portray women who are even today rarely accorded a public forum: miners' and farmers' wives, high school and college students, a waitress, an office worker, and elderly woman, an African-American "girl," a "laundress." All are unemployed as well, adding economic insult to social injury. Providing these marginalized women a public, discursive voice remains a noteworthy accomplishment in itself. More important though, in the context of the skit, the juxtaposition of their unofficial discourse of colloquial yet substantive and meaningful complaint with the more official, officious, and hegemonic language of government and its various representatives acts to relativize both discourses and thus enhance the status of the discourse of the unemployed. The official discourse was at the same time demystified by the workers as they began to understand and use it through the research, writing, and production of the play. While, for the most part, summer school student discourse presents the voice of worker protest and desire as male, The Prelude does express concerns typically of importance to women. The farmer's wife complains about the living conditions of her children, "they'd be better dead / than grow up in a sty." The waitress expresses sisterly sympathy at these complaints.

Gender is not designated for many of the roles in this script, and since few men were involved with the summer school, women more than likely played almost all parts. The variety of roles offered them an expanded array of subject positions as well as a greater awareness of the common problems of different kinds of workers. Through these roles, the actors often strengthened the voices of the oppressed, and when speaking as judges and Supreme Court justices they also experienced the powerful discourse of androcentric hegemony. Significantly, a "Male Voice" is called for in the stage directions to speak the masterful discourse of Constitutional law. In terms of Bakhtinian theory, the centripetal discursive force of this conservative voice is offset by the centrifugal refrain of the collective, feminine "Voices Off Stage" who appropriate the words of the Constitution and the Declaration of Independence.[50] As the "Voices" proclaim the urgency of the country's most neglected ideals, "justice, tranquility . . . blessings of liberty," the feminized reciting acquires an ironic and humorous tone while testimony from the unemployed reveals how hollow these hallowed words have become, perhaps especially to women. By the end of the skit and after hearing from the previously marginalized, the very meaning of the Declaration of Independence has been transformed, and the words "duty of the people, to alter, abolish it" chanted by the "Voices" justifies revolutionary action.

Audience and actors alike were probably pleasantly surprised to find themselves ridiculing powerful government figures in this skit. In both becoming and mocking Republicans, Democrats, politicians, and judges, spectators and actors began to see these groups from a more familiarized yet paradoxically critical (estranged) perspective that domesticates previously sanctified discourse and power structures. This dual experience of familiarization and estrangement experienced by both the actors and audience is again "carnivalesque" in nature.[51] Wearing costumes of the "other," the rich and the powerful, is a defiant, if not empowering, aspect of traditional carnival, and adorning the robe of a justice in The Prelude has the same effect.

The complex interplay of race, class, and gender in the short sequence containing the "negro girl" is a more problematic discursive manoeuvre. The passage begins with references to the bodily oppression experienced by members of the working class, both black and white, male and female. The "old woman" complains of the heat, the "negro" inquires about aching feet. The one protests that she is "too old to work," the other that she is "too black." Both are trapped in bodies that the prevailing powers deem unacceptable. The "waitress" reveals a triple blindness of class, race, and gender in her declaration to the African American that "You've got the same right as ANYONE else. Why don't you raise hell about it?" Ironically, as a white working-class woman, the waitress herself doesn't have the same rights as her male counterpart and certainly not as the male bourgeois "ANYONE" she seems to be referring to. She is also blind to the racist social structures and laws that oppress African Americans. Her ignorance is partially allayed by the "negro girl's" revelation about what can happen to African Americans when they protest. She cites ways the white racist majority has denied blacks their Constitutional rights, through the chain gang, lynching, and misuse of judicial power. As is typically the case with summer school discourse, the class perspective is thus privileged over that of gender and race. Differences among workers are ignored in favor of a centripetal, white, androcentric voice of working-class protest. Or perhaps it is the unifying experience of bodily oppression endured by all workers and referred to at the beginning of this sequence rather than the power of androcentric rhetoric that led working women to privilege class over issues of gender and race in this instance.

The skit quite successfully defuses a common bourgeois strategy for controlling the working class, that is pitting worker against worker for an ever decreasing wage. For example, the WPA worker complains that the meager "six dollars a month" given to the high school student "should have been ours." Then the laundress exclaims, "I'm one up," since she is making "six bucks a week"—a sharp decline, however, from her previous twelve. This antiworker discourse that mirrors the competitive individualist rhetoric of the patriarchal bourgeoisie is subverted in several ways. For one thing, the WPA worker also informs his (?) listeners that plenty of money "went / to the great War Powers!" and not to the Americans who needed it, thus directing workers' anger away from each other. Then the unemployed begin to voice together a series of worker demands: the NRA, a Child Labor Amendment, a minimum wage, antilynching legislation. By the end of the skit, these individual complaints are subsumed in the collective demands of the "unemployed," a voice stronger and united.

Workers Enter the Critical Conversation

Although providing an analysis of a play in contemporary critical terms may hopefully yield insights of interest to today's scholars, in terms of historiography, it is also important to see how the creators of this piece may have evaluated it or may have been responding to critical voices of the age in producing it. Of course, in its heyday, workers' theater was rife with debates over aesthetic and political issues such as: What should be the ultimate purpose of workers' theater; or What was the most useful theatrical style, expressivist or socialist realist? Students at the summer school debated these same issues. Here is the way student Nina Lamousen framed critical questions for her worker classmates in the 1934 issue of *Shop and School*.

What Do You Think?

Do we go to the theater with the expectation of being entertained, of being taken into the world of make-believe, of being able to forget for a few hours the drabness of life; to be shown a picture of a better future, to be given new ideas, to be moved to a better way of living?

What do we expect from a workers' theater? Should it be a wailing wall where they go over their sufferings and misery in a dramatic, highly intensified form? What is the psychological effect of it?

Should a worker be shown the jerky movements of machines? But is it not the mechanization that he dreads, his whole body being tense in protest? Jerky movements of impressionistic dances—convulsions of decadence—do they appeal to him who stepped not so long ago out of the realm of folklore and round dances?

Or would a worker better enjoy rhythmic movements and music that flows in harmonious cadence, which straightens out the furrows of the brow, untangles and eases the nerves strung and overtaxed in mechanical speed-up?

The very name "workers' theater" suggests a certain kind of play, suggests propaganda to propagate ideas, to spread them. What is the chance to attract the general public? Interested workers will come, but they already know this side of life. What of the general public that should be there?

How should we attract them? Should we present our ideas in a crude, though true-to-life picture, or should we select the elegant setting of black and pink and lavender a la *Aria da Capo* even if Tragikos is there, ever present?

Or is the satire better? It gives us a feeling of superiority, but gives to the audience a chance to laugh, though they are laughing at their own faults. Laughter takes out the sting of antagonism. Would the general public accept it?

What is the better way? What do you think?[52]

The women workers' possible replies to Lamousen's questions are suggested in their summer school productions. There is no doubt that the workers wanted to be entertained at the theater, especially to laugh. Their pieces were also rhetorical and aimed at prompting the spectators—in the case of the summer school theater, these were mainly students and faculty—to participate in the workers' cause by joining unions and becoming active in them; the pieces were also educational in that they presented information crucial to workers' understanding of political and economic issues. Finally, the pieces were oppositional in that they presented a workers' discourse to counterconservative ideology. The summer school theater was not generally a "wailing wall," although grievances and hardships were certainly voiced. The resulting psychological effect was energizing, not despairing. Although the scenic devices were simple and adaptable, their descriptions do not suggest crudeness, on the one hand, or elegance, on the other, but basic, minimal use of available materials to create a strong scenic image. Satire and parody were preferred modes of discourse, again giving both the workers and any bourgeois audience members a chance to laugh, although in the case of the bourgeoisie, "they [would be] laughing at their own faults," while the workers would experience "a feeling of superiority." This high level of emotional satisfaction was also an important requirement of summer school theater and indicates its function as a discourse of desire for the women workers.

The Legacy of Dramatic Discourse

Students and faculty at the Bryn Mawr Summer School thus built a heteroglossic drama program that included a great variety of discursive experiences promoting student development and social change. In fact, they seemed to have practiced sixty years ago what Clar Doyle argues for in his recent book aimed at today's drama educators. Sounding remarkably like faculty and students at the summer school in his recognition of dramatics as a tool for social justice, he writes that "a critical drama should help students examine their own life experiences through the reflective analysis of role playing and improvisation. . . . Drama must become, in the process of schooling, a movement toward a consciousness of what might be. In so doing, drama can aid in bringing about needed social changes that through critical consciousness could result in a freer human development."[53] It can indeed be argued that the summer school theater accomplished these goals, as well as those of building a workers' culture and more powerful subjectivities for the women workers. Moreover, the social legislation that improved workers' lives in the 1930s was fought for and won because workers came to believe in their own vision and collective power. In helping to instill this belief in more than 1,600 working women over the years from 1921 to 1938, the Bryn Mawr Summer School contributed to a "freer" human development.

ten Italian-American Cookbooks

Authenticity and the Market

Stephanie Almagno, Nedra Reynolds, and John Trimbur

For anthropologists like Claude Levi-Strauss, the daily practices of cooking and eating are more than biological necessities. These practices are also invested with social meaning and cultural value. According to Levi-Strauss, "the cooking of a society is a language in which it unconsciously translates its structure —or else resigns itself, still unconsciously, to revealing its contradictions."[1] For Levi-Strauss, a Promethean myth about the theft, control, and application of fire provides a mediating link to resolve, rhetorically if not actually, the contradictions between humans and animals, culture and nature, life and death, the cooked and the raw. To think of cooking as a language, however, tends to focus on its cognitive status—the totem, as Levi-Strauss says, "is good to think as well as to eat"[2]—and to neglect how cooking also articulates material practices. The control and application of fire result in cooking practices that mediate not only a scheme of conceptual polarities but also the dependence of society on its primary food producers by creating a cuisine and instituting a practice of eating.

Throughout much of human history, food production and food preparation are stitched together as continuous practices that coordinate the rhythms of work with seasonal cycles and communal rituals of solidarity and mutual aid. As human societies, however, elaborate divisions of labor by which individuals and groups are increasingly removed from direct engagement with the production of food—whether by hunting and gathering, pastoralism, or farming— the cultural practices of food preparation and consumption diversify, taking on new meanings and values. In commercial cultures, trade creates exotic distance between cooking ingredients and their places of production, amplifying the use of food as an available means of conspicuous consumption to mark class and status differences. Such market-based cuisines loosen foodstuff from the local relations of primary producers and consumers, inserting middlemen and elongating the circuits of distribution and exchange. The incorporation of indigenous ingredients and cuisines into the "universal market" makes food preparation appear to have achieved autonomy from food production. In the global market, the cuisine becomes increasingly cosmopolitan, absorbing and commodifying local ethnic traditions, offering consumers dizzying possibilities of choice, and multiplying the symbolic exchange value of food and the cultural messages its preparation conveys.

Mary Douglas says that "if food is to be treated as a code, the message it encodes will be found in the pattern of social relationships being expressed. The message is about different degrees of hierarchy, inclusion and exclusion, boundaries and translations across boundaries."[3] The message that a market-based cuisine encodes can be seen in a number of cultural hierarchies that organize the production and consumption of food. Gourmet food and the haute cuisine of five-star restaurants, for example, have traditionally been the province of male chefs, whose specialized practices elevate food preparation to the status of an art and dining to a habitus of knowing and symbolically significant consumption. On the other hand, the everyday preparation of food in the domestic household belongs largely to female providers, a part of the larger reproduction of labor power that the family enacts as one of its primary functions. Moreover as Pierre Bourdieu notes, food preparation enacts social distinctions along class lines. According to Bourdieu, the middle and upper-middle classes emulate aristocratic tastes that regard dining as an aestheticized activity, with significant value invested in the visual presentation of food, the use of exotic and expensive ingredients, and difficult cooking techniques. For the working classes, though, dining is a worldly activity that focuses on the body, with value invested in the volume and hardiness of food rather than its aesthetics.[4]

Research on food and foodways typically represents the cultural practices of cooking and eating as symbols and performances of group identity, treating issues such as the boundary definitions of a group, persistence and change in culinary habits, the transportability of ethnicity across regions, and the expansion of culinary affinity groups. Scholars from a variety of fields—folklore, American studies, ethnography, nutrition, women's studies, public health, history, and sociology—see food as "a nexus for the convergence of traditional disciplinary methods and insights,"[5] to unlock the cultural meanings of food preparation and consumption. One of the most interesting developments in this line of research has been the recuperation of the cookbook as a telling site of women's experience.

Cookbooks, of course, have long been an indispensable aid to kitchen management, but only recently have feminist researchers such as Susan Leonardi explored the relationship of "the giving of a recipe" to reading and writing—

as communicative acts of exchange. Leonardi describes the 1931 edition of *The Joy of Cooking* as the literary production of "embedded discourses," which codify recipe sharing as a practice uniting women across social classes: "The establishment of a lively narrator with a circle of enthusiastic and helpful friends reproduces the social context of recipe sharing—a loose community of women that crosses the social barriers of class, race, and generation. Many women can attest to the usefulness and importance of this discourse: mothers and daughters—even those who don't get along well otherwise—old friends who now have little in common, mistresses and their 'help,' lawyers and their secretaries—all can participate in this almost prototypical feminine activity."[6] Anne Goldman, however, questions whether recipe sharing, as Leonardi sees it, is always so reciprocal. Goldman asks, "When does recipe sharing . . . become recipe borrowing, with only a coerced 'consent' from the domestic 'help?'"[7] Goldman wants to read cookbooks not so much as instances of a "prototypical feminine activity" but instead as a "culturally contingent" form of writing that ranges from the "culture plunder" of global food traditions by First World cookbook authors to "autoethnographic" accounts of women's "conscious labor" reproducing ethnic and communal traditions through food preparation. For Goldman, the question of whether a cookbook "embodies" or "obliterates" a culture depends on the particular relation of forces at work in its production, circulation, and reception.

In this chapter, we want to look at three recent (and commercially successful) Italian-American cookbooks as problems of popular literacy. The cookbooks we will be considering—Helen Barolini's *Festa*, Nancy Verde Barr's *We Called It Macaroni*, and Francesca Romina's *Mangia, Little Italy!*—can be read, from Goldman's perspective, as autoethnographies that express a local cuisine and culture. They are richly detailed and illustrated accounts of food preparation by New World Italians that give voice to traditional kitchen discourse and the oral transmission of cooking lore from mother to daughter. By the same token, though, following Leonardi, we could read the Italian-American cookbooks as cross-class recipe sharing—with *Festa, We Called It Macaroni*, and *Mangia, Little Italy!* translating the everyday culinary practices of Italian-American cooks into the vernacular of mass culture through the same topoi of recipe sharing from mother to daughter that Irma Rombauer uses in *The Joy of Cooking*.

In fact, the functions Goldman and Leonardi ascribe to cookbooks may not be opposed so much as they point to contradictory aspects of Italian-American cookbooks. Italian-American cookbooks such as *Festa, We Called It Macaroni*, and *Mangia, Little Italy!* are simultaneously recollections and celebrations of the foodways of a particular ethnic-class community and a commodification of ethnicity as an object of consumption in the American metropolis. In this sense,

Italian-American cookbooks pose the problem of the "popular" as a cultural and economic process that appropriates elements from working-class and subordinate cultures in order to rework them as respectable objects in a cosmopolitan culture of consumption.

A Short History of the American Cookbook

The earliest cookbooks in the English-speaking New World appeared in the eighteenth century. As early as 1742, The Compleat Housewife by Eliza Smith, published fifteen years earlier in England, was brought to North America and published by William Parks's printing house in Williamsburg, Virginia. An immediate best-seller, The Compleat Housewife was followed by other English cookbooks, such as Housekeeper's Companion by Hannah Glasse, The Frugal Housewife by Susannah Carter, and The New Art of Cookery, According to Present Practice by Richard Briggs.

While these cookbooks sold well, none offered instruction for preparing foods native to North America. What is commonly considered the "first truly American cookbook,"[8] Amelia Simmons's American Cookery was published in 1796, with recipes for such indigenous American fare as spruce beer, pumpkin pie, cranberry sauce, and roasted wild turkey. Simmons's cookbook began a tradition of American cookbooks adapted to local conditions and ingredients. In the 1800s, cookbooks such as The Virginia Housewife by Mary Randolph, The Practice of Cookery, Adapted to the Business of Everyday Life by Mrs. Delgairns, The American Frugal Housewife by Lydia Child, and Miss Beecher's Domestic Receipt Book by Catherine Beecher, sister to Harriet Beecher Stowe, recorded an American cuisine suited to the American kitchen.

The titles of these popular eighteenth- and nineteenth-century cookbooks indicate the understanding in the antebellum era that to cook was to run a domestic economy. Simmons says that American Cookery is "calculated for the improvement of the rising generation of Females in America,"[9] and the cookbook contains extensive advice about domestic matters, as wells as recipes. In the pre-Victorian family, housewives performed essential economic work managing the household, growing food, and keeping domestic animals. Simmons's detailed directions on how to preserve butter in the summer, for example, reveals the work entailed in dealing with local producers: "To have sweet butter in dog days and thro' the vegetable seasons, send stone pots to honest, neat, and trusty dairy people, and procure it pack'd down in May, and let them be brought in in the night, or cool rainy morning, covered with a clean cloth wet in cold water, and partake of no heat from the horse, and set pots in the coldest part of your cellar or in the ice house." In addition, Simmons appears particularly alert to the effect of overheated horses on the quality of food. She warns: "Veal bro't to market in panniers or in carriages is to be preferred to that bro't in bags, and flouncing on a sweaty horse." In *American Cookery*, Simmons's housewife is a vigilant figure, keeping a close eye on food suppliers and guarding the family's resources. In the fall when apples ripen, a diligent housewife must be prepared to defend the household's private property—"to preserve the orchard from the intrusion of boys &c. which is too common in America."[10]

Cookbooks defined and codified what it meant to be a housewife, elaborating rules of etiquette and decorum and offering advice on everything from nutrition and herbal remedies to child-rearing and the frugal management of the home. Frugality was perhaps the key term in the domestic economy of the middling classes, located between the extremes of wealth and poverty in the colonial and early national periods. Frugality did not mean simply saving money by getting the best deals at the market, as its contemporary uses might suggest. In the pre-Victorian family, housewives were producers as much as consumers, actively engaged in managing the relation of the household economy to the local market. By producing subsistence foods, housewives maintained a measure of autonomy from the market. Frugality meant in part staying out of debt by producing your own food and selling the surplus in the cash economy. Simmons, for example, advocates the domestication of wild rabbits, arguing that the "cultivation of rabbits would be profitable in America if the best methods were pursued—they are a very prolific and profitable animal."[11]

The earliest American cookbooks recommended frugality and the "profitable" production and use of American food sources. By the middle of the nineteenth century, however, two other types of cookbook had begun to appear. One is the compiled cookbook, a collection of recipes put together for fund-raising purposes.[12] The first compiled cookbooks appeared during the Civil War. Ladies Aid Societies gathered recipes in collections to sell at fund-raising bazaars for war relief, instituting a longstanding tradition that links domestic recipes to women's public charitable work. By the end of the nineteenth century, well over two thousand titles had been published by charitable organizations such as the Women's Poultry Club, the Auxiliary Society of the Hebrew Sheltering Guardian Society, and the New York Orphan Asylum.

The second type is the ethnic cookbook. The earliest of these, according to William Woys Weaver, is *Die Geschickte Hausfrau*, a thirty-eight-page collection of Pennsylvania-German cookery, published in 1848.[13] Interestingly, Weaver disqualifies two earlier cookbooks, Madame Utrecht-Friedl's *La Petite Cuisiniere Habile*, published in New Orleans in 1840, and *Novissimo Arte de Cochina*, published in Philadelphia in 1845, as "elite" cookbooks that had appeared earlier in Paris and Mexico. By Weaver's account, an "ethnic" cookbook, as opposed to an "elite" one, records the everyday cookery of a folk. This distinction, however, is difficult to sustain. The fact of the matter, as Weaver admits, is that *Die Geschickle Hausfrau* combined recipes from nineteenth-century Pennsylvania-German oral tradition with new foods from Anglo-American cookbooks. From its inception, the "ethnic" cookbook was not the direct and authentic expression of folk culture that could be contrasted to elite forms but rather the result of hybrid practices that drew on contemporary print as well as traditional oral sources.

The Formation of Italian-American Cookery

In the 1999–2000 *Subject Guide to Books in Print*, there are nearly 6,000 listings under the heading "cookery," and over 500 of these are titles appearing for the first time. The categories include every state and region in the United States and probably every ethnic, racial, and religious group represented in the population, from Amish to Indonesian to Yugoslavian. Consumers can buy 74 cookbooks on Florida cookery, 18 on cooking with beer and 5 with marine algae, 148 Jewish cookbooks, 8 Norwegian, 45 Thai, and 6 books on cooking for the physically handicapped. The most popular sellers of international cuisine, numbering in the hundreds of cookbooks currently in print, are Chinese, French, and Italian. Of these, Italian has the largest number of entries with 376.

These numbers represent a remarkable reevaluation of what Americans cook, as well as what they eat when they go out. By contrast, virtually no recipes for foreign dishes of any kind turn up in a survey of *Good Housekeeping* magazine in 1890, and in 1913 "only ten out of 1200 recipes in the popular *Around the World Cookbook* could be considered Italian by even a generous-minded reader."[14] Over the span of the twentieth century, Italian cookery has come to dominate the huge market for ethnic food in the United States. By the late 1980s, as *Advertising Age* reports: "Italian food . . . remains the most popular ethnic food in America. Figures say that in 1984, 13.5% of the American population ate Italian food at home and 8.8% ate it away from home, as compared to 1973 figures of 4.5% in home and .8% away. In the late 1980s retail sales of Italian foods topped $1.6 billion."[15]

An irony of the apparent success of Italian food in the American culinary market is the fact that it is based not only on the preservation of Old World styles of cooking but also on the invention of a distinctly New World Italian-American cuisine. The Italian immigrants who came to the United States in the 1890s and early 1900s did not bring with them what might properly speaking be called Italian food. Instead, they brought the cooking of a region, a particular *paese*. The two largest regional groups of immigrants—from Campania (the province around Naples) and Sicily—shared such staple ingredients as tomatoes, onions, garlic, cheese, and olive oil with others from the southern provinces Calabria and Abruzzi, while northerners continued to cook the cornmeal staple polenta and to use lard or butter rather than oil.

Since first-generation immigrants tended to live in neighborhoods with people from their region of Italy, the concentration of southern Italians in American cities created a new market for imported and domestic foodstuffs and a new niche for food suppliers of all sorts—grocers, butchers, bakers, fish mongers, and so on. Italian immigrants started gardens to produce the fruit, vegetables, and spices that would grow in New World climates. The adjustment of food habits to the availability and expense of ingredients influenced decisively what we now call "Italian food." A hybrid of cooking practices from the southern regions adapted to growing conditions and market realities in the American metropolis, Italian cuisine as we commonly know it was born not in Italy but in the Little Italies of the New World.

Historian Harvey Levenstein argues that Italians succeeded in resisting "the forces of assimilation" by "adapting their food habits to the American environment, creating a cuisine that was distinctive enough to retain old country flavors yet attractive enough to turn the tables, as it were, and influence the tastes of the host country." For Levenstein, Italians "thus became one of the few ethnic groups in the United States who retained and indeed cultivated distinctively non-Anglo-Saxon modes of cooking and eating through the second and even the third generations after immigration."[16] In turn, through a "kind of cultural compromise," by the 1920s food processing companies such as Franco-American, Heinz, Kraft, and Campbell were mass producing canned and packaged Americanized Italian food. During the Great Depression, macaroni and cheese and spaghetti and meatballs became meatless and meat-stretching staples in middle- and working-class households in the host country, promoted by social workers, nutritionists, and food writers as economical, healthful, and easy to prepare.

As Levenstein notes, this dual success of Italian-American food—in terms both of preserving its "Italianness" and of influencing mainstream American cooking—depended on reversing the moral evaluation at the turn of the century that represented Italian food as unhealthy, unsanitary, and disorderly. With the waves of immigration from eastern and southern Europe between 1890 and 1920, Old World foodways figured in social workers' and settlement house activists' discourse as one of the key words of cultural assimilation. Upper-class philanthropists and middle-class reformers concerned with the living conditions of recent immigrants in the urban slums of the late nineteenth and early twentieth centuries began to teach "household economics" as a means of self-improvement and Americanization. In 1904 Robert Woods, head of South End House, the most important settlement house among Boston's Italians, attributed the apparently rising death rates of New England Italians to the move from an outdoor life in a sunny climate to life in slum tenements and "their over-stimulating and innutritious diet"—"precisely the opposite sort of feeding," Woods says, "from that demanded by our exhilarating and taxing atmospheric conditions." For this reason, changing the Italian diet was for Woods "the chief step in bringing about the adaptation of the Italian type of life to America."[17]

Woods's sentiments were widely shared in the period before World War I. Teaching immigrants to cook in the American style became a major focus of settlement house workers and reformers such as Jane Addams and Florence Kelly. Faced with the resistance of Italian women to American-style cooking, Addams advocated public school cooking classes as a means of Americanization—to side step the mothers by making their children into agents of assimiliation. As Addams explains, an Italian girl trained to cook American foods in school can "help her mother to connect the entire family with American food and household habits."[18]

Some reformers took their message directly to the streets. In 1912 the New York Association for Improving the Condition of the Poor put together an exhibit in an Italian area of lower Manhattan to show residents the deficiencies in their diet and to present "an Americanized dietary with the deficiencies corrected."[19] One of the central notions of the exhibit, erroneous but standard for its time, was the belief that foods lost nutritional value when they were mixed together during cooking. Throughout the country, social workers, settlement house workers, home demonstration agents, and other middle-class reformers articulated a politics of cooking in the name of a genteel WASP cuisine that presented its food—meat, vegetables, and starches—on a grid, according to a neatly separated and clearly delineated logic that Foucault would have appreciated. In turn, such micro-technologies of power constructed out of Italian cookery's mix of flavors and ingredients a culinary "other" that is not only unsanitary and "innutritious" but also disorderly, unregulated by the categorical divisions in mainstream food preparation and presentation.

Other reformers tried to change shopping practices, as well as dietary habits. Leaflets distributed by the Boston Women's Municipal League warned about the lack of sanitation in the street markets and small stores. The New York Association for Improving the Condition of the Poor circulated a leaflet in Italian warning that the produce purchased from street vendors and open-air stalls was likely to be germ-infested. In 1911 Eva White, head of Boston's Peabody House, lamented, "No matter what inducements the larger stores of the city offer, [Italians] will trade with none but their own people."[20] White's apparent dismay that Italian immigrants refused to shop in the emerging supermarkets of the North American metropolis, to buy the packaged goods and processed foods produced and distributed by the emergent corporations, is revealing, for what White casts as the clannishness of Italians not only resists Waspish ways of shopping and preparing food but also subverts in crucial respects the economic dependence of recent immigrants on waged labor and the universal market.

One of the problems facing American capitalism at the turn of the century was to integrate immigrants into the routines of factory work, breaking them of what Antonio Gramsci calls the "bad habits" of nonindustrial life and promoting the "good habits" of industrial discipline. As John Clarke points out, while this attempted transformation involved most visibly correcting such bad work habits as "irregularity, poor time keeping, 'Blue Mondays,' holidays taken according to the customs of the 'old country,' and so on," the problem of Americanizing an immigrant work force extended "into forms of sociability, religion, politics, patterns of domestic economy, sexual divisions of labour, child socialization and linguistic communities."[21] From this perspective, the struggle between New World Italians and Americanizing reformers over food and shopping involves a very real attempt on the part of immigrant Italians to maintain control over their domestic economies and to resist their integration into the corporate structures of the supermarkets and chain stores.

New World Italians devised various means to maintain a degree of local autonomy from dependence on wage labor and the commodities of the national market. These included subsistence production, such as fruit and vegetable gardening, fishing, winemaking, and raising animals, as well as developing an ethnic petite bourgeoisie of green grocers, butchers, bakers, and dry goods merchants to produce, import, and trade foodstuffs geared to Italian households. Such domestic and local economies, embedded in family and neighborhood networks, provided Italian immigrants with a measure of independence. They also virtually guaranteed, as we have seen, conflicts with state power in such arenas as schooling, family life, public hygiene, and home economics. By seeking to subjugate the popular knowledges of Italian immigrants—replacing traditional skills, investing authority in the expertise of social workers and nutritionists instead, building trust in institutions such as the schools, settlement houses, and food store chains—public officials and middle-class reformers sought to integrate Italian immigrants' ways of life into the state and the market. The ethnic class culture of New World Italians, in contrast, consisted of accommodations, evasions, hedges, subversions, and outright resistance to the relations of identification and dependence offered by mainstream institutions. As we will see in the next section, the Italian-American strategies of local subsistence, as they are played out in families and neighborhoods, are in part what make recent Italian-American cookbooks such *as Festa, We Called It Macaroni,* and *Mangia, Little Italy!* so popular—because they suggest a way of life that holds on to some local autonomy in the face of a relentless universal market.

Cookbooks as Memoirs: Authenticity and Marketability

Helen Barolini, Nancy Verde Barr, and Francesca Romina have written their cookbooks as celebrations of Italian-American culture a generation or two in the past, when the old timers were settling Little Italy in New York City, the North End in Boston, and Federal Hill in Providence, Rhode Island. Romina calls *Mangia, Little Italy!* a cookbook-memoir, and the recipes are interspersed among family photographs and stories of her ancestors: "Grandma Josephine's Arrival in America," "Grandma's New Life in Little Italy," and "Great Aunt Conchetta Jilts a Suitor."[22] By the same token, Barr dedicates *We Called It Macaroni* to the culture heroes and heroines, the "first Italian-Americans who knew that food meant so much more than eating,"[23] and includes old photos of store fronts, street scenes, and neighborhood life, as well as "Memories" from Italian-Americans in Providence. Helen Barolini's *Festa* is subtitled *Recipes and Recollections of Italian Holidays* and, unlike the other two, abandons the conventional cookbook categories (Appetizers, Soup, Pasta, Main Courses, Vegetables, Bread, and Sweets) to arrange the recipes chronologically, according to a ritual calendar of holidays and festivals.

Barolini draws the connection between food and memory that informs all three books: "*Mangiando, ricordo* [While eating, I remember]. My memory seems more and more tied to the table, to a full table of good food and festivity, to the place of food and ritual and celebration in life. . . . Food is the medium of my remembrances." The task each writer sets herself is to write down what has before only been passed down orally, to get a record before memory fails. The function of the cookbooks is thereby in part custodial and archival. As Barolini says, when her non-Italian son-in-law wondered aloud at Christmas Eve about the tradition of the seven fish courses, "what gave me pause was my daughter" when she began to "call into doubt the tradition of the seven fishes": "The seven fish dishes of Christmas Eve? Good Lord, even if everything else goes by the board, that is one occasion that is solemn in any Italian household. That's when it occurred to me that these menus and memories should be set down or else, indeed, they would first be doubted and then lost for good."[24] In this regard, the three cookbooks begin at a moment of crisis, and their exigence is to avert a tragic doubt and forgetting, to perform what Barr calls a "modern restoration of what might otherwise have been lost."[25]

Establishing this sense of urgency—warranted in Barolini's case by her maternal responsibilities toward her doubting daughter—lends legitimacy to what could be seen otherwise as violating tradition by recording knowledges that are oral and practical rather than literate in character. As Joe De Giulio, Jr. says, "when my mother was cooking, she never used recipes. She knew what she was doing. She didn't look in a box or at index cards. Everything came out of her memory, out of her mind, out of her feel and touch." This idea of cooking by memory and feeling instead of by written recipes is reinforced by Americo Rossi, "They never wrote anything down. They cooked by feeling a little bit of this and a little of that."[26]

It is out of character, moreover, for Italian-American women to write at all. The photographs of signs, brand names, storefronts, trademarks, and restaurants that give We Called It Macaroni its documentary look are the external public record of Italian-American foodways, in much the same way photo albums, legal documents (birth certificates, marriage licenses, death registers), and church records of baptisms and confirmations are the external public record of the otherwise unwritten domestic experience of Italian-American women. In The Dream Book: An Anthology of Writings by Italian American Women, Helen Barolini considers why Italian-American women have not recorded their domestic or personal experience: "This is the paradox: Italian American women are at the core of their families and they are the ones who have most subordinated themselves to the well-being of the total entity Family above self. But, being at the heart of things, it is they who . . . are best suited to make literary use of material implicit in family struggles. What provides the thematic material is, ironically, the greatest obstacle to the writing." Italian-American women, Barolini continues, are rarely diarists or journal keepers. Their introspection is largely limited to the "condoned relief of the confessional, in which the male figure exonerates and blesses them."[27] To write these cookbooks, then, would seem to involve what might be considered from one perspective an untoward and unsanctioned act of going public with private domestic matters (Romina's Mangia, Little Italy!, after all, is subtitled Secrets from a Sicilian Family Kitchen) and putting the unwritten into print. At the same time, the collection and recording of recipes can be seen as an act of self-effacement, in which the cookbook writer is simply a vehicle for a threatened tradition that requires a written form if it is to survive.

This paradox, in turn, is transferred to readers: are we actually being brought into the family ("Now everyone can have a Sicilian grandmother!" the back cover of Mangia, Little Italy! exclaims), or are we voyeurs to a spectacular commodification of ethnicity? Readers may recall that this is in many respects the dilemma of cookbooks with which we began (and one that points to the dilemmas of popular literacy more generally): Are these cookbooks an "authen-

tic" account of Italian-American cookery and ways of life, or are they appropriations by the publishing industry that amount to niche marketing of the exotic in a cosmopolitan consumer culture that is hungry for novelty? This is a
difficult—and perhaps unanswerable—question, at least to the extent that it
depends on such polarized terms of inquiry. The problem of whether we as
readers are entitled to feel that we are confidantes to an intimate and reciprocal exchange of recipes or must instead regard ourselves as at best connoisseurs
acquiring new knowledge to add to the metropolitan fund of information hinges
on our understanding of the rhetoric of authenticity and its relation to the
market.

Any cookbook, by the nature of the genre, is a guide that enacts a kind of
pedagogy about food preparation and the operation of the domestic economy.
From Amelia Simmons's eighteenth-century frugal housewife to Irma Rombauer's mid- twentieth-century "canny mother"[28] in The Joy of Cooking or the late-
twentieth-century sophisticates of the "nouvelle cuisine," cooking has always
involved an apparently inevitable idealization of the kitchen as a workplace of
self-improvement that transmits cultural knowledge between generations. Festa,
We Called It Macaroni, and Mangia, Little Italy! are no exceptions. What distinguishes
them, though, from mainstream cookbooks is a nostalgia for the past and how
the old-timers did it that suffuses their pages with an elegiac glow.

In many respects, the three cookbooks call up the aura of "something I
think is missing these days," as Donna Scarletti Rizzo puts it in We Called It
Macaroni: the family gatherings, the neighborhoods where everyone knows each
other, shopping from local merchants, growing your own herbs and vegetables,
canning in the fall, and making everything from scratch. "It seems a shame,"
Joe De Giulio, Jr. says, "that in the society we live in today everything is quick,
everything is fast . . . so push-buttoned, so microwave." Along similar lines,
Irma Pacifico Verde says, "Your social life used to be centered around the table.
Now they don't do that. They just eat and run." At the emotional center of these
cookbooks are profound feelings of regret about modern times and what has
been lost: "The neighborhood was one big family, every family was yours. There
was no such thing as locks on doors, everybody socialized with each other,
everybody borrowed from each other, everybody paid back what they borrowed."[29]

This sense of what Raymond Williams calls a "knowable community" has
been taken up recently by advocates of communitarianism and family values.
And, in certain ways at least, the Italian-American cookbooks would seem to fit
in neatly with their conservative agendas. The patriarchal arrangements are
manifest in many of the "Memories" in We Called It Macaroni: "When I was a
child, my father would get home kind of late—eight o'clock during the week.

I couldn't have supper without my father. We all had to wait and have supper with my father. It was important to sit there at that dinner table and talk. Any problems that I had in school and so on would come up at the dinner table. Even though my father worked very many hours, it was that time that we had together." In addition, the passage of time spent eating together is extended and ritualized: "A meal to my parents was very important. It was marvelous. We would be an hour, hour and a half at the table. Just sitting there and not rushing anything." This vision of family meals and families sticking together has, of course, turned into one of the dominant representations of Italian-American life, from the *Godfather* trilogy to the three cookbooks that concern us here. "Another thing that was so marvelous was that you visited your aunts whether you wanted to or not. Holidays, you went down, wished them a happy holiday. Families were very close."[30]

The point that must be made here is that while the ethnic class culture of New World Italians, as memorialized in the cookbooks, did indeed rest on "close" family values that are patriarchal ("When you're married you please your husband. Right? So I learned to cook more my mother-in-law's way than my mother's"[31]), these are by no means the family values of the suburban nuclear family. Family dinners are not matters of "quality time" seized from two-career parents' work schedules and their children's equally frenetic schedules of school activities, soccer practice, and community service. Instead, the popular appeal of Italian-American cookbooks rests on a utopian vision of independence from the mainstream institutions of a corporate and bureaucratic society.

The familiar relations of family and neighborhood provided the underpinnings of a way of life that enabled Italian immigrants to hold on to at least a measure of autonomy from waged labor, the state, and the market. The "Memories" in *We Called It Macaroni* repeatedly mention the types of food the New World Italians produced to feed families and to sell for cash: the herb pots kept on tenement window sills, the gardens, preserving tomatoes, making wine, fishing. But unlike the nineteenth-century frugal housewife, the New World Italians relied on more than just the household to preserve their relative autonomy. For example, mutual aid societies of *paesani* from the various villages and regions of Italy provided financial assistance in times of death or unemployment and kept local customs alive. And, as Barr notes, in some instances neighbors revived the precapitalist commons: "There was a well-known family who had a lot of property and people would go there and make a garden. A lot of the people from my parents' area who lived in apartments without land would go there to garden."[32]

There is no doubt in our minds that the publishing companies that produced these cookbooks—Harcourt, Knopf, and Chronicle Books—shrewdly per-

ceived a market niche for "authentic" Italian-American cookery, warranted by
the kind of historical and ethnographic detail we have been drawing on in this
chapter. At the same time, we cannot help thinking that the popularity of the
three cookbooks depends, in at least some degree, on the way *Festa, We Called It
Macaroni,* and *Mangia, Little Italy!* locate the practices of food production and food
preparation outside the dominant institutions of the market. Part of the charm
of the cookbooks, indeed, is the way they represent the local neighborhood
markets where Italian Americans shopped and socialized daily as part of an
urban village where relations were familiar and personal. As Nancy Verde Barr
writes, "Since native dialects and food customs varied, the immigrant chose a
store where his language and his cooking needs would be understood—and,
most important, where he could trust his 'paesan' and count on him for credit
in hard times. I can remember, as a little girl, wondering why my grandmother
sent me past what seemed to be two or three perfectly good shops to buy what
she needed from her own 'paesan'."[33]

The sense of intimacy that the cookbooks trade on is, of course, in many
respects a manufactured one that typically accompanies such recipes as "Nonna's
Meat Sauce" or "Nonna's Lasagna" with wedding and other photos of Nonna
and Papa.[34] At the same time, the cookbooks represent a vindication of the New
World Italians' resistance to the official literacy of the social workers, settlement house reformers, home demonstration agents, and nutritionists, whose
leaflets, posters, street exhibits, and recipes sought to Americanize the foodways brought from the old country. By ignoring and evading—or simply being
unable to read—what the reformers pressed on them, both in Italian and in
English, the New World Italians maintained in living memory and experience
foodways that were unwritten and, in many ways, unwritable matters of feeling and practical knowledge. This resistance—and the measure of autonomy it
secured for Italians in the New World—as the three cookbooks recognize, calls
for a vindication that is both necessary, as a re-representation of the old-timers
and their historical moment, and inevitably ironic, as their authenticity is validated by the popularity of the cookbooks in the market.

eleven **Joe Shakespeare**

The Contemporary British Worker-Writer Movement

Nicholas Coles

Joe Smythe's *Come and Get Me* (1979) was the first book I came across from the contemporary worker-writer movement in Britain: sixty pages of poems about living and working in Manchester and on the northern railways, printed on cheap paper, the type that is heavier on some pages than others, with a black-and-white cover photo of a young boxer standing fists-up next to a tableau of trophies. The poems were playful, political, surreal sometimes, told in what the author calls "a remembering voice, a scraping-the-bottom-of-the-barrel voice, a street-rough 'hung-'em-in-anywhere voice." On the book's back cover, Smythe announces his relation to established literary convention with ironic self-deprecation: "If there is any poetry here, regard it as a happy accident: if Art is what you're after, ask for your money back, better still, give me to someone you don't like. . . . For twenty-five pence what do you expect? Joe Shakespeare?" The blurb is signed, nevertheless: "Joe Smythe, poet and railway guard."[1]

The book's publisher is Commonword, "a writers workshop for working people," based in Manchester. An afterword describes Commonword and the politics of the book's production:

> The poems in this book are not the work of a professional writer. Joe Smythe who wrote them is a railway guard. Commonword who produced and published the book is not out to make a profit.
>
> These points are important. Professional writers, by definition, make their living out of using words. In practice this means they will have risen to the top of our "educational" system; 99% of them will be middle class; their views, on the whole, will be acceptable to the people who control the media and the publishing houses. The outlook of most writers is therefore extremely narrow, and the experience of the majority of people, who are not like them, is ignored.—"Most people ignore most art because most art ignores most people."

The past [several] years, however, has seen a growth in a new sort of writing: writing for and by working people. There is now a national federation of over twenty worker writer groups. Joe Smythe is a member of Commonword, one of these groups.

We hold regular workshop meetings at which people get together to read and discuss their own work. And we try to find outlets for this work both in our own publications and in public readings. Poems, stories, life histories: the important thing is communication, not making a profit.[2]

In the twenty years since this passage was written, the Federation of Worker Writers and Community Publishers (FWWCP) to which it refers has expanded to about fifty groups, and the class-based popular literacy its members enact has become an important cultural movement in Britain—important mainly for its impact on the lives of its participants, but also for its less direct influences on such cultural practices as adult literacy, community education, bookselling practices, and government arts funding. If the clearly drawn class lines of Commonword's 1979 literary manifesto now look more blurred—with a far stronger working-class presence in mainstream publishing and media, for example—the worker-writer movement represented by FWWCP member groups may well have played a significant part in that cultural shift.

My aim in what follows is, first, to describe the work of this movement, as much as possible in the language of the participants, drawn from FWWCP publications and from my interviews with members of worker-writer groups.[3] Second, I want to raise some implications of this form of community-based writing and publishing for current work in English studies and adult literacy. The FWWCP is a remarkable instance, to borrow the words of John Trimbur's prospectus for this volume, of the ways "ordinary (and extraordinary) readers, speakers, and writers use literacy to articulate identities and social aspirations, to produce alternative forms of cultural knowledge, and to cope with the asymmetries of power that regulate the conduct of cultural life."[4] I am particularly interested here in what the work of the Federation groups suggests about motivations and structures for developing writing and publication when it is not required for academic credentialing or job advancement, and not provided by institutions; when it is, rather, engaged in for purposes defined by the participants and according to their own principles of organization. This is, as Anne Ruggles Gere says of the American writers groups she studied, a literacy "constructed by desire."[5] It is also a literacy shaped by a sharp sense of difference from, and in many ways of opposition to, the arrangements by which large sectors of cultural life in Britain—schooling, literature, publishing—have customarily been regulated.

Federation

The groups of "ordinary (and extraordinary) writers" that comprise the FWWCP, or "the Fed" as it is known to those involved, began to form in the early 1970s, as part of a broad turn away from national and party politics and toward local initiatives and cultural politics. Some groups arose from "initiatives to provide bookshops for huge, urban and chiefly working-class populations hitherto lacking them." Other groups emerged in conjunction with community-organizing efforts—such as a rent strike by tenants in a Liverpool Council estate —that required the writing and printing of fliers and bulletins. In Brighton, for instance, QueenSpark began as a "campaign to stop Brighton Council turning the Royal Spa into a casino, and to get a nursery school, day nursery, and park center instead."[6] The campaign's newsletter would gather and publish residents' reminiscences of the Spa, and this face-to-face contact and storytelling led to the writing of full length memoirs and books of local history and politics that now make up much of QueenSpark's booklist.[7] Still other groups grew out of traditional forms of educational provision for adults, such as literacy programs, local history workshops, and Workers Education Association classes, in which students would decide to continue and take control of the work after a course was over or a tutor had moved on.

The Federation of Worker Writers and Community Publishers was founded by twelve such groups in 1976 to provide a "collective, national voice" to the local workshops and (in the words of its constitution) "to further the cause . . . by all means possible." These means have included supporting the development of new workshops, publishing collections of members' writing for national distribution, holding annual general meetings and regional "training days," and coordinating fund-raising and liaison with "such persons and bodies as may be appropriate," including Arts Councils, trades unions, and education authorities. Since attracting funding for a full-time coordinator, the Fed also publishes a quarterly magazine, newsletter, and "broadsheet" of new writing and maintains the Web site mentioned in note 2.

In their most recent invitation to membership, the FWWCP's mission and aims are put this way:

> For nearly twenty-five years, the Federation of Worker Writers and Community Publishers (The Fed) has established itself as one of the leading voices for community writing and publishing. Working with and on behalf of our membership, we encourage an inclusive approach to creativity.
>
> The Fed's aim is to further working-class writing and community publishing,

and has a membership of independently organized writers' workshops and community publishers in Britain and abroad. Members . . . share these characteristics:

- to make writing and publishing accessible.
- to publish work by and for a particular community or group of people.
- to offer support to groups and individuals in their writing development, and distribute and promote writing through publishing and performance.
- to encourage people to take an active, cooperative and democratic role in writing, performing and publishing.
- to enable often marginalized groups to express themselves.[8]

The FWWCP Constitution, adopted in 1978 and regularly amended, offers the following "broad definition" of the key terms "working class" and "community publishing":

> The term "Working Class" is open to various definitions and this is a matter essentially for member organizations to determine, subject to the right of other members and the Federation as a whole to question and debate. We favour a broad definition. By "working class writing" we mean writing produced within the working class and socialist movement or in support of the aims of working class activity and self-expression. By "community publishing" we understand a process of producing and distributing such writing in cooperative and mutual ways (rather than competitive and private), primarily for a working class readership. The Federation is committed to the policy and practice of equal opportunities and is therefore opposed to any form of discrimination on the grounds of race, colour, creed, gender, class, sexuality, disability, or age. In implementing this policy the Federation positively works to provide a forum for the discussion of issues connected with working class writing, racism, sexism, disability and age.

These sentences represent more than a standard antidiscrimination disclaimer. In conversations with Fed members, I've encountered a range of views on the working-class status of the organization and on the relations of class and writing, with, nearly always, a strong stress on the value of "question and debate" about this and other issues. Laura Corbalis, a former coordinator of the member group Bristol Broadsides, who also served on the Fed's executive board, recalls:

> A lot of the arguing over the past five years at Fed Annual General Meetings is about what is working class and between people who wanted to abandon the subtitle working class and people who wanted to keep it. And what does it mean to be working class? Do you have to pass a test to be a member, does having it there alienate people who aren't working class but belong in the Fed for whatever reason? And in the end we kept it because . . . it does broadcast an oppositional stance. I'm very aware . . . that anybody in the Fed would give you a different answer, but in my view what we did was keep "working-class" but as a kind of shorthand for

anybody who finds themselves because of their identity in an oppositional stance to this culture. So although it doesn't immediately proclaim itself as such, we understand it as encompassing women and black people and people with disabilities and gay people. Who of course may be middle class.[9]

The diversity Corbalis points out is strikingly evident at any Fed gathering. Among the writing workshops sponsored by the FWWCP's affiliates are groups of black, Asian, women, senior-citizen, gay and lesbian, disabled, and teenage writers. Groups joining the Federation in 1990s included Survivors Poetry, providing "workshops and performances by and for survivors of the mental health system," and Big Issue, a "homeless people's writing project," which puts out Britain's national street newsweekly.

A sampling of Fed member groups indicates the range of the Federation's "broad definition" of working-class membership. Each name can also be read as a sign for a particular group's sense of its cultural location and the direction of its work:

Arts Disability Wales
Basement Writers, London E1
Big Issue Writers
Commonword, Manchester
Ethnic Communities Oral History Group, London SW6
Forest Artworks, Gloucestershire
Hybrid Writers, Durham
London Voices
Night Writers, Hackney Women's Center, London E8
Yer Own Stuff Press, Nottingham
Oxford Scribblers/Bloomin' Arts
Spread the Word, London
Survivors Poetry Scotland
Working Press, London SE11
Writer First Time, Bedford
Write Now, Birmingham
Yorkshire Art Circus.[10]

Overseas "associate member" groups have included Bunchu Books in Capetown, South Africa, which was affiliated with the African National Congress; Home-front Belles, Canberra, Australia, a group begun in a battered women's refuge; and Grup d'Autoedicio de Materials per Aprenents (roughly, "group for self-publishing of materials written by learners"), Barcelona, Spain. Four United

States groups have recently applied for Fed membership, two in Philadelphia, and two in Youngstown, Ohio, as a result of a 1999 United States tour by Fed writers and organizers.

Workshops

The FWWCP is in fact an even larger formation than the count of fifty "member groups" suggests, since many groups run several distinct writers' workshops. Manchester's Commonword, for instance, had in 1992 four core workshops— the Monday Night Group, Womanswrite, Identity Writers' Workshop, and North-ern Gay Writers, and a new "Asian women writers' group." Bristol Broadsides, when I visited in the early 1990s, comprised nine workshops: seven of these were based in different neighborhoods in the city, meeting weekly in librar-ies, pubs, and community centers.[11] The Bristol workshops are described in a brochure as "friendly and informal settings, where people can read, discuss, and criticize each others' poems, stories, plays, autobiography, or whatever else they might bring along. All are free and open to anyone, whether they've been writing for a day or a decade."

Though some workshops may be initiated by a coordinator, most are for-mally leaderless, rotating among their members the responsibility for getting the session started, keeping time, and so on. Typically, members take turns reading their work aloud, while fellow-writers offer response and critique. Workshops provide the support and the pressure writers sometimes need from each other, as Bertel Martin, a member of the Bristol Broadsides' Black Writers group, explains:

> There can be like this sense within the group that we're meeting, so you have to have something new. And then that urge to have to have something new means, does it pass what you've done before? And so you then feel you're not contribut-ing to the group if you're not producing, and that can make you feel guilty, and that means some people stay away. . . . Writing doesn't end just with what you put down on paper, it's also what you say about the work, that's just as important. And that's the way you end up trying to actually encourage people to come, even if they haven't got anything new. There's going to be new people there, there's going to be people whose work they had experience of before, and their views on that. To actually help those people see that it's not just producing work, which means that literature's moving on, it's the fact that as an individual, as a black person, as a per-son who's involved with a workshop your comments are actually feeding on and helping other people, and those people improve—and that's adding onto the lit-erary canon, or the literary dynamics.[12]

(I want to take up later some implications of Martin's concept of literature, its "canon" and "dynamics.")

Publishing

Beyond the direct support and challenge of the weekly workshop, participation in a Fed group also provides access to a broader public through opportunities for publication. Article 4 of the FWWCP Constitution stipulates, "To qualify for membership, organizations should have published work in some form, or be in the process of doing so." "In some form" is an important qualification, since some groups have a primary orientation to performance, through public readings and/or local radio, for instance. Nearly all the groups, however, are engaged in the production and distribution of books and magazines: initially these were often duplicated and stapled; in recent years they are mostly bound as paperbacks and attractively designed. I estimate that FWWCP members had by the mid-1990s published roughly 1,000 titles, with a total unit production of more than a million volumes. In its fifteen years of operation (1977–1992), Bristol Broadsides alone published more than forty books, either single-authored or collections, by writers in its workshops. Memoir, local history, and poetry predominate their booklist, but a selection of titles indicates other genres, as well as a range of subjects and themes:[13]

Wilfred Scott, *To a Farmer Born* (1987)—memoirs of a West Country boyhood

Bristol as We Remember It (1987)—transcribed conversations among older residents of the Barton Hill neighborhood.

A Southmead Festival of Words (1986)—poetry, fiction, and reminiscences from writers on the North Bristol Council Estate of Southmead.

Bristol's Other History (1983)—articles about the city's tradition of radical movements by a local history workshop; includes Madge Dresser, "Black and White on the Buses: The 1963 Colour Bar Dispute in Bristol."

DOWN to EARTH and ON its FEET: People's Poetry in Performance (1987)—words and photographs from the 1986 Avon Poetry Festival.

Let's Hurry Up and Get This Relationship Over. . . . So I can Get On With Decorating the Hallway (1987)—an anthology of "love poetry."

Terry Lee, *Grease & Grime* (1985)—a book of short stories about "the seamier side of life" by an unemployed engineer.

Fred's People: Young Bristolians Speak Out (1980)—writings by members of a literacy group for "early school-leavers."

St. Paul's People Talking to children from St. Barnabas School (1983)—interviews by

elementary school children with older residents of the St. Paul's neighborhood.

Tears and Joy (1981) by parents of disabled children, and *A Celebration of Differences:
A Book by Physically Handicapped People* (1985).

Shush—Mum's Writing (1978) and *The Dinner Lady and Other Women* (no date)—collections from the Women Writers Workshop.

Joyce Storey, *Joyce's War* (1990)—an autobiography set in World War II Bristol,
winner of the Raymond Williams Community Publishing Award and republished by Virago in 1992.

Other forms of publication not represented on Bristol Broadsides's list but
produced by Fed groups include illustrated storybooks for children, broad-
sheets, postcard sets, comic books, calendars with local photographs and cap-
tions, spoken-word cassette tapes, bilingual books in English and Urdu or Hindi,
large-format books by people with learning difficulties, neighborhood walking guides, and, from London's Age Exchange, collections of traditional health
remedies and recipes by "Caribbean elders." The FWWCP also instituted a Federation Book Club to promote distribution beyond the groups' local communities
and followed this up with a regular "broadsheet" of writing from member
groups.

Distribution

A strong feature of the Fed's work that marks it as an alternative to "Establishment literature" and commercial publishing is the way in which writers are
involved in the decisions and processes of publication and distribution. Choices
about who and what to publish, which can be difficult especially in times of
shrinking local arts budgets, are usually made collectively by editorial groups
of workshop members. The writers to be published participate to whatever extent they can in the editing, layout, and design of the book, with actual production handled by local printers.

Distribution and marketing are primarily local and face-to-face: the writers themselves share responsibility for bringing their works to their audiences.
The publication of a new book is typically celebrated with a launching party, a
collectively written account of the Federation's early years, described by the
authors of *The Republic of Letters* as follows:

Launching a book made in this way is an important social celebration. Rather than
being an exercise in publicity management, a launching is an occasion for bringing all the people who helped create the book together: writers, lay-out people,

typists, printers, other writers in the project, friends, families, neighbours and so on. The reading of part of the text is, of course, the highlight. There have been launchings in pubs, community centres, cafes, railway station buffet rooms, trade union buildings, cinemas, where large numbers of people have gathered to listen to an evening of readings of autobiography, poetry, new writings. . . .

Under Oars, a lighterman's autobiography published by Stepney Books and Centerprise jointly, was launched in a Thames-side pub and attended by dozens of retired and still working lightermen, trade union officials, families and friends, many of whom hadn't seen each other for twenty or thirty years. Parts of the book were read by the author's son to a packed pub listening in complete quiet. . . . Every Birth it Comes Different was launched in the Centerprise coffee bar, packed by Hackney Reading Centre students, their families and friends, and visitors from other centres, and the evening was an extraordinary blend of private and public; women read aloud written accounts of the birth of their children to eighty or more people.

Characteristic distribution methods extend the community-building function of the launchings and demonstrate how "different work, reflecting popular experience; different writers, whom you may know and can certainly meet; different distribution, through local centers and face-to-face contacts—all these have created new reading publics."[14] Quoting, again, from The Republic of Letters:

Examples tell the story best. Poetry is supposed to be a minority interest and yet the collection of poems by Vivian Usherwood sold over 10,000 copies, of which it is likely that nearly half were sold from one bookshop, Centerprise in Hackney. They were bought in dozens by friends of his, by relations, by other black teenagers and parents, by school teachers who used them in the classroom and by people who were prepared to try out such an attractive small collection at such a cheap price. The first edition was sold for 5p. It had a printed cover, was duplicated inside, folded and stapled by hand. . . . Another example— in 1974 a retired carpenter, Albert Paul, took a manuscript of his early autobiography to the Brighton community newspaper, QueenSpark. They decided to publish it and the book was typed, designed, pasted up, cut and stapled by local voluntary labour. The pages were printed by a small local press. 2,000 copies were sold within three months, the majority in one small neighbourhood. It was sold door to door mostly, and Mr Paul himself sold 700 to friends and in cafes and streets.

QueenSpark have set a lot of store by this method of selling as a logical extension of the aim to make all the processes of producing and distributing visible, to challenge the concessions to commercial structure that are involved when selling through bookshops.[15]

QueenSpark, for example, adopted one of the traditional European forms of local distribution, selling its books and pamphlets on stalls in Brighton's weekly outdoor markets. Forest Artworks, a Fed affiliate in Gloucestershire's Royal

Forest of Dean, developed a publishing partnership with area libraries whereby local residents would bring in their writings, which were then mounted and exhibited and later bound and cataloged into the library's holdings of regional materials. The WWW has recently opened much wider avenues for distribution, for groups with access to the technology. Roughly half of Fed member groups have Web sites, on which excerpts from publications can be read and downloaded, extending circulation well beyond the group's local community. QueenSpark is now experimenting with books written collectively on-line through its "multimedia history" project.

Authorship

The concept of authorship enacted in these methods of production and distribution is different from, and in many ways opposed to, that in commercial publishing. The function of autobiography here, for instance, is not primarily to draw attention to the specialness of the individual writer and to market his or her story to a large and anonymous audience on the basis of that specialness, but rather to articulate experiences that may be common to many members of a known community, and to do so with the explicit intention of drawing out more such stories from that audience. "Every reading is always permeated by the assumption that listeners are now potential writers themselves."[16] In the introduction to Bristol Lives, Bob Pitt addressed his readers this way: "Hopefully you too will be inspired to put down your memories and experiences on paper or on tape. All our experiences are important. Perhaps they may not be published tomorrow or broadcast next week, but in years to come they may provide part of a unique record of Bristol and its people. So look to your local Writers Workshops, Community History Projects and Local History Groups. Memories shouldn't just leave us to wallow in the past but give us the experience with which to change the future for ourselves and all Bristol People."[17] One of the motivations, then, that many worker-writers bring to their work is to record memories, including memories of political struggles, movements, and migrations that may have gone unmarked by professional historians. This recording serves to assert that their experience of these histories is valuable as knowledge that can be drawn on for the development of their communities: "We know that other Somali women have different experiences. We ask these women, who have so much history, to write their knowledge down, for themselves, for their children, and for their people."[18] Of course, converting "experiences" into "knowledge" by writing it down is not an easy process for many of those involved in this project. For some, the struggles of authorship begin not only with learning spoken English but with the rigors of transcribing oral stories and thoughts into writing. The Somali women's literacy group I visited in 1994, organized by Manchester's Gatehouse Books, was beginning this process with a sharing of recipes, and the dishes made from them, before moving on to collecting stories of their homeland and immigration to Britain. But they were nevertheless planning to produce a publication, following Gatehouse's central strategy of enabling literacy learners to publish books for the use of other students.[19]

For some, the struggles of authorship arise in the disruption of settled family or community patterns that may come with a family member's increasing involvement with writing. As the authors of *Feds under the Bed* put it: "Change brings conflict and it's clear in all writers groups, that people who join them sometimes get under pressure at home."[20] "The most common . . . is the pressure on women from husbands to stay at home rather than go out to a writer's workshop—or any other independent activity where different values operate from those at home. It does also occasionally work the other way around. Men are sometimes thought odd to be wasting their time on such an eccentric activity as writing. Some people keep secret their involvement in writing, telling nobody until this is revealed by publication."[21] A poem on the front cover of *Shush: Mum's Writing*, from the Bristol Women Writers Workshop, handles such conflict with a light irony, as it both sketches the family context in which such texts are produced and points to the gains that can accompany publication:

> Sit down be quiet read a book
> Don't you dare to speak or look
> Shush Mum's writing
> She's left the dishes in the sink
> All she does is sit and think
> Shush Mum's writing
> Nothing for dinner nowt for tea
> And all she ever says to me is
> Shush Mum's writing
> But what's all this Mum's wrote a book
> Why not buy one have a look
> No need to shush now we can shout
> And tell all our friends about
> MUM'S WRITING

The pride in seeing their mother published, which the writer ascribes to her children (who knows with how much accuracy), is only one of the possible reactions to having a family member in print. Ron Barnes, writing and publishing in the mid-1970s with London's Centerprise Books, recalls the response to publication of his first book *License to Live*: "Distant relatives who I had not seen for years phoned to congratulate me. They felt sure I was on my way to fame and fortune. 'We hope so, especially the fortune bit.'" His second book, *Coronation Cups and Jam Jars*, which moved beyond personal autobiography into family history, "unfortunately had quite an adverse effect on some of my relatives. . . . I had spoken about things that should never be mentioned, in or outside the family. 'In print as well, what a disgrace.'"[22] And there are risks in exposure beyond the family incurred by first-time authorship, as Roger Mills, author of *A Comprehensive Education*, makes clear: "If you've written something it becomes public property, really. If I write, if I state some opinion . . . then you've got the right to come up to me and say, 'What's this you say here? I think you're totally wrong.' You've laid yourself open far more than if you just said it in a pub. If you've said it in print it's open for anyone to come up to you and say, 'Justify this!'"[23]

Gains

If, in the words of *Feds under the Bed*, "the whole process of writing changes people [and] it's not all happy times," the outcome of authorship most often cited in interviews and in the prefaces to FWWCP books involves gains in self-confidence:

> At least twenty women have passed through the Women Writers Workshop in the last eighteen months. Some have journeyed from as far as Yate to be here; others have only had to step round the corner. Some of us are single parents, some married, some black, some white & some disabled, some old, some young. All of us feel impelled to write.
>
> Besides going into print we have read our work in public. This was something most of us believed we could never do, but we did. Publishing our own work was also something we didn't think possible, but it was.
>
> We have learnt a lot. There have been many changes and confrontations during the compilation of this book. None of it has been easy, much of it pleasurable. We have argued, listened, laughed & cried—& written. It has been life with all its raw edges, not altogether rosy. We are proud of our achievement and look forward to sharing it with you.[24]

Fed members are aware that to stress "confidence" as a central gain of involvement in worker-writer groups is to risk marginalizing the writing as "therapy." And yet, excerpts such as this imply that the confidence that comes with writing, performing, and publishing extends well beyond private self-esteem. When people who describe themselves as shy or poorly educated come "out of the closet" (in the phrase used by many of the writers I met) with their desire to write, or with their already composed private writings, they are claiming some cultural space for themselves and for "people like us." They present themselves as subjects rather than objects of others' literary or historical attentions or inattentions; they see themselves as having histories, which are connected to other larger histories; and sometimes they can act as literate agents in shaping those histories. Roger Drury, coordinator of Forest Artworks in Gloucestershire's Royal Forest of Dean, described how residents responded to the conservative government's proposal to "privatize" the Forest (a well-known "beauty spot" with an independent tradition of iron mining and sheep grazing on Crown lands) with an outpouring of written protest, not only in letters to the weekly paper but also in poems and songs. Reminiscences of life and work in the Forest were being collected and published as part of an ongoing "diaries project" in support of the campaign against privatization.[25]

Other, smaller campaigns on the domestic front can be no less political, as Anne Fazackerley makes clear in "Why I Write Poetry": "I must have told my husband half a dozen times how I felt about him going to prison and leaving me to cope with the children on my own. He used to read my letters and dismiss them as petty nagging. So I wrote him a poem 'I've heard it all before' explaining my grievances. Suddenly it sunk in. He realized that if I felt strongly enough about it to burst into poetry, then I must be serious."[26]

Schooling

In an afterword to the anthology Don't Judge This Book by Its Cover, Keith Birch of the Merseyside Association of Writers Workshops, explains that the confidence generated by participation in writing and publishing groups is especially significant in light of the writers' damaging experiences with schooling, and particularly with the schools' imposition of standard English. Birch also articulates commonly held FWWCP beliefs about the processes of writing and the function of editing:

> Working-class writing is a form of writing expressed by people without any writing background, that is to say by people who, through poor teaching standards, left school at the earliest possible moment with English teachers' comments on work and school reports, usually in red ink, indelibly stamped on their minds:

"Bad grammar!" . . . *"Can't spell!"* . . . *"Poor punctuation!"* . . . etc.—People who, as children with a natural eagerness to learn, had been brainwashed into believing that writing belonged to an elite class of people, that form and structure were more important than content. That imagination was alright as long as you had a College or University education to go with it. That *"Writing isn't for the likes of us."*

Don't think I'm advocating a form of writing that'd be unintelligible to any reader—what I'm promoting, and writers' workshops are encouraging, is that everyone can "write" and that everyone has interesting tales to tell. The stumbling block to writing is premature editing. With all those bad memories of school, we compose our stories in our minds and are then unable to transfer them to paper because we are worried about the spelling, the grammar, this won't "look right," etc.

Writers' workshops encourage, through supportive, constructive and honest criticism. Members are urged to write down the ideas first, and worry about the rest later. They bring their work into the group meetings and read it out for criticism, then re-write until happy they can do no more to improve their work.

After the first few stumbling attempts, confidence begins to grow and a natural inclination to 'get better' begins to show itself. Dictionaries are consulted, more thought and planning goes into the structure of the piece, and for some this is a time to have another go at English, with a different approach this time.[27]

It is tempting to suggest, on the basis of Birch's critique of the disciplines of schooling, that the alternative work represented by the FWWCP should be emulated in schools and universities. The worker-writer movement is, after all, an educational as well as a cultural-political formation. And as Gregory, a former teacher and now lecturer in Education, points out: "Community writing/ publishing activity, viewed as *collective self-education*, has begun to realize in practice what teachers have regularly been exhorted to arrange," including "promoting collaboration in the writing process," complete with response groups, cooperative revision, delayed editing, and student publishing.[28] The "workshop" is the social and pedagogical center of Fed groups, as it is also the dominant mode in American creative writing programs, and in the "whole language" approach to literacy learning in schools.

However, because cultural contexts and personal histories, especially British experiences of class, in and out of school, combine to give this work its particular meanings and values, I am frankly undecided about its application to traditional educational contexts. Rather, I see the work as broadly significant, first, as a reminder of how much "writing in society" (to borrow a title of Raymond Williams) is going on around us every day, and for purposes other than those with which we are most familiar: academic qualification, career advancement, or commercial publication.[29] Gere, in her study of diverse American writers' groups, comes to a similar reflection: "Although it remains largely invisible and inaudible to us, writing development occurs regularly and successfully outside classroom walls."[30] The desire to write—in other words, to "get better" at writing—is not (or is not only) school-bred. Second, the movement offers a demonstration of other fundamental purposes people have for engaging in literacy: the pleasures of self-expression, and of communicating and sharing understandings, feelings, and memories; and the cultural work of building community, reclaiming history, and participating in social change.[31]

Beyond these broad implications, I want to take Birch's offer to "have another go at English" in a more particular sense. The worker-writer movement offers those of us who work in English a politically pointed, extracurricular stance from which to look critically at some key terms in our field, terms that organize much of our professional practice even as we constantly revise and redefine them. Specifically, I want to reflect on "literature," "literacy," and "popular culture," in light of what I have seen of the movement's work.

Literature

The title of one of the workshops at the Fed's 1992 annual general meeting invited participants to "Forget literature, write a book instead." The cover of The Republic of Letters carries a bold diagonal slash with the words: "GUARANTEED 'no solid literary merit'—Arts Council of Great Britain." But the history of the FWWCP's relations with the literary establishment—institutions of literary study, commercial publishing, and government arts funding—has been marked by conflict and ambivalence more painful than these ironies imply. On one hand is the commitment announced in the Federation's slogan, "working to make writing and publishing accessible to all," and its aim to "encompass all forms of the written word." This has entailed a conscious rejection of the relevance of the term "Literature," and all that its capital "L" has signified, to their practice. On the other hand, the struggle for recognition by the literary establishment— most crucially by the Literature Division of the Arts Council of Great Britain, which until 1992 regularly refused to fund the work of the Federation—required the assertion that the Fed was indeed producing "literature," and was in fact contributing to and enacting a necessary democratic redefinition of literary work.

I discussed this redefinition with Nick Pollard, a member of Heeley Writers in Sheffield and editor of FEDeration magazine:

> This is not going to be the stuff of Penguin Modern Classics. There isn't the application and the discipline in the writing people do. What you could say, however, is that . . . Federation stuff is perhaps superliterary, that if you look at what Barthes is

saying about the exchange between the reader and the writer, and *jouissance*, you've got this exchange between the two—that's what the workshop process is about. People are reading their stuff in workshop or they're reading stuff in pubs. Or they're doing what's happening with QueenSpark, they write their book and say, "Well, this is what it was like," and somebody else says, "No it wasn't, it was like this," so you've got that kind of exchange. So I don't think you can really say that it's literature. It's more a sort of participatory culture.[32]

Bristol Broadsides' Bertel Martin, however, accepts the term "literature" as applicable to his experience in that it marks the "importance" of the work of this "participatory culture":

Initially you just write out, you're not really conscious of there being this great canon behind you, because a lot—well, for me, anyway—a lot of it was just I didn't see what I was doing as being associated with any of that. But then there comes a stage when, as you receive criticism, as you receive positive criticism, you develop your confidence, and actually—you don't feel, "Well, yeah, I'm as good as, or I'm better than"—any of that. But you certainly get a sense of, "Yeah, I'm a part of that, I'm a different voice added into all of that canon." And then once you realize that . . . then you suddenly are more aware of the importance of what you're saying, and you can feel more of how you need to do it right, rather than rely on just sort of general ways you used to put things down before.[33]

For Martin, what marks the work as literature is neither success in publication nor an abstract (and usually class-based) concept of literary quality, but rather the level of criticism, and consequent revision, applied in the social process of the work's composition. Here again is Martin's comment on the literary politics of workshop practice: "Writing doesn't end just with what you put down on paper, it's also what you say about work, that's just as important. . . . It's not just producing work which means that literature's moving on, it's the fact that as an individual, as a black person, as a person who's involved with a workshop whose comments are actually feeding on and helping other people, and those people improve—and that's adding onto the literary canon, or the literary dynamics."[34] This redefinition returns "literature" to one of the earliest meanings traced by Raymond Williams in his *Keywords* entry, where the word refers broadly to the social "dynamics" (in Martin's phrase) of reading and writing, rather than to particular books, genres, or qualities of writing: "*Literature*, that is to say, corresponded mainly to the modern meanings of *literacy*."[35] The difference, and the source of conflict with the "literary establishment," is that the Fed's practice of literature extends its opportunities to a working-class majority, rather than to the "talented few" supported by the Arts Council, whose response to the FWWCP's initial request for funding reads in part:

It may seem unfair to you that some people are more talented than others, and indeed it is unfair; however, it remains a fact that talent in the arts has not been handed out equally by some impeccable heavenly democrat. You are right to think that the Arts Council views itself as a patron of the arts. This is, indeed, our function. It is important that we do all we can to increase audiences for today's writers, *not that we increase the number of writers*. There are already too many writers chasing too few readers. Although the real writer will always emerge without coaxing, it is not so easy to encourage new readers into existence.[36]

Literacy

The success of the FWWCP, both in increasing the number of writers and in encouraging new readers, has contributed to a rethinking of official provisions for adult literacy in Britain. As in the United States, British literacy programs were aimed primarily at developing "functional literacy" through the one-to-one teaching of volunteer reading tutors, mini-courses that prepare for job training, and workplace programs that teach employees to read manuals and file reports. Addressing the limitations of this emphasis on the functional, Jane Mace, who has designed and studied adult literacy programs in Britain, including FWWCP affiliates, writes that "the full range of literacy purposes and possibilities available to any of us has barely been described, let alone promoted." She notes the traditional emphasis on reading, the more passive or receptive form of literacy, over writing, the more active and participatory form. She says, however, that "the effort to re-establish writing as central to literacy education" encounters these customary resistances (exemplified in the Arts Council letter quoted above): "The 'imposed' literacy of our education and cultural experience after primary school largely concerns the reading of other people's writing. Anything which concerns writing for imaginative or reflective purposes belongs to an area of adult life called 'leisure' (which, in terms of funding, belongs on the very edges of serious education for adults)." For the future, she proposes to designers of community-based programs that "literacy education means persuading adult students that they are writers as well as readers, that they have an entitlement to be read, as well as to read others. Literacy education, on this basis, means a journey towards confident, critical and active authorship."[37] Adult literacy students writing in FWWCP workshops may have needed such persuasion when they first made the break from individualized workbook instruction, but they are now taking control of their own education in remarkable ways. A shining example is Pecket Well College, a Fed affiliate near Hebden Bridge, in Yorkshire. Pecket Well is the first residential college in Britain for people with learning difficulties. Its old stone building, a former cooperative store in the Pen-

nine hills, has been made fully accessible. It is run by a management committee of students and tutors who together make all decisions about curriculum
and administration. One founding member of this team is Florence Agbah,
who immigrated to Britain at nineteen having never been to school in her native
Ghana. She has authored two slim books of autobiography, titled *My Way*, and
leads workshops at the College on life-writing, as well as dressmaking. When I
met her, she was meeting with other women members of the management
committee to plan a women-only weekend course for the College, called
"Breaking Free."

Another Pecket Well founder is Peter Goode, an artist and poet who divides
his life into eras "before" and "after" coming to literacy in his mid-fifties. His
book *The Moon on the Window*, subtitled "The Book of Gobbledegook," is beauti-
fully produced, complete with facsimiles of his drafts, on envelopes and other
scrap paper, in invented spelling. Goode is also now a workshop leader, in schools
and prisons, and has recently started a writers group, through Unit 51 in Hud-
dersfield, for people living with addictions. Their work is published in *Straight
Ahead*, a large-format journal produced by Pecket Well. "The aim of this paper
is an honest, factual, & uncensored look at drug use and abuse" is printed in
huge capitals on the cover.

I discussed the process of students' active engagement in literacy work
with Joe Flanagan, another member of Pecket Well's management committee.
Permanently laid off—"made redundant" is the telling English term—at fifty-
two, Flanagan enrolled in Adult Basic Education to learn to read and write. He
quickly became dissatisfied with the elementary reading materials, the lessons'
emphasis on literal decoding, and, above all, the condescension and dependency
of one-to-one tutoring. He wanted, he said, "to discuss," to talk with other
readers about what they liked and didn't like, and why. With several other students, and with the help of a tutor, Gillian Frost, who went on to work with
them in creating Pecket Well, Flanagan started a magazine, *Not Written Off*, for
adult literacy students in Calderdale. The experience of discussing what would
go into the magazine (rather than leaving these decisions to the tutor) and of
writing back to contributors recommending changes (but only, he pointed out,
after they had been assured the piece would be published) provided a turning
point for Flanagan: "A whole world—there's no other way to describe it—a
new world opened up, a world where I had a say." Although reading is still
difficult for Flanagan, he has composed a substantial autobiography, with the
help of an oral-history interviewer, and a chapter on "Tackling a Long Piece of
Work" in *Opening Time*, a resource pack for people learning to read and write.
Flanagan says he would like to see the word "'literacy' buried for good": "I

don't want the system deciding what you're going to learn. If you go to basic education classes now they ask you what you want to learn, when do you want to start. They don't tell you what you can have, take it or leave it. And that is because of us. Because we fought for that."[38]

Popular Culture

As distinct from the official literacy provision Flanagan critiques here, the worker-writer movement can, I think, be seen as an activist, oppositional form of "cultural literacy": a popular cultural literacy produced by and for "the majority of people" (in the words of the preface to Joe Smythe's book). As such, the Fed not only represents a counterpoint to conservative constructions of "cultural literacy," which still have such currency in the United States, it also offers an opening for redefinition of what is studied in English departments as "popular culture": popular fiction, pop music, television, movies, advertising —those productions, in other words, of mass commercial culture that are de signed for consumption, usually assumed to be unmediated and uncritical, by "the majority of people." These artifacts have been studied in much the same way as the traditional objects of study in English, with more attention to their formal structures and ideological tendencies than to the contradictory complexities of their actual reception and use. The existence of a widespread working-class literary culture of self-representation counterposes to our essentially consumerist definition the recognition that "popular culture" is continuously produced and disseminated by "ordinary" people, with little or no access to official means of production. Studying the products and processes of that culture allows us to see something of the complexity and partiality of ordinary people's appropriation of commercial and educational cultures, as they go about creating forms for their own purposes. As the authors of *The Republic of Letters* put it: "Established cultural institutions are not simply one-way conveyor belts for ruling class ideology: nor are working class people and communities blank slates upon which those cultural institutions can, at will, write. Cultural relations are matters of negotiation, contest, struggle."[39] No small sample can do justice to the pleasure and power, to say nothing of the range, of the work produced by those involved in this cultural movement. (Interested readers are urged to visit the FWWCP Web site at www.fwwcp.mcmail.com and follow its links to member groups.) I shall close, nevertheless, with a single poem by Commonword's Joe Smythe, poet and railway guard, in which he reflects on the writing of *The Peoples Road*:

Third Shunt

Eleven times I tried to write
another poem for The Peoples Road.
Five hours within myself
trains were moving,
signals changed,
night gathered immense wagons
in a string of stars,
sun shuffled
shunting dawns,
and I could not write.
I had forgotten myself
in the studied books,
lost my own experience in the history of others,
become the old events,
and I could not write.
There's learning for you.
The road itself had taught
to live is to be
perception first, then memory.
I remember these lives within
from a sense of being
one with the road,
which book is peopled
at this twelfth success
with what I saw when the eyes were mine.

twelve **Changing the Face of Poverty**

Nonprofits and the Problem of Representation

Diana George

> Constructively changing the ways the poor are represented in every
> aspect of life is one progressive intervention that can challenge every-
> one to look at the face of poverty and not turn away.
> —BELL HOOKS, *Outlaw Culture*.

ENCLOSED: No Address Labels to Use Up.
No Calendars to Look At.
No Petitions to Sign.

And No Pictures of Starving Children.

FIGURE I

Text from the outer envelope of a 1998 Oxfam appeal

As I write this, Thanksgiving is near. I am about to go out and fill a box with
nonperishables for the annual St. Vincent De Paul food drive. Christmas lights
already outline some porches. Each day my mailbox is stuffed with catalogs
and bills and with appeals from the Native American Scholarship Fund, the Salvation Army, WOJB—Voice of the Anishinabe, the Navaho Health Foundation,
the Barbara Kettle Gundlach Shelter Home for Abused Women, Little Brothers
Friends of the Elderly, Habitat for Humanity, and more. One *New Yorker* ad for
Children, Inc. reads, "You don't have to leave your own country to find third-

world poverty." Alongside the ad copy, from a black-and-white full-page photo, a young girl in torn and ill-fitting clothes looks directly at the viewer. The copy continues, "Just travel along the hillsides and down through the valleys where the Appalachian coal mines have been shut down. Sad, hungry faces of little children, like Amy's, will haunt you."

The Oxfam promise that I quote above—to use no pictures of starving children—is surely an attempt to avoid the emotional overload of such images as the one Children, Inc. offers (fig 2). Still, those pictures—those representations of poverty—have typically been one way nonprofits have kept the poor before us. In a culture saturated by the image, how else do we convince Americans that —despite the prosperity they see all around them—there is real need out there? The solution for most nonprofits has been to show the despair. To do that they must represent poverty as something that can be seen and easily recognized: fallen down shacks and trashed out public housing, broken windows, dilapidated porches, barefoot kids with stringy hair, emaciated old women and men staring out at the camera with empty eyes. In such images, poverty is dirt and rags and helplessness. In mail, in magazines, and in newspapers, ads echoing these appeals must vie for our time, attention, and dollars with Eddie Bauer, Nordstrom's, the Gap, and others like them whose polished and attractive images fill our days.

In the pages that follow, I offer one way of understanding how the images nonprofits must rely on may, as Stanley Aronowitz has noted about so many public appeals, result in charity but not activism—not in real structural change or an understanding of the systems that remain in place to keep many in poverty even while the culture at large is a prosperous one.[1] I begin with a discussion of what it means to rely on an image to represent an argument about something as complex as poverty and social responsibility—and how nonprofits must convince potential benefactors that they are dealing with the most needy, with the "deserving" and not the "undeserving" poor. In the second part of this essay, I examine a particular representation of poverty—publicity videos produced by Habitat for Humanity—in order to suggest that reliance on stereotypes of poverty can, in fact, work against the aims of the organization producing them. Finally, I look at alternate representations of poverty, especially those offered by the poor themselves and by men and women who work among the poor in this country. If it is possible, as bell hooks suggests above, to constructively change the ways the poor are represented, then such a change must begin with those whose lives are defined by need.

You don't have to leave your own country to find third-world poverty.

Just travel along the hillsides and down through the valleys where the Appalachian coal mines have been shut down. Sad, hungry faces of little children, like Amy's, will haunt you.

For just $21 a month, through Children, Inc., you can sponsor a girl or boy in desperate need. You can help provide food, warm clothes, health care, school needs. And maybe a toy or two. And we'll send you your child's story, address and picture.

Write or call, but please, don't look the other way.

Write to: Mrs. Jeanne Clarke Wood
Children, Incorporated, P.O. Box 5381
Dept. Y2A8, Richmond, Va. 23220 USA

☐ I wish to sponsor a ☐ boy, ☐ girl, in
   ☐ Asia, ☐ Latin America, ☐ Middle East,
   ☐ Africa, ☐ USA, ☐ Greatest need.

☐ I will give $21 a month ($252 a year).
   Enclosed is my gift for a full year ☐,
   the first month ☐. Please send me the
   child's name, story, address and picture.

☐ I can't sponsor, but I will help $_____
☐ Please send me further information.

Name _____
Address _____
City _____
State _____ Zip _____

☐ Check ☐ Am. Express ☐ Visa ☐ MasterCard

Card No. _____ Expiration Date _____

Signature _____

1-800-538-5381
CHILDREN, INC.
Serving Needy Children Since 1964

U.S. gifts are fully tax deductible.
Annual financial statements are available on request.

FIGURE 2

"We Must *See* Them": The Problems of Representation

Consumer's Union Executive Director Rhoda H. Karpatkin explains her motive for commissioning Eugene Richards's 1985 photo documentary *Below the Line: Living Poor in America* with a workplace anecdote: "In the Consumers Union lunchroom one day, I asked several of my suburban coworkers if they see people who are hungry or homeless. Many do not. Yet we must *see* them before we can care about them. And we must care about them before we are moved to end the intolerable conditions that mark their lives."[2] That motive—to *show* the reality of hard lives in order to move others to act or, at least, react—is an old one.

We might reach back to the paintings of eighteenth-century French moralist Jean-Baptist Grueze, who equated much poverty with moral decay, or to similar representations by Greuze's English contemporary William Hogarth, whose paintings and engravings of English street life linked abject poverty to an unholy and unrepentant lifestyle, one that might lead to the horrors of *Gin Lane*, or the dismal life and ultimate execution of the Idle Apprentice. Or, better yet, we could look to Sir William Beechey's 1793 portrait of the Ford children giving alms to a ragged boy they have encountered in the lane on the edge of their estate.[3] Painted in the manner of Gainsborough, these pretty, delicate upper-class children lean forward to place a coin in the hand of a young beggar—his rags barely covering him, his chest curved inward against hunger and cold.

Paintings, however, are easily understood as interpretations, even fictions —in the case of Grueze and Hogarth, they are eighteenth-century morality tales intended to uplift the monied class at the same time that they reconfirm old prejudices and fears. As industrialization concentrated more poverty and crime in the cities, nineteenth-century journalists and reformers turned to other ways of uncovering the truth and despair of urban poverty, once again, in order to move others to action or at least to sympathy.

Whatever his methods—and they are contested—moving readers to sympathy, if not reform, was certainly a motive for Henry Mayhew when in 1850–1851 he published the first of four volumes of interviews, stories, and firsthand descriptions detailing the lives of London's poor and working poor.[4] In his introduction to the final volume *Those That Will Not Work*, Mayhew writes of beginning with the aim of not simply contributing new facts or with only the hope of making "the solution of the social problem more easy to us, but, setting more plainly before us some of its latent causes, [to] make us look with more pity and less anger on those who want the fortitude to resist their influence."[5] Mayhew reveals with this short statement, and even with the title of this volume, the ambivalence with which even reformers or journalists sympathetic to the plight of the poor approached their subject. "Those that will not work": are they victims to be pitied, or are they simply a drain on resources, a site of criminal behavior, or worse? What Mayhew asks is that his readers, in the least, temper their anger.

At the turn of this century, American novelist and journalist Jack London traveled to England to look again at London street life, to do more than Mayhew and actually *become* one of the London homeless. His accounts, as well, provide almost too vivid moments of the actuality of living in destitution. At one point as London walks beside two men who keep picking things up from the sidewalk, he is so taken aback when he understands what they are doing that he pauses in shock and, for his reader, puts his revelation into italics: "*They picked up stray crumbs of bread the size of peas, apple cores so black and dirty one would not take them to be apple cores, and these things these two men took into their mouths, and chewed them, and swallowed them; and this, between six and seven o-clock in the evening of August 20, year of our Lord 1902, in the heart of the greatest, wealthiest, and most powerful empire the world has ever seen.*"[6] For London, in contrast to Mayhew, there was little question of who or what was to blame. Writing in a moment of social realism with such contemporaries as Theodore Dreiser and Frank Norris, whose short stories and novels placed the individual at the mercy of an American capitalist machine out of control, London collects the stories of England's street people, thrown out to hunger and cold when industry has no more use for them: "The unfit and the unneeded! Industry does not clamor for them. There are no jobs going begging through lack of men and women. . . . Women and plenty to spare, are found to toil under the sweat-shop masters for tenpence a day of fourteen hours. Alfred Freeman crawls to muddy death because he loses his job. Ellen Hughes Hun prefers Regent's Canal to Islington Workhouse. Frank Cavilla cuts the throats of his wife and children because he cannot find work enough to give them food and shelter."[7] It is a bleak world made all the more bleak by the assuredness with which London offers his readers little hope.

For reformers, the firsthand account has perennially been the most compelling, for it is through such stark representations that writers and, even more so, photographers challenge their audiences to dare deny the truth before them. Photojournalist Jacob A. Riis's 1890 publication *How the Other Half Lives*, the first thoroughgoing attempt at documenting poverty using photography, certainly marked a turning point for social reform. Using his camera as a way to capture New York tenement life, Riis showed the filth, decay, chaos, and dangerous crowding of which most Americans knew nothing. For Riis, the tenements were "the nurseries of pauperism and crime that fill our jails and police courts; that throw off a scum of forty thousand human wrecks to the island asylums and workhouses year by year; that turned out in the last eight years a round half million beggars to prey upon our charities; that maintain a standing army of ten thousand tramps with all that that implies; because, above all, they touch the family life with deadly moral contagion." Quite bluntly, Riis challenged his readers: "What are you going to do about it?"[8] Riis's photographs are such unflinching documents that they are often credited with forcing housing reform in New York's tenement district.

It was that bluntness, the promise of photography to show what we might not otherwise see, that gave the publisher of Helen Campbell's *Darkness and Daylight; or Lights and Shadows of New York Life* the courage to boast that here we have a volume of uncommon faithfulness to the harsh face of street life in 1892 New York, brought even more vividly into view by "recent developments in photography [which] have rendered it possible to catch instantaneously all the details of a scene with the utmost fidelity." "It is said," writes this publisher, "that figures do not lie. Neither does the camera. In looking on these pages, the reader is brought face to face with real life as it is in New York; not AS IT WAS, but AS IT IS TO-DAY. Exactly as the reader sees these pictures, just so were the scenes presented to the camera's merciless and unfailing eye at the moment when the action depicted took place. Nothing is lacking but the actual *movement* of the persons represented."[9] Despite the publisher's assurance that we have before us what was captured by the untainted lens of the camera, the illustrations for *Darkness and Daylight* are, in fact, engravings made from the photos of Bellevue Hospital photographer O. G. Mason, photojournalist Riis, and others. Still, the claim is crucial to the book's argument that we must be able to *see* the poverty (and depravity) that fills the streets of New York in order to truly understand it and, ultimately, to be moved to end it. The motive is a humanistic one—the belief that seeing is not only believing but understanding as well. Furthermore, such a belief constitutes a faith that, once understood, the problem can—indeed will—be solved.

In depicting the poor, whether in literature, journalism, painting, or photography, representations swing between imaging the impoverished as dangerous, intemperate, low-life street thugs, or as helpless victims. Often, the two representations are somehow set together, as in Mayhew's depiction of those who will not work but whose lives must still be looked on with pity. Helen Campbell's volume—while it has much in common with Riis's *How the Other Half Lives* and even takes some of its engravings from those and similar photographs—actually is the story of a Christian temperance mission, suggesting that the true horror of New York Street life begins and ends in the bottle. The pages of this dense book are headed with such running titles as "Human Beasts in Filthy Dens."[10] Of the reformers I mention above, it is only London who rarely strays from the insistence that the impoverished he sees are victims of a larger system. His refrain, "Then the thing happens," is London's way of reminding his

Help Feed The Homeless This Thanksgiving

For 105 years, the Milwaukee Rescue Mission has been providing food, shelter and compassionate care to Milwaukee's homeless. This season we expect hundreds of homeless men, women, and children to come to our door seeking help. For only $1.56 the Mission can provide a hungry, homeless person with a hot meal. Your gift can make a real difference in someone's life.

Yes, I want to help the homeless this Thanksgiving.

Name _____

Address _____

City _____ State _____

Zip _____ Phone _____

☐ $15.60 to provide food and shelter this Thanksgiving season
☐ $31.20 to provide food and shelter this Thanksgiving season
☐ $156.00 to provide food and shelter this Thanksgiving season
☐ $____ to provide food and shelter this Thanksgiving season

MRM
Milwaukee Rescue Mission

Your tax-deductible gift can be made payable to:

Milwaukee Rescue Mission • Dept. 1114
830 N. 19th Street • Milwaukee, WI 53233 • (414) 344-2211

FIGURE 3

readers that the homeless wanderers he spends his days with are only an unfortunate incident away from having been self-supporting working-class or middle-class men and women.

For Hogarth and Grueze, the connection was clear: an immoral life led inevitably to a degraded condition. A return to morality was a return to prosperity and the warmth of hearth and home. Such stories of Penitent Magdalenes and Prodigal Sons might well seem appropriate moralistic tales for eighteenth-century class-conscious English society, and not at all related to what we understand of poverty in the United States today. And yet, the Appalachian child posing for *Children, Inc.* and the unwashed, unshaven, homeless man cautiously leaning into his coffee in a Milwaukee Rescue Mission photo[11] are likely to evoke much the same response as those eighteenth-century images: pity and almsgiving mixed with slight disapproval (fig. 3).

The issue at hand and the difficulty for nonprofits, then, is how to make real the dimensions of poverty and evoke the desire to give or to act without turning benefactors away. The question of seeing remains at the heart of problems of representation. What exactly is it that we see? Here I find Henry Mayhew's words once again useful for understanding what it is we might see. As he introduces that final volume devoted to "those that will not work," Mayhew tells his readers,

> The attainment of the truth, then, will be my primary aim; but by the truth, I wish it to be understood, I mean something *more* than the bare facts. Facts, according to my ideas, are merely the elements of truths, and not the truths themselves; of all matters there are none so utterly useless by themselves as your mere matters of fact. A fact, so long as it remains an isolated fact, is a dull, dead, uninformed thing; no object nor event by itself can possibly give us any knowledge, we must compare it with some other, even to distinguish it; and it is the distinctive quality thus developed that constitutes the essence of a thing.[12]

If we think, then, of representation in the way cultural theorist Stuart Hall has explained it—as constitutive of reality or meaning rather than as an attempt to replicate a "fact" already there—easy to see and understand—then Mayhew's remarks must lead us to ask what it is we are representing in the images of poverty most in use by today's nonprofits. What, then, is the essence of this thing *poverty* as it takes form in the popular imagination?

Certainly this century's most extensive and thoroughgoing attempt to represent poverty in the United States has been the Farm Security Administration's vast photo project documenting the face of rural poverty throughout the Depression and Dust Bowl years. Following the tradition of earlier documentarists like Riis and Lewis Hine, photographers including Walker Evans, Dorothea Lange, Arthur Rothstein, and others of the FSA created some of the most recognized images we have of America in hardship. These images continue, I would argue, to set the limits for representations of poverty today. Yet, even those images, as historian James Curtis notes in his full-length study of FSA photography, are not mere "facts" recorded with the unflinching eye of the camera lens. The clientele for these images—like the clientele for today's nonprofits—was primarily urban and middle class, and these images, "and entire photographic series," Curtis writes, were manipulated "to conform to the dominant cultural values" of this clientele.[13]

In his analysis of Dorothea Lange's photograph of Florence Thompson, generally known as *Migrant Mother* or *Migrant Madonna*, Curtis points particularly to the photographic choices Lange made that were "undoubtedly influenced by prevailing cultural biases."[14] The FSA documentary project portrayed the human spirit, the indomitable will of individuals who refused to yield to troubles they could not control, and *Migrant Mother* was certainly that. Florence Thompson, Curtis tells us, was traveling with her husband and seven children in the migrant work camps of California when Lange encountered her, and the choices Lange made in coming to that final shot that is now so recognizable were crucial for the way the image has been read over the years. The series of shots Lange took leading up to the final image indicates, for example, that she made the decision to leave a teenage daughter out, to compose the final group in a classic Madonna and child manner, to eliminate the clutter of the makeshift shelter and more—decisions that, in essence, placed Florence Thompson and her children clearly into the class of *deserving* over undeserving, or shiftless, or any other less acceptable representation that might have been made from the same family. This is an image that America not only accepted but embraced as emblematic of human courage and strength. In fact, this image remains so familiar that in 1998 the United States Postal Service chose it as one of several that would represent the thirties in a run of stamps commemorating each decade of the twentieth century.

In any number of nonprofit appeals, we can see versions of *Migrant Mother*, or of the shacks and bare dirt yards and delicate children in tattered clothing so familiar in Walker Evans's FSA photos. The issue is not that such conditions did not exist then. They did. They do today as well. And yet to rely primarily on these kinds of images while the country, the economy, the conditions, and the dimensions of poverty and need have changed considerably is to limit the ways nonprofits might respond to the need that is there.

Habitat for Humanity: A Case in Point

I have chosen Habitat for Humanity publicity videos for my focus because Habitat is a popular and far-reaching nonprofit with affiliates not only in the United States but throughout the world. Its goal is not a modest one: Habitat for Humanity aims to eliminate poverty housing from the globe. More than that, Habitat puts housing into the hands of the people who will be housed—into the hands of the homeowners and their neighbors. This is not another program aimed at keeping people in what has become known as the poverty or welfare cycle.

To be very clear, then, I am not criticizing the work of Habitat for Humanity. It is an organization that has done an amazing job of addressing what is, as cofounder Millard Fuller tells us again and again, a worldwide problem. What I would draw attention to, however, is how that problem of inadequate housing and its solution are represented, especially in publicity material produced and distributed by the organization, and how those representations can feed into the troubles that Habitat continues to have as it attempts to change the ways Americans think of helping others. What's more, the kinds of visual arguments Habitat and other nonprofits use to advocate for action or change have become increasingly common tools for getting the message to the public, and yet, I would argue, these messages too often fail to overturn cultural commonplaces that represent poverty as an individual problem that can be addressed on an individual basis. Habitat's catch phrase—A Hand Up, Not a Hand-Out—appeals to a nation that believes anyone can achieve economic security with just the right attitude and set of circumstances.

Habitat's basic program has a kind of elegance. Applicants who are chosen as homeowners put in sweat equity hours to build their home and to help build the homes of others chosen by Habitat. The organization then sells the home to the applicant at cost (that cost held down through Habitat's ability to provide volunteer labor and donated materials) and charges a small monthly mortgage that includes no interest. Unlike public assistance, which is raised or lowered depending on the recipient's circumstances, most Habitat affiliates do not raise mortgage payments when homeowners get better jobs or find themselves in better financial shape. And once the house is paid for, it belongs to the homeowner.

Obviously, in order to run a program like this one, Habitat must produce publicity appeals aimed at convincing potential donors to give time, money, and material. Print ads, public service television and radio spots, commercial appeals linked to products like Maxwell House coffee, and publicity videos meant to be played for churches, volunteer organizations, and even in-flight video appeals on certain airlines are common media for Habitat.

Habitat publicity videos are typically configured as problem-solution arguments. The problem is that too many people have inadequate shelter. The solution is community involvement in a program like Habitat for Humanity. The most common setup for these productions is an opening sequence of images —a visual montage—in which we see black-and-white shots of rural shacks, of men and women clearly in despair, and of thin children in ragged clothing. The voice-over narrative of one such montage tells us the story:

> Poverty condemns millions of people throughout the world to live in deplorable and inhuman conditions. These people are trapped in a cycle of poverty, living in places offering little protection from the rain, wind, and cold. Terrible sanitary conditions make each day a battle with disease and death. And, for this, they often pay over half their income in rent because, for the poor, there are no other choices. Daily, these families are denied a most basic human need: a decent place to live. The reasons for this worldwide tragedy are many. They vary from city to city, country to country, but the result is painfully the same whether the families are in New York or New Delhi.[15]

It is a compelling dilemma.

Organizations like Habitat for Humanity, in order to convey the seriousness of this struggle and, of course, to raise funds and volunteer support for their efforts in addressing it, must produce all sorts of publicity. And in that publicity they must tell us quickly what the problem is and what we can do to help. To do that, Habitat gives us a visual representation of poverty, a representation that mirrors the most common understandings of poverty in America.

Now, there is nothing inherently wrong with that representation unless, of course, what you want to do (as Habitat does) is convince the American people to believe in the radical idea that those who have must care for the needs of others, not just by writing a check, but by enabling an entirely different lifestyle. For Americans, it is truly radical to think that our poorer neighbors might actually be allowed to buy a home at no interest and with the donated time and materials of others. It is a radical notion that such a program means that these neighbors then own that house and aren't obliged to do more than keep up with payments in order to continue owning it. And it is a radical idea that Habitat does this work not only in our neighborhoods (not isolated in low-income housing developments) but throughout the world. Habitat International truly believes that we are all responsible for partnering with our neighbors throughout the world so that everyone might eventually have, at least, a simple decent place to live. Like the philosophy behind many nonprofits, Habitat's is not a mainstream notion.

Still, that representation of poverty—clinging as it does to commonplaces drawn from FSA photographs in this century, from Jacob Riis's nineteenth-century photos of urban poverty, and from documentaries of Third World hunger—has serious limitations, which must be obvious to those who remember the moment that the Bush administration confidently announced that, after looking everywhere, they had discovered no real hunger in the United States. And that myth that poverty cannot/does not actually exist in the heart of capitalism has once again been reinforced in the 1998 Heritage Foundation report in which Robert Rector echoed the perennial argument that there is little true poverty in this country ("Myth").[16] Heritage Foundation's finding comes despite figures from the National Coalition for the Homeless ("Myths and Facts About Homelessness"), which tell us that in 1997 nearly one in five homeless people in twenty-nine cities across the United States was employed in a full- or part-time job.[17]

In her call for a changed representation of poverty in America, bell hooks argues that in this culture poverty "is seen as synonymous with depravity, lack and worthlessness." She continues, "I talked with young black women receiving state aid, who have not worked in years, about the issue of representation. They all agree that they do not want to be identified as poor. In their apartments they have the material possessions that indicate success (a VCR, a color television), even if it means that they do without necessities and plunge into debt to buy these items."[18] Hers is hardly a noble image of poverty, but it is a true one and one that complicates the job of an organization like Habitat that must identify "worthy" applicants. This phenomenon of poverty in the center of wealth, in a country with its national mythology of hearty individuals facing the hardness of the Depression with dignity and pride, is certainly a part of what Manning Marable challenges when he asks readers not to judge poverty in the United States by the standards of other countries. Writing of poverty among black Americans, Marable reminds us that "the process of impoverishment is profoundly national and regional."[19] It does little good to compare the impoverished of this country with Third World poverty or, for that matter, with Depression Era poverty.

The solution in these Habitat videos is just as visible and compelling a representation as is the problem. The solution, it seems, is a modern-day barn raising. In clip after clip, Habitat volunteers are shown lined up to raise walls, to hammer nails, to cut boards, to offer each other the "hand up not a hand out," as these publicity messages tell us again and again. Like the barn-raising scene from Peter Weir's *Witness*, framed walls come together against blue skies. People who would normally live in very different worlds come together to help a neighbor. It is all finished in record time: a week, even a day. Volunteers can come together quickly. Do something. Get out just as quickly.

The real trouble with Habitat's representation, then, is twofold: it tells us that the signs of poverty are visible and easily recognized. And it suggests that one of the most serious results of poverty (inadequate shelter) can be addressed quickly with volunteer efforts to bring individuals up and out of the poverty cycle.

Of course, if Habitat works, what could be wrong with the representation? It is an organization so popular that it receives support from diametrically opposed camps. Newt Gingrich and Jesse Jackson have both pounded nails and raised funds for Habitat. This is what Millard Fuller calls the "theology of the hammer." People might not agree on political parties and they might not agree on how to worship or even what to worship, Fuller says, but they can all agree on a hammer. All can come together to build houses. Or, can they?

As successful as Habitat has been, it is an organization that continues to struggle with such issues as who to choose for housing, how to support potential homeowners, and how to convince affiliates in the United States to tithe a portion of their funds to the real effort of Habitat: eliminating poverty housing throughout the world, not just in the United States. And, even in the United States, affiliates often have trouble identifying "deserving" applicants or convincing local residents to allow Habitat homes to be built in their neighborhoods. There are certainly many cultural and political reasons for these problems, but I would suggest that the way poverty continues to be represented in this country and on tapes like those videos limits our understanding of what poverty is and how we might address it.

That limitation holds true for those caught in poverty as well as those wanting to help. What if, as a potential Habitat applicant, you don't recognize yourself or you refuse to recognize yourself in those representations? As Stanley Aronowitz points out in *The Politics of Identity*, that can happen very easily as class identities, in particular, have become much more difficult to pin down since World War II, especially with an expansion of consumer credit that allowed class and social status to be linked to consumption rather than to professions or even wages. In his discussion of how electronic media construct the *social imaginary*, Aronowitz talks of the working class with few media representations available to them as having fallen into a kind of "cultural homelessness."[20] How much more true is that of the impoverished in this country who may be neither homeless nor ragged, but are certainly struggling every day to feed their families, pay rent, and find jobs that pay more than what it costs for daycare?

I have been particularly interested in this last question because of a difficulty I mentioned earlier, that of identifying appropriate applicants for Habitat homes or even getting some of the most needy families of a given affiliate to apply for Habitat homes. When I showed the video *Building New Lives* to Kim Puuri, a Copper Country Habitat for Humanity homeowner and now member of the affiliate's Homeowner Selection Committee, and asked her to respond, she was very clear in what she saw as the problem:

> When I see those pictures I usually think of Africa or a third world country and NOT the U.S. It's not that they can't be found here, it's just that you don't publicly see people that bad off other than street people. If they could gear the publicity more to the geographical areas, it may make more of an impact or get a better response from people. It would mean making several videos. It may not be so much of a stereotype, but an association between Habitat and the people they help. People viewing the videos and pictures see the conditions of the people and feel that their own condition may not be that bad and feel they probably wouldn't qualify.[21]

What this Habitat homeowner has noticed is very close to what Hall describes. That is, the problem with this image, this representation, is not that it is not real enough. The problem has nothing to do with whether or not these are images of poverty as it exists in the world. There is no doubt that this level of poverty does exist in this country and elsewhere despite the Heritage Foundation's attempts to demonstrate otherwise. The problem is that this representation of poverty is a narrow one and functions to narrow the ways we might respond to the poor who do not fit this representation.

The representation I have been discussing is one that insists on constructing poverty as an individual problem that can be dealt with by volunteers on an individual basis. That is the sort of representation common in this country, the sort of representation Paul Wellstone objects to in a recent call to action when he says "We can offer no single description of American poverty." What it takes to break through such a representation is first, as Stuart Hall suggests, to understand it as a representation, to understand it as a way of imparting meaning. And the only way to contest that representation, to allow for other meanings, other descriptions, is to know more about the many dimensions of poverty in America. "More than 35 million Americans—one out of every seven of our fellow citizens—are officially poor. More than one in five American children are poor. And the poor are getting poorer," Wellstone writes.[22] But we can be certain that much of that poverty is not the sort pictured in those black-and-white images. And if it doesn't look like poverty, then how do we address it? How do we identify those "deserving" our help?

Indeed, as Herbert Gans has suggested, the labels we have chosen to place on the poor in this country often reveal more than anything "an ideology of undeservingness," by which we have often elided poverty and immorality or laziness or criminality. "By making scapegoats of the poor for fundamental problems they have not caused nor can change," Gans argues, "Americans can also postpone politically difficult and divisive solutions to the country's economic ills and the need to prepare the economy and polity for the challenges of the twenty-first century."[23] These are tough issues to confront and certainly to argue in a twenty-minute video presentation aimed at raising funds and volunteer support, especially when every piece of publicity must make a complex argument visible.

On the Way to Changing the Face of Poverty

Reflecting on more than thirty years of working among the poor, Dorothy Day once wrote, "Poverty is a strange and elusive thing. . . . We need always to be thinking and writing about it, for if we are not among its victims its reality fades from us."[24] Of course, that impulse—to keep the poor before us—is precisely what has led to the many firsthand accounts and documentary photographs and sociological studies and publicity videos like those I have mentioned above. But Day, who devoted her entire life to working with the poor, continues on in a passage quoted here at length for its directness and clear-headed understanding of what it means now, and has meant in the past, to be truly in need:

> So many good souls who visit us tell us how they were brought up in poverty, but how, through hard work and cooperation, their parents managed to educate all the children—even raise up priests and nuns for the Church. They contend that healthful habits and a stable family situation enable people to escape from the poverty class, no matter how mean the slum they may once have been forced to live in. The

argument runs, so why can't everybody do it? No, these people don't know about the poor. Their concept of poverty is of something as neat and well ordered as a nun's cell.

Poverty has many faces. People can, for example, be poor in space alone. . . . Then there are those who live under outwardly decent economic circumstances but are forever on the fearful brink of financial disaster. . . . No matter how high wages go, a sudden illness and an accumulation of doctor and hospital bills, for example, may mean a sudden plunge into destitution.[25]

What Day tells us here recalls Jack London's warning: "Then the thing happens." It is a reminder that the poor are not only always among us, but at any time might be us. At any time so many Americans living on the very edge of financial health might be plunged into destitution.

I suspect some readers wonder why I continue to emphasize the very ordinary nature of those who live in poverty and why I not only consider it so important that nonprofits work to break older stereotypes, but that recipients of those nonprofit appeals learn to read the images of poverty with the knowledge that they are stereotypes and do limit our understanding of need. More than one of the many colleagues and friends I have besieged with my talk of poverty and nonprofit appeals has asked an important question: If nonprofits don't use images that show hunger and need, then how are they to get across the urgency of their message? How do they raise money or awareness? It is a question I have not always answered well or completely. I do believe, however, that an answer might lie in two areas: first, in a knowledge of the actual consequences of relying on those stereotypes to carry a message of need; and second, in an understanding of what we have sometimes called the "visual imperative" of the electronic media.

Once again, as long as people give to nonprofits to support poverty programs, what does the image matter? Does "the vocabulary of poverty," as Michael B. Katz claims, really impoverish the political imagination?[26] I offer one very quick example of how that vocabulary, that stereotype, does indeed impoverish the political imagination. Early in 1999, the Michigan legislature put on fast-track Governor John Engler's most recent plan to cut back the assistance rolls in his state. Engler proposed drug testing for all welfare recipients. Those tested positive would be sent to rehabilitation programs. If they fail to attend those programs or if they are found to continue drug use, they will be dropped from welfare rolls. Despite federal studies that indicate that only about 5 percent of welfare recipients are serious drug and alcohol abusers ("Welfare Drug Test"),[27] this legislation feeds into the notion that if someone is on assistance, there must be something wrong with that person, something that once fixed will make each individual a contributing, self-supporting member of the community.

Democrats' proposed amendments to the Engler bill weren't much better. Amendments asked that only those applicants who have not found a job after participating in Michigan's Work First program be screened "for potential drug and alcohol abuse, learning disabilities, illiteracy, domestic violence, actual or imminent homelessness and mental illness."[28] Clearly, the operative notion here is that only the most deviant, disabled, or disinclined to learn make up the ranks of those who cannot find work.

Although many would argue that such legislation is unconstitutional, it was no idle threat. By July 1999, the legislature had passed Engler's bill and drug testing had begun. Readers might well recall that John Engler's name came to national prominence during his first term in office when he began what has continued to be a deep slashing of public assistance and welfare rolls. His back-to-work or workfare programs have caught on throughout this country, and Engler has been heralded as a governor who takes people off welfare and puts them back into the workplace.

Barbara Ehrenreich's most recent experiment in which she became—Jack London-like—a low-wage employee, not to find out "how the other half lives" but to test out policies like Engler's that claim that "work will lift poor women out of poverty while simultaneously inflating their self-esteem and hence their future value in the labor market," vividly illustrates how impoverished this particular political imaginary actually is. Not only do most jobs held by low-wage employees offer no security and few or no benefits; they are simply not jobs that will provide a living wage. Ehrenreich explains, "According to the National Coalition for the Homeless, for example, in 1998 it took, on average nationwide, an hourly wage of $8.89 to afford a one-bedroom apartment, and the Preamble Center for Public Policy estimates that the odds against a typical welfare recipient's landing a job at such a 'living wage' are about 97 to 1."[29] These are not good odds, and they point again to the reality Dorothy Day wrote of so many years ago: it is important to help individuals, and individuals can certainly raise themselves up out of poverty, but helping the individual without addressing larger structural problems will do little more than help the individual.

The second concern I point to—understanding the role of the media in communicating need—may be even more crucial in changing the face of poverty, for it points directly to how the media work within certain "givens." Speaking on the difficulties of getting United States news media to carry the 1983 story of the Ethiopian famine, communication scholar Brian Winston addresses one of those givens—what he calls the media myth of being in the "grip of the visual imperative."[30] Winston argues that, if we closely analyze the news media, we will discover that it is only such stories as Third World hunger that are caught in the grip of this visual imperative. Many other kinds of stories get long play with stock—even dull—footage. He names political election stories or stories of economics for which the media will find a number of images that we could not call compelling—the President getting off a plane, for example, or oil wells in a Kansas field. According to Winston, if we were instead to tell the story of hunger as a real story of problems of wealth and distribution and the like, then there would be all kinds of images that would work: wheat fields, graphs, ships moving grain, and more. Instead, however, the story of hunger and poverty exists on the level of crisis reportage so that, according to Winston, this kind of story is *located* in the image.

"Famine," Winston argues, "is a biblical word. We don't have famines in the West. Famines can only come into our collective consciousness . . . if it's in biblical terms." As if to reinforce Winston's point, Michael Buerke, whose BBC report did finally break the Ethiopian famine story in 1984, says much the same: "The curious thing—it came out in the first film we did—is that biblical business. People looked like those depicted in the color illustrations in my old school Bible. Sort of sackcloth color and a certain nobility of features."[31] Winston is much harsher in his assessment. He calls many of these images "masturbatory" images of hunger—a pornography of starvation.

If not those images, then what? Well, I would return to Habitat homeowner Kim Puuri's suggestion that Habitat might have to start making different videos or publicity pieces for different areas/different audiences. In that suggestion, Puuri is actually calling our attention to the most serious problem of such broad representations: they depict poverty as a crisis that we can recognize and address now with just a call, a contribution, a few hours of our time. In addition, these images depict poverty as something that happens to others, people outside the ordinary. As the Michigan legislation suggests, these people are addicts, illiterates and, worse yet, potentially *violent* addicts and illiterates.

Since I have focused many of my comments on Habitat for Humanity publicity, I feel compelled to turn first to Habitat for alternate representations of the people who apply for and get Habitat homes. My own local affiliate published the following fund-raising Christmas card for the 1997 Christmas season (fig. 4). The images of these families are remarkable only for the fact that they are our neighbors. This area, known as the Copper Country, is small enough that families receiving this appeal would recognize some or all of the families pictured on the card. They would have worked with them; many would even be related to them. They are people we know whose financial circumstances are not unlike that of many of their neighbors. What Copper Country Habitat is doing with a card like this one is, in some ways, risky. It is, after all, much easier to imagine need that is far away and desperate in ways that can be seen. Instead,

We send thanks—
and thoughts & prayers
for a fine Holiday
and a Good Year—
to your family
from all of ours…

FIGURE 4

the Kangas family

the Deforge-Harma family

this affiliate is counting on the community to know that need looks a lot like the every day. It looks a lot like the people they live with and work with. In fact, it is the people they live and work with.

Other local affiliates do much the same. I have been especially impressed by the work of Chicago's Uptown affiliate. Uptown renovates old apartment houses and turns them into condos. In forming its homeowner's association, Uptown Habitat homeowners have written their own newsletters, written rules for the condo group, advocated for police attention to the crime outside their doorways, and more. The newsletter *HabiChat* published by Uptown Habitat looks much like many of the newsletters of neighborhood associations throughout suburban America. It includes announcements for Spring Clean-up, marriage and birth announcements, resources for parenting troubles, and more. Such newsletters, sent out as they are to the entire affiliate and not kept isolated within the homeowners association, work to remind Habitat volunteers and donors that Habitat's best work is fundamental to the lives of ordinary people working at one or more low-wage jobs and just trying to get by in safe, inexpensive, decent housing.

Of course, that is Habitat. Despite its goal to eliminate poverty housing on the globe, Habitat can rarely address the needs of the most impoverished. After all, a Habitat homeowner must come up with even a little money for a mortgage, and there are millions of Americans who cannot do that. What of those others? What about that man in the Milwaukee Rescue Mission ad I mentioned earlier? This is clearly a man with little enough to eat much less the resources for a house payment or even the energy for "sweat equity." Perhaps he is a part of those "undeserving" poor, the drunks and addicts Engler would like to push off Michigan's assistance rolls.

Again, I would call attention to how the homeless depict themselves. I offer one last, true story: Outside the San Francisco Hilton just after Christmas a year ago, I bought my third copy of *Streetwise: A Publication of the Coalition on Homelessness San Francisco*. It is not unlike papers sold by homeless men and women in several cities throughout this country. As I tucked the paper into my books, a short, well-dressed woman waiting for a cab turned to ask me if someone was handing out free things. "No. It's a paper. It costs a dollar." In anger, she came closer to me and yelled, "You *paid money* for that trash?"

Stunned both by the suddenness and the volume of her anger, I neglected to ask if she'd read the article on prisons and shelters signed by "Art B, One Homeless Guy, one of the 14,000 in San Francisco living in a shelter or under the freeways." It was pretty good, I wanted to tell her, but she was already off in her cab.

In these street papers, written as this one is by "the homeless and formerly homeless," we are presented with yet another image of desperate poverty. Perhaps because the homeless themselves write articles seeking to uncover the very structures that keep homelessness and poverty alive and well in our cities, some potential readers are driven to the kind of anger I witnessed. More likely, it is that the very sight of a homeless person, so very obviously in need of food, shelter, a recovery program, or more, is enough to frighten away the lady in the cab.

In Tucson during the past year, the City Council threatened to clear the medians of homeless people selling papers. The Council claimed these men and women represented a safety threat. In response Casa Maria, Tucson's Catholic Worker House, distributed a flyer calling for action to block the Council order. In it, Casa Maria accused the Council of acting on the basis of "aesthetics" rather than from any real concern over safety and pointed to the fact that many of the people who sell those papers have actually been able to pay rent and provide themselves with basic necessities just by being allowed to stand on those medians and sell newspapers. Brian Flagg, a worker from Casa Maria, wrote recently "We won this one! It was cool—We filled their meeting with church people & uppity tramps!"[32]

It might indeed take uppity tramps, local newsletters, and committed activists like Brian to change constructively the ways the poor are represented, as bell hooks asks that we do. As well, however, it will take a clear understanding of need in its many forms, and for this the image of Amy standing in a deserted mining town and looking out from a black-and-white photo does not altogether tell New Yorker readers what they need to know.

thirteen **Popularizing Science**

At the Boundary of Expert and Lay Biomedical Knowledge

Lundy Braun and John Trimbur

It is no mystery to anyone who reads the popular and scientific press these days that biomedicine is big business. In the United States, scientists argue that a large-scale investment in biomedical research and the technological advances that result will not only improve individual health but also increase labor productivity, global competitiveness, and control Medicare costs. Indeed, the Republican-controlled Congress has demonstrated its strong support for science, particularly the biomedical sciences, by awarding the National Institutes of Health (NIH) the largest budget increase for 1999 of any agency in the government. An increase of this magnitude, at the same time that social programs for the poor are being slashed and dismantled, is driven by the lure of commercializing biomedical discoveries as well as the broader cultural expectation of conquering disease.

For science policymakers, the sustained flow of tax dollars and labor power needed to realize the potential of biotechnology (even as small biotechnology companies are closing their doors and venture capital is withdrawing support) depends on an informed public. The citizenry, as voters and workers, must be recruited, in effect, to the research enterprise, persuaded of the public's stake in the ongoing work of science. Accordingly, the leading professional organizations in science have called in recent years for campaigns to increase the public's understanding of science.

Traditionally aloof from public involvement, governed (at least in Robert K. Merton's classic account) by norms of disinterestedness and humility,[1] bench scientists would hardly seem likely candidates to be public spokespersons, and yet that is exactly what the scientific organizations are now urging them to do —to "go public," to get out of the laboratory and find public forums where they can communicate the promise of their research. This involvement takes many forms: participation in science education programs in local schools, developing formal and informal lecture series for the public, fostering a collaborative relationship with the popular media, and lobbying Congressional leaders for research support. The National Science Foundation (NSF) has funded "scientifically literate" college students to work in public schools. The National Cancer Institute (NCI) has conducted a series of focus groups with both scientists and members of the general public to assess scientists' ideas on communicating medical research findings and the public's perception of medical research.[2] And recently, M. R. C. Greenwood, Chancellor of the University of California at Santa Cruz and president of the American Association for the Advancement of Science (AAAS), has called on AAAS to initiate a campaign to elect at least one scientist, engineer, or "scientifically literate" person on every school board in the United States.[3]

The idea of scientists communicating with a broad public audience is, to be sure, a laudable one, with its historical roots in nineteenth-century popular traditions of democratic learning and the diffusion of useful knowledge through mechanics institutes, lecture series, lending libraries, and so on. The question remains, though, concerning the nature of the communication and the types of relationships "going public" is meant to establish between scientists and nonexperts. In some cases, such as the creation by former NIH Director Harold Varmus of a Council of Public Representatives, the scientific establishment has sought input from the public, to get advice on policy matters and insight into the public's perception of official science. In the biomedical community, progressive health care workers have developed programs that take advantage of the rich social networks in communities to help improve access and delivery of medical care.[4] Nonetheless, the methods scientists use to communicate to laypeople are based, for the most part, on a unidirectional flow of information —from the scientific experts to the lay public, often times with the media as go-between—where the boundaries between science and nonscience are thought to be clear and unambiguous. The usually unstated goal of this linear transmission model is to inform the public while maintaining the authority of scientists over knowledge-making practices. According to this model, scientists, not the public, are responsible for determining what research questions are worthy of study, which methodological approaches are relevant in addressing these research questions, how scientific data is interpreted, and what policy initiatives derive from scientific findings.

Studies of the popularization of scientific knowledge have analyzed how science writers employ various genres to translate the findings of practicing scientists to educated readers.[5] These analyses are useful in what they can tell us about how the popular as well as the scientific press helps maintain the cultural authority of science by reinforcing the boundary between experts and laypeople, producers and consumers of knowledge. What such analyses fail to explore, however, is how laypeople might reimagine their relationship to scientific expertise and become actively engaged with scientists in constructing scientific knowledge. By focusing largely on discursive practices such as genre analysis and the rhetoric of inquiry, studies of popular science have, for the most part, overlooked the literate practices that lay activists have devised to popularize science. In recent years, "popular epidemiologists" in grassroot toxic waste movements, AIDS activists, and breast cancer organizers have struggled to redefine the relation of laypeople to the biomedical establishment.

In this essay, we explore the relationship between the biomedical research establishment and the public, how this relationship is shaped by popular media accounts of biomedical research, and how popular movements of lay activists are seeking to rearticulate the expert knowledges of official science. As we will see, recent efforts by lay activists to popularize science involve not only the acquisition and circulation of scientific knowledge but also a change in the relationship of nonspecialists to the reading and writing practices of scientific expertise. For lay activists, popularizing science means participating in its knowledge-making practices.

Public Understanding of Science

A variety of terms, including scientific communication, scientific literacy, the rhetoric of science, and science education are currently used by scholars and scientific organizations to represent the relationship of the public to science and scientific communities. The terms point to different communication strategies on the part of official science and different areas of research in the academic disciplines (sociology, communication, science studies, rhetoric, education, and public health). Recently, this scholarship and the efforts of scientists and laypeople to make science public have been thematized by the term "public understanding of science" (with its unfortunate acronym PUS). As we will see, however, what is actually meant by "understanding" in this formulation of the public's relation to the scientific enterprise remains unresolved, a contested term that refers variously to notions of "appreciation," "acquisition of knowledge," and "ability to use."

In the postwar period, with the military victories of World War II attributed to such scientific and technological advances as penicillin, synthetic rubber, and the atomic bomb, public attitudes toward science were generally enthusiastic, although scientists and policymakers considered the public's knowledge lacking in scientific facts. The launching of Sputnik in 1957 only seemed to confirm the fears of the scientific establishment, which led to major investments in scientific research and in educational initiatives such as the "new math" and new science curricula designed to inculcate schoolchildren with scientific ways of reasoning.

The success of this investment was assessed in the 1970s and the 1980s by a series of quantitative surveys administered to adults to test their "scientific literacy."[6] The results shocked scientists and policymakers. Scientific literacy was low in the United States and seemed to be declining, from a high of 14 percent considered scientifically literate in 1979 to a low of 5 percent by 1985. A 1997 NSF survey measuring public attitudes and understanding of science found that many Americans could not define molecules and DNA or even how often the earth revolves around the sun. According to the survey's findings, respondents' interest in science and technology, nearly 70 percent, was at an all-time high, but only one in four Americans understands the nature of scientific investigation well enough to make informed judgments about scientific results reported in the media. In addition, the survey shows that public attitudes toward science and technology are divided, especially over the impact of such technological developments as the use of nuclear power to generate electricity and genetic testing. The upshot for official science, as outgoing NSF director Neal Lane put it, is that "the public has not given science a blank check, and the scientific community needs to communicate its work more clearly and effectively."[7]

Concern among American scientists about the public understanding of science intensified during the 1990s, largely as a result of sharp cuts in the federal budget for scientific research. These cuts not only jeopardized the careers of a generation of basic scientists, but also threatened efforts to develop new therapies for a wide range of diseases. Since the budget cuts for science coincided with new advances in research on the biological mechanisms of cell growth, there was great fear that the opportunity to translate basic research findings from molecular biology and biochemistry to the clinical realm would be lost. Through their professional associations, many basic scientists went public, to persuade ordinary citizens of the biomedical promise of new research findings on the inner workings of the cell and to increase federal funding for basic research, even while draconian cuts in education, welfare, health care, and social services were being implemented. After basic scientists' intense lobbying of Congress, Harold Varmus, a prominent molecular virologist from the University of California at San Francisco (now at Sloan Kettering), made a surprising shift from the laboratory to public policy and was appointed Director of the NIH by President Clinton. Varmus proceeded to appoint a number of basic scientists to crucial leadership positions at the NIH, thus consolidating the highly visible and active role of basic scientists in setting the biomedical research agenda.

This transition from the laboratory to the public forum reveals some of the limits to what basic scientists believe an "understanding" of science entitles the public to say and do. These limits became apparent when two important social movements of patient advocates—AIDs and breast cancer activists—demanded and obtained substantial increases in the allocation of funds targeted to AIDS and breast cancer research. In addition, activists demanded direct involvement in setting the research agenda through participation on committees such as Institutional Review Boards that evaluate the ethics of research on human subjects and study sections that assess the merit of scientific research proposals. For many in the basic research community, the expanded participation of lay-people in the workings of biomedicine amounted to no more than concessions to interest-group politics. Instead of picturing the involvement of lay activists as a widening in the public understanding of science, some in the scientific establishment regarded movements for popular participation in science as a dangerous infringement on basic researchers' freedom to explore the secrets of nature, unfettered by what the scientists thought of as the "special interests" of consumer advocates and disease constituencies.[8]

In the main, "official" science has favored education rather than popular participation as the vehicle of extending public understanding of science. The belief in an ongoing scientific literacy crisis, ostensibly demonstrated by the surveys of adult Americans already mentioned, as well as the declining performances of American elementary and secondary students on international standardized science tests, has offered a powerful instigation for reform in science education—to recruit the best and brightest students, to overcome the alienation of women and minorities from science, and to prepare the citizenry to understand such issues as medical marijuana, genetically engineered food, alternative medicine, and physician-assisted suicide. This felt sense of crisis, however, concerns more than just the public's knowledge of science. For the scientific and biomedical establishment, what is at stake in the public's understanding is the cultural prestige of science—and the fear that a consensus on the authority of basic research and mainstream medical practice needs to be shored up.

To forge such a consensus, mainstream programs for the public understanding of science tend to rely on finished accounts of scientific research, success stories in which knowledge is portrayed as complete, unproblematical, and certain. Mini-medical schools, for example, featuring university medical faculty have popped up across the country to explain the latest breakthroughs in research and clinical practice. According to a report in the *New York Times*, there are forty-five mini-medical programs throughout the United States, drawing thousands of participants and providing scientists with a public forum to present their knowledge and expertise.[9] At costs that keep the programs at least theoretically accessible to a broad audience, participants "experience the excitement of medical school" by learning about new discoveries in genetics and genetic testing, and the latest advances in neurosciences, infectious disease, and immunology. The sponsoring medical schools, in turn, expect that the communication of information from experts to laypeople will increase both the public's understanding of science and its support of the biomedical enterprise.

The mini-medical school's lecture format, of course, is designed to transmit information rather than engage in exchange with the public. Moreover, by focusing on biomedical success stories, in which scientific knowledge is portrayed as fully formed, replicable, and accurate, these programs mask the uncertainty and dynamic nature of scientific research. They promote a public understanding of science that is of a hierarchy of knowledge in which scientific expertise is pictured as "real" and "true," authenticated by laboratory work and clinical studies, where scientific objectivity is immune to the passions of the public forum, above the fragmentary, interested, and incomplete accounts of nonexperts. In turn, the public is cast as passive recipients of a predetermined body of information with little or no attention paid to what the public thinks they need to know, how scientists could most productively share their technical expertise with laypeople, or what the nature of lay knowledges may be.

Policing the Boundaries between Scientific and Popular Knowledge

This polarization of expert and lay knowledges has marked the relationship between official science and the public as one of suspicion and frustration. The communication of scientific information in simplified form, stripped of uncertainty and complexity, leaves the public frustrated because it locates them outside the realm of knowledge-making, marginalized and acutely aware of the asymmetrical distribution of scientific expertise. It should not be surprising, then, that the public's sentiments toward science are frequently ambivalent, ranging from feelings of dependence and vulnerability to eruptions of hostility to the mandates of experts, noncompliance, and passive resistance. By the same token, scientists are frustrated when the information they communicate is not received in a "correct" way, leading to what scientists perceive to be irrational public policy brought about by ignorance and a failure to follow the norms of scientific reasoning. Instead of mutual understanding, we have border skirmishes between experts and laypeople, at the boundary between official and popular science.[10]

The widespread use of alternative medicine by the American public in the face of vehement opposition by the biomedical community offers a good example of such a skirmish—about what legitimately counts as health care and who are the rightful bearers of medical knowledge. It is estimated that $27 billion are spent annually on alternative medical treatments in the United States, nearly equivalent to the amount, $34.4 billion, spent on mainstream medicine. In one study published in 1993, one-third of Americans admitted to the use of alternative therapies, such as massage, acupuncture, herbal remedies, megavitamins, chiropractors, naturopaths, and so on.[11] Even more significant, many of those interviewed did not inform their primary care physicians of these practices. By 1997 the percentage of Americans who used alternative therapies had increased to 42.1 percent.[12]

Scientists and physicians, especially in the United States, view the public's interest in alternative medicine with suspicion and anger, as a "flight-from-reason" that threatens the authority of Western medicine to determine the scientific approach to disease and health. For much of the medical establishment, alternative medicine is just further proof of the public's ignorance of science and, along with creationism, UFOs, feminism, and cultural studies of science, a rejection of reason and objectivity. In a public expression of frustration, Arnold Relman, editor-in-chief emeritus of the *New England Journal of Medicine*, argued that there "are not two kinds of medicine. Nor . . . are there two kinds of thinking, or two ways to find out which treatments work and which do not."[13]

In fact, the public's interest in alternative medicine is not based on a rejection of Western medicine but on a rejection of Relman's argument that there is only one type of medical knowledge worth having. A closer look at the debate over alternative medicine suggests that, rather than reflecting an outright hostility toward medical orthodoxy, the widespread use of alternative medicine reflects a more complex and ambivalent relationship of the public to medical treatment. The public has certainly not abandoned Western medicine but, at the same time, it refuses to exclude the unratified popular knowledges of alternative medicine. Perhaps most frustrating to Relman and other spokespersons for biomedical orthodoxy is that the public's understanding of science recognizes the artificial nature of distinctions between official and popular knowledges. Understandably, the public wants to have it both ways.

There is no question that medical treatment should be based on the best designed studies. Since few alternative therapies have been rigorously tested in clinical trials, the gold standard of mainstream medicine, physicians are legitimately concerned about possible drug interactions in the case of alternative medicines that contain biologically active substances. But more is at stake in the controversy over alternative medicine than potential toxicities—or that alternative treatments might delay the use of more effective ones. Indeed, many mainstream medical treatments have not undergone clinical trials either, and even the most elegant experimental work, whether in laboratory research or clinical trials, may result in uncertainty. The problem with Relman's polarized "kinds of medicine" and "ways of thinking" is that they demand a choice of social allegiances—with us or against us—but offer the public little in the way of handling ambiguity or making sense of differing interpretations, when there is no clear consensus among scientists and physicians.

The recent debate over mammography screening guidelines for women aged 40–49 illustrates what can happen when the evidence is ambiguous. After several highly charged meetings of the National Cancer Advisory Board and much politicking behind the scenes, the National Cancer Institute issued guidelines in 1997 that recommended mammographies every one to two years for women forty years and older. Evidence from randomized controlled clinical trials has clearly demonstrated that screening reduces mortality for women over the age of fifty. These studies are not controversial. On the other hand, evidence of benefit for women under fifty is much less certain, and scientists differ in their interpretation of the data. Not surprisingly, these equivocal results have turned into a heated controversy.

Some scientists argue that evidence of harm due to false positives will outweigh any protective effect of screening for women under fifty. On the other side, advocates of screening, including the American Cancer Society, radiologists, and manufacturers of mammography machines, claim that the benefits are overriding. Faced with such differing interpretations of inconclusive evidence, advocacy groups are split. The National Breast Cancer Coalition, the Center for Medical Consumers, and the National Women's Health Network argue that the scientific evidence is not sufficient to recommend screening for women under fifty, whereas other groups have advocated strongly that screening programs include women under fifty on the grounds that screening is one of the few ways women can control their experience of breast cancer.

For others, however, the real problem is neither the evidence nor the interpretations but the controversy itself. According to Jane Wells, writing in the *British Medical Journal*, "the necessity of screening for breast cancer among women in their 40s has assumed an importance out of proportion to its potential impact on public health." While admitting reasonable differences among experts in interpreting the scientific data, she goes on to question the reasonableness of the public's response. The problem, as she sees it, is that the public found the uncertainty of experimental evidence unacceptable: the "public has been taught to believe in medical and scientific infallibility" and thereby "the expectations of the public and the media contributed to the pressure for definitive guidelines."[14]

In Wells's account of the mammography controversy, the public is an obstacle to sound clinical practice, in part because of their ignorance of science, but also in part because of their unquestioning belief in it. "When trials do not give an unequivocal answer," she says, "when politicians and interest groups become involved, and when the professionals responsible for promoting the public's best interest fail to do so, objectivity is likely to suffer."[15] Rather than acknowledging that the response of the public may be a legitimate way to manage the scientific uncertainty about mammography, the lay public (as well as certain groups of scientists, physicians, and politicians) is blamed for contaminating the establishment of policy informed by objective scientific principles.

Wells is certainly correct that the public has been taught to believe in the infallibility of science, but she fails to locate the origins of this idea in the practice of science itself and how it authorizes experts as the best interpreters of science for the general public. An alternative way of thinking about the debate over mammography screening would suggest that the public did not misunderstand or misinterpret the issues, including the scientific questions, at all. Although guidelines to screen women under fifty may be off the mark, since there is no scientific evidence that such screening increases survival, we would argue that the controversy represents not only a problem in interpreting data but an attempt to renegotiate boundaries, with the nonexpert public taking an active role in defining their relationship with the experts. In the absence of a compelling demonstration, the public was simply doing the only thing available, namely, engaging in the deliberative rhetoric of policymaking, where the boundary between scientific and popular knowledges is a permeable one.

Boundary-making and the Media

As popularizers of science, positioned between scientists and the public, the media plays a crucial role in regulating the boundary between expert and lay knowledges. For their part, scientists and physicians may feel plagued by what they perceive to be crude and inaccurate representations of their work and exaggerated accounts of cures in the press. At the same time, scientists acknowledge that the media is in a powerful position to influence public opinion and, therefore, is an important mechanism for communicating scientific ideas to the public. Seminars on interacting with the media, for example, have become commonplace at professional scientific meetings and, increasingly, are a component of graduate education in the sciences.

In *Selling Science*, Dorothy Nelkin argues that popular accounts of science in the media are characterized by several features, including imagery that replaces content, superficial explanations of the content of research, a focus on the competitive nature of science, and the representation of the scientist as savior.[16] Promises of cure—for cancer, heart disease, arthritis—carry the most dramatic appeal for the public and often end up on the front page of the news, shaping public views on the "miracles" of biomedicine and subsequent feelings of vulnerability and anxiety when medicine cannot solve all the problems of health and disease.

There is no question that science journalism varies greatly in quality. Some accounts are sensationalized, exaggerated, or grossly distorted, whereas others do an excellent job of communicating the best available understanding of biomedical topics in a way that is of value to the public. However, the "difficulty of writing 'popular' articles about science," as Bruno Latour points out, does not hinge finally on matters of accuracy or inaccuracy, responsibility or sensationalism. Instead, the difficulty "is a good measure of the accumulation of resources in the hands of a few scientists . . . . It is hard to popularize science because it is designed to force out most people in the first place."[17] Science journalists must struggle daily with an overwhelming amount of highly technical information, trying to balance their own critical judgment of science, the cultural authority of scientific expertise, and the fragility of their networks with practicing scientists.

Nelkin calls particular attention to the relations between journalists and scientists and how they function together as "wary collaborators" in the popularization of science.[18] On one hand, both groups share a positivist vision of science and a common belief that professional expertise is the final arbiter of what counts as science. In turn, they cast the public variably as passive, duped, dangerous, or irrational consumers of scientific information who are in need of science to make "informed" personal decisions, expected to support rational public policy, but excluded from participation in scientific knowledge-making practices. On the other hand, the norms and values of the two professions differ in their judgment of what is news, what counts as evidence, the distinction between simplification and accuracy, and the relevance of the social and political context to understanding science.

The shifting and ambivalent relationship between scientists and journalists is neither innocent nor disinterested, and "official" science cannot be understood simply as the external source of knowledge that popular science draws on to transmit to the public. Instead, as Nelkin argues, science is a coparticipant with science writers in the construction of a popular science. In some instances, scientists seek to use the media to shape public understanding and advance broad agendas for research. For example, following the publication in the *New England Journal of Medicine* of an article that claimed to find no association between exposure to DDT and PCBs and incidence of breast cancer, the research group's principal investigator, David J. Hunter, suggested to a *New York Times* reporter that "perhaps it was time to question the assumption that much breast cancer is caused by unknown environmental agents"[19]—thereby jumping from the possible elimination of DDT and PCBs in the causation of breast cancer to eliminate environmental agents altogether, a sweeping and, at least in some scientific quarters, highly contested view of the etiology of breast cancer.

Other scientists take on a watchdog role and make it their mission to correct the perceived distortions and misrepresentations of science rampant in the media. This view casts the media as driven by special interest groups, hidden agendas, and an appetite for sensationalism. Recently, for example, investigators claimed that media reporting of relative risk for mortality is particularly liable to distortion, with serious implications for public health policy.[20] The authors cite as evidence of such biased reporting the fact that, although homicide ranks eleventh as a cause of death, it received similar press attention as heart disease, which is the leading cause of death in the United States (ignoring that there might be legitimate reasons for reporting homicide as opposed to heart disease, given that death from heart disease tends to occur in older age groups and is seen as a natural cause of death compared to the more newsworthy homicide, which takes place as an unnatural and shocking event). For Frost, and others, the real issue is who will control the scientific understanding of a public that is easily misled by biased and inaccurate accounts of risk. "*Health professionals,*" they say, "must focus the attention of the news media and the public on the health issues of greatest concern so that the most prevalent receive appropriate attention."[21] Notice that the media and the public are marked as problematical —with health professionals responsible for determining what health issues warrant the greatest concern.

There is an important sense in which scientists' concerns about the media acknowledge that the popularization of science does not simply transmit information, whether accurately or inaccurately, between experts and laypeople but also shapes the relationship between them. While scientists may seek to use or correct science reporting, accounts of popular science provide readers with information from the laboratory and clinic as well as strategies for managing their relationship to the specialized world of biomedicine and the concentration of power and expertise in the hands of health professionals. Media accounts offer readers various ways to recognize themselves in relation to health professionals—for example, as deferential patients, anxious consumers, or do-it-yourself healers—and to compensate for their sense of powerlessness and vulnerability.

The dominant strategy—and certainly the preferred and most common one in the establishment press—is that of deference. For example, a 1996 *New York Times* article "Aspirin Proposed for Suspected Heart Attacks," reports a study that found taking as little as half a regular-strength aspirin at the onset of a suspected heart attack can significantly reduce the risk of death. The article, however, reports these findings and emphasizes, as the dramatic pull quote accompanying the article warns, "patients should not act on their own." Certainly there is the reasonable concern, voiced by one of the physicians interviewed for the article, that "patients might try treating themselves without consulting their doctors"[22] and then simply wait for the symptoms to subside. What is telling for our purposes, though, is how the article addresses the reader. Typical of science coverage in the establishment press, the article offers readers an accurate and responsibly written account of recent biomedical research—and at the same time provides them with a reassuring recognition of themselves as patients under a doctor's care.

In other instances, popular science writing, especially medical advice columns in newspapers and magazines, addresses readers not so much as compliant patients but as anxious consumers. Women's magazines in particular mediate consumer anxieties about current medical practices, such as recommended prevention measures, testing and screening, and treatment. In these popular accounts, the boundary between experts and laypeople, so reassuringly in place in the New York Times article, is figured as less reliable and perhaps treacherous. The Glamour article "How OB-GYNs Fail Women: Read This Before Your Next Checkup" is a typical example, reporting in this case on a survey showing "that doctors are dangerously silent about the most important threat to young women's health," namely sexually transmitted diseases (STDs).[23] The strategy offered readers here is not one of deference but of distrust. By problematizing the authority of physicians, the article casts the reader back on her own resources and the need for vigilant and informed consumerism. To the extent that a young women must rely on herself rather than just her doctor, the lines between experts and laypeople are blurred as agency shifts from the medical establishment to the individual, although she remains atomized and anxious in the face of a health care system where so much could go wrong. Another Glamour article "Your Pap Smear: A Save-Your-Life Guide" acknowledges the pap smear as "one of medicine's success stories," but then goes on to warn women that doctors and cytotechnologists can and do make mistakes. The conclusion is that "you need to do everything you can to reduce the risk of error on your next Pap."[24]

If the genre of medical advice, with its "eight steps" or "eleven warning signs," offers readers a strategy to manage their relationship to doctors and to compensate for their relative powerlessness by becoming active and informed consumers, a third type of popular science—the do-it-yourself remedies offered by tabloids and alternative health magazines—validates popular knowledges by discounting the authority of official ones altogether. Such remedies range from traditional dietary and herbal folklore (some of which are efficacious) to the magical thinking of crackpot wonder cures (some of which are outright dangerous). The tabloid *Weekly World News*, for example, featured in its 24 October 1995 issue the headline news: "Golden Raisins and Gin Cure Arthritis." The cover story reports the findings of the "noted nutritionist Dr. Lorenzo Abatz" that "for reasons we don't completely understand, the combination of gin and golden raisins acts as a healing lubricant in the human body."[25] In the sensationalized pseudoscience of the tabloids, the mysterious power of gin and raisins concocts a kind of magical potion that escapes scientific explanation. Although it may appear at first glance to be simply a denial of scientific authority, the appeal of such magic is in fact an expression of powerlessness, disappointment, and desperation when orthodox medical treatments fail to relieve the pain of arthritis sufferers. Unlike the *New York Times* or *Glamour*, the *Weekly World News* is not just offering a way to mediate between experts and laypeople. Its own peculiar step-by-step directions on how to prepare the gin-soaked raisins are meant to empower readers as self-healers. The relationship of this type of popular science to the medical establishment is made clear in the article's closing passages, where it notes that although the "mainstream medical community has been slow to embrace Dr. Abatz' plan, . . . the Boston-based researcher's files are filled with passionate testimonials."[26] In the do-it-yourself world of tabloid science, the personal witnessing of magical cures is really a compensatory gesture, a kind of wishful thinking in the face of the skeptical orthodoxy of the experts.

Lay Activism and Popularization of Scientific Knowledge

The media's popularization of science negotiates in various ways the exclusion of nonexpert readers from the knowledge-making practices of science. Beginning with Love Canal in the 1970s, however, when residents of Niagara Falls noticed unusual clusters of health problems, which they linked to the dumping of hazardous wastes by local companies, community activists have challenged these formidable barriers between experts and laypeople and in the process helped to shape the intellectual content of the emerging fields of environmental epidemiology and environmental health. More recently, AIDS and breast cancer activists have also sought to blur the line between official and popular knowledges. These struggles, to be sure, have been long and difficult ones that highlight profound differences between lay and professional ways of knowing, while at the same time offering telling examples of popular participation in determining what counts as good science.

Differences in the way scientists and lay activists think about science may be seen in the legal case brought to national attention by the book *Civil Action* and its film version, where residents of Woburn, Massachusetts, charged W. R. Grace Chemical Company and Beatrice Foods that their illegal dumping of trichloroethylene (TCE) had contaminated the drinking water of two wells and caused an unusually high incidence of childhood leukemia. Although Beatrice Foods was found not guilty in the jury trial and W. R. Grace settled out of court for $8 million (a fraction of the anticipated settlement), ultimately the Environmental Protection Agency sued both companies, who were forced to spend millions to clean up the site.

Cancer clusters, as occurred in Woburn, where the etiology of the cancer is unknown, pose a particular challenge to interpret, primarily because the numbers of cases are often too small to draw causal inferences with any certainty and may represent nothing more than chance variation in geographic location of a disease. The suffering of the affected population and their desire to know the origin of their disease, however, are real, no matter what difficulties and uncertainties surround the professional study of disease clusters. For this reason, the Woburn activists' sense of urgency often brought them into conflict with legal and scientific experts over standards of causal proof, the degree of certainty required for action, and the significance of anecdotal evidence.

Equally contentious were negotiations over the appropriate roles of laypeople and professionals in the controversy. Community activism is, in many respects, the antithesis of the dominant idea of how scientific knowledge advances (and explains why scientists often approach cases such as toxic waste contamination with trepidation). For the legal and scientific professionals, lay activists can play an important but limited role in providing information and evidence. Nonetheless, as Phil Brown's study of the Woburn activists argues, their function went beyond that of informants and entered into the actual construction of scientific knowledge, even though their developing scientific expertise was rarely acknowledged by the professionals involved in the case.

Brown shows that the Woburn activists' approach to the scientific problem of the disease cluster—what he terms "popular epidemiology"—is not unlike that pursued by professional epidemiologists. According to Brown, lay involvement in toxic waste cases tends to proceed through a series of methodical steps that resemble conventional scientific inquiry: first, identification of health effects and possible pollutants; second, the formulation of hypotheses to connect pollutants and health effects; third, consensus-building around an hypothesis; fourth, input from scientific experts and government officials; and finally organization to continue the investigation.[27] Although the Woburn activists uncovered the problem in the first place, provided oversight over the activities of the professionals, and recruited outside experts to their cause, they were marginalized once litigation began and never got the opportunity to tell their story in court. Yet, despite the fact that their emergent expertise as popular epidemiologists was silenced by the legal maneuvering of the corporations' lawyers, their questions and investigations made important contributions to the design of future studies and helped to construct the field of environmental health.

It is important to note, moreover, that while the Woburn activists were critical of what they perceived to be the disinterested stance and the neglect of community welfare on the part of official scientists, the activists were in no way antiscience. In fact, they were excited by their developing expertise, as they discovered how science could help them act on behalf of their community. If anything the activists' attempts to popularize science by pursuing their community's own questions and needs call into issue the conventional distinction between political involvement and "good science" and the wall it erects between "neutral" and "objective" experts, on one side, and "biased" and "self-interested" laypeople, on the other.

A further challenge to the validity of this distinction between the supposed rationality of official science and the supposed passions of politics occurred when the AIDS epidemic exploded on the national scene in 1981 and profoundly altered the relationship among scientists, physicians, and the lay public. As Steven Epstein observes, AIDS activists were uniquely positioned to engage the biomedical community for several reasons. AIDS was a deadly disease with a prolonged course that affected young, healthy people who had the physical strength and motivation needed to politicize the disease. Moreover, the first group to be affected in the United States were gay men able to draw on a strong network of gay rights activists, many of whom had prominent positions in government, universities, the arts, and media, for support.[28] Activists thus had the intellectual capital and political connections to challenge the cultural authority of the biomedical establishment with unprecedented vigor.

In his analysis of how AIDS knowledges were constructed during the epidemic, Epstein argues that "knowledge emerges out of credibility struggles." By exploring the credibility struggles played out in the AIDS epidemic, Epstein shows that scientific evidence is an indispensable factor in establishing credibility but that other equally important factors include the credentials of the claims-makers and the plausibility of the claims. The key questions then become who is invested with the appropriate credentials and how does the credentialing process take place? Are the only credentialed actors in a scientific controversy those who have officially sanctioned scientific expertise, or can expertise be developed through interactions between lay activists and the knowledges of science? As a consequence of the organizing efforts of AIDS activists, Epstein argues, there has been a "*multiplication of the successful pathways to the estab-*

lishment of credibility and *diversification of the personnel* beyond the highly credentialed."[29] In other words, the polarized conceptualization of layperson and expert has been problematized, opening up the political process of scientific knowledge-making to previously excluded groups. By politicizing AIDS research in such a visible way, AIDS activists positioned themselves to acquire critical credentials to evaluate the scientific evidence and biological plausibility of claims and thus were able to establish their own credibility as claims-makers. Lay or popular knowledges and expert knowledges thus became inextricably linked and mutually dependent in ways that redefined their relationship to each other.

The transformation of the relationship between the biomedical community and laypeople that AIDS activism started has been continued by breast cancer activists. In 1991 a small group of breast cancer survivors founded the National Breast Cancer Coalition (NBCC), a grassroots coalition that has grown to include approximately 400 organizations and 10,000 individual members nationwide. Like AIDS activists, breast cancer activists were able to draw on a long tradition of feminist political action around women's health issues to launch a social movement that would give breast cancer a position of prominence on the national research agenda.

Several distinctive features of breast cancer, including the lack of any credible knowledge about etiology or means to prevent the disease, as well as the younger age of onset and relatively long survival compared to many other cancers, combined to make this cancer the locus of a broad social movement that is changing how biomedicine is practiced. Breast cancer advocates demanded more information about the disease, faster access to experimental drugs, and active participation in allocating coveted research funds to shape the future of breast cancer research in this country. Because the incidence of breast cancer is high in affluent women, breast cancer survivors were able to use the privileges of their social class as cultural capital to gain access to the halls of Congress, the NIH, and scientific meetings throughout the country.

There are inherent tensions in any social movement centered on disease-related advocacy, and, as Epstein notes, one important tension that must be negotiated is the simultaneous dependence on science and the need to challenge the authority of the experts to find solutions to problems of disease. Recognizing how little is known about breast cancer after so many years of study, breast cancer activists saw that a central feature of their movement was to engage with scientists not just at the level of lobbying for more research funding but, more fundamentally, to obtain a "seat at the table" to influence what research should be done, how it should be done, and who should do it. Perhaps the most radical demand was for activist participation in the design of experimental studies, an area of research previously the exclusive province of the experts.

The NBCC was successful in getting $407 million allocated to breast can-
cer research by fiscal year 1993. Because of parliamentary maneuvers, some of
the money was funneled through the Department of Defense (DOD). The fact
that the DOD's procedures for peer review of grant proposals were not highly
regarded by scientists afforded the NBCC the opportunity to help shape the
composition of the study sections, the groups charged with evaluating the scientific merit of proposals for grant funding, by demanding that at least one
"consumer" representative be included on each study section, as well as on the
committee at the second level of grant approval. Participation on scientific review boards has opened up the closed and insular community of study sections
to the lay public and in the process has redefined the boundaries between expert and lay persons as well as transformed, in its most basic respects, the cultural practices by which scientific knowledge is made.

Public Understanding of Science in Practice

Many in the biomedical community have now come to accept and to appreciate the participation of laypersons in certain aspects of research, treatment, and
prevention of disease. But for laypeople to go beyond accessory roles in biomedical research and to become equal partners in making what we think of as
science requires engagement with the content as well as the political process
of making science. Such participation in the knowledge-making practices of
science, as Epstein suggests, requires not only political clout but a change in
identity. AIDS activists turned themselves, in Epstein's words, from a "disease
constituency" into an "alternative basis of expertise" by moving beyond the
early demands of groups like Act Up for more research, better health care delivery, and faster approval of new drugs.[30] By learning science, AIDS activists, in
effect, have transformed themselves from consumer advocates representing the
interests of patients to lay-experts capable of intervening in the process of
knowledge-making and contesting the prevailing understanding of what counts
as "good science"—in the clinical studies at the NIH, in the manufacturing of
drugs at the pharmaceutical companies, and in the approval of drugs at the FDA.

Education had always been important to breast cancer activists. The support groups for women with breast cancer that proliferated in the late 1970s
and the 1980s recognized the need to understand the scientific aspects of the
disease. Study groups formed and members pored over the medical literature,
realizing in the process that ordinary readers could learn to understand the
specialized discourse of scientific expertise. In the words of one activist, "once
you start reading them [medical journal articles], you get the gist of it."[31] This

desire to popularize science—not by simplifying the scientific literature but by making it accessible to lay readers—led NBCC to establish a program for breast cancer activists to develop a strong and systematic foundation in basic principles of biology, molecular biology, and epidemiology.

Entitled Project LEAD (Leadership, Education, and Advocacy Development), the program teaches scientific principles to breast cancer activists in order to facilitate and enhance their participation in a wide range of scientifically related programs. Each year the NBCC sponsors four workshops with thirty to thirty-five participants from a wide variety of organizations, including breast cancer support and advocacy groups, the Black Women's Health Project, health centers in local communities, state breast cancer coalitions, women's health advocacy groups, and state and local health departments. The majority of the participants are breast cancer survivors.[32]

As we have seen, most models of promoting the public understanding of science involve a top-down, linear approach of transmitting scientific information as fully formed and complete. In contrast, Project LEAD does not simplify scientific knowledge by stripping it of complexity and uncertainty. The workshops popularize science not by acting as an intermediary between science and public, but instead by redefining the participants' reading practices and their relationship to the expert knowledges of official science. Through a combination of lectures, interactive small group sessions, case studies, research seminars with discussion, role-playing, and critical appraisals of the basic science and epidemiologic literature, participants together with faculty grapple with contemporary debates over the causes, prevention, and treatment of breast cancer and how to make sound, though imperfect, policy decisions in the face of inconclusive data and uncertainty. In addition, as a follow-up to the workshops, Project LEAD sponsors a Journal Club that distributes recent experimental articles on breast cancer research and invites readers to participate in an on-line forum and telephone conference calls to discuss the articles with LEAD faculty.

Project LEAD participants develop an emergent lay expertise based on reading practices that enable them to negotiate their relationship to biomedicine without the debilitating dependence and sense of vulnerability we have seen in the deferential and anxious consumer readings offered by the popular media. Drawing on both the rich knowledge of their lived experience of health and disease and the wide-ranging inquiry into the biology of cancer gained in the workshop, Project LEAD participants develop an understanding that goes beyond the mere acquisition of information to a critical appraisal of study design and experimental method in basic research and clinical trials. They learn, that is, to popularize science by demystifying the scientific literature and submitting it to their own questions after the workshop through involvement in the development of research protocols, participation in scientific/peer review of grant proposals, service on Institutional Review Boards and data monitoring committees, scientific advisory committees, and many aspects of clinical trial recruitment. By actively engaging and challenging scientific experts, Project LEAD participants gain the ability to look beyond their own disease experience both to help individual women negotiate the sometimes byzantine world of health care and to lend a powerful voice for a more critical public health, wary of pronouncements of cures and simplistic prevention messages and committed to the health needs of everyone, regardless of race, gender, or social class.

Conclusion

The promise that biomedicine will develop solutions to problems of health and disease is enticing, and everyone—businesspeople, scientists, policymakers, and the public alike—has high expectations. Although their perspectives vary, these groups share the idea that science can deliver "the truth" with certainty. It is precisely the credibility invested in biomedicine—the unquestioning popular faith in science—that creates dependence on the experts, desire for scientific certainty, and anxiety and vulnerability when medicine does not have the answers. Official public understanding of science programs are not movements to help the public explore the complexity of biology and the dilemmas of policymaking in the face of scientific uncertainty. Rather, as we have seen, these official movements are the battleground to reestablish on firmer footing the cultural authority of science to determine who will control the public's understanding and how scientific knowledge will be constructed and transmitted. In contrast, movements of toxic waste, AIDS, and breast cancer activists struggled with the public's dependence on experts by challenging the cultural authority of scientists. By engaging scientific knowledge, they have successfully begun a process of transforming the relationship between the public and the scientific community so that laypeople can take an active role in determining what counts as scientific knowledge.

fourteen **Understanding Popular Digital Literacies**

Metaphors for the Internet

Lester Faigley

> The Internet is the final empowerment of the individual. It allows me
> to have a complete, comprehensive amount of information.
> —Charles Schwab ad on the CBS Evening News
> (25 November 1998)

It seems hard to believe today that the personal computers that have made new
forms of popular literacy possible didn't exist until 1977, when the Apple II
was introduced. (Before then, personal computers had to be assembled from
a kit.) The majority of computers in the late 1970s and the early 1980s still
were behemoths housed in secure, air-conditioned rooms behind thick plate
glass. Many users punched cards and submitted the deck on a "batch" basis,
then waited hours for the output. (The computers were fast; their attendants
weren't.) If you made an error in punching the cards or arranging the deck,
you had to resubmit the batch and wait more hours for the job to be repeated.
Only the lucky few who had access to a terminal connected to the mainframe
computer could avoid the step of punching and submitting the cards. Modem
access from dumb terminals was available twenty years ago, and primitive word
processing was even possible, but to work from home on a 300-baud modem
meant that a full-screen text editor took over a minute to record each change;
thus text editing had to be done "blind" using a programming language with
commands that said the equivalent of "in line 17, character 21, substitute 'p'
for 'j.'" This tedious process required a physical printed text on which you did
your best to keep up with the changes you had made. Sooner or later you lost
track of what was actually in line 17, causing frequent trips to the computation
center to get printouts of the latest version.

An early form of the Internet—the ARPANET—also existed twenty years ago. ARPA is an acronym for Advanced Research Projects Agency in the Department of Defense, which during the 1960s became increasingly interested in a system of intercomputer communication among the various military, academic, and corporate research sites it sponsored. In 1969 the first files were transferred between the University of California at Los Angeles and the Stanford Research Institute, and by 1971, the possibility of e-mail became a research goal.[1] Quickly e-mail among researchers became as important as file sharing. My exposure to the ARPANET came when three colleagues at Texas and I obtained a grant from the Fund for the Improvement of Postsecondary Education in 1980, and I learned that researchers who had federal grants could get an account on the ARPANET. Soon after I signed on, I received a thin directory of everyone on the ARPANET —a collection of midlevel officers at top-secret bases, academics in applied physics laboratories, and researchers in defense industries. Needless to say, I didn't find any key pals on the ARPANET. But I did find that the weapons builders took time out to talk about the latest science fiction book they had read or their other hobbies on bulletin boards.

The growing ranks of computer professionals who did not have access to the ARPANET wanted these same capabilities. One of the most important efforts came at the University of North Carolina and Duke University in 1979, when the team of Steve Bellovin, Mark Horton, and Tom Truscott experimented with a system that allowed articles to be distributed to multiple newsgroup subscribers, a system that later grew into USENET. The initial motivation was the quick distribution of UNIX bug reports. But as USENET grew in the 1980s, so did the range of topics. By 1987 the USENET administrators stumbled into one of the first big censorship fights when they rejected a proposal for a newsgroup (net.rec.drugs) to discuss drugs. Another newsgroup called "gourmand" was rejected because the USENET administrators wanted it to be called "recipes." Those angered by centralized control of what they believed should be freely distributed information started the "alt" newsgroups linked through privately owned and public access servers. Others followed the "alt" model, creating their own newsgroups using the USENET protocols, and soon any central control of newsgroups became a distant memory. By 1994 USENET became a global, decentralized association of systems with over 10,000 newsgroups.

This brief sketch of the development of the Internet suggests how popular literacies developed with the medium from the beginning, within and outside official channels. Although the Internet has become thoroughly commercialized, the growth of e-mail, participation on listservs and chatrooms, the proliferation of personal Web sites, and other forms of popular literacies continue to expand. At this point quoting statistics of Internet use takes on a Carl Sagan air. There are billions of words moving around the planet every day in digital forms of popular literacies that seemingly rose from nowhere. These statistics are brought home when you find an e-mail message from someone (in my case older relatives) whom you doubted would ever own a computer, much less be on-line.

In 1969 an estimated 500 million people around the world watched in amazement as Neil Armstrong and Edwin "Buzz" Aldrin stood on the moon's Sea of Tranquility. The live broadcast of the event was at the time as incredible as the mission itself, and many people who watched the first lunar landing remember it vividly. By contrast, on 11 September 1998, millions went to various sites on the World Wide Web to peek at Kenneth Starr's report to Congress on President Clinton shortly after it was released. CNN's Web site received 340,000 hits a minute before its monitoring system was overwhelmed, and other sites reported record traffic. No document before was read (or at least skimmed) so quickly by so many, but few besides newspaper editors, who had been leap-frogged by the on-line release of the report, found noteworthy the nearly instant publication and consumption of the Starr Report by millions of readers. People simply expected the Starr Report to be published on a medium that almost nobody knew existed at the beginning of 1993, when there were fewer than fifty Web servers.

The Internet has become a part of daily life in developed nations, and yet many scholars of literacy do not feel the need to acknowledge its impacts. Perhaps this quiet acceptance reflects that the Internet is but the latest in a series of electronic communications technologies dating back to the development of the telegraph in the 1840s. Within four years of Samuel Morse's first demonstration of this new technology in the United States, newspapers were using the telegraph for transmitting news. The great advantage of speed was evident from the beginning, and we've never backed away from the desire for faster communication technologies. The Internet came to many as yet another fast electronic technology, joining the telephone, the fax machine, radio, and television. In terms of its functions, it didn't seem different.

The quotidian response to the explosion of popular digital literacies also results from the dominant metaphors for the Internet. During the 1990s the primary metaphors for the Internet were those of the "Information Superhighway" and various metaphors of "community." Both sets of metaphors are spatial; thus both defined the Internet as space, offering competing metaphors of "Cyberspace." The metaphor of Cyberspace gives the Internet an otherworldly quality, conflating a variety of literate activities that occur on the Internet and removing them from the circumstances of their production and reception.

Another reason that people in general have failed to notice the impacts of the Internet on their own practices of literacy is that many mundane acts of personal literacy became much easier to perform with personal computers. When the first Macintoshes were introduced in 1984, desktop publishing became a reality for many amateurs. The printing of a club, church, or neighborhood newsletter that formerly required a laborious process of typing and formatting suddenly was a cinch using a template on a word processing program. That newsletter now can be published on the Web, eliminating the need to print address labels and the costs of postage. Furthermore, because the process of scanning and publishing images has become increasingly simpler, that newsletter can contain many photographs and illustrations. The activities involved in creating Web sites for newsletters as well as many personal Web sites are not subsumed under metaphors of highways or communities. Instead, we might better think of these literacies as activities of craft as practitioners have begun to probe the capacities of new media. Many nonprofessionals have created beautiful, yet highly functional Web sites, exemplifying how the craft tradition can persist in new media and new genre.

But my intent in this chapter is not to survey the forms of personal digital literacies, but rather to examine the claims that underlie metaphors of Cyberspace—specifically the easy conflation of information, power, and democracy.[2] These facile connections, as well as the antiutopian connections of technology to the loss of freedom and corporate and government control, have restricted how we might imagine digital communications technologies being used. James Carey has observed that claims for electrical technologies leading to decentralization, renewed democracy, and re creation of human community have been issued frequently since the nineteenth century. Each new electrical communication technology, beginning with the telegraph and telephone, have brought new dreams of democracy. In this century prophets of the coming electronic revolution have been accompanied by those who cry out that the apocalypse is near unless technology is contained. Techno-utopians and neo-Luddites appear as almost mirror images. In 1964 when Marshall McLuhan in *Understanding Media* pronounced that communications technologies are imploding the world into a global village, Herbert Marcuse in *One-Dimensional Man* described the pessimistic obverse where all forms of dissent in modern society were being controlled and assimilated through technology.

As long as metaphors for the Internet are confined to competing versions of Cyberspace, we will not get far beyond Microsoft's slogan, "Where do you want to go today?" in either its utopian or antiutopian versions. For most users, Cyberspace refers to the collective World Wide Web—not e-mail, MOOS, or other on-line discourse. Metaphors of space are perhaps necessary for making sense of the Web. We "visit" Web "sites" that can be restricted by "firewalls." But at the same time, the Web is not so much a place as a technology—the most powerful publishing technology ever invented. Just as for books, newspapers, and pamphlets, Web sites are produced by people, published from particular locations and visited by people in specific locations. The promise of metaphors of Cyberspace is, in the words of an ad agency, "the final empowerment of the individual." Whether in actuality this phrase means that those who are well off can buy practically anything on the Web, or whether something more is implied, that the small player can have an influence that was not possible or much less possible before the Internet, is something we have to find out by examining what people do both on and off the Internet.

Superhyped Superhighways

When President Clinton signed into law the Telecommunications Act of 1996 on 8 February of that year, he borrowed from his vice president the pen President Eisenhower had used to sign the Interstate Highway Act in 1957. Eisenhower then gave the pen to Senator Albert Gore, Sr., the great champion of building the Interstate system. In President Clinton's words, "The Interstate Highway Act literally brought Americans closer together. We were connected city to city, town to town, family to family, as we had never been before. That law did more to bring Americans together than any other law in this century, and that same spirit of connection and communication is the driving force behind the Telecommunications Act of 1996."[3] Clinton called Albert Gore, Jr. the father of the Telecommunications Act for his success in popularizing the metaphor the "Information Superhighway" during his campaign for the vice presidency in 1992. The "Information Superhighway" gained quick currency in the media in part because previous electronic communications technologies followed the pathways of transportation technologies, beginning with the stringing of telegraph wires beside railroad tracks before the Civil War. But there were other reasons why the Information Superhighway became a deeply resonant metaphor. Al Gore, Jr. had learned well from his father that much political capital could be gained through the rhetoric of highways.

The promotion of the Interstates in the 1950s and 1960s and Gore's enthusiasm for the Information Superhighway in the 1990s continue a long-standing American mythology of the freedom of the open road. Throughout this century the automobile has embodied freedom of action—not just the pleasures of driving around aimlessly for recreation but the possibility of exploring new territories and reaching the frontier. The planners of the Interstate system appealed to the mythology of unrestricted freedom when they promised coast-to-coast highways without stoplights. The 1990s prophets of the Internet and Cyberspace also draw heavily on the mythology of the frontier. The first Cyberspace and the American Dream conference held in Atlanta in August 1994, sponsored by the Newt Gingrich-affiliated Progress and Freedom Foundation, produced the manifesto for a new generation of high-tech political conservatives. In "A Magna Carta for the Knowledge Age," Ester Dyson, George Gilder, George Keyworth, and Alvin Toffler invoke the idealized highway in the American imagination—the highway that leads to the frontier. Their optimism is as unrestrained as their imagery: "The bioelectronic frontier is an appropriate metaphor for what is happening in Cyberspace, calling to mind as it does the spirit of invention and discovery that led ancient mariners to explore the world, generations of pioneers to tame the American continent and, more recently, to man's first exploration of outerspace."[4]

Exploration of the frontier is linked to democracy in this rhetoric. Both Interstates in the 1950s and the 1960s and the Internet today are represented as agents for democracy, carrying on a long-standing American rhetorical trope. From Thomas Jefferson onward, American leaders have maintained that good roads are a prerequisite to democracy. By the end of the last century, good roads were the people's answer to the hated railroad monopolies depicted by Frank Norris in The Octopus. With good roads, farmers could transport their crops directly to local markets and competitive railheads. When the Interstate system was proposed, it was advanced as a means of connecting the nation, stimulating the economy, and eliminating poverty in Appalachia and other regions lacking good roads.

Gore's "Information Superhighway" metaphor thus associated the economic prosperity of the 1950s and the 1960s facilitated by new highways with the potential for vast amounts of commerce to be conducted over the Internet. Gore set out these implications in detail in his speech at the National Press Club on 21 December 1993, announcing the National Information Infrastructure:

> It used to be that nations were more or less successful in their competition with other nations depending upon the kind of transportation infrastructure they had. Nations with deep water ports did better than nations unable to exploit the technology of ocean transportation. After World War II, when tens of millions of American families bought automobiles, we found our network of two-lane highways completely inadequate. We built a network of interstate highways. And that contributed enormously to our economic dominance around the world. Today, commerce rolls not just on asphalt highways but along information highways. And tens of millions of American families and businesses now use computers and find that the 2-lane information pathways built for telephone service are no longer adequate. This kind of growth will create thousands of jobs in the communications industry.[5]

Later in the speech Gore turned to the impediments of implementing his vision of the information superhighway, impediments that have become known as "bumps" or "bottlenecks." These bumps are of two kinds—the technical ones more directly analogous to highways and those imposed by regulatory agencies working under obsolete legislation. Gore was confident that the technical problems could be quickly resolved; his main concern was with the "potholes" of obsolete legislation. Finally Gore used the metaphor of the highway as the road to the future, with the clear message that those not on the highway would not reach the utopia around the corner. By making the highway metaphor the vision of the future, Gore provided a strong, though controversial, rationale for giving the federal government the central power to shape policy even though the system would be built by corporations (the last federally owned backbone of the Internet was turned off in April 1995).

Conveniently forgotten, however, were other effects that superhighways brought. Like the Internet, superhighways themselves were also sold to the public through metaphors. Urban planners of the 1960s saw superhighways as the means to prevent inner cities from continuing to decay. Inner-city blight was recognized as early as the 1930s, and the problem was understood for four decades as one of circulation (hence expressways were called "arterials"). The planners argued that those who had moved to the suburbs would return to the city on expressways. By the end of the 1960s, the engineers were tearing down thousands of units of urban housing and small businesses to build expressways with a logic that was similar to the logic of mass bombing in Vietnam —to destroy the city was to save it.[6] Shortly the effects were all too evident. Old neighborhoods were ripped apart, the flight to the suburbs continued, and the decline of inner cities accelerated rather than abated.

Not everyone in the 1950s and the 1960s saw expressways as the answer to urban dilapidation. Lewis Mumford in 1958 challenged the circulation metaphor. He wrote: "Highway planners have yet to realize that these arteries must not be thrust into the delicate tissue of our cites; the blood they circulate must rather enter through an elaborate network of minor blood vessels and capillaries." Mumford saw that new expressways produced more congestion and aggravated the problem they were designed to overcome, thus creating demand for still more expressways. If road building through cities were allowed to continue, he predicted the result would be "a tomb of concrete roads and ramps covering the dead corpse of a city."[7] In 1959 San Francisco's Board of Supervisors refused to allow any more expressways to be built in their city, leaving the partially completed Embarcadero Freeway literally suspended in midair, and after an eight-year battle in New York City, the Lower Manhattan Expressway was finally rejected a decade later.[8] Today, no Western nation has taken steps as radical as San Francisco's to limit access to the Internet (although Saudi Arabia, Myanmar, and a few other nations have effectively banned the Internet), but there are no shortage of critics who view the rush to the Internet as a flight away from a physical reality in a world that is increasingly violent, ugly, noisy, polluted, and paved over. One of the more strident critics, Mark Slouka, accuses the Internet of magnifying all the ill effects of twentieth-century technologies, culminating in an "attack on reality as human beings have always known it."[9]

Given the exponential growth of the Internet, it is no wonder that it has inspired visions of utopia and apocalypse. The highway lobby of automobile manufacturers, petroleum companies, trucking companies, and building contractors that controlled the United States Congress during the 1950s and the 1960s now is dwarfed in comparison to the powerful transnational corporations involved in privatizing the Internet. President Clinton promised that the Telecommunications Act of 1996 would "help to create an open marketplace where competition and innovation can move as quick as light." Just the opposite has been the result. The new media megaliths created by the frenzy of mergers are battling each other for control of Cyberspace. And even the giants are running scared. In March 1997, Gerald Levin, the chairman of Time Warner, which controls Warner Brothers movies, Time Warner cable, Time and People magazines, HBO, CNN, and Ted Turner Broadcasting, observed that the real competition is all the giants versus Microsoft.[10] In May 1998, the United States Department of Justice entered the fray by suing Microsoft for anticompetitive practices, and at the end of one of the most important antitrust trials in American history, a federal judge ruled in November 1999 that Microsoft was monopolistic. While the outcome of these battles is far from over, all players are betting on a future in which nearly everyone in the world who has any disposable income will own a computer that is connectable to nearly every other computer in the world.

On-line Communities

For the corporate marketing giants, the lone computer user choosing to click or not to click on the multitude of sites on the World Wide Web is the embodiment of the fragmented media market. Advertising has become an ensemble of entertainment and three-dimensional marketing. To gain the loyalty of that computer user, the advertiser has to offer an array of consumable objects— wear the T-shirt, collect the cup, go to the concert or sports event, carry the tote bag, enter the contest, dial the 800 number, get the plastic figures when you buy a "Happy Meal." Clicking on a Web site simply adds to the list. The media megaliths saw immediately the potential of the World Wide Web because they were already engaged in webs of cross-media promotions. Contrary to the vision of the Internet as a global bazaar for thousands of small businesses, the only big commercial winners in the long run are likely to be the big players because only they control all the pieces—what is called "synergy" in the corporate world.

In the late 1960s and the early 1970s, advocates of cable television envisioned two-way interactive systems that would facilitate political participation, improve education, and overcome social isolation. Seldom-viewed community-access channels are a legacy of this optimism. But the major result of cable television has been much more of the same. If the Internet is going to offer people more than an endless supply of products, services, pay-per-view movies, and interactive games, then it will have to prove to be a means of overcoming the isolation and narrow self-interest of a society based on consumption. This recognition of how the Internet will be used in shaping future social and political landscapes brought community as the primary oppositional metaphor in debates over the impacts of the Internet in the 1990s.

The arguments of the celebrants and critics share a common critique of urban space. All take as points of departure the war zones that our major cities have become and the alienated individualism of our suburbs, where people are likely to know more about the lives of celebrities than about the lives of their neighbors. Critics of the Internet blame technology for the state of the present. Celebrants argue either that the poverty and blight of the present are lingering remains of the smokestack era (Toffler's "Second Wave" decaying industrial world that is being replaced by the technological utopia of the "Third Wave"), or that the world is now so transformed by technology that we have no choice but to seek salvation through technology. The latter is the position of John Perry Barlow, who typically begins articles and interviews with an account of growing up on a cattle ranch in Wyoming, inheriting that ranch, and watching it and Pinedale, the community where he lived, be inundated by the economic and cultural forces of contemporary America. Then he discovered the Internet. Barlow writes that:

> In 1987, I heard about a "place" I could visit without leaving Wyoming. Inside the WELL [Whole Earth 'Lectronic Link] was, it seemed, almost everything one might find going on in a small town. I was delighted. I felt I had found the new locale of human community—never mind that the whole thing was being conducted in mere words by minds from whom the bodies had been amputated. The commons, or something like it, had been rediscovered. Once again, people from the 'burbs had a place where they could encounter their friends as my fellow Pinedalians did at the post office. They could put down roots that could not be ripped out by forces of economic history. They had a collective stake. They had a community.[11]

Finding the WELL was a conversion experience for Barlow. He became a co-founder of the libertarian Electronic Frontier Foundation and is a leading spokesman for leaving the Internet unregulated. Barlow rejects the highway metaphor since the Interstate system was planned by the Federal government. He ignores the military origins of the Internet and portrays it as an organism that has grown largely on its own without planning or government supervision.

To his credit, Barlow does recognize the warts on his beloved Internet. Writing in 1995, he regrets that "there is not much human diversity in cyberspace, which is populated by white males under 50 with plenty of computer-terminal time, great typing skills, strongly held opinions, and excruciating face-to-face shyness, especially with the opposite sex." He grants that many elements "essential to the formation and preservation of real community" are missing in cyberspace. But in the end Barlow says we have no choice because "in five years, everyone who is reading these words will have an e-mail address, other than the determined Luddites who also eschew the telephone and electricity." Barlow says that we're better off going to the Internet open-minded and excited rather than being dragged reluctantly.[12]

People are hardly being dragged to the Internet now. In the many thousands of listservs, newsgroups, threaded Web forums, and personal Web sites, more words are published electronically each day than are published in print worldwide—a fact that enthusiasts like Barlow celebrate as the overcoming of barriers to communication and that skeptics like Slouka decry as a morass of Babel in which reflective thought disappears. What is overlooked in these pronouncements of the Internet as our salvation or our demise is that significant new practices of literacy have come into existence along with the Internet. In 1981 Thomas Miller and I conducted a survey of 200 college-educated people writing on the job, stratified according to type of employer and type of occupation. We found that everyone in an occupation that requires a college education wrote on the job and wrote frequently. Nearly three-fourths of the people sampled claimed to devote 10 percent or more of their work time to writing, but few reported to write much while off the job.[13] For many people who have access to the Internet, that situation has changed. They may be using work time for personal writing, but they are nonetheless writing for purposes other than work.

Another celebrant of virtual communities, Howard Rheingold, explains this phenomenon by claiming that the Internet provides a "place" in people's lives that functions as a site for conversation similar to the ways that corner bars, coffee houses, and town squares provided these places in the past. Rheingold applies the distinction Ray Oldenburg proposes in *The Great Good Place*, that there are three essential places in life—the places where people live, the places where they work, and the places where they gather for conviviality. Many of these third places have fallen victim to the culture of the automobile. When urban dwellers fled to the suburbs, they did not re-create third places because their dispersed housing did not facilitate these places and too much of their time was consumed by driving. Now this social transformation has spread to the small towns of North America, where the strip malls on the highways on the outskirts of town have all the business, leaving the downtowns as empty skeletons.

Rheingold, like Barlow, discovered his "third place" on the WELL. Rheingold writes that "finding the WELL was like discovering a cozy little world that had been flourishing without me, hidden within the walls of my house; an entire cast of characters welcomed me to the troupe with great merriment as soon as I found the secret door." He says that the WELL felt like an "authentic community" from the start, and he describes firsthand emotional experiences online, including participating in a parenting support group where a friend had just learned his son was diagnosed with leukemia. Rheingold finds in virtual communities that people "use words on screens to exchange pleasantries and argue, engage in intellectual discourse, conduct commerce, exchange knowledge, share emotional support, make plans, brainstorm, gossip, feud, fall in love, find friends and lose them, play games, flirt, create a little high art and a lot of idle talk"—indeed "just about everything people do in real life."[14]

Rheingold maintains that virtual communities provide a solution for the absence of informal public life in America, the kind of place that was lost when "the malt shop became a mall." There is no question that the Internet is an efficient medium for connecting people who have common interests, especially highly specialized interests, and in that respect, the Internet can develop a sense of community. But Rheingold wants to claim more. The climactic moments in both Barlow's and Rheingold's accounts of life in virtual communities are highly emotional events. Barlow describes the sympathy he received from around the world when he announced the death of his lover. Rheingold narrates the virtual grieving and rituals that followed the suicide of one of the most active and controversial participants on the WELL. Rheingold quotes Barlow's remark that "you aren't a real community until you have a funeral" to certify the WELL's status as a community.[15] Both Rheingold and Barlow make nostalgic appeals to the image of small towns of the past.

Certainly it is possible to feel a genuine emotional loss over the death of a person one has never met, but that hardly qualifies as the making of a "real" community. In rural communities like Pinedale, Wyoming, in Barlow's memories, the fact of living in close proximity over many years and generations and coping with common problems produces a shared sense of place. Virtual communities have such no essential basis. Instead they form along lines of shared interests and beliefs, and many seem to be little more than venues for self-disclosure and self-display rather than projects to build a collective sense of a group. Virtual communities may even work against the traditional notion of a neighborhood because they provide another alternative to talking with people who live around us.

Rheingold has been sensitive to criticism of virtual communities, and in his recent publications he has pointed to examples of people who have used computer networks to address common problems. But by citing such examples, Rheingold exposes the inadequacy of his nostalgic notion of a virtual community. The practices of organizations such as the National Rifle Association to mobilize special-interest factions using communications technologies hardly represent communities in any public collective sense and rather are more an indicator of increasing privatization of public life. Similarly, the emotional need to write about personal life is much in evidence on the Internet, but it is also much in evidence on the broadcast media. The viewers of Oprah or the listeners of various talk radio shows are not usually described as a community. Shared emotional experiences are one aspect of a community, but it is hardly a defining criterion. The irony of defenses of virtual communities like Rheingold's and Barlow's is that in their nostalgia for the past they raise precisely those aspects of community that make virtual communities appear as simulacra of small-town life. Small towns they are not.

A New Public Sphere?

If the metaphor of community is unsatisfactory for describing the gigabytes of discourse that flow across the Internet every day, those of us interested in the history and practices of various literacies are still left with the problem of how to theorize the massive and varied self-sponsored discourse of the Internet. Rheingold's metaphor of the third place as virtual coffee house does recall Jürgen Habermas's important work on public discourse. Although Rheingold does not cite Habermas's *Structural Transformation of the Public Sphere*, his argument has parallels to Habermas's contention that third places in the seventeenth and eighteenth centuries were critical sites for public discourse. Habermas laments the loss of public spaces for rational public discourse with the goal of achieving consensus.

Habermas's advocacy of rational public discourse as the basis of democratic polity has been frequently attacked. In a collection on Habermas's concept of the public sphere, Nancy Fraser points out that open public discussion was never a reality since bourgeois discourse was socially stratified and excluded women. Furthermore, Fraser argues that any notion of public discourse must necessarily be multiple at a time when old nation-states are fragmenting and many groups are asserting their identities.[16] In the same volume, Habermas addresses these criticisms by modifying his articulation of the public sphere, granting that it is implausible to theorize complex societies as associations writ large. His reconciliation is a "discourse-centered concept of democracy," where political disputes are still resolved by rational discussion but where the goal of organization through consensus is abandoned. He describes the discourse-centered approach as "the interplay between a constitutionally instituted formation of the political will and the spontaneous flow of communication unsubverted by power, within a public sphere that is not geared toward decision making but toward discovery and problem resolution and that in this sense is nonorganized."[17]

Even though Habermas has long been a critic of technology, his reformulation of the public sphere moves toward the valorization of the Internet as inherently democratic precisely because it is nonorganized and nonregulated. In the revival of Ann Rand-style libertarianism among Internet enthusiasts, we find deep suspicion of large institutions and a celebration of the ability of the individual to speak to many. Give people unrestricted access to the Internet and participatory democracy will automatically follow. Unrestricted access, however, is highly problematic. Within the United States and Canada, the dominance of young, affluent, and well-educated men on the Internet appears to be lessening, and users are becoming more representative of the population, with the number of women up to 42 percent in a survey conducted by Nielsen Media Research in December 1996 and January 1997.[18] Nevertheless, lines to the Internet do not run from every neighborhood. The United States Department of Commerce found in 1995 that the households of rural poor (incomes less than $10,000) have the lowest levels of computer penetration—only 4.5 percent—and of the households with computers, fewer than one in four had modems. Among households of the poor in central cities, only 7.6 percent had computers. In less-developed nations, of course, the statistics are far more stark. Access to the Internet in large areas of Asia, South America, and Africa is still a rarity.

The libertarian position is that access is strictly a matter of bandwidth, and soon bandwidth will be plentiful and available to everyone. The libertarian right attacks the mass media with the vehemence of the farmers' spleen for railroads a century earlier. George Gilder describes the mass media as a feudal system: "The media class composed of the Hollywood glitterati and the East Coast network elites is the product of a specific technology: mass broadcasting based on the analog transmission of images and other information. Essentially, the current system is a top-down hierarchy where all the intelligence is concentrated at a few networks or studios and transmitted in standardized form from those central locations to 'dumb terminals,' where people assemble to watch it on the idiot box or on the otherwise blank cinema screen."[19] Gilder forecasts that the feudal system will be overthrown by advanced personal computers and the Internet. When each terminal has the potential to become a transmitter, everyone can become a multimedia producer.

Even if Internet technologies become so inexpensive that anyone who wants access can have it, the question remains: what sort of techno-utopia will result? For the marketing megaliths like Time Warner, that utopia will happen when the buying habits of individuals can be tracked and highly personalized marketing can be offered. Much harder to find on the Internet is the kind of sustained rational public discourse on civic issues that is Habermas's version of the idealized public sphere.

Hacktivism

It is no surprise that political interest groups from across the spectrum have moved quickly to the Web as their primary venue for publishing their views (see the list of issues on www.yahoo.com/Society_and_Culture/Issues_and_Causes). These groups were already quite effective in using both print and electronic technologies to advance their positions. At a time when misery and poverty are becoming exacerbated in developing nations and increasing in developed nations, the test case for those who promise a technological utopia can be stated thus: if those who are now left out can enter into larger discourses, they can eventually change the material circumstances of their lives.

One prominent example that has unfolded alongside the development of the Internet is the rebellion by the Ejército Zapatista de Liberación Nacional in southern Mexico that began on New Year's Day 1994. The Zapatista uprising occurred on the day the North American Free Trade Agreement (NAFTA) came into effect and took the Mexican government by surprise. The rebels seized four towns in Chiapas, including San Cristóbal de las Casas, a town of about 100,000, and long popular with European tourists. In other years, the news of the uprising likely would have been suppressed in Mexico and little noticed abroad. But the Zapatistas didn't follow the usual script for rebellions of indigenous peoples. From the outset they made innovative use of communications technologies, faxing their Declaration of War to newspapers, to radio and television stations, and to the international press, gaining extensive coverage. They held theatrical press conferences, where men, women, and children wore black ski masks and their primary spokesperson, Subcomandante Marcos, appeared with a pipe sticking out of his mask and a Zapata-style bandolero. The international media and the opposition press within Mexico made the Zapatistas instant heroes, forcing the Mexican government to declare a cease-fire on 9 February.

The Zapatistas followed the initial round of publicity by placing many documents on the Internet, offering their critique of the government and the global economic restructuring codified by NAFTA. They provided depth and context for their struggle, explaining why it is crucial to have a sustainable peasant agriculture if the rain forests of Chiapas and the culture of the Mayan people who live there are to be preserved. In these efforts the Zapatistas were greatly assisted by academics in Mexico, the United States, and other nations, who continue to support Web sites and translate communiqués. The results of the Zapatista rebellion have been disappointing, but if the Zapatistas have failed to win a just settlement, the government likewise has failed to restore its credibility with other uprisings occurring elsewhere in Mexico during the 1990s. The Zapatista rebellion has also been influential in inspiring critiques of modernization policies in other Latin American countries.

More recent test cases have come in the authoritarian nations of Asia, most prominently in China, which recognize the economic importance of the Internet but wish to impose rigid censorship. The inherent contradictions in this policy are becoming evident in China, which is rushing to connect schools and businesses to the Internet. The government in Beijing initially thought it could achieve this end by establishing an internal network with highly censored connections to the outside. They have discovered to their displeasure just how difficult filtering the Internet can be. They have banned high profile news sources like the BBC and the *New York Times*, but are much less effective in blocking access to a multitude of small sites that provide alternative views. In frustration, the Chinese government has turned to crude brutality in singling out individuals who it claims are providing addresses of Chinese users to dissident publications and subjecting those accused to secret trials.[20] Of course, dissidents from outside China can send e-mail to users within China using the same spamming practices of advertisers in the West. Furthermore, the Chinese people are becoming increasingly sophisticated users of the Internet and find alternative sources on their own. Like other people around the world, they too went to the Web to read the sections of the Starr report that were not printed in government newspapers.

The Internet poses a fundamental dilemma for Chinese leaders, who want to become an economic superpower in the twenty-first century while remaining in strict control over more than a billion people. The government wants its citizens to use the Internet to form partnerships and engage in commerce with people throughout the world, yet at the same time forbids its citizens from reading foreign newspapers lest they encounter a story about the Dalai Lama or any of hundreds of other forbidden topics. To the government's great displeasure, they have found out the hard way that the Internet can be an important tool in coordinating protests, just as fax machines proved to be effective in co-ordinating the Intifada protests on the West Bank. Elsewhere in Asia, the Internet allowed students protesting President Suharto to combine their efforts and distribute information, speeding his downfall in May 1998. Citizens in Malaysia went to the Web in September 1998, when Malaysian Prime Minister Mahatir Mohamad fired and arrested his popular deputy Anwar Ibrahim. Dozens of Web sites critical of the Malaysian government went up almost overnight and pro-vided news reports that countered the state-controlled media.

Despotic governments assume people will believe what they are fed through the established media, but the Internet allows citizens access from other view-points. In the past, dissidents required significant resources to print and distrib-ute an opposition newspaper or run a radio station, but now with a computer and a modem, dissidents can put up a Web site on a server in another country within hours or even minutes. The various "free" servers offered by fast-growing Net companies like Geo-Cities and Tripod have become a great resource for Asian dissidents. Those clever enough can establish these Web sites with fake names, masking their electronic trails by frequently changing their e-mail ad-dress. Filtering the Web is no easy task, even for a nation like China that has limitless human resources to search the Web for subversive sites. Few govern-ments are willing to go to the extremes of Myanmar's military junta, which now sentences people to prison terms up to fifteen years for possessing a com-puter that can be connected to the Internet. Other nations have realized that they will have to downsize the degree of control they exercise over external in-formation sources. Singapore has maintained its largely symbolic authority to censor the Internet, but now restricts its efforts to blocking pornographic sites.

The irony of Western visions of the Internet as a great forum for partici-patory democracy is that if these visions are even partially realized, they will occur in nations without traditions of democracy. In these nations, forums for public discourse are still critical for political evolution. The examples of the dissidents in Asia and rebels in Chiapas challenge those in the West to imagine what desirable futures the Internet might help to facilitate and then to organ-ize people to achieve those futures. We should remember our recent past. In the 1960s, it was only when people in urban neighborhoods began talking to each other and organizing did the widespread destruction of housing, busi-nesses, and parks in order to build freeways come to a stop.

Notes

Introduction: Popular Literacy: Caught Between Art and Crime

1. Samuel R. Delaney, *Times Square Red, Times Square Blue* (New York: New York University Press, 1999), 148, 111.

2. For revisionist literacy theory, see Harvey Graff, *The Literacy Myth: Cultural Integration and Social Structure in the Nineteenth Century* (New Brunswick, NJ: Transaction, 1991); Brian Street, *Literacy in Theory and Practice* (Cambridge: Cambridge University Press, 1984); and Shirley Brice Heath, *Ways with Words* (Cambridge: Cambridge University Press, 1983). Studies in the history of the book and reading have mushroomed in recent years. Some of the most important works are Robert Darnton, "What Is the History of Books?" *Reading in America: Literature and Social History*, ed. Cathy N. Davidson (Baltimore: Johns Hopkins University Press, 1989), 27–52; Roger Chartier, *The Order of Books* (Stanford: Stanford University Press, 1994); Elizabeth Eisenstein, *The Printing Press as an Agent of Change*, 2 vols. (Cambridge: Cambridge University Press, 1979); and Cathy N. Davidson, *Revolution and the Word: The Rise of the Novel in America* (New York: Oxford University Press, 1986).

3. Leslie Fiedler, *What Was Literature? Class Culture and Mass Society* (New York: Simon and Schuster, 1982); John Cawelti, *Adventure, Mystery, and Romance* (Chicago: University of Chicago Press, 1976).

4. Angela McRobbie, "Jackie: An Ideology of Adolescent Femininity," *Mass Communication Review Yearbook*, vol. 4, ed. Ellen Warhella and D. Charles Whitney (Beverly Hills: Sage, 1983), 251–71. Fiske's work can be found in John Fiske, *Reading the Popular* (Boston: Unwin Hyman, 1989).

5. T. J. Clark, *The Painting of Modern Life: Paris in the Age of Manet and His Followers* (Princeton: Princeton University Press, 1984), 234, 238.

6. John Clarke, *New Times and Old Enemies: Essays on Cultural Studies and America* (New York: Harper Collins, 1991), 93.

7. Ibid., 110.

8. Quotes from this paragraph are from Linda Greenhouse, "In Broad Ruling, Court Prohibits Banning of Homeowners' Signs," *New York Times* (14 June 1994), A1, B9 (emphasis in original).

9. Quoted in Greenhouse, "In Broad Ruling," A1, B9.

10. Michael Walsh, *Graffito* (Berkeley: North Atlantic, 1996), 87.

11. Quoted in Walsh, *Graffito*, 3.

12. Quoted in Walsh, *Graffito*, 7.

13. Quoted in Walsh, *Graffito*, 36.

14. See Robert Goldman and Stephen Papson, *Sign Wars: The Cluttered Landscape of Advertising* (New York: Guilford, 1996), 259–60.

15. Quoted in Henry Chalfant and James Prigoff, *Spraycan Art* (London: Thames and Hudson, 1987), 10.

16. Raymond Williams, *Keywords: A Vocabulary of Culture and Society* (New York: Oxford University Press, 1976), 237. Also see Peter Burke, *Popular Culture in Early Modern Europe* (New York: Harper and Row, 1978).

17. Michel de Certeau, *Heterologies: Discourse on the Other* (Minneapolis: University of Minnesota Press, 1997), 135.

18. Ibid., 136.

Chapter 1: Porque no puedo decir mi cuento:
Mexican Ex-votos' Iconographic Literacy

Epigraphs at this chapter opening are cited respectively from: "Voto o tabella votiva," in *Dizionario di erudizione storico ecclesiastica* (Venezia: n.p., 1861); Jorge Durand and Douglas S. Massey, *Miracles on the Border: Retablos of Mexican Migrants to the United States* (Tucson: University of Arizona Press, 1995), 3.

1. Gloria Fraser Giffords, *Mexican Folk Retablos,* rev. edn. (Albuquerque: University of New Mexico Press, 1992), 4. Further references to this source are given in the text.

2. Durand and Massey point out yet another, and I would suggest related, important difference: santos and ex-votos as markers of class: "Mexican santo painting . . . arising from evangelical roots, supplied icons to devout members of an elite criollo class (and only later mestizos) during a brief 100-year period. . . . The ex-voto grew from very different roots and arose to satisfy deeper human needs using a flexible artistic style that was not wedded to a particular time or place. . . . Whereas santos arose from a conservative institution's need to evangelize and an elite's desire to objectify its piety, ex-votos arose from a spontaneous desire on the part of the people to placate supernatural forces they believed controlled their fates" (*Miracles on the Border,* 9). Further references to this source are given in the text.

3. In the twentieth century, these two traditions, the commissioning of the ex-voto and the artist's anonymity, which in plausible argument were rooted in historical conditions of literacy, have been interrupted and reinvented. Dr. Emanuela Angiuli, a much-respected scholar of ex-votos, informed me during a recent conversation in Italy that technological advances, mainly photography, have made it possible for some "miracolati" to stage the accident with accuracy. Paint is splattered on the ground or on the victims, if necessary, and individuals reenact the happening, placing themselves in the exact position they claim to have been at the time. Professional photographers or relatives fix the reconstructed happening. As Enzo Spera points out in "Ex Voto Fotografici ed Oggettuali" (*Puglia Ex Voto,* ed. Emanuela Angiuli [Lecce: Congedo Editore, 1977], 233–40), this development eliminates the mediating function of the "pittore in pietà" (the retablista) in both his painterly and scribal function (233). I shall return to this later. In other recent versions of ex-votos, images of the Virgin Mary or other saints are pasted on a sheet of paper, next to or above a photograph of the supplicant (fig. 2). The texts explain the happening. There is evidence that some Mexican ex-votos as well are being produced by the supplicants themselves (Giffords, *Mexican Folk Retablos,* 144–45).

4. Actually, in terms of function and location, I would suggest that ex-votos are

closer to *milagros* than to santos. Milagros are votive offerings of tin plate or silver (the preciousness of the material is a marker of class and economics) reproducing anatomical shapes: feet, hands, heads, hearts, breasts, eyes, legs, arms, kidneys. Like ex-votos, they are left at places of devotion to give thanks for a favor received (fig. 3). (In Italy, milagros are called "ex-voto oggettuali.") These offerings, now coveted by folk-art historians and art dealers, have been used by sociologists and historians of medicine to assess the diffusion of medical knowledge across time, cultures, and classes. The cultural antecedents of milagros can be traced to ancient civilizations where these objects were believed to have the power to intercept the anger that gods might have been directing toward humans.

5. In comparison with other Italian regions, Puglia has several sanctuaries with large numbers of ex-votos. Among the oldest is the Santuario della Madonna Incoronata, which began to be built, very humbly, in 1002, one year after "Mary, Mother of God" appeared on the last Saturday of April 1001 to a poor shepherd called *Strazzacappa* (tattered coat) and asked him that the place of apparition become a site of veneration. Another version of the story has Mary appear to a nobleman, the Count of Ariano Irpino, and to a shepherd who had lost two oxen and found them kneeling at the foot of the oak tree where the vision took place. In both stories, after the apparition, a statue of a black Madonna (*la Madonna bruna*) was found in or at the foot of the tree. The Byzantine-style statue, carved in wood, had probably been brought from the East to be spared destruction during the iconoclastic period. On one of the original walls enclosing what is left of the tree on or by which the Madonna appeared, there is a plaque that lists the names of some of those who over the centuries came in pilgrimage to the sanctuary: among the names are Saint Francis of Assisi, Saint Catherine of Siena, Saint Bernard, and Pope John XXIII. In other words, this sanctuary's existence is marked in ecclesiastical as well as popular history. Another sanctuary whose walls can be read as pages of *historia* (scholarly history) and *people's stories* (popular history) is Monte Sant'Angelo. Almost all ex-votos, mostly offered in the last two centuries, have been taken down from the cave walls wherein the original statue of the Archangel Michael (seventh and eighth centuries)—sword in one hand, scale in the other—is still kept, apparently untouched by the water infiltrations that have damaged instead the humble drawings and words of ex-votos. But another kind of ex-voto has withstood the test of time and is recorded in history and art history books. On the walls of the corridors leading to the place of prayer, traces of hands etched in the rock can be seen. They are said to be the hands of humble pilgrims and of Crusaders who on their way to war passed by the sanctuary to ask that the Archangel Michael grant them a safe return.

6. A few months ago, while in Italy, I went back to those sanctuaries in search of answers for some of the questions this project has raised for me. The experience was rich and draining, and too difficult to put into words. In the sanctuary where I first saw them, the Madonna Incoronata, the ex-votos had been moved out of their original location and hung on the walls of a portico in an adjacent building, housing offices, and stores. I felt distanced from them, until I fixed on them the eye of the camera—the telescopic lens tunneled out the incongruity of the new context and tunneled me into a pool of memories I thought I had left behind.

7. In so much as ex-votos are markers of class, the ones I saw in Puglia document the rural and agricultural experiences of its (poor) inhabitants. The ex-votos preserved in the sanctuary of Madonna della Consolata, in Turin, reproduce instead urban and in-

dustrial accidents and record the prayers of people (soldiers and their families) affected by World War I and World War II. As Franco Bolgiani points out ("Santuaris, ex voto e cultura 'poplare'" [1983], 50), because the Consolata Sanctuary is located within the city walls and because as a center of prayer it attracted (and attracts) more heterogenous groups of people (high bourgeoisie and aristocrats), the ex-votos displayed on its walls record more complex social stratification and traffic of influences. In so far as the economically affluent class also commissioned ex-votos to the local popular artist or to a nonpopular artist who would produce a naif rendering of the miraculous event according to normalizing popular schemes, ex-votos become an interesting site of inquiry into mutual borrowings, attractions, oppositions, and influences between what gets defined as the popular and the nonpopular. (See also, in the same volume, Laura Borello, Elio Ruggero, who provides a useful survey of various sociological "schools," and the provocative studies by Emanuela Angiuli, Ettore De Marco, Anna Maria Tripputi, Enzo Spera, and Giovanni Battista Bronzini in *Puglia Ex-Voto* 1977).

8. In Italy ex-votos are considered "cultural patrimony."

9. I realize the extent to which my desire to collect ex-votos may cast suspicion on my relationship to them. This concerns me, and, even if only briefly, I want to address this issue. I am aware that both collecting them as artifacts and casting them as texts of scholarly research may be seen as cultural maneuvers that de Certeau would expose as acts of violence (more on this later). But I would like to suggest that their (relative) invisibility, if they were not collected and studied, might be another form of violence. Perhaps it is time to reclaim a less tainted and venal understanding of collecting, one that enables and results from a way of knowing that is a form of gathering, harvesting; a way of knowing that (pace Foucault) is an expression of deferential appreciation and a source of pleasure—tactile, visual, intellectual—a pleasure that comes precisely from and is conveyed through numbering the collected items—cataloguing, arranging, displaying, surveying, and interpreting them. Although Mexican, I collect and study the ex-votos that have become a part of my life; they have been the means for me to know, to rememory, a set of cultural practices that have connecting power.

10. I am thinking here not only of the limits that the convention of the written text (limits pertaining to its possible length, literacy in general, and specifically the literacy of this genre) imposes on what can be conveyed to others, but also of the more problematic and less tangible "convention" of ex-votos to which Moroni refers: "[to offer] a representative oblation . . . a public testimonial of gratitude, or of special devotion to sacred images [that functions] as healthy incitement to ask for graces" (see the 1890 dictionary entry that stands as the first epigraph to this essay). Although the Moroni definition invoked here applies to Italian ex-votos, I want to suggest that even in the case of Mexican ex-votos their production and publication were finally accepted by the Church for similar reasons of containment and control. See Durand and Massey, *Miracles on the Border*, 15.

11. I am *not* using "humble" as a term of condescension. In *Selections from Cultural Writings* (ed. David Forgacs and Geoffrey Nowell-Smith, trans. William Boelhoner [Cambridge: Harvard University Press, 1991]), Gramsci exposes the deployment of this term by Italian intellectuals whose relationship toward the "people" has traditionally been one of "paternal and divine superiority," one that indicates "the self-sufficient sense of his undiscussed superiority. It is like the relationship between two races, one considered superior and the other inferior, like the relationship between adult and child in the

old schools or, worse still, like that of a 'society for the protection of animals' or like that between the Salvation Army and the cannibals of Papua" (293–94). Gramsci acknowledged Alessandro Manzoni's "democratic" attitude toward the "humble," one that in his historical novel I Promessi Sposi led him to give accounts of "subaltern classes" about whose history "there are no traces . . . in the historical documents of the past" (294). As it should become apparent, my argument about ex-votos is not one that names them "humble" in the "'self-sufficient' sense of . . . undiscussed superiority" (293).

12. For a detailed account of the origins of these votive paintings, the transformations they underwent from their European origins to their Mexicanization, and especially for the cultural and artistic consequences of "the shift in the class background and ethnic origins of both patrons and clients," see Durand and Massey, Miracles on the Border, 5–22. With few exceptions, many Italian ex-votos can be seen as representative of the "cultura della miseria" (culture of the wretched).

13. The question of how ex-votos, said to have been produced first in Italy, took root in Mexico, and wherever else, is one I would like to pursue at another time. I would like to engage in a nontotalizing fashion the issue of how similar economic, cultural, and religious conditions might have made this transfer possible. What interests me are the phenomenon of seeming recognition of an otherwise foreign or alien culture, the sudden unexpected feeling of connectedness, and the accompanying problematicity of this moment.

14. Michel de Certeau, "The Beauty of the Dead: Nisard," Heterologies: Discourse on the Other (Minneapolis: University of Minnesota Press, 1997), 119. Further references to this source are given in the text.

15. In my work with pedagogy I am becoming increasingly uneasy with the effects of the (relative) absence of student texts in theoretical discussions of composition. This absence is often explained and defended as being theoretically motivated by a commitment to not appropriating these texts, to not speaking for them. But I think we need to reconsider and reevaluate the effects and consequences of this ethical stance.

16. Carlo Ginzburg, The Cheese and the Worms: The Cosmos of a Sixteenth-Century Miller, trans. John and Anne Tedeschi (New York: Penguin, 1982), xvii–xviii.

17. What my research interest casts as lack of coverage, Giffords, whose main interest is santos, sees as greater coverage: "While there is very little written about the [santo], the related ex-voto enjoys more publicity. Because ex-votos portray dramatic moments and include written texts, they are favorites among writers and collectors of Mexican art and folklore." She does, however, specify that "with the exception of Roberto Montenegro's book Retablos de Mexico, written material on the ex-voto is descriptive rather than analytic" (Mexican Folk Retablos, 177).

18. It should be noticed that Giffords's seminal and groundbreaking book was first published in 1974, Mexican Folk Retablos: Masterpieces on Tin (Tucson: University of Arizona Press, 1974).

19. At the same time, this raises the problematic issue of the commonly accepted notion that the visual is more easily communicative than the written.

20. In his Prison Notebooks (Quaderni dal Carcere), Antonio Gramsci wrote these observations about folklore in response to a 1928 text (Problemi fondamentali del folclore) by Giovanni Crocioni: "One can say that until now folklore has been studied primarily as a 'picturesque' element. . . . Folklore should instead be studied as a 'conception of the

world and life' implicit to a large extent in determinate (in time and space) strata of society and in opposition (also for the most part implicit, mechanical and objective) to 'official' conceptions of the worlds (or in a broader sense, the conceptions of the cultured parts of historically determinate societies) that have succeeded one another in the historical process. (Hence the strict relationship between folklore and 'common sense,' which is philosophical folklore.)" (*Selections from the Prison Notebooks*, ed. and trans. Quintin Hoare and Geoffrey Nowell Smith [New York: International Publishers, 1971], 188–89). Gramsci's understanding of folklore has shaped in major and positive ways readings of ex-votos by many post–World War II Italian scholars, especially those who approach folklore from a political perspective.

21. I am reminded here of John Berger's response to Seymour Slive's study of Frans Hals. Although in that case Slive writes about a work of highbrow art, it seems to me that Montenegro's reading of ex-votos is driven by the same desire to make them instances of the unchanging human condition. See John Berger, *Ways of Seeing* (New York: Penguin, 1977), 11–16.

22. Giffords also says: "[Montenegro's] words point up important differences between the painting of retablos and the painting of ex-votos. The retablo, with its simple format illustrating a single figure, could be copied exactly from many sources. The miraculous cure or rescue depicted on the ex-voto, however, had to be constructed solely from the imagination. It is true that the holy persons pictured on ex-votos could be copied from traditional sources, but the paintings as a whole were the products of the artists' own creativity. Many problems of perspective, color, and shading are handled in a fresh, new way which would not have been possible with copying, and solutions to problems in depicting the narrative—such as showing two or three simultaneous scenes of action—offer striking originality" (144).

23. Here is an example. In the introduction to *Ebbi Miracolo*, a volume that reproduces 145 ex-votos that have survived the periodical ransackings of the Sanctuary of San Michele Archangelo on the Gargano promontory (seventh and eighth centuries) and precarious environmental conditions, Filippo De Michele stresses the religious function of ex-votos and calls into question any reading of them that proposes them as signs of anything but faith: "We'll let the superior intelligence of skeptics and mis-believers produce abstruse readings resulting from fervid imagination, and philosophical disquisitions of the interpretive 'anthropological and sociological' type. Ex-votos contain a sacrosanct, incontrovertible fundamental reality: faith. [That is] the supplicant's simple, unwavering, deep faith. Ex-votos must be framed by and looked at from the perspective of faith; if read and observed from another perspective they are falsified, their essential traits are changed: they no longer are 'ex-voto.' Because they have religious value, because they are expressions of faith, ex-votos become 'signs'" (Antonio Troiano and Filippo de Michele, *Ebbi Miracolo* [Napoli: Grafiche Lithosud, 1992], 47). Deeply embedded in Catholicism, I nevertheless find myself resisting (and feeling guilty for resisting) this kind of coercive religious reading, one that, for me at least, reduces and flattens the heterogeneity of conflicted needs, desires, functions, and aims that make me yearn for faith's sustenance.

24. Jean Charlot "Mexican Ex-Votos" *Magazine of Art* 42 (1949), 141. Durand and Massey use the generic term "retablo" for both ex-votos and santos. They substitute the term "ex-voto" only when they wish to distinguish ex-votos from santos (*Miracles on the Border*, 6).

25. Sandra Cisneros, "Little Miracles, Kept Promises," *The Story and Its Writer: An Introduction to Short Fiction*, ed. Ann Charters (n.p.: Bedford Books, 1995), 322.

26. Thomas J. Steele, *Santos and Saints: The Religious Folk Art of Hispanic New Mexico* (Santa Fe, N.M.: Ancient City Press, 1994), 8.

27. One wonders how a story painting of a young girl marked with acne, or of a nalgas-less man, would look on the walls of a sanctuary.

28. Reading the short story, one can assume that the offerers write their own requests/complaints/implorations. The local dialect and faulty spelling here can be seen less as the flavor of the primitive (or, from my viewpoint, as a marker of unjustly inadequate education) and more perhaps as the presence of oral inflections.

29. I said earlier that my mother introduced me to the culture of ex-votos when she took me with her on pilgrimage to various sanctuaries. But my mother never got to leave her ex-voto. The miracle she was praying for was never granted. Even if it had, she probably would not have commissioned an ex-voto. Her high level of literacy excluded her from this specific devotional and thanksgiving practice. She might have instead left a milagro in precious metal, or she might have done or commissioned a different kind of votive offering: a religious figure embroidered in gold and silver thread and encased in a precious frame; or a precious garment for the particular saint or Madonna to wear. And the story of the offering might have been told and retold privately by family members to other family members and close friends. Clearly, my rendering of what happened and did not happen is class inflected.

30. See Steele, *Santos and Saints*.

31. "The importance and popularity of a Sanctuary is almost always linked to the mass of ex-votos brought by the devout" (Giovanni De Meo, *L'Incoronata di Foggia* [Foggia: Edizioni Santuario dell' Incoronata, 1995], 115).

32. Here I am casting a more positive light on what de Certeau names as a "retreat" and "last recourse": the function of religiosity for the poor. Responding to Bolleme's remark that "Catholicism is the religion of the poor people" and that the God of the almanacs is the "God of the poor," de Certeau argues that the growing popular religiosity (in eighteenth-century France) could be actually seen as "the retreat of the popular culture into the only language still available for its expression after the triumph of reason, which desires to negate it. The language of religion would then be the last recourse of a culture that could no longer find expression, that was being forced to fall silent or mask itself so a different cultural order could be heard" (de Certeau, "Beauty of the Dead," 131).

33. Durand and Massey raise similar questions about the retablista's anonymity: "Despite the relatively large number of retablos [ex-votos] now in museums, galleries, private collections, and churches . . . little is known about the people who actually paint them (Sanchez Lara 1990). Although the lack of information is understandable in the case of santos, whose creators can be assumed to have expired years ago, it is less defensible in the case of ex-votos, because these works continue to be produced today.

"Knowing little about *retablistas*, as the artists are called, detracts from a full and complete understanding of the genre, because as Charlot (1949: 139) observes, 'Anonymity veils the origin of much folk art and allows the sophisticate to make much of the product and little of the producer'" (*Miracles on the Border*, 29).

34. Nancy Wall, "Retablos and Santos," *Tucson Guide* vol. 17 (1999), 76.

Chapter 2: Gypsy Fullstop Punctuates Imperialism

The epigraph at this chapter opening is cited from Stanley Diamond, *In Search of the Primitive: A Critique of Civilization* (New Brunswick, N.J.: Transaction, 1974), 4.

1. Charles Keil, *Tiv Song: The Sociology of Art in Classless Society* (Chicago: University of Chicago Press, 1979); Colin Turnbull, *The Forest People* (New York: Simon and Schuster, 1962); Robert K. Dentan, *The Semai: A Non-violent People of Malaya* (New York: Holt, Rinehart, and Winston, 1968); Steven Feld, *Sound and Sentiment: Birds, Weeping, Poetics, and Song in Kaluli Expression* (Philadelphia: University of Pennsylvania Press, 1982).

2. Bracketed words in italics, signed C. K., are editorial comments, not Gypsy Fullstop's text.

3. This is a Tiv word or expression that probably refers to "the Creation."

Chapter 3: Popular Literacy in the Middle Ages: *The Book of Margery Kempe*

1. Shirley Brice Heath, *Ways with Words* (Cambridge: Cambridge University Press, 1983); Sylvia Scribner and Michael Cole, *The Psychology of Literacy* (Cambridge, Mass.: Harvard University Press, 1981); E. D. Hirsch, Jr., *Cultural Literacy: What Every American Needs to Know* (Boston: Houghton, 1987); Geneva Smitherman, *Talkin and Testifyin: The Language of Black America* (Detroit: Wayne State University Press, 1977); Walter Ong, S.J., *Orality and Literacy* (London: Methuen, 1982); and Eric Havelock, *The Literate Revolution in Greece and Its Cultural Consequences* (Princeton: Princeton University Press, 1982). Heath, Scribner and Cole, Hirsch, Smitherman, Ong, and Havelock represent perhaps the most respected and well-known templates of literacy research, research implicitly based on a comparison with schooled literacy. The only research that seems free of technological determinism is M. T. Clanchy, *From Memory to Written Record: England 1066–1307* (Cambridge, Mass.: Harvard University Press, 1979).

2. For another view of medieval popular literacy, see Glenn, "Medieval Literacy Outside the Academy: Popular Practice and Individual Technique," *College Composition and Communication* 44 (Dec. 1993), 497–508.

3. Like *litterati*, *illitterati* is an uncalibrated term insufficient to indicate the rank, importance, expertise, or education of those people so described. See Franz H. Baüml, "Varieties and Consequences of Medieval Literacy and Illiteracy," *Speculum* 55 (1980), 237–65, which provides an examination of such terminology.

4. Brian Stock, *Listening for the Text: On the Uses of the Past* (Baltimore: Johns Hopkins University Press, 1990), 37.

5. Ruth Crosby, "Oral Delivery in the Middle Ages," *Speculum* 11 (1936), 88 [88–110].

6. These Latin proclamations were posted publicly, making way for the gradual "transition to literate practices for the majority and shows how the 'literate mentality' was ushered in through familiar forms" (Brian Street, *Literacy in Theory and Practice* [Cambridge: Cambridge University Press, 1984], 120).

7. *The Uses of Literacy in Early Medieval Europe*, ed. Rosamond McKitterick (Cambridge: Cambridge University Press, 1990), 333.

8. Mary Carruthers, *Book of Memory: A Study of Memory in Medieval Culture* (Cambridge: Cambridge University Press, 1990), 10.

9. Brian Stock, *The Implications of Literacy* (Princeton: Princeton University Press, 1983), 7.

10. H. J. Chaytor, *From Script to Print* (Cambridge: Cambridge University Press, 1945); M. T. Clanchy, *From Memory to Written Record: England 1066–1307* (Cambridge: Cambridge University Press, 1979); Harvey J. Graff, *The Legacies of Literacies* (Bloomington: Indiana University Press, 1981); and *Literary Practice and Social Change in Britain, 1380–1530*, ed. Lee Patterson (Berkeley and Los Angeles: University of California Press, 1990) have written eloquently about early modern literacies and literate practices.

11. Lynn is located within the Norfolk area, an area that seems to have led the way in the civic revival of English, and to have abandoned the use of Latin and French. Julian of Norwich (mentioned in n. 13) was also from this area.

12. In "Franciscan Spirituality: Vision and the Authority of the Scripture" (Ph.D. diss., Indiana University, 1985), Denise Despres writes that "the Franciscans encouraged the laity to meditate freely on the Gospels and to use their imaginations. They instructed penitents to mesh individual history with the sacred history of the Scripture, for only by experiencing life with Christ could the sinful fully understand the sympathy Christ had for the human condition, and the nature of the supreme sacrifice he willingly chose through love" (3). Franciscan affective piety, then, emphasized fellowship with Jesus and individual participation. And in her telling, Margery becomes an actual participant in scriptural history. Regardless of twenty-first-century suspicion with regard to Margery's spirituality, she was practicing within an established and respected fifteenth-century tradition of affective piety.

13. For an analysis of her contributions to rhetorical technique, see Glenn, "Author, Audience, and Autobiography: Rhetorical Technique in *The Book of Margery Kempe*," *College English* 53 (Sept. 1992), 540–53.

14. Julian of Norwich (1343–1415) seems to have been the first woman to write about herself as an anchoress, but she did not write her life story. Although better educated than Margery, she was also dependent on an amanuensis, to whom she dictated her *Revelations of Divine Love*, sometimes referred to as her *Book of Showings*.

15. Of course, verse was another matter. But supporting the effectiveness of Margery's realism is her use of prose, which accommodates matters of fact in ways that poetry, with its rhymes and rhythms, simply cannot. In *From Script to Print*, H. J. Chaytor writes that during the Middle Ages "to tell a story in prose was to invest it with an air of realism . . . ; it became clear that a family chronicle, written in verse, would vastly gain in authority and dignity, if it were rewritten in prose; it would, in fact, become real history" (85).

16. I am not saying that only or all women in religious orders were educated; neither case is true.

17. As her *Book of Margery Kempe* demonstrates, Margery became well versed in saints' lives, especially those of women: Saint Bridget of Sweden (d. 1373), whose chapel Margery visits in Rome; Saint Catherine of Siena (d. 1380); Saint Katherine of Sweden (d. 1391); Bl. Dorothea of Prussia (d. 1394); Saint Frances of Rome (d. 1440). As David Knowles explains in *The English Mystical Tradition* (London: Burns, 1961): "Lynn, at this time at the height of its medieval prosperity, was one of the chief ports of communication with North Holland and the Baltic ports, while East Anglia was remarkable as the home of many recluses, men and women, and as the scene of the preaching and other spiritual activities of several of the most distinguished friars of the period. Margery Kempe was therefore almost ideally placed for the life of devotion; she had an abundance of potential directors and *conferenciers*, and she could readily acquire knowledge of the lives and works of the holy women of Europe in the last generation. Though she was

almost certainly unable to read, we know that her directors read to her frequently. She herself either mentions by name or quotes all the English mystics of our survey" (142–43).

18. Meech and Allen, Proem. 2a.23–30; 2b.1–2 (all quotations are my own modernizations from this edition; subsequent references to this source will be cited in the text).

19. Thanks to a reviewer, I more clearly understand how any measure of Margery's own orthographic expertise is beside the point, particularly since I have neither proof nor circumstantial evidence that Margery was absolutely excluded from all writing lessons, that she could or could not form a letter of the alphabet. Whatever her measure of orthographic expertise, however, she seems to have preferred dictation as her means of composing.

20. Franz H. Bäuml, "Medieval Literacy and Illiteracy," 43–44.

21. This practice resonates with the Vai letter-writers/letter-readers of the Scribner and Cole study (Psychology of Literacy, 73).

22. Scholars disagree on the exact date of each transcription, but all concur that in the 1430s Margery was over sixty years old when she hired the first scribe and began looking back over half a century. The twosome had nearly completed the dictation and reading-back process when the scribe died suddenly. She soon hired a second scribe, who found the first scribe's work illegible, so he wrote out the second transcription.

23. And her text continues to vex many readers today.

24. Rosamond McKitterick, The Carolingians and the Written Word (Cambridge: Cambridge University Press, 1989), 138. McKitterick goes on to explain: "The necessary quantities of parchment, quill or reed pens and ink were relatively easily obtainable, in that the sheep, cow, goat, rabbit or squirrel skins for the parchment, the common reed . . . and goose quills for the pens, and gall nuts, organic salts of iron, and lampblack for the ink were in abundant supply" (138). But she clarifies the benefits of such abundance with a direct correlation between the material wealth of a center and its book production: successful and productive libraries, scriptoria, and learning centers depended on their own land and livestock holdings (141).

25. In her chapter "The Production and Possession of Books: An Economic Dimension," McKitterick tells us that "the pigments and their raw materials used in the most richly decorated books were emphatically not just from local sources. There can be no doubt that the owner of a mediaeval manuscript would have some inkling at least of the costliness of the paints and the technical perfectionism expended upon the preparation of parchment, ink and pigments" (146). In addition, "a binding could represent more than a material complement of the sacred text; personal wealth and status also found an outward symbol in the ornateness of the covers of books. Nor should the significance of bejewelled covers be forgotten; given the symbolic meaning attached to particular gems, the jewels on a book could act as a reflection of the splendour of heaven" (147). It is when we understand books as intellectual and commercial commodities that we more easily understand contemporary medieval literature, such as Chaucer's allusion to the value of books in the Wife of Bath's Prologue: the Wife of Bath's fifth husband struck her deaf and to the floor after she ripped three pages from his prized possession (his book of wicked wives).

26. Carruthers, Book of Memory, 8.

27. Knowles, The English Mystical Tradition, 144 (emphasis added).

28. In this chapter as well as chapters 17 and 62, references are made to Margery's

being read to. In this case, the priest read her the Bible, commentaries of the Church Fathers (the doctors); the *Revelations of St. Bridget of Sweden*; Walter Hilton's *Scale of Perfection*; Richard Rolle's mystical treatises, *The Prick of Love* and *The Fire of Love*, both of which seem to have been ascribed to Saint Bonaventure.

29. H. J. Chaytor, *From Script to Print*, 116.

30. Plato, *Euthyphro, Apology, Crito, Phaedo, Phaedrus*, trans. H. N. Fowler (Cambridge, Mass.: Harvard-Heinemann, 1977), 405–580. 31. Since she had a newborn son and a living husband at the time, her announcement of her decision to wear white and thereby signify a reclamation of her (spiritual) virginity was considered scandalous behavior by lower churchmen and townspeople alike (chap. 15).

32. Clarissa Atkinson, *Mystic and Pilgrim: The Book and the World of Margery Kempe* (Ithaca, N.Y.: Cornell University Press, 1983), 218.

33. Stock, *Implications*, 18.

34. Lollardism is the religious movement best known for making translations of Latinate biblical texts available to the common people, readers and nonreaders alike.

35. Margery herself often prays for sermons: "If I had gold enough, I would give every day a noble to have every day a sermon, for thy word is more worthy to me than all the good in this world" (58.69a.21–23).

36. Opposition, mocking, and routing were practices consistent not only with Jesus' life but with saints' lives as well—life stories that Margery apparently used to model her own. It seems clear that the stories of female saints, an extremely popular form of oral and written literature in the Middle Ages, helped Margery live out her vocation by placing before her a group of holy women who not only defied their society but won closeness to Jesus by doing so. In chapter 18, Margery meets with Julian of Norwich, and in chapter 39, she recounts her meeting with Saint Bridget's maid.

37. Lollards denied the existence of Purgatory, a denial that affected many other Christians. Most Christians, however, continued to believe in Purgatory and in the special circumstances for circumventing it. Margery's decision to wear white clothes could have indicated either her chaste living or her salvation without time in Purgatory.

38. Franciscan participatory meditation requires the penitent to envision or recreate scriptural events. These consciously embellished scenes, then, are a source of solace and affirmation.

39. Philippe Lejeune, "Women and Autobiography at Author's Expense," trans. Katherine Jensen, in *The Female Autograph*, ed. Domna Stanton (Chicago: University of Chicago Press, 1984), 208 [204–18]. Carolyn Heilbrun, *Writing a Woman's Life* (New York: Norton, 1988), 18.

Chapter 4: Giving Voice to the Hands: The Articulation of Material Literacy in the Sixteenth Century

This paper was inspired and informed by the work of James A. Bennett, Owen Hannaway, and Neil Kamil, especially in the form I read it during a seminar directed by Owen Hannaway at the Folger Library, Washington, D.C., in 1988. The bulk of this paper was prepared for publication in 1992, and since then there has been a great resurgence of interest in Palissy. The most important recent works are *Bernard Palissy 1510–1590: L'Écrivain, Le Réformé, Le Céramiste*, ed. Frank Lestringant (Coédition Association Internationale des Amis d'Agrippa d'Aubigné, 1992); Leonard N. Amico, *Bernard Palissy: In Search* of *Earthly Paradise* (Paris: Flammarion, 1996); and the recent exhibition catalog, *Une Or-fèverie de Terre: Bernard Palissy et la Céramique de Saint-Porchaire: Musée National de la Renaissance, Chateau D'Écouen* (Paris: Seuil, 1997). Literature in the history of science on early modern prac-titioners has grown even more rapidly and a relatively recent useful bibliography can be found in Steven Shapin, *The Scientific Revolution* (Chicago: Chicago University Press, 1996). My notes reflect only some of this exciting new work on Palissy and other prac-titioners.

1. Quoted in Lon R. Shelby "The Geommetrical Knowledge of Mediaeval Master Masons," *Speculum* 47 (1972), 395–96.

2. Bernard Palissy, *The Admirable Discourses*, trans. Aurele la Rocque (originally publ. 1580; Urbana: University of Illinois Press, 1957), 94, 148.

3. On this point, see Eugene S. Ferguson, "The Mind's Eye: Nonverbal Thought in Technology," *Science* (1977): 827–36, and his recent book *Engineering and the Mind's Eye* (Cambridge, Mass.: MIT Press, 1992) in which he argues that engineers (and before them artisans) design and work by means of a kind of trained intuition.

4. I will use the masculine pronoun throughout this paper because the artisans I discuss are male. It should not be assumed, however, that this implies there were no fe-male artisans. There were many female artisans, but only in rare cases did they become masters in their craft.

5. Dietlinde Goltz, "Die Paracelsisten und die Sprache," *Sudhoffs Archiv* 56 (1972), 337–39.

6. See Alexander Bruno Hanschmann, *Bernard Palissy der Künstler, Naturforscher und Schriftsteller* (Leipzig: Dieterich'sche Verlagsbuchhandlung, 1903); and Thomas Clifford Allbutt, "Palissy, Bacon, and the Revival of Natural Science," *Proceedings of the British Acad-emy* (1913–14): 234–47. For a modification of this view, see Wallace Kirsop, "The Leg-end of Bernard Palissy," *Ambix* 9 (1961): 136–54, and H. R. Thompson, "The Geographical and Geological Observations of Bernard Palissy the Potter," *Annals of Science* 10 (1954): 149–65.

7. Palissy achieved this verisimilitude by molding these creatures "from life," a process that involved making plaster casts of entire freshly killed animals to form a mold for the clay. See Ernst Kris, "Der Stil 'Rustique:' Die Verwendung des Naturab-gusses bei Wenzel Jamnitzer und Bernard Palissy," *Jahrbuch der Kunsthistorischen Sammlungen in Wien*, NF 1 (1928): 137–207, and, more recently, the extensive archaeological evidence unearthed at the site of Palissy's workshop in Paris, in the issue of *Revue de L'Art* 78 (1987) devoted to Bernard Palissy, and Amico, *Bernard Palissy*, esp. 86–96.

8. Palissy, *Recepte véritable*, in Henry Morley, *Palissy the Potter* (2nd edn. London: Chap-man and Hall, 1855), 317–18. It is not known if Palissy produced a garden to his design here, and it is not clear if he ever completed a grotto. For a discussion of this thorny question, see Amico, *Bernard Palissy*.

9. Psalm 104, the Bible, King James Version. Palissy may also have gained inspira-tion for his garden from a contemporary book, entitled *Songe de Polyphile*, but this is a matter of controversy. See *Bernard Palissy: Mythe et Réalité* (Niort, Saintes: Musées d'Agen, 1990), 32–33; Bernard Palissy, *Recepte véritable* (Geneva: Librairie Droz, 1988), intro. Keith Cameron, 26–28; and Keith Cameron, "L'originalité de Bernard Palissy," in Lestringant, *Bernard Palissy*.

10. In the St. Bartholomew's Day Massacre of 1572, Palissy was spirited out of Paris to the lands of the Duke of Bouillon in the principality of Sedan, where he lived and worked for four or five years before returning to Paris. *Bernard Palissy: Mythe et Réalité*, 21.

11. Romans 1:19–21.

12. Augustine, *Confessions*, bk. 13, chap. 32.

13. Keith Cameron discusses this in his introduction to Bernard Palissy, *Recepte véritable* (Geneva: Librairie Droz, 1988), 15–16.

14. Palissy, *Admirable Discourses*, 194. He describes the saltworks in the chap. "On Common Salt," 136–45. For an overview of the *gabelle*, see Morley, *Palissy*, 88–96.

15. Palissy, *Admirable Discourses*, 29.

16. Aristotle, *Nicomachean Ethics*, trans. H. Rackham (2nd edn. Cambridge, Mass.: Harvard University Press, 1982), I.5.1–7; 6.3.2–4.

17. On these issues, see Barbara J. Shapiro, *Probability and Certainty in Seventeenth-Century England* (Princeton, N.J.: Princeton University Press, 1983); and Henry G. Van Leeuwen, *The Problem of Certainty in English Thought 1630–1690* (The Hague: Martinus Nijhoff, 1963).

18. *Nicomachean* 6.4.

19. *Nicomachean* 6.4.4–5.

20. This brief overview does not do justice to the great amount of literature that has appeared recently on this development. Paolo Rossi, *Philosophy, Technology, and the Arts in the Early Modern Era*, trans. Salvator Attanasio (New York: Harper & Row, 1970) has in many ways not been superseded. See also the cogent summation by Reijer Hooykaas, "The Rise of Modern Science. When and Why?" *British Journal for the History of Science* 20 (1987): 453–73. More recent historians investigating this question are James A. Bennett, "The Mechanics? Philosophy and the Mechanical Philosophy," *History of Science* 24 (1986): 1–28; idem, "The Challenge of Practical Mathematics," in *Science, Culture, and Popular Belief in Renaissance Europe*, ed. Stephen Pumfrey, Paolo Rossi, Maurice Slawinski (Manchester: Manchester University Press, 1991), 176–90; William Eamon, *Science and the Secrets of Nature: Books of Secrets in Medieval and Early Modern Culture* (Princeton: Princeton University Press, 1994); Michael Hunter, *Science and Society in Restoration England* (Cambridge: Cambridge University Press, 1983); Pamela O. Long, "The Contribution of Architectural Writers to a 'Scientific' Outlook in the Fifteenth and Sixteenth Centuries," *Journal of Medieval and Renaissance Studies* 15 (1985): 265–98; idem, "Power, Patronage, and the Authorship of Ars," *Isis* 88 (1997): 1–41; Bruce T. Moran, "German Prince-Practitioners: Aspects in the Development of Courtly Science, Technology, and Procedures in the Renaissance," *Technology and Culture* 22 (1981): 253–74; and Steven Shapin, *A Social History of Truth: Civility and Science in Seventeenth-Century England* (Chicago: University of Chicago Press, 1994).

21. Juan Luis Vives, *Deradendis disciplines*, trans. Foster Watson (originally publ. 1531; Totowa, N.J.: Rowman and Littlefield, 1971), bk. 4, chap. 6, 209. On this subject, see also Rossi, *Philosophy, Technology*.

22. Reijer Hooykaas, *Humanisme, Science et Réform: Pierre de la Ramée (1515–1572)* (Leiden: E. J. Brill, 1958), 95–96; 20–21; 30.

23. Quoted in Allen G. Debus, *The French Paracelsians: The Chemical Challenge to Medical and Scientific Tradition in Early Modern France* (Cambridge: Cambridge University Press, 1991), 9.

24. Paracelsus, "The Seven Defensiones," 4th defense, *Four Treatises of Theophrastus von Hohenheim, called Paracelsus*, trans. C. Lilian Temkin (Baltimore: Johns Hopkins University Press, 1941), 29.

25. Walter Pagel, s.v. "Paracelsus," *Dictionary of Scientific Biography*, ed. Charles Gillispie, 18 vols. (New York: Scribner, 1970–86).

26. On this point, see Pamela H. Smith, *The Business of Alchemy: Science and Culture in the Holy Roman Empire* (Princeton: Princeton University Press, 1994).

27. The literature on Paracelsus is large and growing, but see in particular Walter

Pagel, *Paracelsus: An Introduction to Philosophical Medicine in the Era of the Renaissance,* 2nd edn. (Basel: Karger, 1982); idem, *Das medizinische Weltbild des Paracelsus: Seine Zusammenhänge mit Neuplatonismus und Gnosis* (Wiesbaden: Franz Steiner Verlag, 1962); Kurt Goldammer, *Paracelsus: Natur und Offenbarung* (Hanover: Theodor Oppermann Verlag, 1953); and Owen Hannaway, *The Chemists and the Word: The Didactic Origins of Chemistry* (Baltimore: Johns Hopkins University Press, 1975), esp. 43–45. B. J. T. Dobbs, *The Foundations of Newton's Alchemy* (Cambridge: Cambridge University Press, 1975), and *Alchemical Death and Resurrection: The Significance of Alchemy in the Age of Newton* (Washington, D.C.: Smithsonian Institution Libraries, 1990); Allen G. Debus, *The Chemical Philosophy,* 2 vols. (New York: Science History Publications, 1977).

28. Pagel, *Paracelsus,* 57.

29. Walter Pagel has shown the influence of the Hermetic corpus (a body of texts supposed by its Renaissance translators and commentators to be contemporaneous with Moses) on Paracelsus in helping him articulate these gnostic ideas. See also Frances Yates, *Giordano Bruno and the Hermetic Tradition* (Chicago: University of Chicago Press, 1964). I would now see Paracelsus's ideas as influenced as much by the "vernacular epistemology" of artisans and other practitioners as by Hermetic concepts. Evidence for this is suggested by Stefan Rhein, "'Mein bart hat mer erfaren dan alle euer hohe schulen'?: Ein Zwischenruf zur Quellenfrage bei Paracelsus," and Gundolf Keil, "Mittelalterliche Konzepte in der Medizin des Paracelsus," in *Paracelsus: Das Werk—Die Rezeption,* ed. Volker Zimmermann (Stuttgart: Franz Steiner Verlag, 1995), 99–104 and 173–93. See also Pamela H. Smith, "Artists as Scientists: Nature and Realism in Early Modern Europe," *Endeavour* 24 (2000): 13–21.

30. Paracelsus, *Labyrinthus medicorum errantium* (1538) in *Paracelsus: Essential Readings,* trans. Nicholas Goodrick-Clarke (Wellingborough, U.K.: Crucible, 1990), 104.

31. Paracelsus's notion of *experientia* and *scientia* is discussed in Pagel, *Paracelsus,* 60. He quotes Paracelsus: "Scientia ist in dem, in dem sie Gott geben hatt: Experientia ist ein Kuntschafft von dem, in dem Scientia probiert wirt."

32. For the following reading of Palissy, I draw on the important work of Neil D. Kamil, "War, Natural Philosophy and the Metaphysical Foundations of Artisanal Thought in an American Mid-Atlantic Colony: La Rochelle, New York City, and the Southwestern Huguenot Paradigm, 1517–1730" (Ph.D. diss., Johns Hopkins University, 1988).

33. The following dialogue is from Palissy, *Admirable Discourses,* 188–203.

34. See Arthur Geoghegan, *The Attitude toward Labor in Christianity and Ancient Culture* (Washington, D.C.: Catholic University of America Press, 1945). Scholars who have investigated the increased value placed on labor and the mechanical arts in the Middle Ages include Elsbeth Whitney, *Paradise Restored: The Mechanical Arts from Antiquity through the Thirteenth Century,* Transactions of the American Philosophical Society, vol. 80 (Philadelphia: American Philosophical Society, 1990); George Ovitt, *The Restoration of Perfection: Labor and Technology in Medieval Culture* (New Brunswick: Rutgers University Press, 1987); and Jacques Le Goff, *Time, Work, and Culture in the Middle Ages,* trans. Arthur Goldhammer (Chicago: Chicago University Press, 1980).

35. Kamil, "War, Philosophy, and Foundations," Cellini quote: 396–97; 450.

36. Palissy, *Recepte véritable,* cited in Morley, *Palissy,* 372.

37. Morley, *Palissy,* 325.

Chapter 5: Social Place and Literacies in John Foxe's *Actes and Monuments*

In all quotations from contemporary sources, the spellings and punctuations have been modernized. Thanks are due to Michael Kauffmann, Crystal Bartolovich, and Annette Lareau for their help in preparing this essay.

1. Haller also notes that the book was "to be set up for all to read in city orphanages and the halls of city companies." *A Book of Certain Canons* (London: John Daye, 1571) quoted in William Haller, *The Elect Nation: The Meaning and Relevance of Foxe's Book of Martyrs* (New York: Harper and Row, 1963), 22. The longstanding legend that the *Book of Martyrs* was available in every parish church is, however, merely legend. See Leslie M. Oliver, "The Seventh Edition of John Foxe's *Acts and Monuments*," *The Papers of the Bibliographical Society of America* 37 (1943), 244–48.

2. A collated scholarly edition is now planned. Sponsored by the British Academy John Foxe Project, this edition will be in electronic form. See http://www.shef.ac.uk/ uni/projects/bajfp/main/aim.html. For textual history, see Warren Wooden, *John Foxe* (Boston: Twayne Publishers, 1983); William Haller, *The Elect Nation*; Mark Breitenberg, "The Flesh Made Word: Foxe's *Acts and Monuments*," *Renaissance and Reformation* 25:4 (1989): 381–407.

3. Keith Thomas, "The Meaning of Literacy in Early Modern England," in *The Written Word: Literacy in Transition*, ed. Gerd Baumann (London: Clarendon Press, 1986), 17.

4. David Cressy, "The Environment for Literacy: Accomplishment and Context in Seventeenth-Century England," in *Literacy in Historical Perspective*, ed. Daniel P. Resnick (Washington, D.C.: Library of Congress, 1983), 27. Yet Cressy's book *Literacy and the Social Order: Reading and Writing in Tudor and Stuart England* (Cambridge: Cambridge University Press, 1980), important as it is, ultimately reinstantiates this dichotomy because of its quantitative desires: after considering many "indirect" means of understanding early modern literacy—such as references to and regulations concerning reading and writing practices, he settles on the "direct" means of counting the number of men and women who could sign their names. Yet as his own evidence suggests, this information gives us no information about reading, since the two skills were taught separately in this period. Writing was a technology taught primarily in schooled settings; reading was taught in a variety of unschooled settings and was often the focus of religious-driven literacy. See Thomas, "The Meaning of Literacy," and Francois Furet and Jacques Ozouf, *Reading and Writing: Literacy in France from Calvin to Jules Ferry* (Cambridge: Cambridge University Press, 1982).

5. John Foxe, *The Acts and Monuments*, ed. Stephen Reed Cattley, 8 vols. (London: Seeley, 1837–41), 1:30. Further references to this source are cited in the text.

6. Quoted in John R. Knott, *Sword of the Spirit: Puritan Responses to the Bible* (Chicago: University of Chicago Press, 1980), 22.

7. I discuss the transmission of the English Bible at length in *Margins and Marginality: The Printed Page in Early Modern England* (Charlottesville, Va.: University of Virginia Press, 1993).

8. Alfred W. Pollard, *Records of the English Bible* (London: Oxford University Press, 1911), 263.

9. Stephen Greenblatt, *Renaissance Self-Fashioning: From More to Shakespeare* (Chicago: University of Chicago Press, 1980), 86.

10. See Frances Yates, *The Art of Memory* (Chicago: University of Chicago Press, 1966) for a description of the various "learned" systems for memorization. These systems

generally relied on spatial systems; memory was aided by constructing a mental "room" furnished with the various details that must be recalled.

11. See Greenblatt, *Renaissance Self-Fashioning*, chap. 2, for a discussion of the ability of the martyrs to seize the "symbolic initiative" from their interrogators.

12. Thomas Harding, *Rejoinder to Jewel* (n.p., 1567), quoted in Warren W. Wooden, *John Foxe* (Boston: Twayne, 1983), 12.

13. Robert Parsons, *A Treatise of Three Conversions* (n.p., 1603–04), 3:24.

14. Breitenberg, "The Flesh Made Word," 388.

15. William Lamont, *Godly Rule: Politics and Religion, 1603–1660* (London: Macmillan, 1969), 67.

16. Richard Helgerson, *Forms of Nationhood: The Elizabethan Writing of England* (Chicago: University of Chicago Press, 1992), 288; Christopher Hill, *Tinker and a Poor Man: John Bunyan and His Church, 1628–1688* (New York: Knopf, 1989), 122.

17. An excellent collection of essays on Foxe's reception has been edited by David Loades: *John Foxe: An Historical Perspective* (Brookfield, Vt.: Ashgate Press, 1999); see also Loades, ed., *John Foxe and the English Reformation* (Aldershot: Ashgate Press, 1997).

Chapter 6: Recasting the Culture of Ephemera

The author would like to acknowledge the generous support and guidance of the American Antiquarian Society (AAS), the Brown University Library, the Getty Center for the History of Art and the Humanities, the National Endowment for the Humanities, and the Winterthur Museum and Library. The manuscript material referenced in this essay comes chiefly from three sources, and the following textual citation format will apply throughout: the Harris Collection of American Poetry and Plays at the Brown University Library (BULH); the Downes Collections at the Henry Dupont Winterthur Museum and Library (WLDC); and the American Antiquarian Society (AAS). Readers interested in locating and retrieving specific items may do so by noting the institutional abbreviation and accompanying suffix, or, in the case of uncataloged collections (like AAS), contextual references. For example, in the case of Mary Abba's mid-nineteenth-century album (BULH, MS Harris Codex 1242), BULH refers to the Harris Collection of American Poetry and Plays at the Brown University Library and MS Harris Codex 1242 refers to the library's own identification number.

1. Werner Muensterberger, *Collecting: An Unruly Passion: Psychological Perspectives* (Princeton, N.J.: Princeton University Press, 1994), 3–48, 5.

2. Barton Levi St. Armand, *Emily Dickinson and Her Culture: The Soul's Society* (Cambridge: Cambridge University Press, 1984), 5.

3. Jean Baudrillard, "The System of Collecting," in *The Cultures of Collecting*, ed. John Elsner and Roger Cardinal (London: Reaktion Books, 1994), 8.

4. Mihaly Csikszentmihalyi and Rochberg-Halton, *The Meaning of Things: Domestic Symbols and the Self* (Cambridge: Cambridge University Press, 1981), 139.

5. Nick Groom, *The Making of Percy's Reliques* (Oxford: Clarendon Press, 1999), 35.

6. In her book, *On Longing: Narratives of the Miniature, the Gigantic, the Souvenir, the Collection* (Baltimore: Johns Hopkins University Press, 1984), Susan Stewart, explaining the creation of "nostalgic desire" (p. 145), overstates the case for the ahistorical qualities of collections, which, she says, replace "history with classification, with order beyond the realm of temporality" (p. 151). Many collections are arranged chronologically and are inspired by a basic impulse to review the past.

7. Krzysztof Pomian, *Collectors and Curiosities: Paris and Venice, 1500–1800*, trans. Elizabeth Wiles-Portier (London: Polity Press, 1990), 30.

8. Ronald J. Zboray, "Antebellum Reading and the Ironies of Technological Innovation," in *Reading in America: Literature and Social History*, ed. Cathy N. Davidson (Baltimore: Johns Hopkins University Press, 1989), 180–200.

9. William C. Seitz, *The Art of Assemblage* (New York: Museum of Modern Art, 1961), 10.

10. The problem of quantifying increases in general literacy is complex. I refer merely to a higher percentage of the United States population being able to read and write, which was brought about by the creation of normal schools, the beginning of public education in America. For the problem of quantifying literacy in the nineteenth century, see Harvey J. Graff, *The Literacy Myth: Cultural Integration and Social Structure in the Nineteenth Century* (New Brunswick: Transaction, 1991), 269–324. See also David Vincent, *Literacy and Popular Culture: England 1750–1914*.

11. Susan Stewart, *Nonsense: Aspects of Intertextuality in Folklore and Literature* (Baltimore: Johns Hopkins University Press, 1979), 4.

12. An illuminating nineteenth-century commonplace book from Wilmington, Delaware, for example, contains a laid-in, printed scrap about the rejuvenative qualities of domestic life; on the reverse is the following notice: "Was committed, as a Runaway, to the Public Goal of New-Castle County, of the 29th inst. a Negro boy who calls himself Daniel Young, supposed to be 17 or 18 years of age, pretty stout made, rather yellow of complexion, has lost one of his fore teeth and has an impediment in his speech" (WLDC, doc. 584).

13. Walter Benjamin, "Unpacking My Library," in *Illuminations*, ed. Hannah Arendt (New York: Schoken Books, 1985), 60–61.

14. Susan Miller, *Assuming the Positions: Cultural Pedagogy and the Politics of Commonplace Writing* (Pittsburgh: University of Pittsburgh Press, 1998), 21.

15. John R. Searle, *Speech Acts: An Essay in the Philosophy of Language* (Cambridge: Cambridge University Press, 1969), 16.

16. Jerome J. McGann, *Social Values and Poetic Acts: The Historical Judgment of Literary Work* (Cambridge, Mass.: Harvard University Press, 1988), 139.

17. Hayden White, "Interpretation in History," in *Tropics of Discourse: Essays in Cultural Criticism* (Baltimore: Johns Hopkins University Press, 1987), 66–67.

18. Todd S. Gernes, "The Assembled Book and the History of Active Reading," paper read at conference for Society for the History of Authorship, Reading and Publishing, Worcester, Mass., 21 July 1996.

19. Roger Chartier, *The Order of Books: Readers, Authors, and Libraries in Europe between the Fourteenth and Eighteenth Centuries*, trans. Lydia G. Cochrane (Stanford: Stanford University Press, 1994) 8.

20. Ibid., 22.

21. Roger Chartier, *Forms and Meanings: Texts, Performances, and Audiences from Codex to Computer* (Philadelphia: University of Pennsylvania Press, 1995), 15.

22. Todd S. Gernes, "Recasting the Culture of Ephemera: Young Women's Literary Culture in Nineteenth-Century America" (Ph.D. diss., Brown University, 1992). See also Alison M. Scott, "'These Notions I Imbibed from Writers': The Reading Life of Mary Ann Wodrow Archibald (1762–1841)" (Ph.D. diss., Boston University, 1995).

23. Michael Bath, *Speaking Pictures: English Emblem Books and Renaissance Culture* (London: Longman, 1994), 33.

24. Mary Carruthers, *The Book of Memory: A Study of Memory in Medieval Culture* (Cambridge: Cambridge University Press, 1994), 9.

25. Ibid., 186.

26. Frances A. Yates, *The Art of Memory* (Chicago: University of Chicago Press, 1966), 128–73.

27. Joan Marie Lechner, *Renaissance Concepts of the Commonplaces: An Historical Investigation of the General and Universal Ideas Used in All Argumentation and Persuasion with Special Emphasis on the Educational and Literary Tradition of the Sixteenth and Seventeenth Centuries* (Westport, Conn.: Greenwood Press, 1974). Interestingly, many early American literary anthologies were fashioned after commonplace books. See, for example, *The American Common-Place Book of Prose, A Collection of Eloquent and Interesting Extracts from the Writings of American Authors* (Boston: S. G. Goodrich, 1828).

28. Michael Bath, *Speaking Pictures: English Emblem Books and Renaissance Culture* (London: Longman, 1994), 33; Joel B. Altman, "'Preposterous Conclusions': Eros, Enargeia, and the Composition of Othello," *Representations* 18 (1987): 129–57.

29. Carruthers, *Memory*, 80–188.

30. Ann Blair, "Humanist Methods in Natural Philosophy: The Commonplace Book," *Journal of the History of Ideas* 53 (1992): 547–48.

31. Ann Moss, "Commonerplace-Rhetoric and Thought-Patterns in Early Modern Culture," in *The Recovery of Rhetoric: Persuasive Discourse and Disciplinarity in the Human Sciences*, ed. R. H. Roberts and J. M. M. Good (London: Bristol Classical Press, 1993), 56.

32. Clifford K. Shipton, *Biographical Sketches of Those Who Attended Harvard College in the Classes 1764–1767*, vol. 16 (Boston: Massachusetts Historical Society, 1972), 481.

33. Enos Hitchcock, *Memoirs of the Bloomsgrove Family: In a Series of Letters*, vol. II (Boston: Thomas and Andrews, 1790), 189–90; 257.

34. *Encyclopedia; or a Dictionary of Arts, Sciences, and Miscellaneous Literature*, vol. V (Philadelphia: Thomas Dobson, 1798), 217–18. I have updated the eighteenth-century typography in this passage for clarity.

35. "Common Place Books," *American Annals of Education and Instruction* 2 (July 1832): 34–35.

36. Carruthers, *Memory*, 169.

37. *The Parlor Book; or Family Encyclopedia of Useful Knowledge and General Literature* (1835) contains Rev. John Lauris Blake's illustrative definition of "Memory": "MEMORY. Memory implies two things: first, a capacity of retaining knowledge; and, secondly, a power of recalling that knowledge to our thoughts when we have occasion to apply it to use. When we speak of retentive memory, we use it in the former sense; when of a ready memory, in the latter. Without memory, there can be neither knowledge, arts, nor sciences; nor any improvement of mankind in virtue, or morals, or the practice of religion. Without memory, the soul of man would be but a poor, destitute, naked being, with an everlasting blank spread over it, except the fleeting ideas of the present moment" (578–79).

38. Rev. John Todd, *Index Rerum; or Index of Subjects* (1835; rpt. Northampton, Mass.: Bridgman and Childs, 1868), n.p.

39. John Locke, *The Works of John Locke*, vol. III (London: Awsham Churchill, 1722), 485.

40. Stewart, *Nonsense*, ix.

41. Miller, *Positions*, 2.

42. Felicity A. Nussbaum has productively used "commonplaces" as a metaphor to

discuss women's autobiographical writing. "Eighteenth-Century Women's Autobiographical Commonplaces," in *The Private Self:Theory and Practice of Women's AutobiographicalWritings*, ed. Shari Benstock (Chapel Hill: University of North Carolina, 1988), 147–71.

43. Kenneth A. Lockridge, *On the Sources of Patriarchal Rage: The Commonplace Books of William Byrd and Thomas Jefferson and the Gendering of Power in the Eighteenth Century* (New York: New York University Press, 1992), 48.

44. Mikhail Bakhtin, "The Problem of Speech Genres," in *M. M. Bakhtin: Speech Genres and Other Late Essays*, ed. Caryl Emerson and Michael Holquist, trans. Vern W. McGee (Austin: University of Texas Press, 1990), 60.

45. Mary Lynn Steven Heininger et al., *A Century of Childhood, 1820–1920* (Rochester, N.Y.: Margaret Woodbury Strong Museum, 1984).

46. Alistair Allen and Joan Hoverstadt, *The History of Printed Scraps* (London: New Cavendish Books, 1982), 12–20; Gernes, "Scrapiana Americana," *Winterthur Magazine* 42 (Spring 1996): 17–18.

47. Lydia Maria Child, *The Girl's Own Book* (New York: Clark Austin & Co., 1833), 152–53.

48. Gould pitched his wares to "Lady Agents": "Beautiful little landscapes, Groups, comic, Sentimental, Dogs, Birds, Little Girls and Boys; in different sizes, calculated for ornaments for The Scrap books, furnished to Agents at from 1 cent to 10 cents each, according to size, six samples for 25 cents. A very large variety . . . of large Chromos and Paintings. Agents and Peddlers, your especial attention I would call to this style of picture, there is a handsome profit on them and you can carry a large assortment without being burdened by the bulk, for this reason I would recommend this class of goods to Lady Agents, and it is a class of goods which ladies thoroughly understand the beauties, therefore, they cannot fail to have good success in selling them" (*J. Jay Gould's Catalogue of Chromos,Album Gems, Lithographs, Picture Frames, Picture Books, Story Books, Card Printers, Little Landscape Chromos, Photographs, Games, Embossed Pictures, Flower Seeds, Novelties, &c.* [Boston: 1875], 8).

49. Henry Glassie, *Patterns in the Material Folk Culture of the Eastern United States* (Philadelphia: University of Pennsylvania Press, 1968), 6.

50. E. W. Gurley, *Scrap Books and How to Make Them* (New York: Authors' Publishing, 1880), 5–6.

51. Campbell's recipe for making a scrapbook illustrates, at a very basic level, the constructionist art of assemblage: "Cut the pictures out very carefully, and plan how to arrange them before you begin work. Sometimes one can be put in the middle, with smaller ones at each corner. To paste neatly you want smooth paste, a small but broad brush, and a soft clean cloth. Lay the picture on its face, on a paper spread on the table. Take only a little paste on the brush at once, and cover the back of the picture thoroughly; then lift it carefully and lay it in its place, dabbing it smooth with the small cloth, pressing it down, and wiping away any particle of paste about the edges. Paste but one side at a time, and, when nearly dry, iron smooth with a warm iron, then the other side can be filled if you want both covered. A book of animals can be made, the pictures colored before or after pasting; and it is very easy, now that the pictures are so plenty, to have them on special subjects. A nice rainy-day game is to take one of these scrapbooks, and make up stories about the pictures; the best time for this being the twilight, when you cannot see any longer to work comfortably" (Helen Campbell, *The American Girl's Home Book of Work and Play* [New York: G. P. Putnam's Sons, 1884], 3–4). This book, interestingly, was a revision and updating of Lydia Maria Child, *The Little Girl's Own Book* (New York: E. Kearney, 1843).

52. Olive E. Dana, "One Woman's Way with Scrap-Books," *The Writer: A Monthly Magazine for Literary Workers* 5 (January–December 1891), 239.

53. Patricia P. Buckler and C. Kay Leeper, "An Antebellum Woman's Scrapbook as Autobiographical Composition," *Journal of American Culture* 14 (Spring 1991): 1–8.

54. Thanks to Barton L. St. Armand for pointing this out to me.

55. Ellen Gruber Garvey, *The Adman in the Parlor: Magazines and the Gendering of Consumer Culture, 1880s to 1910s* (Oxford: Oxford University Press, 1996), 16–50.

56. Eddie Wolfram, *History of Collage: An Anthology of Collage, Assemblage, and Event Structures* (New York: Macmillan, 1975), 9.

57. James L. Elderdice, "One Way of Making a Scrapbook," *The Youth's Companion* 57 (June 1884), 234.

58. Muneharu Kitagaki, "English Periodical Essays and Hawthorne: A Few Suggestions," *The Hawthorne Society of Japan Newsletter* 9 (April 1990): 1–2.

59. The first young woman to gain prominence in the field of amateur journalism was Miss L. Libbie Adams, better known as "Nettie Sparkle." Adams, who wrote poetry, fiction, and spunky editorials, edited and published *The Youthful Enterprise* from 1874 to 1878 in Carbondale, Pennsylvania, and, later, in Elmira, New York. *The Youthful Enterprise* was a semimonthly paper published "by a girl 14 years old who [was] its Editress, Printer, and Proprietress." In her scintillating editorials, Sparkle discussed the subjugation of women, women's suffrage, dress reform, intellectual uplift, and young women's right to publish. "One reason for the intellectual narrowness of women," she decried, echoing Wollstonecraft, "and their extreme subjection to prejudice and slavery to custom, is mental indolence" and the habitual denigration of women's ideas by men. Nettie Sparkle could write with the irreverence of Mark Twain or the smug gentility of Lydia Sigourney, as she provoked her readers to reconsider women's fashions, the dangers of reading "sensational trash," or the "mental capacities" of the sexes. Truman J. Spencer, *A Cyclopedia of the Literature of Amateur Journalism* (Hartford: Truman J. Spencer, 1891), 6–7.

60. Campbell, *Girl's Home Book*, 20.

61. Gurley, *Scrap Books*, 54–56.

62. Anne Ruggles Gere, "Common Properties of Pleasure: Texts in Nineteenth-Century Women's Clubs," in *The Construction of Authorship: Textual Appropriation in Law and Literature*, ed. Martha Woodmansee and Peter Jaszi (Durham: Duke University Press, 1994), 392.

63. An anonymous New York scrapbook (WLDC, fol. 123), which was created by pasting over an older shoemaker and tanner's account book, contains an essay (ca. 1863) on the importance of systematic reading, within a rich context of scraps on various topics. Included is a description of the "home amusement" of "photographic recreations," which consisted of making amateur prints from daguerreotypes by creating an ambrotype (negative) of the original, chemically treating the paper, and letting it sit in the sunlight, a process that could also be executed with leaves. Other scraps discussed divorce, husband catching, reading, novels, teaching, history, identifying parts of ships, young women in their twenties, fashion, and the Civil War.

64. "Many Albums Kept by Women," rpt. from the *New York Sun; Current Literature* 34 (June 1903): 741.

65. A telling example can be found in *The Secret Eye: The Journal of Ella Gertrude Clanton Thomas, 1848–1889*, ed. Virginia Ingrahm Burr (Chapel Hill, N.C.: University of North Carolina Press, 1990). On Friday, 31 July 1863, Thomas wrote, "During this summer I

have been much interested in pasting a scrapbook. I have two filled and cannot buy another in Augusta altho I have material enough to fill several more. A great many important events which occur in our country's history I would allude to more fully in my journal if it was not so much easier a plan to paste the printed account. In writing now I have an eye always to the future when I shall read portions to my children or submit the book to their perusal—I regret now that I have permitted so much of the year 1863 to pass unrecorded" (216). Thanks to Amy Thomas for calling my attention to this entry.

66. *Mark Twain's Notebooks and Journals: Volume II* (1877–1883), ed. Frederick Anderson, Lin Salamo, and Bernard L. Stein (Berkeley and Los Angeles: University of California Press, 1975), 12, n.2.

67. Charles Francis Potter, "Autograph Album Rimes," in *Wagnalls Standard Dictionary of Folklore, Mythology and Legend*, ed. Maria Leach (New York: Funk and Wagnalls Co., 1949), 94–96; See also Charles Francis Potter, "Round Went the Album," *New York Folklore Quarterly* 4 (1948): 4–14.

68. Max Rosenheim, "The Album Amicorum," *Archaeologia* 62 (1910): 251–308; W. K. McNeil, "The Autograph Custom: A Tradition and Its Scholarly Treatment," *Keystone Folklore Quarterly* 13 (Spring 1968): 29; J. K. Cameron, "Leaves from the Lost Album amicorum of Sir John Scot of Scotstarvit," *Scottish Studies* 28 (1987): 35–48.

69. To nineteenth- and twentieth-century Germans of the middle class, the *Stammbuch*, or genealogical book, belonged to the household, and inscribing it was usually a family affair. American folklorist Charles Francis Potter, observing New York families of German descent in 1949, reported the persistence of the folk custom and noted that all accessible family members must be the first to inscribe a new autograph album. In earlier times, the German *Stammbuch* had official connotations and contained marriage, birth, and death certificates (Potter, "Album Rimes," 94). Another eighteenth- and nineteenth-century parallel is the *Fraktur* of the Pennsylvania Dutch, "pen and ink drawings or lettering [on birth and baptismal certificates, letters, manuscripts, or broadsides], embellished with bright colors which contrast sharply with proximate colors. . . . In addition, New Year's wishes, occasional letters, religious mottoes, and scriptural verses were included in the vast array of Fraktur" (William T. Parsons, *The Pennsylvania Dutch: A Persistent Minority* [Boston: Twayne Publishers, 1976], 160–62).

70. McNeil, "The Autograph Custom," 30.

71. Bill of sale: John C. Riker to Hezekiah S. Archer, 1 August 1856, John C. Riker Papers, Long Island Room, Queens Borough Public Library, Jamaica, New York.

72. For example, one typical, lithographed introduction, printed in the shape of a scroll, read: "To Poets, Painters, Enigma and Conundrum Makers &c.; and all who wish to shine in this our literary Society. Wanted. A number of very neat drawings, in any style you are most proficient in; to fill up the blank paper in this Album. Also a few good stanzas on different subjects of a sentimental nature: Enigmas, Conundrums &c. will be likewise admitted. P.S. Originals are strongly recommended and dispatch must not be lost sight of" (Elizabeth Packard, "Album," AAS).

73. For a useful and well-illustrated discussion of the ornamental aspect of women's education, see Suzanne L. Flynt, *Ornamental and Useful Accomplishments: Schoolgirl Education and Deerfield Academy 1800–1830* (Deerfield, Mass.: Pocumtuck Valley Memorial Assoc. and Deerfield Academy, 1988).

74. Thorstein Veblen, *The Theory of the Leisure Class* [1899] (Boston: Houghton Mifflin, 1974), 46.

75. *Catalogue of the Officers and Students of Smithville Seminary* (Providence: H. H. Brown, 1841), 10–16.

76. David Park Curry, "Rose-Colored Glasses: Looking for 'Good Design' in American Folk Art," in *An American Sampler: Folk Art from the Strong Museum* (Washington, D.C.: National Gallery of Art, 1987), 28.

77. Jerome J. McGann, "Theses on the Philosophy of Criticism," in *The Beauty of Inflections: Literary Investigations in Historical Method and Theory* (Oxford: Clarendon Press, 1988), 343.

78. Jonathan Edwards, "The Nature of True Virtue," in *Jonathan Edwards: Representative Selection with Introduction Bibliography and Notes,* ed. Clarence H. Faust and Thomas H. Johnson, rev. edn. (New York: Hill and Wang, 1963), 349–72.

79. Lucretia Bailey Yaghjian, "Writing Practice and Pedagogy Across the Theological Curriculum: Teaching Writing in a Theological Context," *Theological Education* 33 (1997): 53.

80. Sarah Bridgeman, for example, copied the following note in her commonplace book (ca. 1830), introducing a lengthy hand-copied extract about the human heart of Jesus: "Dear Mrs. D, I have been reading an extract in a scrapbook & send you, that it seems to suit our reflections this morning as we are able to communicate the dying love of Jesus at his table. I think the description here is perfectly sublime—it has touched my hard heart—and I cannot refrain from sending it to you to read before you go to church—it is so badly written I am ashamed to send it—but it was only intended for my own eye, and with the hope it might do me good whenever I read it—I give it to your care—and you must make all allowance—oh let us draw near today—with humble hearts—and pray for your unworthy sister E—" (WLDC, doc. 10).

81. *Catalogue of the Officers, Teachers and Pupils of the Charlestown Female Seminary, for the Year, Ending August 1846* (Boston: Howe's Sheet Anchor Press, 1846), 15–16.

82. Gary Saul Morson and Caryl Emerson, *Mikhail Bakhtin: Creation of a Prosaics* (Stanford: Stanford University Press, 1990), 35.

83. Lev Vygotski, *Thought and Language,* trans. and ed. Alex Kozulin (Cambridge, Mass.: MIT Press, 1986), 113–15.

84. Gernes, "Poetic Justice: Sarah Forten, Eliza Earle, and the Paradox of Intellectual Property," *New England Quarterly* 71 (June 1998): 229–65.

85. Michel De Certeau, *The Practice of Everyday Life,* trans. Steven Rendall (Berkeley and Los Angeles: University of California Press, 1998), 21.

86. William Gilmore, *Reading Becomes a Necessity of Life: Material and Cultural Life in Rural New England, 1780–1835* (Knoxville: University of Tennessee Press, 1989), 286. The relevant verse from the New-England Primer, placed next to the emblem of the Bible, reads, "This Book attend, / Thy Life to mend." *The New-England Primer: A Reprint of the Earliest Known Edition,* ed. Paul Leicester Ford (New York: Dodd, Mead, and Co., 1899), n.p.

Chapter 7: "We Can Never Remain Silent":
The Public Discourse of the Nineteenth-Century Press

1. With the exceptions of *Freedom's Journal* and *A Red Record*, all quotes attributed to specific newspapers are from selections available in *The Black Press 1821–1890: The Quest for National Identity,* ed. Martin Dann (New York: G. P. Putnam's Sons, 1971). Since the major-

ity of articles and editorials were unsigned in the nineteenth-century African-American press, I use "writer" to refer generally to contributors.

2. Martin Dann, *The Black Press*, 11, 12.

3. J. William Snorgrass, "America's Ten Oldest Black Newspapers," *Negro History Bulletin* 46 (January-March 1983): 11–14; Roland Wolseley, *The Black Press, U.S.A.*, 2nd edn. (Ames: Iowa State University Press, 1990), 38.

4. Dann, *The Black Press*, 15.

5. *The Black Press in the South, 1865–1979*, ed. Henry Lewis Suggs (Westport, Conn.: Greenwood, 1983), 423.

6. Wolseley, *The Black Press, U.S.A.*, 39.

7. Penelope L. Bullock, *The Afro-American Periodical Press 1838–1909* (Baton Rouge: Louisiana State University Press, 1981), 11.

8. Dann, *The Black Press*, 22.

9. Lawrence Fortenberry, "*Freedom's Journal*: The First Black Medium," *The Black Scholar* (November 1974): 33–37.

10. Dann, *The Black Press*, 15.

11. Fortenberry, "*Freedom's Journal*," 33–34.

12. *Freedom's Journal*, 16 March 1826.

13. "Proposals for Publishing the *Freedom's Journal*," 6 April 1827.

14. Dann, *The Black Press*, 13.

15. Colonization schemes drew intense disagreements within the black community; some individuals wanted to fight to strengthen the rights and privileges that had been hard won, and they had no desire to leave a familiar, if imperfect, home for a foreign land. Others, such as John Russwurm, became disillusioned with the notion of free blacks within the United States and wanted to emigrate to northern Africa and other locations. These debates also led to unlikely agreements and collaboration between free northern blacks and proslavery forces who were seeking a way to rid the southern states of free and manumitted African Americans.

16. Wolseley, *The Black Press, U.S.A.*, 25.

17. Cornish, "Why We Should Have a Paper," 4 March 1837.

18. *Aliened American*, ed. Howard Day, Samuel Ward, and J. W. C. Pennington (Cleveland, 1853). In Dann, *The Black Press*, 50–52.

19. Gossie Harold Hudson, "Black Americans vs. Citizenship: The Dred Scott Decision," *Negro History Bulletin* 46 (January–March 1983): 26–28.

20. Jane H. Pease and William H. Pease, *They Who Would Be Free: Blacks' Search for Freedom, 1830–1861* (Urbana: University of Illinois Press, 1974), 213–18, 227.

21. *Weekly Anglo-African*, 23 July 1859.

22. Dann, *The Black Press*, 74.

23. *Weekly Anglo-African* 15 October 1859.

24. "The Irrepressible Conflict," *Weekly Anglo-African*, 3 December 1859.

25. *Weekly Anglo-African*, 3 December 1859.

26. Bullock, *The Afro-American Periodical Press*, 30–31.

27. *Emancipator*, 13 January 1835.

28. *Mirror of Liberty*, August 1838.

29. Daniel, *The Black Press*, 155.

30. *Douglass' Monthly* (November 1862), 1.

31. *Tribune*, 18 July 1865.

32. *The New National Era*, Washington, 27 January 1870; 25 January 1872. In Dann, *The Black Press*, 155–56, 95.

33. *Globe*, 20 October 1883.

34. Ibid.

35. *Colored American*, 10 October 1840.

36. Gerda Lerner, *Black Women in White America: A Documentary History* (New York: Vintage Books, 1972), 196–98.

37. Ida B. Wells Barnett, *A Red Record* (Chicago: Donohue and Henneberry, 1895); rpt. in Lerner, *Black Women*, 199–205.

38. Ibid., 200–03.

39. Ibid., 205.

40. Wolseley, *The Black Press, U.S.A.*, 209.

Chapter 8: "Stolen" Literacies in *Iola Leroy*

1. *Iola Leroy* was long thought to be Harper's only novel, but three others have recently been republished: Frances E. W. Harper, *Minnie's Sacrifice; Sowing and Reaping; Trial and Triumph*, ed. Francis Smith Foster (Boston: Beacon Press, 1994). There may be others.

2. Frances Ellen Watkins Harper, *Iola Leroy or Shadows Uplifted*, intro. Hazel V. Carby (Boston: Beacon Press, 1987), 7.

3. Harper, *Iola*, 34.

4. See Barbara Christian, *Black Women Novelists: The Development of a Tradition* (Westport, Conn.: Greenwood Press, 1980).

5. See Hazel V. Carby, *Reconstructing Womanhood: The Emergence of the Afro-American Woman Novelist* (Oxford: Oxford University Press, 1987).

6. See P. Gabrielle Forman, "'Reading Aright': White Slavery, Black Referents, and the Strategy of Histotextuality in *Iola Leroy*," *Yale Journal of Criticism* 10 (Fall 1997): 327–54.

7. See Foster, "Introduction," *Minnie's Sacrifice*.

8. Harper, *Iola*, 48.

9. See Alice Walker, "If the Present Looks Like the Past, What Does the Future Look Like?" in *In Search of Our Mother's Gardens: Womanist Prose* (New York: Harcourt, Brace, Jovanovich, 1983), 290–312.

10. Forman, "'Reading Aright'," 333.

11. For a thorough analysis of Harper's oratory, see Shirley Wilson Logan, *"We Are Coming": The Persuasive Discourse of Nineteenth-Century Black Women* (Carbondale, Ill.: Southern Illinois University Press, 1999).

12. I would like to thank Myriam Chancy for suggesting this comparison.

Chapter 9: Plays of Heteroglossia: Labor Drama
at the Bryn Mawr Summer School for Women Workers

The epigraph is from the student publication *Shop and School* (1938).

1. Diane Price Herndl, "The Dilemmas of a Feminist Dialogic," in *Feminism, Bakhtin, and the Dialogic*, ed. Dale M. Bauer and S. Jaret McKinstry (Albany: State University of New York Press, 1991), 9.

2. Rita Heller, "The Women of Summer: The Bryn Mawr Summer School for

Women Workers, 1921–1938" (Ph.D. diss., State University of New Jersey, 1986), 39. Florence Hemley Schneider, *Patterns of Workers' Education: The Story of the Bryn Mawr Summer School* (Washington, D.C.: American Council on Public Affairs, 1941), 102.

3. Esther E. Peterson, "Bryn Mawr Summer School, 1937: Dramatics" (Bryn Mawr: Bryn Mawr Summer School for Women Workers, 1937), 1.

4. Linda Nochlin, "The Paterson Strike Pageant of 1913," *Theatre for Working-Class Audiences in the United States, 1830–1980*, ed. Bruce A. McConachie and Daniel Friedman (Westport, Conn.: Greenwood Press, 1985), 87.

5. Daniel Friedman, "A Brief Description of the Workers' Theatre Movement of the Thirties," *Theatre for Working-Class Audiences*, 114.

6. Ibid., 111, 114.

7. Ibid., 114.

8. Douglas McDermott, "The Workers' Laboratory Theatre: Archetype and Example," *Theatre for Working-Class*, 126.

9. Ibid., 111.

10. Ibid., 128.

11. Michael Goldstein and Douglas McDermott, "The Living Newspaper as Dramatic Form," *Modern Drama* 7 (May 1965), 84.

12. Friedman, "Brief Description," 115.

13. McConachie and Friedman, *Theatre for Working-Class Audiences*, 14, 12.

14. Ibid., 14.

15. Victoria Grala, "Dramatics," *Shop and School* (Bryn Mawr: Bryn Mawr Summer School, 1937), 34.

16. McConachie and Friedman, *Theatre for Working-Class Audiences*, 12.

17. Friedman, "Brief Description," 111.

18. "Experiments in Labor Dramatics at the Bryn Mawr Summer School for Women Workers in Industry" (Bryn Mawr: Bryn Mawr Summer School, 1932), 1.

19. Hilda Worthington Smith, *Women Workers at the Bryn Mawr Summer School* (New York: Affiliated Summer Schools for Women Workers in Industry and American Association for Adult Education, 1929), 167.

20. Karyn L. Hollis, "Autobiographical Writing at the Bryn Mawr Summer School for Women Workers," *College Composition and Communication* 45 (1994), 56.

21. Jean Carter, "Labor Drama," *Journal of Adult Education* (1935), 179.

22. Carter, "Labor Drama (Introduction)," *Affiliated Schools Scrapbook* (1 March 1936), 1.

23. Lyn Goldfarb, "Memories of a Movement: A Conversation," *Sisterhood and Solidarity: Workers Education for Women, 1914–1984*, ed. Joyce L. Kornbluh and Mary Frederickson (Philadelphia, Pa.: Temple University Press, 1984), 335, 330.

24. Grala, "Dramatics," 34.

25. Smith, *Opening Vistas in Workers' Education: An Autobiography* (Washington, D.C.: self-published, 1978), 138.

26. Carter, "Labor Drama (Introduction)," 4, 3 (emphasis mine).

27. Esther E. Peterson, "Dramatics and Recreation" (Bryn Mawr: Byn Mawr Summer School for Women Workers, 1936), 5.

28. Smith, "Autobiography," 167.

29. "Minutes: Instruction Committee Meeting" (Bryn Mawr: Bryn Mawr Summer School for Women Workers, 1932), 1, 3.

30. Peterson, "Dramatics and Recreation," 1, 3.

31. Carter, "Report to Faculty of Bryn Mawr Summer School of Plans Following Staff Conference Held on the Campus, May 15–16, 1937" (Bryn Mawr: Bryn Mawr Summer School for Women Workers, 1937), 2.

32. Peterson, "Dramatics and Recreation," 2.

33. Hollace Ransdell, "Amateur Dramatics in the Labor Movement," *Affiliated Schools Scrapbook* (March 1936), 3.

34. Hollis, ""Autobiographical," 39.

35. Haroldine Humphreys, "The Play Spirit in Acting," *Bryn Mawr Alumnae Bulletin* (2 October 1922), 17.

36. Ruthella Stambaugh, "The Chronicle," *Bryn Mawr Echo* (1928), 39–43.

37. *Echo* (1929), 19.

38. Florence M. Pharo, "Syllabus-English" (Bryn Mawr: Byrn Mawr Summer School for Women Workers, 1930), 4.

39. Ruth Epstein, Margaret Sofia, and Jean Carter, "Calendar," *Shop and School* (1930), 53.

40. Congressperson Martin Dies of Texas was staunchly anti-Communist, anti-labor, and anti-immigrant. He later chaired the House Un-American Activities Committee.

41. Peterson, "Dramatics and Recreation," 2.

42. Ibid., 2.

43. Ibid., 6.

44. Carter, "Report to Faculty of Bryn Mawr Summer School," 2.

45. *Shop and School* (1937).

46. *Shop and School* (1938).

47. In 1932, Angelo Herndon, a nineteen-year-old Communist, organized an interracial hunger march in Atlanta, Georgia. He was arrested for attempting to incite insurrection, a capital crime. His defense became a cause célèbre in the 1930s. Nevertheless, a white supremacist judge and jury sentenced him to twenty years in prison. After a lengthy appeals process, the Supreme Court reversed his conviction in 1937. (Mark D. Naison, *Encyclopedia of the American Left*, ed. Mari Jo Buhle, Paul Buhle, and Dan Georgakas [Chicago: University of Chicago Press, 1992], 307.)

48. The Guffey-Snyder Act of 1935 provided for government regulation of the mining industry. Miners' rights to organize and bargain collectively were extended; production, work hours, and wages were regulated. It was declared unconstitutional in 1936.

49. For an excellent discussion of the relationship between drama and carnival in a specific context, see Randy Martin, *Socialist Ensembles: Theater and State in Cuba and Nicaragua* (Minneapolis: Bergin and Garvey, 1994), 113–23.

50. M. M. Bakhtin, *The Dialogic Imagination*, ed. Michael Holquist, trans. Caryl Emerson and Michael Holquist (Austin: University of Texas Press, 1981), 272.

51. Bakhtin, *Rabelais and His World*, trans. Helene Iswolsky (Bloomington: Indiana University Press, 1984), 10.

52. Nina Lamousen, "What Do You Think?" *Shop and School* (Bryn Mawr: Bryn Mawr Summer School for Women Workers, 1934), 20.

53. Clar Doyle, *Raising Curtains on Education: Drama as a Site for Critical Pedagogy* (Westport, Conn.: Bergin and Garvey, 1993), 80.

Chapter 10: Italian-American Cookbooks: Authenticity and the Market

1. Claude Levi-Strauss, "Culinary Triangle," *Partisan Review* 33 (1966), 595.

2. Levi-Strauss, *Totemism* (Boston: Beacon Press, 1962), 89.

3. Mary Douglas, "Deciphering a Meal," *Myth, Symbol, and Culture*, ed. Clifford Geertz (New York: Norton, 1971), 61.

4. Pierre Bourdieu, *Distinction: A Social Critique of the Judgement of Taste* (Cambridge, Mass.: Harvard University Press, 1984), 177–200.

5. Linda Keller Brown and Kay Mussell, introduction, *Ethnic and Regional Foodways in the United States: The Performance of Group Identity*, ed. Brown and Keller (Knoxville: University of Tennessee Press, 1984), 13.

6. Susan J. Leonardi, "Recipes for Reading: Summer Pasta, Lobster à la Riseholme, and Key Lime Pie," *PMLA* 104 (1989): 342–43.

7. Anne Goldman, "'I Yam What I Yam': Cooking, Culture, and Colonialism," *De/Colonizing the Subject: The Politics of Gender in Women's Autobiography*, ed. Sidonie Smith and Julia Watson (Minneapolis: University of Minnesota Press, 1992), 172.

8. Mary K. Taylor, "America's First Cookbook," *Early American Life* (February 1991), 40.

9. Amelia Simmons, *American Cookery* (Green Farms, Conn.: Silverleaf, 1984), 14.

10. Ibid., 76, 85, 98.

11. Ibid., 102.

12. See Lynne Ireland, "The Compiled Cookbook as Foodways Autobiography," *Western Folklore* 40.1 (1981), 107–14.

13. William Woys Weaver, "*Die Geschickte Hausfrau*: The First Ethnic Cookbook in the United States," *Food in Perspective*, ed. Alexander Fenton and Trefor M. Owen (Edinburgh: John Donald, 1981), 343–63.

14. Harvey Levenstein, "The American Response to Italian Food, 1880–1930," *Food and Foodways* 1 (1985), 5, 6.

15. Sewell Whitney, "Ethnic Products Satisfy Craving for Something New," *Advertising Age* (19 September 1985), 47–48.

16. Levenstein, "American Response," 2, 19.

17. Quoted in ibid., 8.

18. Jane Addams, *Twenty Years at Hull House* (New York: Signet, 1976), 253.

19. Quoted in Levenstein, "American Response," 9.

20. Ibid., 9.

21. John Clarke, *New Times and Old Enemies: Essays on Cultural Studies and America* (New York: HarperCollins, 1991), 56.

22. Francesca Romina, *Mangia, Little Italy! Secrets from a Sicilian Family Kitchen* (San Francisco: Chronicle Books, 1998).

23. Nancy Verde Barr, *We Called It Macaroni: An American Heritage of Southern Italian Cooking* (New York: Knopf, 1990), iii.

24. Helen Barolini, *Festa: Recipes and Recollections of Italian Holidays* (San Diego: Harcourt, 1988), 13.

25. Barr, *We Called It Macaroni*, xvii.

26. Ibid., 124, 308.

27. Helen Barolini, introduction, *The Dream Book: An Anthology of Writings by Italian American Women*, ed. Helen Barolini (New York: Schocken, 1985), 27.

28. Leonardi, "Recipes for Reading," 341.

29. Barr, *We Called It Macaroni*, 124.

30. Ibid., 163, 88.

31. Ibid., 237.

32. Ibid., 308.

33. Ibid., 284–85.

34. Ibid., 79, 137.

Chapter 11: Joe Shakespeare: The Contemporary British Worker-Writer Movement

1. The book jacket provides no other biographical information; however, Gerry Gregory has interviewed Smythe and offers the following details: "Joe Smythe is a Manchester railway guard (after years of unsettled employment). An 'omnivorous' reader from the start, he got interested in poetry after being given a volume of Shakespeare. Contact with the Commonword (Manchester) group led to remarkable developments: in 1979 two volumes of poetry were published (*Come and Get Me* and *Viva Whatsisname*). In the same year, he conceived the idea of publishing a further volume in 1980 to mark the 150th anniversary of the Liverpool-Manchester Railway. He approached the [National Union of Railwaymen], who promptly agreed and gave him three months sabbatical to get on with the project. Working the 'night shift' while his family were asleep upstairs, Joe met the deadline with *The People's Road*" (Gerry Gregory, "Community Publishing as Self-Education," in *Writing in the Community: Written Communication Annual*, ed. David Barton and Roz Ivancic, vol. 6 [Newbury Park, Ca.: Sage, 1991], 137).

2. Because most of the research for this account was done in the early 1990s, I have provided updated information where appropriate. The best current source of FWWCP information is the regularly updated Web site at <www.fwwcp.mcmail.com>.

3. John Trimbur, private correspondence, 1994.

4. QueenSpark can be visited on-line at <www.queensparkbooks.org.uk/booklist.html>.

5. Anne Ruggles Gere, "The Extracurriculum of Composition," *College Composition and Communication* 45: 1 (1994), 80.

6. Gregory, "Community Publishing as Self-Education," 113.

7. FWWCP information brochure, 1999.

8. Not all the groups listed here are current members. While some groups fold and others join, the membership has been at about fifty groups over the past ten years. Current information is available from FWWCP, 67 The Boulevard, Tunstall, Stoke-on-Trent, ST6 6BD, England.

9. Laura Corbalis, interview by author, Bristol, 1993.

10. The past tense is needed here because Bristol Broadsides dissolved in 1992. Commonword, however, is still going strong and can be visited on-line at <rylibweb.man.ac.uk/data1/sy/jw/cword.html>.

11. Gregory offers the following summary, based on his wide reading of community-published texts: "The large perennial themes of literature appear abundantly in community publications: birth, childhood, adolescence, work, love, marriage, war, bereavement, and so on. Certain matter and themes predominate: working-class home life and conditions; the solidarity and claustrophobia of community relationships; street-

wise childhood, and a schooling 'nasty, brutish, and short'; relationships with authorities; the experience of women and of minorities—or of both combined" ("Community Publishing as Self-Education," 114).

12. Bertel Martin, interview by author, Bristol, 1993.

13. Gatehouse can be visited on-line at <www.gatehousebooks.org.uk>.

14. David Morley and Ken Worpole, eds., *The Republic of Letters: Working Class Writing and Local Publishing* (London: Comedia, 1982), 40–41.

15. Ibid., 42–43.

16. Ibid., 41.

17. Bob Pitt, introduction to *Bristol Lives* (Bristol: Bristol Broadsides, 1987).

18. Quoted in Gregory, "Community Publishing as Self-Education," 135.

19. As a tutor in Workers Education Association courses in the late 1940s, Raymond Williams noted "the substantial number of wage-earners who at the 3rd or 4th meeting produce their novel or autobiography, short stories or poems—an enormous amount of unknown writing of this sort goes on" (*Politics and Letters* [London: Verso, 1979], 78).

20. Roger Drury, et al., *Feds under the Bed: A Performance Devised for the FWWCP to Celebrate 21 Years of Activity . . . and a Lot of Words under the Pen* (unpublished MS, 1997), 13.

21. Morley and Worpole, *The Republic of Letters*, 58.

22. Gregory, "Community Publishing as Self-Education," 128.

23. Quoted in Gregory, "Community Publishing as Self-Education," 127.

24. *The Dinner Lady and Other Stories* (Bristol: Bristol Broadsides, n.d.), preface.

25. Roger Drury, interview by author, Cinderford, Gloucestershire, 1994.

26. *Once I Was a Washing Machine* (Stoke-on-Trent: FWWCP, 1989), 84.

27. Keith Birch, "The Growing Phenomenon of Working-Class Writing on Merseyside," in *Don't Judge This Book by Its Cover!* (Liverpool: Merseyside Association of Writers Workshops, 1990), 154.

28. Gregory, "Community Publishing as Self-Education," 134.

29. The fact that the Federation not only survived but grew and diversified during the Thatcher years of official hostility to workers' culture and causes testifies to the depth and tenacity of these motivations. While my focus in this account of the FWWCP is primarily on its enactment of "popular literacy," I think it's important to note that the Fed's resilience has everything to do with its democratic structure and openness to difference. Laura Corbalis explains: "This is my theory about why the Fed has survived Thatcher is because it's—it has a lot to do with it being a cultural organization instead of a political party, and I think the reason we were able to argue positively over the past several years about sex and class and race is because not being a political party, we didn't have the pressure of having to come up with a line. So at the end of every year, a lot of us would go home [from the annual general meeting] really cross, but still feeling like there was a place for us in the Fed, because an official line had not been arrived at that would force people to leave, which is what repeatedly happens in political parties, and feminist groups, and so on. That's one of its strengths, is that it can tackle those things and tolerate a very broad range of positions. But also because I think it's a demonstration of why we were right in the 70s to get into local action, because it has such solid roots, in people's own neighborhood. So I suppose in a way it mirrors early trade-union history and does for people what early trade unions did—it gives a lot of face to face personalized communal neighborhood support, and you can go as far as

you like in that—in your city, in your region, you can get involved in the national organization if you want to."

30. Gere, "The Extracurriculum of Composition," 78.

31. By the mid-1990s, however, these gains were in practice looking rather modest and fragile in light of the conservative government's regression to a "back to basics" approach, with strict curriculum for adult basic education, and the fragmentation of literacy to a set of "digestible" subskills.

32. Nick Pollard, interview by author, Sheffield, 1984.

33. Bertel Martin, interview by author, Bristol, 1993.

34. Ibid.

35. Raymond Williams, *Keywords: A Vocabulary of Culture and Society* (Oxford: Oxford University Press, 1976), 151.

36. The words of Charles Osborne, Literary Director, Arts Council of Great Britain, 1979, are quoted in *The Republic of Letters*, 135–36 (emphasis added). I should note here that the Federation's application to the Arts Council was successful in 1992. Under the Literature Division's new director, Alisdair Niven, the FWWCP received a grant to fund a full-time development worker, and that support has continued.

37. Jane Mace, *Talking about Literacy: Principles and Practice of Adult Literacy Education* (London: Routledge, 1992), xiv, xvii, xvi–xvii.

38. Joe Flanagan, interview by author, Halifax, 1993.

39. *The Republic of Letters*, 96.

Chapter 12: Changing the Face of Poverty:
Nonprofits and the Problem of Representation

1. Stanley Aronowitz, interview in the video production *Consumer Hunger: Part III Selling the Feeling* (Maryknoll, N.Y.: Maryknoll World Productions, 1988).

2. Eugene Richards, *Below the Line: Living Poor in America* (Mount Vernon, N.Y.: Consumers Union, 1987), 215.

3. Richard Leppert, *Art and the Committed Eye: The Cultural Functions of Imagery* (Boulder, Co.: Westview Press, 1996), 173–76.

4. Henry Mayhew, *London Labour and the London Poor* (New York: Penguin Books, 1985).

5. Ibid., 447.

6. Jack London, *The People of the Abyss*, facs. edn. (New York: Garrett P, MSS Information Corp., 1970), 78.

7. Ibid., 287–88.

8. Jacob A. Riis, *How the Other Half Lives: Studies among the Tenements of New York* (New York: Dover, 1971), 2.

9. Helen Campbell, *Darkness and Daylight; or Lights and Shadows of New York Life: A Woman's Story of Gospel, Temperance, Mission, and Rescue Work "In His Name"* (Hartford, Conn.: A. D. Worthington, 1892), viii–ix, x–xi (emphasis in the original).

10. Ibid., 99.

11. "Help Feed the Homeless This Thanksgiving," *Milwaukee Rescue Mission* ad appeal, *Milwaukee Journal Sentinel* (Saturday, 14 Nov. 1998), 8A. To be fair to the Milwaukee Rescue Mission, this photograph has been replaced in more recent ads by photos of mothers with children and other single homeless men. In a telephone interview, Pastor Patrick Vanderburgh, Executive Director of Milwaukee Rescue Mission, indicated that the mis-

sion has wrestled with the problem of how best to represent the need that is out there. Since this is a fundraising ad, the representation must move the public to charity, but according to Pastor Vanderburgh, even photos of mothers with children have not been nearly as successful in raising funds as this photo of a homeless man who very obviously fits the public's common idea of a street person.

12. Mayhew, *London Labour*, 448.

13. James Curtis, *Mind's Eye: Mind's Truth: FSA Photography Reconsidered* (Philadelphia: Temple University Press, 1989), viii–ix.

14. Ibid., 52.

15. *Building New Lives* (Americus, Ga.: Habitat for Humanity International). This and other Habitat videos are directed primarily at potential volunteers for the organization or might be used to inform local residents about the work of Habitat.

16. Robert Rector, "The Myth of Widespread American Poverty," *The Heritage Foundation Backgrounder* (18 Sept. 1998), no. 1221. This publication is available on-line at <http://www.heritage.org/library/backgrounder/bg1221es.html>.

17. Cited in Barbara Ehrenreich, "Nickel and Dimed: On (Not) Getting by in America," *Harper's* (January 1999), 44. See also Christina Coburn Herman's *Poverty Amid Plenty: The Unfinished Business of Welfare Reform* NETWORK, A National Social Justice Lobby (Washington, D.C., 1999), from NETWORK's National Welfare Reform Watch Project, which reports that most studies of welfare use telephone surveys even though a substantial percentage of those needing aid do not have phone service (41 percent in the NETWORK survey had no operative phone) and, therefore, are not represented in most welfare reform reports. This report is available on-line at <http://www.network-lobby.org>.

18. bell hooks, "Seeing and Making Culture: Representing the Poor," *Outlaw Culture: Resisting Representations* (New York: 1994), 169.

19. Manning Marable, *How Capitalism Underdeveloped Black America* (Boston: South End Press, 1983), 54.

20. Stanley Aronowitz, *The Politics of Identity. Class, Culture, Social Movements* (New York: Routledge, 1992), 201.

21. Kim Puuri, personal correspondence with author.

22. Paul Wellstone, "If Poverty Is the Question," *Nation* (14 April 1997), 15.

23. Herbert J. Gans, *The War Against the Poor* (New York: Basic Books, 1995), 6–7.

24. Dorothy Day, *Loaves and Fishes: The Inspiring Story of the Catholic Worker Movement* (Maryknoll, N.Y.: Orbis Books, 1997), 71.

25. Ibid., 71–72.

26. Michael B. Katz, *The Undeserving Poor: From the War on Poverty to the War on Welfare* (New York: Pantheon Books, 1989), 3.

27. "Welfare Drug Test Bill on Fast Track," *Detroit News* (4 Feb. 1999) <http://www.detnews.com>Metro/State edition.

28. Ibid.

29. Ehrenreich, "On (Not) Getting By," 38.

30. Interviewed in the video production *Consuming Hunger: Part I—Getting the Story* (Maryknoll, N.Y.: Maryknoll World Productions, 1988). These comments and the discussion that follows are drawn from the three-part video *Consuming Hunger* about media representations first of the famine crisis in Ethiopia and then of media representations of hunger in America culminating in the 1986 media event *Hands Across America*. At the

time of this taping, Brian Winston was serving as Dean of Penn State's School of Communication.

31. *Consuming Hunger.*

32. Brian Flagg, personal correspondence with author.

Chapter 13: Popularizing Science: At the Boundary of Expert and Lay Biomedical Knowledge

Lundy Braun would like to acknowledge all the people who have made Project LEAD so successful: the core faculty, Ben Anderson, Kay Dickersin, Margaret Mead, Bob Millikan, Jennifer Pietenpol, Susan Troyan, and Anna Wu; NBCC staff and former staff, Sara Collina, Margo Michaels, Jane Reese-Coulborune; Fran Visco, President of the National Breast Cancer Coalition; and, finally, the participants who by sharing their compelling stories taught me so much. We would also like to thank Phil Brown for his careful reading of an earlier version of this essay.

1. For his thinking on the scientific ethos, see Robert K. Merton, *The Sociology of Science: Theoretical and Empirical Investigations*, ed. Norman W. Storer (Chicago: University of Chicago Press, 1973), especially "The Normative Structure of Science," 267–78, and "Priorities in Scientific Discovery," 286–324.

2. "Communicating Science to the Public: Whose Job Is It Anyway," *Journal of the National Cancer Institute* 90 (1998), 1509–11.

3. Sally Lehrman "AAAS Head Wants to See Scientists on School Boards," *Nature* 397 (1999), 374.

4. James C. Thomas, et al. "Lay Health Advisors: Sexually Transmitted Disease Prevention through Community Involvement," *American Journal of Public Health* 88 (1998), 1252–53.

5. See, e.g., Greg Myers, *Writing Biology: Texts in the Social Construction of Scientific Knowledge* (Madison: University of Wisconsin Press, 1990), esp. 141–92.

6. Jane Gregory and Steve Miller, *Science in Public: Communication, Culture, and Credibility* (New York: Plenum Press, 1998), 5.

7. "Americans Are Interested in Science; Lack Understanding of the Basics," *Journal of the National Cancer Institute* 90 (1998): 1127.

8. For example, in *A Passion for DNA: Genes, Genomes, and Society* (Cold Spring Harbor, N.Y.: Cold Spring Harbor Laboratory Press, 2000), Nobel Laureate and first Director of the Human Genome Project James D. Watson criticizes the widespread public opposition in the 1970s to recombinant DNA research as uninformed meddling with the advancement of science. The problem, Watson says, is that the public's lack of "emotional ease with the gene and the geneticists who study it" combined with the "political hang-ups" of left-wing scientists to foment a popular movement raised serious questions about recombinant DNA research—and in some cases blocked it, at least temporarily.

9. Christine Day, "A Medical Education for Ordinary People," *New York Times* (24 Nov. 1998): D8.

10. See, e.g., Brian Wynne's case study of the misunderstanding between hill sheep-farmers in the Lake District of England and government scientists investigating the radioactive contamination of their flocks, "Misunderstood Misunderstandings: Social Identity and Public Uptake of Science," *Misunderstanding Science? The Public Reconstruction of*

Science and Technology, ed. Alan Irwin and Brian Wynne (Cambridge: Cambridge University Press, 1996), 19–46.

11. David M. Eisenberg, et al., "Unconventional Medicine in the United States: Prevalence, Costs, and Patterns of Use," *New England Journal of Medicine* 328 (1993): 246–52.

12. Eisenberg, et al., "Trends in Alternative Medicine Use in the United States, 1990–1997" *Journal of the American Medical Association* 280 (1998): 1569–75.

13. Arnold S. Relman, "A Trip to Stonesville," *New Republic* (14 Dec. 1998): 37.

14. Jane Wells, "Mammography and the Politics of Randomized Controlled Trials," *British Medical Journal* 317 (1998): 1228.

15. Ibid.

16. Dorothy Nelkin, *Selling Science: How the Press Covers Science and Technology* (New York: Freeman and Co., 1995), 5–7

17. Bruno Latour, *Science in Action* (Cambridge, Mass.: Harvard University Press, 1987), 52.

18. Nelkin, *Selling Science*, 7.

19. David J. Hunter, et al., "Plasma Organochlorine Levels and the Risk of Breast Cancer," *New England Journal of Medicine* 337 (1997): 1253–58; Gina Kolata, "Study Discounts DDT Role in Breast Cancer," *New York Times* (30 Oct. 1997): A19.

20. Karen Frost, Erica Frank, and Edward Maibach, "Relative Risk in the News Media: A Quantification of Misrepresentation," *American Journal of Public Health* 87 (1997): 842–45.

21. Ibid., 844 (emphasis added).

22. Warren E. Leary, "Aspirin Proposed for Suspected Heart Attacks," *New York Times* (19 June 1996): C9.

23. Leslie Laurence, "How OB-GYNs Fail Women: Read This Before Your Next Checkup," *Glamour* (October 1997): 292–94.

24. Stephanie Young, "Your Pap Smear: A Save-Your-Life Guide," *Glamour* (August 1997): 208 (emphasis added).

25. Ann Victoria, "Banish Arthritis Forever," *Weekly World News* (24 Oct. 1995): 9.

26. Ibid.

27. Phil Brown, "Popular Epidemiology and Toxic Waste Contamination: Lay and Professional Ways of Knowing," *Journal of Health and Social Behavior* 33 (1992): 269–71.

28. Steven Epstein, *Impure Science: AIDS, Activism, and the Politics of Knowledge* (Berkeley and Los Angeles: University of California Press, 1996), 10.

29. Ibid., 3.

30. Ibid.

31. Roberta Altman, *Waking Up, Fighting Back: The Politics of Breast Cancer* (Boston: Little, Brown, and Co., 1996), 303.

32. For a fuller description of Project LEAD, see Kay Dickersin, et al. "Development, Implementation and Evaluation of a Science Training Course for Breast Cancer Activists: Project LEAD (Leadership, Education and Advocacy Development)" (MS).

Chapter 14: Understanding Popular Digital Literacies:
Metaphors for the Internet

1. Peter H. Salus, *Casting the Net: From ARPANET to Internet and Beyond* (Reading, Mass.: Addison-Wesley, 1995).

2. James W. Carey, *Communication as Culture Essays on Media and Society* (Boston: Unwin Hyman, 1989).

3. William J. Clinton, "Remarks by the President in Signing Ceremony for the Telecommunications Act Conference Report," 8 February 1996, The White House, Office of the President, 14 December 1998.

4. Ester Dyson, George Gilder, George Keyworth, and Alvin Toffler, "A Magna Carta for the Knowledge Age," *New Perspectives Quarterly* 11:4 (Fall 1994): 28.

5. Albert Gore, "Remarks by Vice President Gore at the National Press Club," 21 December 1993, <http://www.dataalchemy.com/txt/POLITICS/ALGORE.SPC.htm> 14 December 1998.

6. Phil Patton, *Open Road: A Celebration of American Highway* (New York: Simon and Schuster, 1986), 102.

7. Lewis Mumford, *The Highway and the City* (New York: Harcourt, Brace, 1963), 236, 238.

8. Helen Leavitt, *Superhighway—Superhoax* (Garden City, N.Y.: Doubleday, 1970), 58–64.

9. Mark Slouka, *War of the Worlds: Cyberspace and the High-Tech Assault on Reality* (New York: Basic Books, 1995), 4.

10. Frank Rich, "Stand-Up Synergy," *New York Times* (6 March 1997): A23.

11. John Perry Barlow, "Howdy, Neighbours," *Guardian* (24 July 1995): 11.

12. Ibid., 37.

13. Lester Faigley and Thomas P. Miller, "What We Learn from Writing on the Job," *College English* 44 (1982): 557–69.

14. Howard Rheinhold, *The Virtual Community: Homesteading on the Electronic Frontier* (New York: Harper Perennial, 1993), 3.

15. Ibid.

16. Nancy Fraser, "Rethinking the Public Sphere: A Contribution to the Critique of Actually Existing Democracy," *Habermas and the Public Sphere*, ed. Craig Calhoun (Cambridge, Mass.: MIT Press, 1992), 109–42.

17. Jürgen Habermas, "Further Reflections on the Public Sphere," *Habermas and the Public Sphere*, 451.

18. Rajiv Chandrasekaran, "Internet Use Has More than Doubled in Last 18 Months, Survey Finds," *Washington Post* (13 March 1997): E3.

19. George Gilder, "Overthrowing Hollywood and the Broadcast E lites," *New Perspectives Quarterly* 12:2 (Spring 1995): 20.

20. Teresa Poole, "China Uses Jail Threat to Keep Control of Internet," *Independent* 1 (3 Dec. 1998): 18.

Works Cited

Addams, Jane. *Twenty Years at Hull House*. New York: Signet, 1976.

Agbah, Florence. *My Way*. Stevenage: Avanti Books, 1987.

The Aliened American, Cleveland, 9 April 1853. Dann 50–52.

Allen, Alistair and Joan Hoverstadt. *The History of Printed Scraps*. London: New Cavendish Books, 1982.

Altman, Joel B. "'Preposterous Conclusions': Eros, Enargeia, and the Composition of *Othello*." *Representations* 18 (Spring 1987): 129–57.

Altman, Roberta. *Waking Up, Fighting Back. The Politics of Breast Cancer*. Boston: Little, Brown, and Co., 1996.

"Americans Are Interested in Science; Lack Understanding of the Basics." *Journal of the National Cancer Institute* 90 (1998): 1127–28.

Anderson, Frederick, Lin Salamo, and Bernard L. Stein, eds. *Mark Twain's Notebooks and Journals.Volume II* (1877–1883). Berkeley: University of California Press, 1975.

Angiuli, Emanuela. "Ex Voto in Biblioteca." Angiuli.

———, ed. *Puglia ExVoto*. Lecce: Congedo Editore, 1977.

Aristotle. *Nicomachean Ethics*. 2nd edn. Trans. H. Rackham. Cambridge: Harvard University Press, 1982.

Aronowitz, Stanley. *The Politics of Identity: Class, Culture, Social Movements*. New York: Routledge, 1992.

Atkinson, Clarissa W. *Mystic and Pilgrim: The Book and the World of Margery Kempe*. Ithaca: Cornell University Press, 1983.

Baden, Anne D. "Drama." *Shop and School* (1938): 46.

Bakhtin, Mikhail. *The Dialogic Imagination*. Ed. Michael Holquist. Trans. Caryl Emerson and Michael Holquist. Austin: University of Texas Press, 1981.

———. *M. M. Bakhtin: Speech Genres and Other Late Essays*. Ed. Caryl Emerson and Michael Holquist. Trans. Vern W. McGee. Austin: University of Texas Press, 1990.

———. *Rabelais and His World*. Trans. Helene Iswolsky. Bloomington, Ind.: Indiana University Press, 1984.

Barlow, John Perry. "Howdy, Neighbours." *The Guardian* 24 July 1995: 11.

Barnett, Ida B. Wells. *A Red Record*. 1895. Lerner 199–205.

Barolini, Helen. "Introduction." *The Dream Book: An Anthology of Writings by Italian-American Women*. Ed. Helen Barolini. New York: Schocken, 1985. 1–30.

———. *Festa: Recipes and Recollections of Italian Holidays*. San Diego: Harcourt, 1988.

Barr, Nancy Verde. *We Called It Macaroni: An American Heritage of Southern Italian Cooking*. New York: Knopf, 1990.

Bath, Michael. *Speaking Pictures: English Emblem Books and Renaissance Culture*. London: Longman, 1994.

Baudrillard, Jean. "The System of Collecting." *The Cultures of Collecting*. Ed. John Elsner and Roger Cardinal. London: Reaktion, 1994. 7–24.

Bäuml, Franz H. "Medieval Literacy and Illiteracy: An Essay toward the Construction of a Model." *Germanic Studies in Honor of Otto Springer*. Ed. Stephen J. Kaplowitt. Pittsburgh: K & K, 41–54.

———. "Varieties and Consequences of Medieval Literacy and Illiteracy." *Speculum* 55 (1980): 237–65.

Benjamin, Walter. *Illuminations*. Ed. Hannah Arendt. Trans. Harry Zohn. New York: Schocken, 1985.

Birch, Keith. "The Growing Phenomenon of Working-Class Writing on Merseyside." *Don't Judge This Book by its Cover!* Liverpool: Merseyside Association of Writers Workshops, 1990.

Blair, Ann. "Humanist Methods in Natural Philosophy: The Commonplace Book." *Journal of the History of Ideas* 53.4 (1992): 541–51.

Bolgiani, Franco. "Santuario, Ex Voto e 'Cultura Popolare.'" *Gli Ex Voto della Consolata*. Torino: Biblioteca di Studi Storico Religiosi Erik Peterson, 1983.

Borello, Laura. "Alcune Considerazioni sugli Ex Voto Oggettuali della Consolata." *Gli Ex Voto della Consolata*. Torino: Biblioteca di Studi Storico Religiosi Erik Peterson, 1983.

Bourdieu, Pierre. *Distinction: A Social Critique of the Judgment of Taste*. Cambridge: Harvard University Press, 1984.

Breitenberg, Mark. "The Flesh Made Word: Foxe's Acts and Monuments." *Renaissance and Reformation* 24 (1989): 381–407.

Bristol Lives. Bristol: Bristol Broadsides, 1987.

Bronzini, Giovanni Battista. "Fenomenologia dell'Ex Voto." *Anguili*.

Brown, Linda Keller and Kay Mussell. "Introduction." *Ethnic and Regional Foodways in the United States: The Performance of Group Identity*. Ed. Brown and Keller. Knoxville: University of Tennessee Press, 1984. 3–18.

Brown Phil. "Popular Epidemiology and Toxic Waste Contamination: Lay and Professional Ways of Knowing." *Journal of Health and Social Behavior* 33 (1992): 267–81.

Buckler, Patricia P. and C. Kay Leeper. "An Antebellum Woman's Scrapbook As Autobiographical Composition." *Journal of American Culture* 14.1 (1991): 1–8.

Buhle, Mary Jo, Paul Buhle, and Dan Georgakas. *Encyclopedia of the American Left*. Chicago: University of Chicago Press, 1992.

Building New Lives. Americus, Ga.: Habitat for Humanity International, vhs video.

Bullock, Penelope L. *The Afro-American Periodical Press 1838–1909*. Baton Rouge: Louisiana State University Press, 1981.

Burke, Peter. *Popular Culture in Early Modern Europe.* New York: Harper and Row, Cambridge University Press, 1996. 19–46.

Burr, Virginia Ingraham, ed. *The Secret Eye: The Journal of Ella Gertrude Clanton Thomas, 1848–1889.* Chapel Hill: University of North Carolina Press, 1990.

"Calendar." *Byrn Mawr Daisy* 2.4 (1922): 15.

"Calendar." *Shop and School* (1929): 16–24.

"Calendar of Events." *Shop and School* (1937): 36.

Cameron, J. K. "Leaves from the lost Album amicorum of Sir John Scot of Scotstarvit." *Scottish Studies* 28 (1987): 35–48.

Campbell, Helen. *The American Girl's Home Book of Work and Play.* New York: G.P. Putnam's Sons, 1884.

———. *Darkness and Daylight; or, Lights and Shadows of New York Life. A Woman's Story of Gospel, Temperance, Mission, and Rescue Work 'In His Name.'* Hartford, Conn.: A.D. Worthington & Co., 1892.

Carby, Hazel V. *Reconstructing Womanhood: The Emergence of the Afro-American Woman Novelist.* New York: Oxford University Press, 1987.

Carey, James W. *Communication as Culture Essays on Media and Society.* Boston: Unwin Hyman, 1989.

Carter, Joan. "Labor Drama." *Journal of Adult Education* 7 (April 1935): 179–82.

———. "Labor Drama (Introduction)." *Affiliated Schools Scrapbook* 1 (March 1936): 1–4.

———. "Report to Faculty of Bryn Mawr Summer School of Plans Following Staff Conference Held on the Campus, 15–16 May 1937." Bryn Mawr: Bryn Mawr Summer School for Women Workers, 1937. 1–6.

Carruthers, Mary. *The Book of Memory: A Study of Memory in Medieval Culture.* Cambridge: Cambridge University Press, 1990.

Casa, Kathryn. "Commerce Challenges Charity." *National Catholic Reporter.* 28 Mar. 1997: 4–5.

Cawelti, John. *Adventure, Mystery, and Romance.* Chicago: University of Chicago Press, 1976.

Chalfant, Henry and James Prigoff. *Spraycan Art.* London: Thames and Hudson, 1987.

Chandrasekaran, Rajiv. "Internet Use Has More Than Doubled in Last 18 Months, Survey Finds." *Washington Post* 13 Mar. 1997, final ed.: E3.

Charlestown Female Seminary. *Catalogue of Officers, Teachers, and Pupils of the Charlestown Female Seminary.* Boston: Howe's Sheet Anchor Press, 1846.

———. *The Annual Report of the Whiting Association or Social Circle (Originally Tract Society) of the Charlestown Female Seminary.* Hingham: Farmer's Press, 1847.

Chartier, Roger. *Forms and Meanings: Texts, Performances, and Audiences from Codex to Computer.* Philadelphia: University of Pennsylvania Press, 1995.

———. *The Order of Books: Readers, Authors, and Libraries in Europe between the Fourteenth and Eighteenth Centuries.* Trans. Lydia G. Cochrane. Stanford: Stanford University Press, 1994.

Chaucer, Geoffrey. *Canterbury Tales. The Complete Poetry and Prose of Geoffrey Chaucer.* Ed. John H. Fisher. New York: Holt, 1977. 1–397.

Chaytor, H. J. *From Script to Print.* Cambridge: Cambridge University Press, 1945.

Child, Lydia Maria. *The Girl's Own Book*. New York: Cark Austin, 1833.

————. *The Little Girl's Own Book*. New York: E. Kearney, 1843.

Christian, Barbara. *Black Women Novelists: The Development of a Tradition*. Westport, Conn.: Greenwood Press, 1980.

Cisneros, Sandra. "Little Miracles, Kept Promises." *The Story and Its Writer: An Introduction To Short Fiction*. Ed. Ann Charters. Boston: Bedford, 1995.

Clanchy, M. T. *From Memory to Written Record: England 1066–1307*. Cambridge: Harvard University Press, 1979.

Clarke, John. *New Times and Old Enemies: Essays on Cultural Studies and America*. New York: Harper Collins, 1991.

Clinton, William. "Remarks by the President in Signing Ceremony for the Telecommunications Act Conference Report." 8 February 1996. The White House, Office of the President. 14 Dec. 1998. (http://www1.whitehouse.gov/WH/EOP/OP/telecom/release.html).

Colored American, New York, 1 July 1831; 4 March, 8 April 1837; 10 October 1840.

"Commonplace Book." *Encyclopedia; or a Dictionary of Arts, Sciences, and Miscellaneous Literature*. Vol. 5. Philadelphia: Thomas Dobson, 1798.

"Common Place Books." Ed. William C. Woodridge. *American Annals of Education and Instruction* 2 (1 July 1832): 305–10.

"Communicating Science to the Public: Whose Job Is It Anyway." *Journal of the National Cancer Institute* 90 (1998): 1509–11.

Consuming Hunger. Part I: Getting the Story. Part II: Shaping the Image. Part III: Selling the Feeling. Maryknoll, N.Y.: Maryknoll World Productions, 1988.

"Course of Study." Bryn Mawr: Bryn Mawr Summer School for Women Workers, 1922. 1–8.

Cressy, David. "The Environment for Literacy: Accomplishment and Context in Seventeenth-Century England and New England." *Literacy in Historical Perspective*. Ed. Daniel P. Resnick. Washington, D. C.: Library of Congress, 1983.

————. *Literacy and the Social Order: Reading and Writing in Tudor and Stuart England*. Cambridge: Cambridge Univ. Press, 1980.

Crosby, Ruth. "Oral Delivery in the Middle Ages." *Speculum* XI (1936): 88–110.

Csikszentmihalyi, Mihaly and Eugene Rochberg-Halton. *The Meaning of Things: Domestic Symbols and the Self*. Cambridge: Cambridge University Press, 1981.

Curry, David Park. "Rose-Colored Glasses: Looking for 'Good Design' in American Folk Art." *An American Sampler: Folk Art from the Strong Museum*. Washington: National Gallery of Art, 1987. 24–41.

Curtis, James. *Mind's Eye. Mind's Truth. FSA Photography Reconsidered*. Philadelphia: Temple University Press, 1989.

Dana, Olive E. "One Woman's Way with Scrap-Books." *The Writer: A Monthly Magazine for Literary Workers* 5 (1891): 238–39.

Dann, Martin. Ed. *The Black Press 1827–1890: The Quest for National Identity*. New York: G. P. Putnam's Sons, 1971.

Day, Christine. "A Medical Education for Ordinary People." *New York Times*. 24 Nov. 1998: D8.

Day, Dorothy. *Loves and Fishes: The Inspiring Story of the Catholic Worker Movement*. Maryknoll, N.Y.: Orbis Books, 1997.

Debus, Allen G. *The French Paracelsians: The Chemical Challenge to Medical and Scientific Tradition in Early Modern France*. Cambridge: Cambridge University Press, 1991.

De Certeau, Michel. *Heterologies: Discourse on the Other*. Minneapolis: University of Minnesota Press, 1997.

————. *The Practice of Everyday Life*. Trans. Steven Rendell. Berkeley: University of California Press, 1988.

Delany, Samuel R. *Times Square Red, Times Square Blue*. New York: NYU Press, 1999.

Deleuze, Gilles and Felix Guattari. *Kafka: Toward a Minor Literature*. Trans. Dana Polan. Minneapolis: University of Minnesota Press, 1986.

DeMarco, Ettore. "Sociologia dell'Ex Voto." Angiuli.

DeMeo, Giovanni. *L'Incoronata di Foggia*. Foggia: Edizioni Santuario dell'Incoronata, 1975.

Dentan, Robert K. *The Semai: A Non-violent People of Malaya*. New York: Holt, Rinehart, and Winston, 1968.

Despres, Denise Louise. "Franciscan Spirituality: Vision and the Authority of Scripture." Diss. Indiana U, 1985.

Diamond, Stanley. *In Search of the Primitive: A Critique of Civilization* New Brunswick, N.J.: Transaction, 1974.

Dickersin Kay, et al. "Development, Implementation and Evaluation of a Science Training Course for Breast Cancer Activists: Project LEAD (Leaderhip, Education and Advocacy Development)." Mss. *The Dinner Lady and Other Stories*. Bristol: Bristol Broadsides, no date.

Doyle, Clar. *Raising Curtains on Education: Drama as a Site for Critical Pedagogy*. Westport, Conn.: Bergin and Garvey, 1993.

Douglas, Mary. "Deciphering a Meal." *Myth, Symbol, and Culture*. Ed. Clifford Geertz. New York: Norton, 1971. 61–86.

Dramatics Project Group Bryn Mawr. "Labor Dramatics Scrapbook fo the Dramatic Project Group at the Bryn Mawr Summer School." Bryn Mawr: Bryn Mawr Summer School for Women Workers, 1933.

Drury, Roger, et al. *Feds under the Bed: A performance devised for the FWWCP to celebrate 21 years of activity .. and a lot of words under the pen* (unpublished MS, 1997).

Durand, Jorge and Douglas S. Massey. *Miracles on the Border: Retablos of Mexican Migrants to the United States*. Tucson: University of Arizona Press, 1995.

Dyson, Esther, George Gilder, George Keyworth, and Alvin Toffler "A Magna Carta for the Knowledge Age." *New Perspectives Quarterly*. 11:4 (Fall 1994): 26–37.

Edwards, Jonathan. *Jonathan Edwards: Representative Selections*. Ed. Charles H. Faust and Thomas H. Johnson. New York: Hill and Wang, 1963.

Ehrenreich, Barbara. "Nickel-and-Dimed: On (not) Getting By in America." *Harper's Magazine*. January 1999. 37–52.

Eisenberg, David M., et al. "Trends in Alternative Medicine Use in the United States, 1990–1997." Journal of the American Medical Association 280 (1998): 1569–75.

———. "Unconventional Medicine in the United States: Prevalence, Costs, and Patterns of Use." New England Journal of Medicine 328 (1993): 246–52.

Elderdice, James L. "One Way of Making a Scrapbook." The Youth's Companion 57.23 (June 1884): 234.

Emancipator, New York, 13 January 1835. Bullock 31.

Epstein, Ruth, Margaret Sofia, and Jean Carter. "Calendar." Shop and School (1930): 50–54.

Epstein Steven. Impure Science. AIDS, Activism, and the Politics of Knowledge. Berkeley: University of California Press, 1996.

Evans, Walker. Walker Evans: Photographs for the Farm Security Administration. 1935–1938. New York: Da Capo, 1973.

"Experiments in Labor Dramatics at the Bryn Mawr Summer School for Women Workers in Industry." Bryn Mawr: Bryn Mawr Summer School for Women Workers, 1932.

Faigley, Lester, and Thomas P. Miller. "What We Learn from Writing on the Job." College English 44 (1982): 557–69.

Feld, Steven. Sound and Sentiment: Birds, Weeping, Poetics, and Song in Kaluli Expression. Philadelphia: University of Pennsylvania Press, 1982.

Fiedler, Leslie. What Was Literature?: Class Culture and Mass Society. New York: Simon and Schuster, 1982.

Finders, Margaret. Just Girls: Hidden Literacies and Life in Junior High. Urbana, Ill.: NCTE, 1998.

Fiske, John. Reading the Popular. Boston: Unwin Hyman, 1989.

____ . Understanding the Popular. Boston: Unwin Hyman, 1989.

Flynt, Suzanne L. Ornamental and Useful Accomplishments: Schoolgirl Education and Deerfield Academy 1800–1830. Deerfield, Mass.: Pocumtuck Valley Memorial Association and Deerfield Academy, 1988.

Forman, P. Gabrielle. "'Reading Aright': White Slavery, Black Referents, and the Strategy of Histotextuality in Iola Leroy." Yale Journal of Criticism 10 (1997): 327–54.

Fortenberry, Lawrence. "Freedom's Journal: The First Black Medium." The Black Scholar (November 1974): 33–37.

Foxe, John. The Acts and Monuments. Ed. Stephen R. Cattley. 8 vols. London, 1837–41.

Fraser, Nancy. "Rethinking the Public Sphere: A Contribution to the Critique of Actually Existing Democracy." Habermas and the Public Sphere. Ed. Craig Calhoun. Cambridge: MIT Press, 1992. 109–42.

Freedom's Journal, New York, 16 March 1826; 6, 20 April 1827.

Friedman, Daniel. "A Brief Description of the Workers' Theater Movement of the Thirties." McConachie and Friedman. 110–19.

Frost, G. and C. Hoy. Opening Time Resource Pack. Manchester: Gatehouse, no date.

Frost, Karen, Erica Frank, and Edward Maibach. "Relative Risk in the News Media: A Quantification of Misrepresentation." American Journal of Public Health 87 (1997): 842–45.

Furet, Francois and Jacques Ozouf. *Reading and Writing: Literacy in France from Calvin to Jules Ferry.* Cambridge: Cambridge Univ. Press, 1982.

Gans, Herbert J. *The War Against the Poor.* New York: Basic Books, 1995.

Garvey, Ellen Gruber. *The Adman in the Parlor: Magazines and the Gendering of Popular Culture, 1880s to 1910s.* New York: Oxford University Press, 1996.

Gere, Anne Ruggles. "Common Properties of Pleasure: Texts in Nineteenth-Century Women's Clubs." *The Construction of Authorship: Textual Appropriation in Law and Literature.* Eds. Martha Woodmansee and Peter Jaszi. Durham: Duke University Press, 1994. 383–99.

———. *Intimate Practices: Literacy and Cultural Work in U.S. Women's Clubs, 1880–1920.* Urbana: University of Illinois Press, 1997.

———. "Kitchen Tables and Rented Rooms: The Extracurriculum of Composition." *College Composition and Communication* 45 (1994): 75–92.

Gernes, Todd S. "Poetic Justice: Sarah Forten, Eliza Earle, and the Paradox of Intellectual Property." *New England Quarterly* 71.2 (1998): 229–65.

———. "Recasting the Culture of Ephemera: Young Women's Literary Culture in Nineteenth Century America. Diss. Brown U, 1992.

———. "Scrapiana Americana." *Winterthur Magazine* 42.1 (1996): 17–18.

Giffords, Gloria Fraser. *Mexican Folk Retablos.* Alburquerque: University of New Mexico Press, 1974.

Gilder, George. "Overthrowing Hollywood and the Broadcast Elites." *New Perspectives Quarterly* 12:2 (Spring 1995): 20–23.

Gilmore, William. *Reading Becomes a Necessity of Life: Material and Cultural Life in Rural New England, 1780–1835.* Knoxville: University of Tennessee Press, 1989.

Ginzburg, Carlo. *The Cheese and the Worms: The Cosmos of a Sixteenth-Century Miller.* Trans. John and Anne Tedeschi. New York: Penguin, 1982.

Glassie, Henry. *Patterns in the Material Folk Culture of the Eastern United States.* Philadelphia: University of Pennsylvania Press, 1968.

Glenn, Cheryl. "Author, Audience, and Autobiography: Rhetorical Technique in *The Book of Margery Kempe.*" *College English* 53 (September 1992): 540–53.

———. "Medieval Literacy Outside the Academy: Popular Practice and Individual Technique." *College Composition and Communication* 44 (Dec, 1993): 497–508.

The Globe. New York, 20 October 1883. Dann 167–68.

Goldfarb, Lyn. "Memories of a Movement: A Conversation." *Sisterhood and Solidarity: Workers Education for Women, 1914–1984.* Kornbluh and Frederickson. 326–42.

Goldman, Anna. "'I Yam What I Yam': Cooking, Culture, and Colonialism." *De/Colonizing the Subject: The Politics of Gender in Women's Autobiography.* Ed. Sidonie Smith and Julia Watson. Minneapolis: University of Minnesota Press, 1992. 169–95.

Goldman, Robert and Stephen Papson. *Sign Wars: The Cluttered Landscape of Advertising.* New York: Guilford, 1996.

Goldstein, Michael and Douglas McDermott. "The Living Newspaper as Dramatic Form." *Modern Drama* 7 (May 1965): 82–94.

Goltz, Dietlinde. "Die Paracelsisten und die Sprache." *Sudhoffs Archiv* 56 (1972): 337–52.

Goode, Peter. *The Man on the Moon.* Hebden Bridge: Open Township Press, 1989.

Goodridge, Grace. *Scissors and Paste: Designs for Cutting and Pasting with Suggestions for the Work.* Chicago: A. Flanagan, 1899.

Gore, Albert. "Remarks by Vice President Gore at the National Press Club." 21 Dec. 1993. 14 Dec. 1998. <http://www.dataalchemy.com/txt/POLITICS/ALGORE.SPC.htm>.

Graff, Harvey J. *The Legacies of Literacies.* Bloomington: Indiana University Press, 1987.

———. *The Literacy Myth: Cultural Integration and Social Structure in the Nineteenth Century.* New Brunswick, N.J.: Transaction, 1991.

———. "Reflections on the History of Literacy: Overview, Critique, and Proposals." *Humanities in Society* 4 (Fall 1981): 303–33.

Grala, Victoria. "Dramatics." *Shop and School* (1937): 34–35.

Gramsci, Antonio. *Selections from Cultural Writings.* Eds. David Forgacs and Geoffrey Nowell-Smith. Trans. William Boelhower. Cambridge: Harvard University Press, 1991.

———. *Selections from Prison Notebooks.* New York: International, 1971.

Greenblatt, Stephen. *Renaissance Self-Fashioning: From More to Shakespeare.* Chicago: University of Chicago Press, 1980.

Greenhouse, Linda. "In Broad Ruling, Court Prohibits Banning of Homeowners' Signs." *New York Times.* 14 June 1994: A1, B9.

Gregory, Gerry. "Community Publishing as Self-Education," in David Barton and Roz Ivancic, eds., *Writing in the Community. Written Communication Annual,* Vol. 6. Newbury Park, Ca.: Sage, 1991, 109–42.

Gregory, Jane and Steve Miller. *Science in Public. Communication, Culture, and Credibility.* New York: Plenum Press, 1998.

Groom, Nick. *The Making of Percy's Reliques.* Oxford: Clarendon Press, 1999.

Gurley, E. W. *Scrapbooks and How to Make Them.* New York: The Authors' Publishing Co., 1880.

Habermas, Jürgen. "Further Reflections on the Public Sphere." *Habermas and the Public Sphere.* Ed. Craig Calhoun. Cambridge: MIT Press, 1992. 421–61.

———. *The Structural Transformation of the Public Sphere: An Inquiry into a Category of Bourgeois Society.* 1962. Trans. Thomas Burger and Frederick Lawrence. Cambridge: MIT Press, 1989.

Hall, Stuart. *Representation and the Media.* video production. Boston: The Media Education Foundation. 1996.

Haller, William. *Foxe's Book of Martyrs and the Elect Nation.* London: Jonathan Cape, 1963.

Harper, Frances E. W. *Iola Leroy, or, Shadows Uplifted.* 1892; rpt. intro. Hazel V. Carby, Boston: Beacon Press, 1987.

———. "Let There Be Justice." *Transactions of the National Council of Women of the United States Assembled in Washington. D. C. February 22, 1891.* Lerner 194.

———. *Minnie's Sacrifice; Sowing and Reaping; Trial and Triumph: Three Rediscovered Novels.* 1869, 1876–77, 1888–89; rpt. ed. and intro. Frances Smith Foster. Boston: Beacon Press, 1994.

Havelock, Eric. *The Literate Revolution in Greece and Its Cultural Consequences*. Princeton: Princeton University Press, 1982.

Heath, Shirley Brice. *Ways with Words*. Cambridge: Cambridge University Press, 1983.

Heilbrun, Carolyn G. *Writing a Woman's Life*. New York: Norton, 1988.

Heininger, Mary Lynn Steven, et al. *A Century of Childhood, 1820–1920*. Rochester, N.Y.: Margaret Woodbury Strong Museum, 1984.

Helgerson, Richard. *Forms of Nationhood: The Elizabethan Writing of England*. Chicago: U. of Chicago Press, 1992.

Heller, Rita. "Blue Collars and Bluestockings: The Bryn Mawr Summer School for Women Workers, 1921–38." Kornbluh and Frederickson. 109–45.

"Help Feed the Homeless this Thanksgiving," *Milwaukee Rescue Mission* ad appeal. *Milwaukee Journal Sentinel*. 14 November 1998: 8A.

Herman, Christina Coburn. *Poverty Amid Plenty: The Unfinished Business of Welfare Reform*. NETWORK. A National Social Justice Lobby. Washington, D.C., 1999.

Herndl, Diane Price. "The Dilemmas of a Feminist Dialogue." *Feminism, Bakhtin, and the Dialogic*. Ed. Dale M. Bauer and S. Jaret McKinstry. Albany: SUNY Press, 1991. 7–25.

Herrmann, Helen. "Joint Meeting of Curriculum Committee and 1933 Bryn Mawr Faculty in New York City." Bryn Mawr: Bryn Mawr Summer School for Women Workers. 1933.

Hill, Christopher. *A Tinker and a Poor Man: John Bunyan and His Church, 1628–1688*. New York: Knopf, 1989.

Hirsch, E. D., Jr. *Cultural Literacy: What Every American Needs to Know*. Boston. Houghton, 1987.

Hitchcock, Enos. *Memoirs of the Bloomsgrove Family. In a Series of LETTERS to a respectable CITIZEN of PHILADELPHIA*. Vol. 2. Boston: Thomas and Andrews, 1790.

Hollis, Karyn. "Liberating Voices: Autobiographical Writing at the Bryn Mawr Summer School for Women Workers, 1921–1938." *College Composition and Communication* 45 (1994): 31–60.

hooks, bell. "Seeing and Making Culture: Representing the Poor," *Outlaw Culture: Resisting Representations*. New York: London, 1994. 165–72.

Hooykaas, R. *Humanisme, Science et Réform. Pierre de la Ramée (1515–1572)*. Leiden: E.J. Brill, 1958.

Hudson, Gossie Harold. "Black Americans vs. Citizenship: The Dred Scott Decision." *Negro History Bulletin* 46 (January–March 1983): 26–28.

Humphries, Haroldine. "The Play Spirit in Acting." *Bryn Mawr Alumnae Bulletin* 2 (1922): 16–17.

Hunter, David J, et al. "Plasma Organochlorine Levels and the Risk of Breast Cancer." *New England Journal of Medicine* 337 (1997): 1253–58.

Ireland, Lynne. "The Compiled Cookbook as Foodways Autobiography." *Western Folklore* 40.1 (1981): 107–14.

It's Unconstitutional. Prelude. Bryn Mawr: Bryn Mawr Summer School for Women Workers, 1936.

Jensen. *The Female Autograph*. Ed. Domna C. Stanton. Chicago, University of Chicago**
    check this: incomplete**

Kamil, Neil D. "War, Natural Philosophy and the Metaphysical Foundations of Artisanal
    Thought in an American Mid-Atlantic Colony: La Rochelle, New York City, and the
    Southwestern Huguenot Paradigm, 1517–1730." Ph.D. diss. Johns Hopkins Univer-
    sity, 1988.

Katz, Michael B. *The Undeserving Poor: From the War on Poverty to the War on Welfare*. New York:
    Pantheon, 1989.

Keil, Charles. *Tiv Song: The Sociology of Art in a Classless Society*. Chicago: University of Chicago
    Press, 1979.

Kitagaki, Muneharu. "English Periodical Essays and Hawthorne: A Few Suggestions." *The
    Hawthorne Society of Japan Newsletter* 9 (April 1990): 1–2.

Knott, John R. *Sword of the Spirit: Puritan Responses to the Bible*. Chicago: University of Chicago
    Press, 1980.

Knowles, David. *The English Mystical Tradition*. London: Burns, 1961.

Kolata Gina. "Study Discounts DDT Role in Breast Cancer." *New York Times* 30 Oct. 1997:
    A19.

Kornbluh, Joyce L. and Mary Frederickson, eds. *Sisterhood and Solidarity: Workers Education for
    Women, 1914–1984*. Philadelphia: Temple University Press, 1984.

Ladies' Art Company. *Miniature Diagrams of Quilt Patterns*. 2nd ed. St. Louis: H. M. Brockstedt,
    1879.

Lamont, William. *Godly Rule: Politics and Religion, 1603–1660*. London, Macmillan, 1969.

Lamousen, Nina. "What Do You Think?" *Shop and School* (1934): 20.

Latour Bruno. *Science in Action*. Cambridge: Harvard University Press, 1987.

Laurence, Leslie. "How OB-GYNs Fail Women: Read This Before Your Next Checkup."
    Glamour Oct. 1997: 292–95.

The Leader, Charleston, 24 December 1856. Dann 89.

Leary, Warren E. "Aspirin Proposed for Suspected Heart Attacks." *New York Times* 19 June
    1996: C9.

Leavitt, Helen. *Superhighway—Superhoax*. Garden City, N.Y.: Doubleday, 1970.

Lehrman, Sally. "AAAS Head Wants to See Scientists on School Boards." *Nature* 397
    (1999): 374.

Lejeune, Philippe. "Women and Autobiography at Author's Expense." Trans. Katherine
    Jensen. *The Female Autograph*. Ed. Domna C. Stanton. Chicago: University of Chicago
    Press, 1984. 205–18.

Leonardi, Susan J. "Recipes for Reading: Summer Pasta, Lobster a la Riseholme, and Key
    Lime Pie." *PMLA* 104 (1989): 340–47.

Leppert, Richard. *Art and the Committed Eye: The Cultural Functions of Imagery*. Boulder, Co., 1996.

Lerner, Gerda, ed. *Black Women in White America: A Documentary History*. Boston: Little, Brown,
    1996.

Levenstein, Harvey. "The American Response to Italian Food, 1880–1930." *Food and Food-
    ways* 1 (1985): 1–23.

Levi-Strauss, Claude. "The Culinary Triangle." *Partisan Review* 33 (1966): 595–601.

————. *Totemism.* Boston: Beacon, 1962.

Lewenstein Bruce V. "Science and the Media." *Handbook of Science and Technology Studies.* Eds. Sheila Jasonoff, et al. Thousand Oaks: Sage, 1995. 343–60.

Locke, John. *The Works of John Locke.* Vol. 3. London: Awsham Churchill, 1722.

Lockridge, Kenneth A. *On the Sources of Partriarchal Rage: The Commonplace Books of William Byrd and Thomas Jefferson and the Gendering of Power in the Eighteenth Century.* New York; NYU Press, 1992.

Logan, Shirley Wilson. *"We Are Coming": The Persuasive Discourse of Nineteenth-Century Black Women.* Carbondale: Southern Illinois University Press, 1999.

London, Jack. *The People of the Abyss.* Facsimile edition. New York: Garrett Press, MSS Information Corporation, 1970.

The Loyal Georgian, Augusta, 27 January 1866. Dann 91.

Mace, Jane. *Talking about Literacy: Principles and Practice of Adult Literacy Education.* London: Routledge, 1992.

MacKaye, Hazel. "Plays for Workers." *Workers' Education* 4 (1926): 11–18.

"Many Albums Kept by Women." *Current Literature* 34.6 (1903): 741.

Marable, Manning. *How Capitalism Underdeveloped Black America.* Boston: South End Press, 1983.

Marcuse, Herbert. *One-Dimensional Man: Studies in the Ideology of Advanced Industrial Society.* Boston: Beacon, 1964.

Martin, Randy. *Socialist Ensembles: Theater and State in Cuba and Nicaragua.* Minneapolis: University of Minnesota, 1994.

Mayhew, Henry. *London Labour and the London Poor.* New York: Penguin Books, 1985.

McConachie, Bruce A. and Daniel Friedman, eds. *Theater for Working-Class Audiences in the United States, 1830–1980.* Westport, Conn.: Greenwood, 1985.

McDermott, Douglas. "The Workers's Laboratory Theater: Archetype and Example." McConachie and Friedman. 87–95.

McGann, Jerome. *The Beauty of Inflections: Literary Investigations in Historical Method and Theory.* Oxford: Clarendon Press, 1988.

————. *Social Values and Poetic Acts: The Historical Judgment of Literary Work.* Cambridge: Harvard University Press, 1988.

McKitterick, Rosamond. *Carolingians and the Written Word.* Cambridge: Cambridge University Press, 1989.

————, ed. *The Uses of Literacy in Early Mediaeval Europe.* Cambridge: Cambridge University Press, 1990.

McLuhan, Marshall. *Understanding Media: The Extensions of Man.* New York: New American Library, 1964.

McNeil, W.K. "The Autograph: A Tradition and Its Scholarly Treatment." *Keystone Folklore Quarterly* 13.1 (1968): 29–40.

McRobbie, Angela. "Jackie: An Ideology of Adolescent Feminity." *Popular Culture: Past and Present.* Ed. Bernard Waites, et al. London: Croom Helm. 263–83.

Meech, Sanford Brown, and Hope Emily Allen, eds. *The Book of Margery Kempe.* EETS, 212. London: Oxford University Press, 1940.

Miller, Susan. *Assuming the Positions: Cultural Pedagogy and the Politics of Commonplace Writing.* Pittsburgh: University of Pittsburgh Press, 1998.

"Minutes: Instruction Committee Meeting." Bryn Mawr: Bryn Mawr Summer School for Women Workers, 30 April 1932. 1–4.

Morley, David and Ken Worpole, eds. *The Republic of Letters: Working Class Writing and Local Publishing.* London: Comedia, 1982.

Morley, Henry. *Palissy the Potter.* 2d ed. London: Chapman and Hall, 1855.

Morson, Gary Saul and Caryl Emerson. *Mikhail Bakhtin: Creation of a Prosaics.* Stanford: Stanford University Press, 1990.

Moss, Ann. *Printed Commonplace-Books and the Structure of Renaissance Thought.* Oxford: Clarendon Press, 1996.

Mozley, James F. *John Foxe and His Book.* London: Society for Promoting Christian Knowledge, 1940.

Muensterberger, Werner. *Collecting: An Unruly Passion. Psychological Perspectives.* Princeton: Princeton University Press, 1994.

Mumford, Lewis. "The Highway and the City." 1958. Rpt. *The Highway and the City.* New York: Harcourt, Brace, 1963. 234–46.

Myers, Greg. *Writing Biology: Texts in the Social Construction of Scientific Knowledge.* Madison: University of Wisconsin Press, 1990.

Nelkin Dorothy. *Selling Science. How the Press Covers Science and Technology.* New York: Freeman & Co., 1995.

New English Bible.

The New National Era, Washington, 27 January 1870; 25 January 1872. Dann, 155–56, 95.

Nochlin, Linda. "The Paterson Strike Pageant of 1913." McConachie and Friedman. 87–95.

Nussbaum, Felicity A. "Eighteenth-Century Women's Autobiographical Commonplaces." *The Private Self: Theory and Practice of Women's Autobiographical Writings.* Ed. Shari Benstock. Chapel Hill: University of North Carolina Press, 1988. 147–71.

Oktavec, Eileen. *Answered Prayers: Miracles and Milagros Along the Border.* Tucson: University of Arizona Press, 1995.

Oldenburg, Ray. *The Great Good Place: Cafés, Coffee Shops, Community Centers, Beauty Parlors, General Stores, Bars, Hangouts, and How They Get You Through the Day.* New York: Paragon House, 1989.

Oliver, Leslie M. "The *Acts and Monuments* of John Foxe: Studies in the Growth and Influence of a Book." Ph.D. diss. Harvard, 1945.

Oliver, Leslie M. "The Acts and Monuments of John Foxe: Studies in the Growth and Influence of a Book." Ph.D. diss. Harvard, 1945.

———. "The Seventh Edition of John Foxe's *Acts and Monuments.*" *The Papers of the Bibliographical Society of America* 37 (1943): 243–60.

Once I Was a Washing Machine. Stoke-on-Trent: FWWCPress, 1989.

Ong, Walter, S.J. *Orality and Literacy*. London: Methuen, 1982.

————. *Rhetoric, Romance, and Technology*. Ithaca: Cornell University Press, 1971.

Our Homes; How to Beautify Them. New York: O. Judd, 1888.

Palissy, Bernard. *The Admirable Discourses*. 1580. Trans. Aurele la Rocque. Urbana: University of Illinois P. 1957.

————. *Recepte Veritable, par laquelle tous les hommes de France pourront apprendre multiplier et augmenter leurs thrsors. Item, ceux qui n'ont saire tous les habitants de la terre. Item, en ce livre est contenu le dessein d'un jardin autant delectable et d'utile invention, qu'il en fut oncques veu. Item, le dessein et ordonnance d'une ville de forteresse, la plus imprenable qu'homme ouyt jamais parler: compos par maistre Bernard Palissy, ouurier de terre, et inventeur des rustiques figulines du Roy, et de monseigneur le Duc de Montmorency, pair et connestable de France; demeurant en la ville de Xaintes*. La Rochelle: Barthlemy Berton, 1563.

Paracelsus. "The Seven Defensiones." 4th defense. *Four Treatises of Theophrastus von Hohenheim, called Paracelsus*. Trans. C. Lilian Temkin. Baltimore: Johns Hopkins University Press, 1941.

————. *Labyrinthus medicorum errantium*. 1538. *Paracelsus. Essential Readings*. Trans. Nicholas Goodrick-Clarke Wellingborough, U.K.: Crucible, 1990.

The Parlor Book; or Family Encyclopedia of Useful Knowledge and General Literature. New York: John L. Piper, 1835.

Parsons, Robert. *A Treatise of Three Conversions*. 1603–04.

Parsons, William T. *The Pennsylvania Dutch: A Persistent Minority*. Boston: Twayne, 1976.

Patterson, Lee, ed. *Literary Practice and Social Change in Britain, 1380–1530*. Berkeley: University of California Press, 1990.

Patton, Phil. *Open Road: A Celebration of the American Highway*. New York: Simon and Schuster, 1986.

Pease, Jane H. and William H. Pease. *They Who Would Be Free: Blacks' Search for Freedom, 1830–1861*. Urbana: University of Illinois Press, 1974.

The People's Advocate. Washington, D. C., 18 February 1882. Dann 356.

Peterson, Esther E. "Bryn Mawr Summer School, 1937: Dramatics." Bryn Mawr: Bryn Mawr Summer School for Women Workers. 1937.

————. "Dramatics and Recreation." Bryn Mawr: Bryn Mawr Summer School for Women Workers. 1936: 1–6.

————. "The Medium of Movement." *Journal of Adult Education* 7 (1935): 182–84.

Pharo, Florence M. "Syllabus-English." Bryn Mawr: Bryn Mawr Summer School for Women Workers, 1930. 1–21.

Plato. *Euthyphro, Apology, Crito, Phaedo, Phaedrus*. Trans. H. N. Fowler. Cambridge: Harvard-Heinemann, 1977. 405–580.

Pollard, Alfred W. *Records of the English Bible*. London, Oxford, 1911.

Pomian, Krzysztof. *Collectors and Curiosities: Paris and Venice, 1500–1800*. Trans. Elizabeth Wiles-Portier. London: Polity Press, 1990.

Poole, Teresa. "China Uses Jail Threat to Keep Control of Internet." *The Independent* 13 Dec. 1998: 18.

Porter, Esteer. "Dramatics." *Material for Recreation. Bryn Mawr Summer School.* Bryn Mawr: Bryn Mawr Summer School for Women Workers, 1934. 63–65.

Potter, Charles Francis. "Autograph Album Rimes." *Funk and Wagnalls Dictionary of Folklore, Mythology and Legend.* Ed. Maria Leach. New York: Funk and Wagnall, 1949.

———. "Round Went the Album." *New York Folklore Quarterly* 4 (1948): 4–14.

Previti, Jennie. "Mother Goose Depression Nursery Rhymes." *Shop and School* (1933): 16.

Radway, Janice. *Reading the Romance: Women, Patriarchy, and Popular Literature.* Chapel Hill: University of North Carolina Press, 1984.

Ransdell, Hollace. "Amateur Dramatics in the Labor Movement." *Affiliated Schools Scrapbook* (March 1936): 2–4.

Rector, Robert. "The Myth of Widespread American Poverty." *The Heritage Foundation Backgrounder,* 18 September 1998.

Relman Arnold S. "A Trip to Stonesville." *New Republic* 14 Dec. 1998: 28–37.

Rheingold, Howard. *The Virtual Community: Homesteading on the Electronic Frontier.* New York: HarperPerennial, 1993.

Rich, Frank. "Stand-Up Synergy." *New York Times* 6 March 1997, natl. ed.: A23.

Richards, Eugene. *Below the Line: Living Poor in America.* Mount Vernon, N.Y.: Consumers Union, 1987.

Riis, Jacob A. *How the Other Half Lives: Studies Among the Tenements of New York.* New York: Dover, 1971.

Romina, Francesca. *Mangia, Little Italy!: Secrets from a Sicilian Family Kitchen.* San Francisco: Chronicle, 1998.

Rosenheim, Max. "The Album Amicorum." *Archaeologia* 62 (1910): 251–308.

Salus, Peter H. *Casting the Net: From ARPANET to Internet and Beyond.* Reading, Mass.: Addison-Wesley, 1995.

Schneider, Florence Hemley. *Patterns of Workers' Education: The Story of the Bryn Mawr Summer School.* Washington, D.C.: American Council on Public Affairs, 1941.

Scott, Alison M. "'These Notions I Imbibed from Writers': The Reading Life of Mary Ann Woodrow Archibald (1762–1841)." Diss. Boston U, 1995.

Scribner, Sylvia, and Michael Cole. *The Psychology of Literacy.* Cambridge: Harvard University Press, 1981.

Searle, John R. Speech Acts: An Essay on the Philosophy of Language. Cambridge: Cambridge University Press, 1969.

Seitz, William C. *The Art of Assemblage.* New York: Museum of Modern Art, 1961.

Shelby, Lon R. "The Geometrical Knowledge of Mediaeval Master Masons." *Speculum* 47 (1972): 395–421.

Shipton, Clifford K. *Biographical Sketches of Those Who Attended Harvard College in the Classes 1764–1767.* Boston: Massachusetts Historical Society, 1972.

Shush—Mum's Writing. Bristol: Bristol Broadsides, 1978.

Simmons, Amelia. *American Cookery.* 1796. Green Farms, Conn.: Silverleaf, 1984.

Slouka, Mark. *War of the Worlds: Cyberspace and the High-Tech Assault on Reality.* New York: Basic Books, 1995.

Smith, Hilda Worthington. *Women Workers at the Bryn Mawr Summer School.* New York: Affiliated Schools for Women Workers in Industry and American Association for Adult Education, 1929.

———. *Opening Vistas in Workers' Education: An Autobiography of Hilda Worthington Smith.* Washington, D.C.: self-published, 1978.

Smitherman, Geneva. *Talkin and Testifyin: The Language of Black America.* Detroit: Wayne State University Press, 1977.

Smithville Seminary. *Catalogue of the Officers and Students of Smithville Seminary.* Providence, RI: H.H. Brown, 1841.

Smythe, Joe. *Come and Get Me.* Manchester: Commonword, 1979.

———. *The People's Road.* Manchester: National Union of Railwaymen, 1980.

———. "Third Shunt," in *Voices* (Manchester: FWWCP) Vol. 23, Winter 1981, 31.

Snorgrass, J. William. "America's Ten Oldest Black Newspapers." *Negro History Bulletin* 46 (January–March 1983): 11–14.

Spencer, Truman J. *A Cyclopedia of the Literature of Amateur Journalism.* Hartford, Conn.: Truman J. Spencer, 1891.

Spera, Enzo. "Ex Voto Fotograficied Oggettuali." Angiuli.

St. Armand, Barton Levi. *Emily Dickinson and Her Culture: The Soul's Society.* Cambridge: Cambridge University Press, 1984.

St. Augustine. *Confessions.*

Stambaugh, Ruthella. "The Chronicle." *Bryn Mawr Echo* (1928): 39–43.

Steele, Thomas J., S. J. *Santos and Saints: The Religious Folk Art of Hispanic New Mexico.* Santa Fe: Ancient City, 1994.

Stewart, Susan. *On Longing: Narratives of the Miniature, the Gigantic, the Souvenir, the Collection.* Baltimore: Johns Hopkins University Press, 1984.

———. *Nonsense: Aspects of Intertextuality in Folklore and Literature.* Baltimore: Johns Hopkins University Press, 1979.

Stock, Brian. *The Implications of Literacy.* Princeton: Princeton University Press, 1983.

———. *Listening for the Text: On the Uses of the Past.* Baltimore: Johns Hopkins University Press, 1990.

Street, Brian. *Literacy in Theory and Practice.* Cambridge: Cambridge University Press, 1984.

Suggs, Henry Lewis. ed. *The Black Press in the South, 1865–1979.* Westport, Conn.: Greenwood Press, 1983.

Taylor, Mary K. "America's First Cookbook." *Early American Life* February 1991: 40–43.

Thomas James C., et al. "Lay Health Advisors: Sexually Transmitted Disease Prevention through Community Involvement." *American Journal of Public Health* 88 (1998): 1252–53.

Thomas, Keith. "The Meaning of Literacy in Early Modern England." *The Written Word: Literacy in Transition.* Ed. Gerd Baumann. London: Clarendon Press, 1986.

Todd, John, comp. *Index Rerum; or, Index of Subjects.* Northampton, Mass.: Bridgman and Childs, 1868.

Toffler, Alvin. *The Third Wave.* New York: Morrow, 1980.

Tribune. New Orleans, 18 July 1865. Dann 88–89.

Tripputi, Anna Maria. "Gli Ex Voto Dipinti." Angiuli.

Troiano, Antonio and Filippo de Michele. *Ebbi Miracolo.* Napoli: Grafiche Lithosud, 1992.

Turnbull, Colin. *The Forest People.* New York: Simon and Schuster, 1962.

United States Department of Commerce. "Falling Through the Net: A Survey of the 'Have Nots' in Rural and Urban America." Washington, D.C.: U.S. Department of Commerce, July 1995.

Veblen, Thorstein. *The Theory of the Leisure Class.* Boston: Houghton Mifflin, 1974.

Victoria, Ann. "Banish Arthritis Forever." *Weekly World News* 24 Oct. 1995: 8–9.

Vincent, David. *Literacy and Popular Culture, England 1750–1914.* Cambridge: Cambridge University Press, 1989.

The Virginia Star, Richmond, 18 March 1882. Dann 356.

Vives, Juan Luis. *De tradendis disciplinis.* 1531. Trans. Foster Watson. Totowa, N.J.: Rowman and Littlefield, 1971.

Vygotsky, Lev. *Thought and Language.* Trans. Alex Kozulin. Cambridge: MIT Press, 1986.

Walker, Alice. "If the Present Looks like the Past, What Does the Future Look Like?" In *Search of Our Mothers' Gardens: Womanist Prose.* New York: Harcourt Brace Jovanovich, 1983.

Wall, Nancy. "Retablos and Santos: Mexican Folk Art, Old and New." *Tucson Guide.* Winter 1999. 72–76.

Walsh, Michael. *Graffito.* Berkeley: North Atlantic, 1996.

Weaver, William Woys. "*Die Geschickte Hausfrau:* The First Ethnic Cookbook in the United States." *Food in Perspective.* Ed. Alexander Fenton and Trefor M. Owen. Edinburgh: John Donald, 1981. 343–63.

The Weekly Anglo-African. New York, 23 July, 20 August, 15 October, 3 December 1859. Dann 50, 74, 133.

"Welfare Drug Test Bill on Fast Track," *The Detroit News.* 4 February 1999.

Wells, Jane. "Mammography and the Politics of Randomized Controlled Trials." *British Medical Journal* 317 (1998): 1224–30.

Wellstone, Paul. "If Poverty is the Question . . ." *Nation* 14 April 1997: 15–18.

White, Hayden. *Tropics of Discourse: Essays in Cultural Criticism.* Baltimore: Johns Hopkins University Press, 1987.

Whitney, Sewell. "Ethnic Products Satisfy Craving for Something New." *Advertising Age* 19 September 1985: 46–48.

Williams, Clara Andrews. *The House That Glue Built.* New York: Frederick Stokes, 1905.

Williams, Raymond. *Keywords: A Vocabulary of Culture and Society.* Oxford University Press, 1976.

———. *Politics and Letters.* London: Verso, 1979.

————. *Writing in Society*. London: Verso, 1984.

Wolfram, Eddie. *History of Collage: An Anthology of Collage, Assemblage, and Event Structures*. New York: Macmillan, 1975.

Wolseley. Roland. *The Black Press, U. S. A.* 2nd ed. Ames: Iowa State University Press. 1990.

Wooden, Warren. *John Foxe*. Boston: Twayne, 1983.

Yaghhian, Lucretia Bailey. "Writing Practices and Pedagogy Across the Theological Curriculum: Teaching Writing in a Theological Context." *Theological Education* 33.2 (1997): 39–68.

Yates, Francis. *The Art of Memory*. Chicago: University of Chicago Press, 1966.

Young, Stephanie. "Your Pap Smear: A Save-Your-Life Guide." *Glamour*. Aug. 1997: 208–11.

Zboray, Ronald J. "Antebellum Reading and the Ironies of Technological Innovation." Ed. Cathy N. Davidson. *Reading in America: Literature and Social History*. Baltimore: Johns Hopkins University Press, 1989. 180–200.

Contributors

STEPHANIE ALMAGNO is associate professor of English, Writing Center Director, and chair of the humanities department at Piedmont College. She is currently working on a series of children's books.

PATRICIA BIZZELL is professor of English at the College of Holy Cross. Among her recent publications are *The Rhetorical Tradition: Readings from Classical Times to the Present*, 2nd ed., coauthored with Bruce Herzberg, and *The Bedford Bibliography for Teachers of Writing*, 5th ed., coauthored with Herzberg and Nedra Reynolds.

LUNDY BRAUN is associate professor of pathology and of environmental studies and a member of the Faculty Committee on Science Studies at Brown University. Her current research examines the history of race and occupational medicine.

NICHOLAS COLES is associate professor of English at the University of Pittsburgh and director of the Western Pennsylvania Writing Project. He is coeditor, with poet Peter Oresick, of *Working Classics: Poems on Industrial Life* and *For a Living: The Poetry of Work*.

LESTER FAIGLEY holds the Robert Adger Law and Thos. H. Law Professorship in Humanities at the University of Texas at Austin. He was the founding director of both the division of rhetoric and composition and the concentration in technology, literacy, and culture at Texas.

TODD S. GERNES is the director of writing at Providence College. He is currently at work on a cultural biography of visionary artist Charles Walter Stetson and his circle in nineteenth-century Providence.

DIANA GEORGE is professor of humanities at Michigan Technological University. She is coauthor, with John Trimbur, of *Reading Culture*, 4th ed., and editor of the collection *Kitchen Cooks, Plate Twirlers, and Troubadours: Writing Program Administrators Tell Their Stories*. With Dennis Lynch and Marilyn Cooper, she received the 1998 Braddock Award for "Moments of Argument: Agonistic Inquiry and Confrontational Cooperation."

CHERYL GLENN is associate professor of English at Penn State University. Her publications include *Rhetoric Retold: Regendering the Tradition from Antiquity through the Renaissance* and *The St. Martin's Guide to Teaching Writing*. She is completing a book-length project, *Unspoken: A Rhetoric of Silence*.

KARYN HOLLIS is the director of the writing program at Villanova University. Her book on writing at the Bryn Mawr Summer School for Women Workers will be published by Southern Illinois University Press.

CHARLES KEIL is best known for collaborating on books about music—*Urban Blues, Tiv Song, Polka Happiness, My Music*, and *Music Grooves*—and promoting projects that reunite the arts in community-building performances. See <musekids.org> and <128path.org> for updates and recent articles.

NEDRA REYNOLDS is associate professor of English at the University of Rhode Island. She is the author of *Portfolio Keeping: A Guide for Writers* and *Portfolio Teaching: A Guide for Instructors* and a coeditor of *The Bedford Bibliography for Teachers of Writing*, 5th ed. Her recent articles include "Who's Going to Cross this Border? Travel Metaphors, Material Conditions, and Contested Places" (*JAC* 2000).

P. JOY ROUSE is assistant professor of professional and technical writing at Appalachian State University. Her current research interests include nineteenth-century Native American literacy instruction and a collaborative project on domestic partner benefits in the corporate sector.

MARIOLINA RIZZI SALVATORI is associate professor of English at the University of Pittsburgh. In 1999, she was selected as Carnegie Scholar by the Carnegie Foundation for the Advancement of Teaching for her work on "pedagogy of difficulty." This piece is in memory of her mother, Olga Nigri Rizzi.

PAMELA H. SMITH teaches history of early modern Europe and history of science at Pomona College and the Claremont Graduate University. She is author of *The Business of Alchemy: Science and Culture in the Holy Roman Empire*, and is now at work on a book entitled *The Body of the Artisan: Nature, Art, and Science in Early Modern Europe* about artisanal culture and vernacular epistemology in the scientific revolution.

EVELYN B. TRIBBLE is associate professor of English at Temple University. She is the author of *Margins and Marginality: The Printed Page in Early Modern England* and coauthor of the forthcoming *Technologies of Writing from Plato to the Digital Age*.

JOHN TRIMBUR is professor of writing and rhetoric and codirector of the technical, scientific, and professional communication program at Worcester Polytechnic Institute. His publications include *The Call to Write, Reading Culture*, 4th ed., with Diana George, and *The Politics of Writing Instruction* with Richard Bullock and Charles Schuster.

Index